Caribbean Development Dynamics 2025

Please cite this publication as:
OECD/IDB (2024), *Caribbean Development Dynamics 2025*, OECD Publishing, Paris, https://doi.org/10.1787/a8e79405-en.

ISBN 978-92-64-53038-6 (print)
ISBN 978-92-64-88237-9 (PDF)
ISBN 978-92-64-80935-2 (HTML)
ISBN 978-92-64-36835-4 (epub)

Photo credits: Cover design by Aida Buendía using an image from © Guven Ozdemir/gettyimages.fr.

Corrigenda to OECD publications may be found at: https://www.oecd.org/en/publications/support/corrigenda.html.

Foreword

Caribbean Development Dynamics is a new annual flagship report by the OECD Development Centre and the Inter-American Development Bank analysing key development trends in the Caribbean with a comparative and multi-dimensional approach. This publication is the result of fruitful dialogue between the two institutions, which concluded by acknowledging the need for a dedicated report to inform policy dialogue on the development of the Caribbean region.

The report calls for a shift in perspective – from emphasising challenges to casting light on opportunities. It seeks to shape the debate on development opportunities in the Caribbean by providing comparable data, policy recommendations, and a regional perspective highlighting policy options and areas of common interest, while acknowledging diversity as a unique asset.

This 2025 edition, alongside future ones, reflects the growing engagement of the OECD Development Centre and the Inter-American Development Bank with the Caribbean. The OECD Development Centre is expanding its work and membership with the region, while the IDB is carrying out this work under the framework of IDB's Regional Program One Caribbean. This initiative is part of an overall institutional commitment to address regional public goods and advance the development agenda of multiple subregions of Latin America and the Caribbean. The programme leverages resources, co-operation, and economies of scale to tackle shared challenges across the Caribbean region.

Acknowledgements

This report is co-produced by the Inter-American Development Bank (IDB) and the Development Centre of the Organisation for Economic Co-operation and Development (OECD).

The contribution of the OECD Development Centre to the report was led and managed by Sebastián Nieto-Parra and Juan Vázquez Zamora, Head and Deputy-Head, respectively, of the Latin America and the Caribbean Unit. Co-ordination was led by Luis Cecchi, Policy Analyst at the Latin America and the Caribbean Unit, under the guidance of Ragnheiður Elín Árnadóttir, Director, and Federico Bonaglia, Deputy Director.

IDB's contribution was led by David Rosenblatt, Regional Economic Advisor for the Caribbean Country Department and Ian Mills, Unit Chief of the One Caribbean Coordination Unit, under the guidance of Anton Edmunds, Manager for the Caribbean Country Department. Co-ordination was led by Fazia Pusterla, representative of the IDB Group Office in Europe; Carolyn Robert, Strategic Advisor for the Vice-President for Countries; Carina Cockburn, Country Representative in Barbados; Carla Fernández-Durán, Strategic Partnerships and Resource Mobilization Senior Specialist; Bernardo Deregibus, Partnerships and Resource Mobilization Specialist; Daniel Hernaiz Diez de Medina, Strategic Task Force Lead Economist; Nadia Rocha, Principal Advisor and Alejandra Quiñonez, Executive Coordinator, both at the Vice-Presidency for Countries; under the guidance of Anabel González, Vice President for Countries and Matias Bendersky, Manager of the Office of Outreach and Partnerships.

The report benefited from the research, drafting and fruitful collaboration among various authors across these organisations, including: Gerard Alleng (IDB), Jose Antonio Ardavin (OECD), Andrew Auerbach (OECD), Severine Baranger (OECD), Dieter Beuermann (IDB), Federico Bonaglia (OECD), Steve Brito Hernandez (IDB), Adriana Caicedo (OECD), Olivier Cattaneo (OECD), Luis Cecchi (OECD), Rita Da Costa (OECD), Victoria de la Puente (OECD), Bernardo Deregibus (IDB), Ben Dickinson (OECD), Gabriel Di Paolantonio (OECD), Saleh El Kadre (OECD), Abdoulaye Fabregas (OECD), Carla Fernández-Durán (IDB), María Garcin Zaldívar (OECD), Paolo Giordano (IDB), Diego Gonzalez-Bendiksen de Zaldivar (OECD), Laura Gutiérrez Cadena (OECD), Hamadi Hakim (OECD), Daniel Hernaiz Diez de Medina (IDB), Tomas Hos (OECD), Martina Lejtreger (OECD), Zayda Manatta (OECD), Thomas Manfredi (OECD), Nathalia Montoya González (OECD), Mariana Navarro (OECD), Sebastián Nieto Parra (OECD), René Orozco (OECD), Lorenzo Pavone (OECD), Cécilia Piemonte (OECD), Arturo Pita Gussoni (IDB), Joan Prats Cabrera (IDB), Fazia Pusterla (IDB), David Rosenblatt (IDB), Ben Roseth (IDB), Callum Ryan (OECD), Harry Tonino (OECD), Piera Tortora (OECD), Juan Vázquez Zamora (OECD) and Pia Zanetti Balparda (IDB). Rosario Hernando Cruz (OECD), Julia Peppino (OECD) and Javier de Ramón (IDB) provided invaluable administrative support throughout the elaboration of the report.

The content of the report was enriched by the constructive feedback received during the consultation meeting held virtually on the 21st of March and the Caribbean Development Dynamics Working Lunch, held at the OECD on the 22nd of May, at the margins of the International Economic Forum on Latin America and the Caribbean 2024, and with the presence of Enrique Iglesias, President, Fundación Astur, as a special invitee. In addition to the LAC delegates to the Governing Board of the OECD Development Centre, we are grateful to the experts, academics, private-sector representatives and other public servants who joined us during the consultation meeting, the working lunch and bilateral meetings: Olga Julissa Anzueto

Aguilar (Guatemala), Seema Baldewsingh (Suriname), Bevon Bernard-Henry (ACS), Symone Betton Nayo (Jamaica), Mauricio Cabrera Leal (Colombia), Rodrigo Cifuentes (CAF), Monica Colomer (Spain), Colin Michael Connelly (Trinidad and Tobago), Ignacio Corlazzoli (CAF), Joseph Cox (CARICOM), Amélie de Montchalin (France), Lisa Douglas-Paul (ACS), David P. Doyle (Saint Kitts and Nevis), María Durán (CAF), Almudena Fernández (UNDP), Félix Fernández-Shaw (European Commission), Cynthia Filártiga (Paraguay), Malcolm Geere (Foreign, Commonwealth and Development Office), Paul Gomez (Bahamas), Cleviston Haynes (Barbados), Karen Hernández (Dominican Republic), Rafael Hoyuela (CAF), Daniela Ibarra (OAS), Len Ishmael (OECS), Raphael Joseph (Grenade), Florian Luetticken (EEAS in Barbados), Luis Fernando Medina (Colombia), Johakson Moncada (ACS), Natalia Moreno Rigollot (Telefonica), Keith Nurse (College of Science Technology and Applied Arts, Trinidad and Tobago), Nahuel Oddone (ECLAC), Joaquim Pedro Penna (Brazil), Miguel Posadas Arias (AECID), Edgar Picon-Prado (Tony Blair Institute for Global Change), Rodolfo Sabonge (ACS), Issamary Sanchez Ortega (Panama), Jo Spalburg (Caribbean Chamber of Commerce in Europe), Charles Trottmann (AFD) and Maria José Zambrano (AFD).

Finally, many thanks go to the Publications and Communications Division of the OECD Development Centre, notably to Aida Buendia, Delphine Grandrieux, Elizabeth Nash and Henri-Bernard Solignac-Lecomte, for their steadfast patience and expedient work on the production of this report and associated materials. The authors also sincerely appreciate the editing and proofreading activities undertaken by Mark Foss and Clara Young, respectively.

Editorial

The Caribbean is a region rich in opportunities, with immense development potential. Home to almost 10% of the world's coral reefs, approximately 45% of the fish species and 25% of the coral species, its unique biodiversity is an invaluable asset not only for the region, but for the world. While the region faces challenges such as exposure to climate change, limited access to external financing, and connectivity issues, the region's natural resources and potential for growth offer significant prospects for development.

The *Caribbean Development Dynamics is* a new flagship report of the IDB and OECD that highlights the region's development potential and informs national policies and international co-operation. The report calls for a shift in perspective – from seeing Caribbean challenges as limitations to recognising the opportunities they present. The Caribbean is part of the solution to our global challenges.

But, unlocking this potential will require bold policy actions, at both national and regional levels, together with stronger international partnerships.

First, at the national level, the report offers a comprehensive approach to challenges and opportunities. It draws on examples from within and beyond the Caribbean to guide efforts in diversifying economies, strengthening climate adaptation, and promoting job formalisation.

Second, at the regional level, the report highlights the potential benefits of deeper integration in areas like transport connectivity, renewable energies, and disaster risk reduction. The region's diversity is an asset, with opportunities to learn from each other's experiences and comparative advantages. With its integrated view of the Caribbean, the report aims to contribute to crafting a renewed regional perspective.

Finally, at the international level, more inclusive partnerships can bring the Caribbean perspective to the forefront. Though contributing little to climate change, the region faces its greatest impacts. The world should support the Caribbean in protecting its citizens and extraordinary biodiversity. Access to affordable financing remains a challenge, but the region is leading innovative climate finance solutions and shaping global discussions on international financial architecture. Multilateral institutions like the IDB and OECD have been working increasingly as a system and partnering with Caribbean countries in deploying new financial tools and providing policy guidance to mobilise climate finance to help the region strengthen its climate change resilience.

We hope that the report's comparative analysis and policy recommendations, developed in close partnership with regional actors, will help the Caribbean advance a home-grown path towards a more prosperous, resilient and inclusive development.

The report also reflects our collective engagement with the Caribbean. The OECD Development Centre has been expanding its analytical work and membership in the region. The Inter-American Development, for its part, continues to be a significant partner in regional development, recently launching One Caribbean – a regional programme to address common challenges in resilience, citizen and food security, and private sector growth.

We are committed to continue delivering this annual flagship report, in the belief that it will contribute to improving the lives of the Caribbeans.

Mathias Cormann
Secretary-General
Organisation for Economic
Co-operation and Development

Ilan Goldfajn
President
Inter-American Development Bank

Table of contents

Foreword 3

Acknowledgements 4

Editorial 6

Abbreviations and acronyms 12

Executive summary 15

Overview 17

Notes 37

References 37

1 Understanding macro-structural conditions 43

Introduction 44

Macroeconomic conditions are characterised by modest potential growth, coupled with volatility and vulnerability to external shocks 44

The economic structure reflects low levels of productivity and limited diversification and upgrading of the production matrix 53

Key policy messages 60

References 61

2 Improving social conditions 65

Introduction 66

Poverty and inequality remain high, although with large disparities across countries and significant information gaps 66

Labour markets remain largely informal, resulting in poor working conditions and heightened social vulnerability for many 70

Social protection and healthcare systems must be strengthened and adapted to climate vulnerabilities and emerging challenges 75

Education systems have improved in recent decades, yet with challenges in access and completion after lower secondary and in overall learning outcomes 80

Key policy messages 84

Notes 85

References 85

3 Environmental challenges and opportunities for sustainable development 89

Introduction 90

Caribbean countries face unique challenges linked to their geographical location and the vulnerabilities associated with Small Island Developing States 90

Adaptation measures are central to tackling climate vulnerabilities and fostering climate resilience in the Caribbean 97
Harnessing the potential of unique biodiversity and natural endowments: From vulnerabilities to opportunities in the Caribbean 101
Key policy messages 114
Notes 114
References 115
Annex 3.A. 124

4 Stronger institutions for a renewed social contract 127
Introduction 128
Understanding citizens' perceptions to improve policy outcomes 128
Advancing more effective and inclusive institutions in the Caribbean 135
Towards a renewed social contract 143
Key policy messages 149
Notes 151
References 152

5 Financing the development agenda 159
Introduction 160
Tax revenues in the Caribbean can be strengthened to finance the development agenda 160
Rethinking debt management and strengthening fiscal frameworks will help Caribbean countries cope with high debt levels 168
Innovative debt financing mechanisms can mobilise resources to support environmental, social and ocean-related objectives 171
Financial markets need development to improve access to financing 178
Key policy messages 182
Notes 183
References 184

6 Regional integration and international partnerships 191
Introduction 192
Targeted regional strategies can improve trade outcomes for the Caribbean 192
Harnessing the potential of regional co-operation to address common challenges and opportunities 201
International partnerships to support financing for development and climate action in the Caribbean 207
Notes 217
References 217

FIGURES

Figure 1. Average annual economic losses linked to climate-related extreme weather events in the Caribbean (1980-2020) 18
Figure 2. Infrastructure Vulnerability Index 2021: Caribbean and Latin American selected countries 19
Figure 3. Prevalence of moderate or severe food insecurity in Caribbean countries, 2022 21
Figure 4. Distribution of population by household informality, latest available year 22
Figure 5. Potential GDP per capita growth in the Caribbean, Latin America and advanced economies 24
Figure 6. Central government total public debt, selected Caribbean countries and regional averages, 2012 and 2022 25
Figure 7. Debt service-to-tax revenues ratio, 2012 and 2022 25
Figure 8. Contribution of economic sectors to total GDP, 2022 26

Figure 9. Intentional homicides rate in the Caribbean, 2022 28
Figure 10. Women's political representation in Caribbean countries, 2022 29
Figure 11. Tax structure in selected Caribbean economies and Latin America and OECD averages, 2022 30
Figure 12. International GSSSB bond issuance in the Caribbean by type and issuer, 2019 - August 2024 32
Figure 13. Domestic credit to private sector by region 2000-22 and domestic bank credit and deposits as percentage of GDP in the Caribbean, 2022 33
Figure 14. Participation in world exports (percentage) of the Caribbean, Latin America and ASEAN, 1981-2022 34
Figure 15. Transport cost intensity, selected regions and country groups (2016-21) 35
Figure 16. Main external financial flows to the Caribbean, 2000-23 36
Figure 1.1. Potential GDP per capita growth in the Caribbean, Latin America and advanced economies (as estimated by different methods since 1980) 45
Figure 1.2. Evolution of GDP per capita by region and GDP growth standard deviations in the Caribbean, 2000-23 46
Figure 1.3. Labour productivity in the Caribbean and Latin America as a share of the OECD, 1991-2023 47
Figure 1.4. Central government fiscal balance as percentage of GDP, 2013-23 average 48
Figure 1.5. Central government total public debt as a percentage of GDP, selected Caribbean countries and regional averages, 2012 and 2022 49
Figure 1.6. Average inflation rate by monetary regimes in the Caribbean, 2000-23 50
Figure 1.7. Total investment as a percentage of GDP, 2015-23 51
Figure 1.8. Public investment in infrastructure in selected Caribbean countries as a percentage of GDP, 2015-21 52
Figure 1.9. Foreign direct investment net inflows (percentage of GDP), 2013-23 53
Figure 1.10. Contribution of economic sectors to total GDP, 2022 54
Figure 1.11. Tourist arrivals and tourism expenditure as percentage of GDP, 1995-2022 54
Figure 1.12. Current account balance in the Caribbean, 2012-22 55
Figure 1.13. Share of services exports in total exports, 2022 56
Figure 1.14. Goods trade structure by technology intensity in the Caribbean, 2022 57
Figure 1.15. Areas of innovation at the firm level in the Caribbean 58
Figure 1.16. Green innovation at the firm level in Caribbean countries 59
Figure 1.17. Main obstacles affecting firms' operation in Caribbean economies 60
Figure 2.1. Monetary poverty in Caribbean countries, latest year available 67
Figure 2.2. Human Development Index, 1990-2022 68
Figure 2.3. Prevalence of moderate or severe food insecurity (%) in Caribbean countries, 2022 69
Figure 2.4. Employment to population rate, by gender, Caribbean countries 70
Figure 2.5. Young people not in education, employment or training by gender, in selected Caribbean countries, 2020 71
Figure 2.6. Informality rates in selected Caribbean countries, latest available year 72
Figure 2.7. Distribution of population by household informality, latest available year 73
Figure 2.8. Workers living under the national poverty line, by informality status, selected Caribbean countries, latest available year 74
Figure 2.9. Distribution of the population by household informality and welfare quintile, latest available year 75
Figure 2.10. Central government social spending in selected Caribbean economies, 2008-22 76
Figure 2.11. Public expenditures on pensions in selected Caribbean countries, latest available year 77
Figure 2.12. Population structure, 2021 and projected in 2050, Caribbean countries 78
Figure 2.13. Health expenditure per capita and as a percentage of GDP, 2021 79
Figure 2.14. Infant mortality rates, 2020 and 2000 80
Figure 2.15. Government expenditures on education in the Caribbean as a percentage of GDP, 2013-22 81
Figure 2.16. Mean years of schooling of people aged 25 or more, Caribbean countries, 2002-22 82
Figure 2.17. Out-of-school rate for youth of upper secondary school age, 2022 or latest available year 83
Figure 3.1. Vulnerability Index: Caribbean, Latin American, and OECD selected countries, 2021 91
Figure 3.2. Climate-related extreme weather events by type, selected Caribbean countries (1980-2020) 92
Figure 3.3. Annual mean temperature anomalies in the Caribbean, 1960-2023 93
Figure 3.4. Impact of climate hazards, selected Caribbean countries (1980-2020) 94
Figure 3.5. Total GHG emissions by subregions, 1990-2020 96
Figure 3.6. Infrastructure Vulnerability Index 2021: Caribbean, Latin American, and OECD selected countries, 2021 98
Figure 3.7. Renewable electricity generation, selected Caribbean countries, 2010 and 2022 102
Figure 3.8. Technical potential for offshore wind generation, selected Caribbean countries by 2020 103
Figure 3.9. Tourism sector contribution to GDP, average 2015-19 109
Figure 4.1. Satisfaction with democracy in the Caribbean and Latin America, 2014-23 129
Figure 4.2. Corruption Perception Index, Caribbean and Latin America, 2022 130

Figure 4.3. Satisfaction with the quality of public schools, selected Caribbean countries and Latin America, 2014-23 131
Figure 4.4. Top concerns for citizens in Caribbean countries, 2023 132
Figure 4.5. Intentional homicides rate in the Caribbean, 2022 133
Figure 4.6. Security risks indicator, selected Caribbean countries, 2022 134
Figure 4.7. Caribbean citizens consider climate change a very serious problem, 2023 135
Figure 4.8. Government effectiveness in the Caribbean, 2022 136
Figure 4.9. Statistical Performance Indicator (SPI) overall score by region, 2022 137
Figure 4.10. Open data inventory (ODIN) overall score for data coverage and openness, selected Caribbean countries, Latin America and OECD, 2020 138
Figure 4.11. Women's political representation in Caribbean countries, 2022 143
Figure 4.12. Perception of citizens' basic rights protection, selected Caribbean countries, 2014 and 2023 144
Figure 4.13. High levels of trust in the local community, selected Caribbean countries, 2014 and 2023 145
Figure 4.14. Citizens' support for policies to reduce income inequality, selected Caribbean countries, 2023 146
Figure 4.15. Key areas of opportunity in Caribbean NDPs 149
Figure 5.1. Evolution of tax-to-GDP ratios, regional averages and Caribbean countries, 2010-22 161
Figure 5.2. Tax structure in selected Caribbean economies and Latin America and OECD averages, 2022 162
Figure 5.3. Environmentally related tax revenues by main tax base in Caribbean countries, 2022 164
Figure 5.4. Debt service to tax revenues ratio, 2012 and 2022 169
Figure 5.5. Public debt by remaining maturity as percentage of GDP, selected Caribbean countries, 2021 170
Figure 5.6. External public debt stock by creditor (public and private) in Caribbean countries, 2022 170
Figure 5.7. International GSSSB bond issuance in the Caribbean by type and issuer, 2019 - November 2024 172
Figure 5.8. Cumulative CAT bond issuance and geographical coverage of CAT bonds issued, 1996-2022 174
Figure 5.9. Sustainable finance framework development in the Caribbean, 2018-24 178
Figure 5.10. Domestic credit to private sector as percentage of GDP by region 2000-22 and domestic bank credit and deposits as percentage of GDP in the Caribbean, 2022 179
Figure 5.11. Number of deposit accounts with commercial banks per 1 000 adults, 2022 180
Figure 5.12. Banking system efficiency, 2021 181
Figure 5.13. Banking system soundness indicators, 2022 182
Figure 6.1. Main regional and sub-regional organisations with Caribbean membership 193
Figure 6.2. Intra-regional trade as a proportion of total trade, selected regional blocs, 1995-99 and 2015-18 194
Figure 6.3. Participation in world exports (percentage) of the Caribbean, Latin America, and ASEAN, 1981-2022 196
Figure 6.4. Trade facilitation performance, 2022 198
Figure 6.5. Main destinations of Caribbean exports, 2022 or most recent year available 199
Figure 6.6. Transport cost intensity, selected regions and country groups (2016-21) 200
Figure 6.7. Internet users as a percentage of the total population, regional comparison 203
Figure 6.8. Average price of electricity (1 kWh) in the Caribbean, Latin America and the OECD, 2021 204
Figure 6.9. Number and share of intra- and extra-regional immigrants in the Caribbean, 2000-20 206
Figure 6.10. Main external financial flows to the Caribbean, 2000-23 208
Figure 6.11. Percentages of TOSSD resources allocated by Sustainable Development Goals, 2019-22 210

TABLES

Table 3.1. Energy transition 104
Table 3.2. Blue economy 106
Table 3.3. The circular economy 107
Table 3.4. Sustainable tourism 110
Table 3.5. Sustainable transport 111
Table 3.6. Nature-based Solutions 112
Table 3.7. Digital transformation 113
Table 4.1. E-Government Development Index (EGDI), selected Caribbean countries, 2022 139
Table 4.2. National Development Plans, selected Caribbean countries 148

Annex Table 3.A.1. Nationally determined contributions, selected Caribbean countries 124
Annex Table 3.A.2. Climate adaptation in national adaptation plans and long-term strategies, selected Caribbean countries 124

BOXES

Box 1.1. Key policy messages 60
Box 2.1. Key policy messages 84
Box 3.1. Resilient infrastructure in the Caribbean 99
Box 3.2. Key policy messages 114
Box 4.1. Spotlight on Haiti 133
Box 4.2. Key policy messages 150
Box 5.1. Tax transparency in the Caribbean region: Progress and remaining challenges 166
Box 5.2. Barbados debt-for-nature conversion 176
Box 5.3. Key policy messages 182
Box 6.1. Food production as a promising sector to boost intra-regional trade in the Caribbean 195
Box 6.2. Spotlight on the EU Outermost Regions: Strategic sectors and the potential for internationalisation 197
Box 6.3. One Caribbean, the IDB's regional strategy to promote sustainable development 212
Box 6.4. Key policy messages 216

Abbreviations and acronyms

4P	The Paris Pact for People and the Planet
ACS	Association of the Caribbean States
ADB	Asian Development Bank
AECID	Spanish Agency for International Co-operation for Development
AFD	Agence française de développement
AOSIS	Alliance of Small Island States
ASEAN	Association of Southeast Asian Nations
BEPS	Base Erosion and Profit Shifting
BMZ	Germany's Federal Ministry of Economic Co-operation and Development
CAF	Development Bank of Latin America and the Caribbean
CAFTA-DR	Dominican Republic-Central American Free Trade Agreement
CARDTP	Caribbean Digital Transformation Project
CARICOM	Caribbean Community
CAT bonds	Catastrophe bonds
CBF	Caribbean Biodiversity Fund
CBI	Citizenship-by-Investment
CCCCC	The Caribbean Community Climate Change Centre
CCREEE	Caribbean Centre for Renewable Energy and Energy Efficiency
CCRIF	Caribbean Catastrophe Risk Insurance Facility
CCS	Cultural and creative sector
CDB	Caribbean Development Bank
CDEMA	Caribbean Disaster Emergency Management Agency
CEDA	Caribbean Export Development Agency
CIT	Corporate income tax
CRDC	Climate Resilient Debt Clauses
CREWS	Climate Risk Early Warning Systems
CRFM	Caribbean Regional Fisheries Mechanism
CSME	CARICOM Single Market and Economy
CTF	Conservation Trust Fund
CTO	Caribbean Tourism Organisation
DiT	Development in Transition
DVRP	Disaster Vulnerability Reduction Project
EC	European Commission
ECCB	Eastern Caribbean Central Bank
ECCU	Eastern Caribbean Currency Union
ECLAC	Economic Commission for Latin America and the Caribbean

EEAS	European External Action Service
EFSD+	European Fund for Sustainable Development Plus
EGDI	E-Government Development Index
EIB	European Investment Bank
EM-DAT	The International Disaster Database
ERTR	Environmental related tax revenues
EUROSTAT	Statistical Office of the European Union
EWS	Early Warning Systems
FATF	Financial Action Task Force
FDI	Foreign direct investment
GCF	Green Climate Fund
GGIA	EU-LAC Global Gateway Investment Agenda
GHG	Global greenhouse gas
GHGBAU	Greenhouse gas emissions/business-as-usual
Global Forum	Global Forum on Transparency and Exchange of Information for Tax Purposes
GMT	Global minimum tax
GNI	Gross national income
GSSSB	Green, social, sustainability, sustainability-linked and blue bonds
GVCs	Global value chains
GW	Gigawatts
HDI	Human Development Index
IBP	International Budget Partnership
ICT	Information and communication technology
ICZM	Integrated coastal zone management
IDB	Inter-American Development Bank
IEA	International Energy Agency
IFRC	International Federation of Red Cross
ILO	International Labour Organization
IMF	International Monetary Fund
IMO	International Maritime Organization
IOM	International Organization for Migration
IPCC	Intergovernmental Panel on Climate Change
LAPOP	Latin American Public Opinion Project
LUCF	Land-use change and forestry
MNEs	Multinational enterprises
MSP	Marine Spatial Plans
NAP	National Adaptation Plan
NbS	Nature-based solutions
NDC	National determined contribution
ND-GAIN	Notre Dame Adaptation Initiative
NDPs	National Development Plans
NEET	Not engaged in education, employment or training
NPLs	Non-performing loans
NSDS	National Strategies for the Development of Statistics

NSOs	National Statistical Offices
NSSs	National Statistical Systems
NTBs	Non-tariff barriers
OAS	Organisation of American States
OBS	Open Budget Survey
ODA	Official Development Assistance
ODIN	Open Data Inventory
OECD	Organisation for Economic Co-operation and Development
OECS	Organisation of Eastern Caribbean States
OGP	Open Government Partnership
ORs	EU Outermost Regions
PACC 2030	US-Caribbean Partnership to Address the Climate Crisis 2030
PARIS21	OECD Partnership in Statistics for Development in the 21st Century
PISA	OECD Programme for International Student Assessment
PIT	Personal income tax
PPO	Principal payment options
PPP	Purchasing power parities
PPPs	Public-private partnerships
ROA	Return on assets
SDGs	Sustainable Development Goals
SICA	Central American Integration System
SIDS	Small Island Developing States
SLBs	Sustainability-linked bonds
SMEs	Small and medium-size enterprises
SPI	Statistical Performance Indicators
SSCs	Social security contributions
TOSSD	Total Official Support for Sustainable Development
UIS	UNESCO Institute for Statistics
UN MVI	United Nations Multidimensional Vulnerability Index
UNCC	United Nations Climate Change
UNCTAD	United Nations Trade and Development
UNDP	United Nations Development Programme
UNDRR	United Nations Office for Disaster Risk Reduction
UNEP	United Nations Environment Programme
UNFCCC	United Nations Framework Convention on Climate Change
UNODC	United Nations Office on Drugs and Crime
UNOPS	United Nations Office for Project Services
VAT	Value-added tax
WEF	World Economic Forum
WFP	United Nations World Food Programme
WMO	World Meteorological Organisation
WRI	World Resources Institute
WTTC	World Travel and Tourism Council

Executive summary

The Caribbean holds significant untapped potential for sustainable development. While most countries have recorded remarkable socio-economic progress, the region faces unique challenges including high climate vulnerability, limited external financing, and connectivity issues. *Caribbean Development Dynamics 2025* proposes a multi-dimensional approach to unlock the Caribbean's development potential and overcome its main challenges. This approach is strengthened by the increasing engagement of the OECD Development Centre and the Inter-American Development Bank with the region, the latter through the ONE Caribbean programme, a recently launched regional strategic initiative aimed at scaling up impact, leveraging resources, and fostering co-operation and economies of scale to tackle shared challenges.

Build climate resilience and harness the potential of natural endowments

The Caribbean is one of the most vulnerable regions to climate impacts in the world, despite its limited contribution to global greenhouse gas emissions. Climate-related extreme weather events in the region increased by 85% in 2001-20 compared to 1980-2000. Natural disasters cost an annual average of 2.13% of regional GDP from 1980 to 2020, with deep social negative impacts, especially on vulnerable populations. These costs underscore the need to build regional resilience through ambitious adaptation measures, resilient infrastructure, and strong early warning systems. The region's rich biodiversity and natural endowments – hosting almost 10% of the world's coral reefs, and around 45% and 25% of the fish and coral species, respectively – provide the basis for developing new activities in renewable energy, sustainable tourism and transport, the blue and circular economy, and nature-based solutions.

Foster social inclusion and strengthen social protection systems

The well-being of the average Caribbean citizen has improved over the last three decades, although heterogeneity is large across countries. In 2022, the average Caribbean person could expect to live 72.6 years (an increase of 4.2 years since 1990), and to complete 14.1 years of education (an increase of 2.9 years). In addition, the mean GNI per capita stood at 17 280 constant 2021 international USD (a 66% increase compared to 1990). However, important socio-economic gaps remain: almost one in four people are poor in the Caribbean on average, and 37% live in moderate or severe food insecurity (33% in Latin America). On average, almost one worker in two has an informal job (47.2%, against 57% in Latin America) and more than a third (34.1%) of the population lives in households where all workers are informal. Women face many obstacles – from gender-based violence to unequal pay and limited access to education and health care. In 2022, they held 23.7% of parliamentary seats on average (31.7% in Latin America).

Boost productivity, reinforce macroeconomic stability and upgrade production

Potential growth in the Caribbean is relatively low and has been declining. Potential GDP per capita growth is estimated at around 1.4%, slightly above the Latin American average (1.1%) and below that of advanced economies (1.8%). This is associated with limited levels of labour productivity in the Caribbean, representing 46% of the OECD level in 2023. Public debt remains high, although with substantial heterogeneity across countries and with several among them embarked on important consolidation efforts. In 2022, the average central government debt was 78.8% of GDP, well above the average for Latin America (52.9%). Debt service is also high: in 2022, the average debt service-to-tax revenue ratio reached 12.9%, higher than in Latin America (11.5%) and well above the OECD average (4.8%). Caribbean countries are mostly service-based and commodity-exporting economies. In 2022, services represented between 55% and 78% of total GDP for most countries, and tourism was the main economic activity for many of them, representing on average 25.4% of the Caribbean GDP between 2015-19. Natural resources – especially oil and gas – play a significant role in some countries, notably in Guyana, Trinidad and Tobago, and Suriname. Agriculture remains relatively large for Belize, Dominica, the Dominican Republic and Guyana.

Build trust, improve evidence-based policy making and public services

Citizen satisfaction with democracy and public services has declined. In 2023, 65% of people, on average, expressed low satisfaction with the democratic system, an increase of 22.6 percentage points (p.p.) in the last decade. In 2023, only 40% of Caribbeans were satisfied with health services, declining by 15.4 p.p. in the last decade. Satisfaction with education is higher (65.2%, on average in 2023) although it fell by 9.5 p.p. Citizen security is paramount, as several Caribbean countries rank among those with the highest per capita average murder rates globally. The average cost of crime is estimated at 3.7% of the region's GDP. Better data are key for informed policy design, implementation and monitoring. In 2021, only half of the Caribbean countries with data available were implementing a statistical plan. Strengthening national statistical offices and open government practices with intra-regional collaboration and digital transformation will be key in promoting citizen engagement and better public services, and, ultimately, strengthening the social contract.

Mobilise more financial resources to finance development

In 2022, average tax revenues in the Caribbean were 21% of GDP, below Latin America (22.4%) and the OECD (34%). Tax systems can be made more equitable and efficient, by enhancing direct taxation, rationalising tax expenditures and fighting tax avoidance. Caribbean countries have spearheaded the development of innovative debt instruments. Green, social, sustainability, sustainability-linked, and blue bonds represented a cumulative USD 1.5 billion in the region from 2019 to August 2024. Other tools include climate-resilient debt clauses, which allow for payment deferrals following disasters, or debt-for-nature swaps to advance environmental goals while reducing debt. Regulatory frameworks and sustainable finance taxonomies will help ensure transparency and attract investments. Financial depth in the Caribbean remains low, constraining households' and firms' access to finance. Domestic credit to the private sector was 42% of GDP in 2022, below Latin America (55%) and the OECD (149%).

Deepen regional integration and expand international partnerships

The Caribbean's participation in world exports has declined from a peak of 0.35% in 1984 to 0.23% in 2022, with intra-regional trade decreasing to 6.7% of total trade in 2015-18. Developing regional value chains in strategic sectors, reducing non-tariff barriers and improving trade facilitation should be priority areas. Regional co-operation can help address challenges like transport, digital connectivity and disaster risk reduction. Transport costs are high, with logistics costs representing 16-26% of GDP (9% in the OECD). Public-private partnerships can enhance transport connectivity. Regional co-operation can also help build climate resilience, for instance through joint early warning systems. Digital technologies offer an opportunity to drive productivity, production diversification and economic integration. Caribbean countries can also foster a cohesive voice in ongoing discussions to transform the international financial architecture.

Overview

The Caribbean region is exposed to unique challenges but is also full of development opportunities

Caribbean countries face specific threats and vulnerabilities, including high exposure to climate change impacts, limited access to external financing, and connectivity challenges. These issues are, to a large extent, linked to geography. They also reflect the fact that these countries are – or share characteristics with – Small Island Developing States (SIDS). *Caribbean Development Dynamics (CDD) 2025* calls for a shift in perspective: from facing the challenges to actively acknowledging the region's assets and seizing the associated opportunities to boost the development of Caribbean countries.

To that end, the report adopts both a regional and multi-dimensional perspective. The regional lens helps emphasise common challenges and opportunities, pointing to areas with potential for greater co-operation and integration among Caribbean nations. While heterogeneity across Caribbean countries is notable and can be an obstacle, diversity is a valuable asset. A regional perspective helps capitalise on such diversity by identifying areas where countries stand to benefit from each other's experiences and comparative advantages.

The report focuses its analysis on 15 Caribbean countries: Antigua and Barbuda, Barbados, The Bahamas, Belize, Dominica, the Dominican Republic, Grenada, Guyana, Haiti, Jamaica, Saint Kitts and Nevis, Saint Lucia, Saint Vincent and the Grenadines, Suriname, and Trinidad and Tobago. These 15 countries are part of the 39 SIDS. The report analyses them alongside the Latin America and OECD averages. When relevant, the analysis also incorporates the perspective of the "Greater Caribbean", including other countries and territories in the Caribbean basin.

The report also analyses the region from a multi-dimensional perspective, focusing on six key areas of action and exploring the synergies and trade-offs among them. The first three dimensions address the "what": examining the core aspects of development in the Caribbean, including i) environmental; ii) social; and iii) economic conditions. The latter three focus on the "how": i) stronger institutions; ii) increased financing; and iii) enhanced regional integration and international partnerships.

Build climate resilience and harness the potential of natural endowments

Caribbean countries are highly vulnerable to the effects of climate change

The Caribbean is among the world's regions most prone to climate-related extreme weather events. The region is increasingly exposed to climate hazards, including extreme heat, droughts, storms, hurricanes, wildfires and excessive flooding (CSGM/UWI, 2020[1]). From 1980 to 2020, Caribbean countries have suffered 322 disasters triggered by climate-related natural hazards, affecting 24 million people. The number of extreme weather events in the Caribbean in 2001-20 was 85% higher than in 1980-2000 (EM-

DAT, 2024[2]). Haiti, the Dominican Republic and Jamaica experienced 60.2% of total climate hazard events in the region during that period.

The economic costs of climate-related extreme weather events in the Caribbean between 1980 and 2020 represent an annual average of 2.13% of gross domestic product (GDP) (Figure 1).

Figure 1. Average annual economic losses linked to climate-related extreme weather events in the Caribbean (1980-2020)

As a percentage of GDP

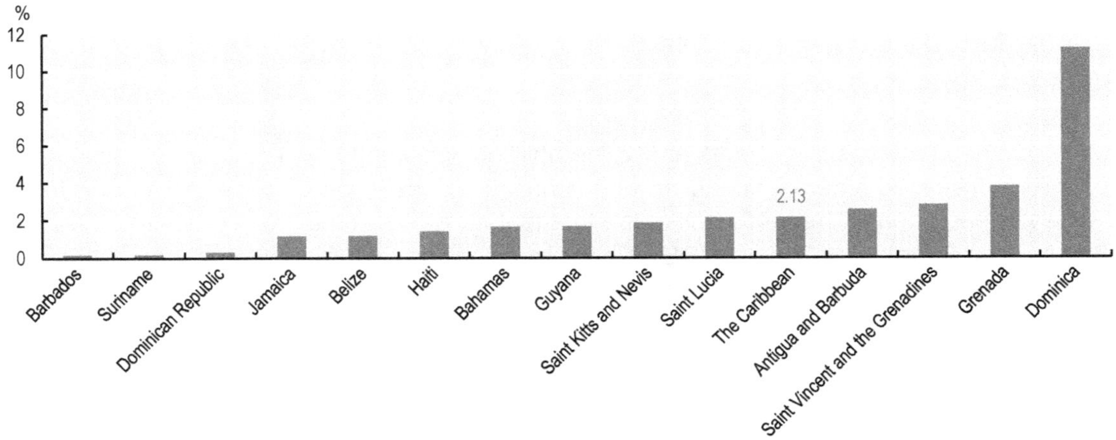

Note: The figure shows the average annual economic costs of climate-related extreme weather events as a percentage of GDP on average from 1980 to 2020. The Caribbean average includes 15 countries: Antigua and Barbuda, The Bahamas, Barbados, Belize, Dominica, Dominican Republic, Grenada, Guyana, Haiti, Jamaica, Saint Kitts and Nevis, Saint Lucia, Saint Vincent and the Grenadines, and Suriname.
Source: Authors' elaboration based on (EM-DAT, 2024[2]; World Bank, 2024[3]).

StatLink https://stat.link/4v5l38

The Caribbean shows, on average, higher vulnerability to climate change than Latin America and the OECD, according to the Notre Dame Adaptation Initiative (ND-GAIN) vulnerability index. Caribbean countries tend to be more exposed (due to their geographical location), more sensitive (given the magnitude of population and sectors affected) and have less adaptive capacity (institutional and infrastructural) to respond to climate hazards (ND-GAIN, 2021[4]). Other metrics – notably the European Investment Bank's Climate Risk Country Scoring Model – also place the Caribbean, alongside the Pacific islands, as facing the highest physical risks globally (EIB, 2021[5]). In addition, Caribbean countries experienced the highest temperature increases in the last three decades in Latin America and the Caribbean (LAC), and rising sea levels are a major threat to the region.

The region is also particularly vulnerable to biodiversity loss, as many of its main economic drivers, such as tourism, agriculture and mineral extraction, are linked to natural resources and the quality of ecosystems (OECD, 2023[6]).

Vulnerable populations are the most affected by climate change consequences. The effects of global warming are accentuating forced migration trends, as well as spatial and gender inequalities. In the Caribbean, environmental disasters caused 5.3 million new internal displacements between 2012 and 2022 (IOM, 2023[7]). High urbanisation rates, unregulated urban expansion and socio-economic residential segregation have forced vulnerable groups into high-risk zones without adequate infrastructure. The increasing effects of droughts on agricultural areas also exacerbate the socio-economic rural-urban divide.

The Caribbean contributed only 0.23% to total GHG global emissions in 2021, a figure closely aligned with the region's share of global GDP (around 0.22%) in that same year (World Bank, 2024[3]). Yet, Caribbean countries have engaged in important mitigation commitments. Under the principle of common but differentiated responsibility, they seek to advance a sustainable and just green transition, which will come with transitional risks[1] (EIB, 2021[5]).

Adaptation measures are central to tackling climate vulnerabilities and fostering climate resilience in the Caribbean

Building climate resilience entails different climate risk management interventions, including resilient infrastructure, early warning systems (EWS) and climate adaptation policy instruments.

Climate-resilient infrastructure is crucial for economic stability, as it can significantly reduce GDP losses by minimising the destruction of capital during natural disasters. Latin American countries perform better than the Caribbean in terms of infrastructure vulnerabilities, with Antigua and Barbuda, Jamaica and Saint Vincent and the Grenadines presenting the highest risks (Figure 2). Several countries in the region are taking steps to develop more climate-resilient infrastructure, enhance the reliability of service provision and extend the lifespan of strategic assets. For instance, Saint Lucia has implemented long-term infrastructure planning strategies; Grenada has a Disaster Vulnerability Reduction Project; and Barbados has developed the Coastal Infrastructural Programme.

Figure 2. Infrastructure Vulnerability Index 2021: Caribbean and Latin American selected countries

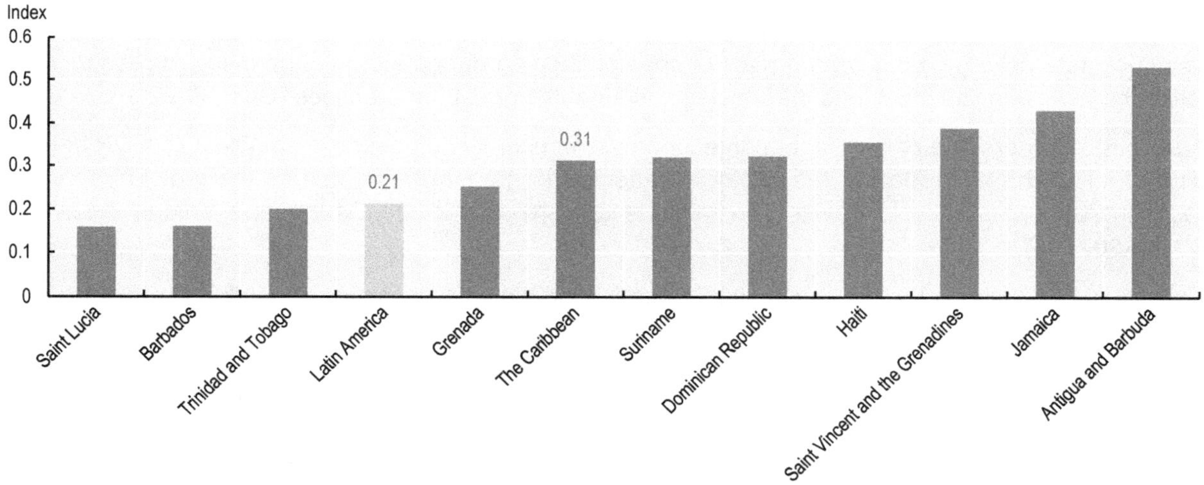

Note: The ND-Gain Infrastructure Vulnerability Country Index captures the vulnerability of coastal and energy infrastructure to climate change.
Source: Authors' elaboration based on ND-GAIN (2021[4]).

StatLink https://stat.link/nsjm3g

EWS are a key element of disaster risk reduction, contributing to protecting communities and infrastructure from natural hazards, minimising disaster losses and boosting resilience (OECD, 2023[6]). Caribbean countries have been frontrunners in developing EWS. Antigua and Barbuda, Dominica, the Dominican Republic, Saint Lucia, and Saint Vincent and the Grenadines have implemented projects to create EWS national assessments and roadmaps with support from different international organisations. Barbados has also implemented EWS projects for several years, adopting a community-based approach to disaster management (UNDRR, 2022[8]).

Several Caribbean countries have advanced their adaptation commitments through National Adaptation Plans (NAPs). These serve as a comprehensive framework to reduce vulnerability from climate change, strengthen resilience and increase adaptive capacity. Grenada (2009), Haiti (2023), Saint Lucia (2018), Saint Vincent and the Grenadines (2019), Suriname (2020) and Trinidad and Tobago (2023) have submitted their NAPs under the United Nations Framework Convention on Climate Change. Saint Lucia and Grenada went further by submitting sectoral NAPs that detail concrete adaptation actions for specific sectors (OECD, 2023[6]).

Unlocking the Caribbean's sustainable development potential: Key areas of opportunity

The rich biodiversity and natural endowments that characterise Caribbean countries provide opportunities for accelerating a green transition that generates economic, social and environmental benefits. These include the energy transition, the blue economy, sustainable tourism, the circular economy, sustainable transport, nature-based solutions to sustainable development challenges and digital transformation.

Transitioning to a more diversified and sustainable *energy mix* in the Caribbean could yield USD 6.1 billion in net benefits, cut fuel oil imports by 260 million barrels, and reduce CO_2 emissions by 41 million tonnes by 2040 with the required investments (USD 11 billion) (Masson, Ehrhardt and Lizzio, 2020[9]). Sustainable transport can reduce dependency on fuel imports, promote energy diversification and efficiency, increase air quality, improve daily commutes and reduce GHG emissions.

The Caribbean is particularly well placed to benefit from the *blue economy* due to its rich marine biodiversity and reliance on ocean-based industries like tourism and fisheries. The region hosts almost 10% of the world's coral reefs, approximately 45% of its fish species and 25% of its coral species (UNEP, 2019[10]). Nature-based solutions, such as wetland restoration and forest conservation, offer robust natural defences against climate risks by reducing the risks of coastal flooding during storms, improving access to water, increasing available fish stock and introducing sustainable agriculture practices (GCF, 2022[11]).

Tourism is a cornerstone of the Caribbean economy, representing on average 25.4% of its GDP between 2015-19. Over the next decade, the sector is expected to grow twice as fast as the regional economy, presenting an opportunity to develop sustainable tourism around the Caribbean's unique biodiversity (WTTC, 2022[12]).

The *circular economy* promotes sustainable production and consumption, contributing to formal job creation, waste transformation, resilient infrastructure and sustainable business models. For example, circular business models are working to transform sargassum, a major threat to local ecosystems and the tourism and fishery sectors, into an economic opportunity. Sargassum could be transformed into different by-products such as fertilisers, raw material for biodegradable plastics, cosmetics, electricity and biomass. Key tools to advance the circular transition include economic incentives, green public procurement, regulatory improvements and data monitoring.

Digital transformation can drive economic growth, improve governance, and enhance disaster resilience, connecting island nations with each other and with global markets and services. However, high infrastructure costs demand innovative solutions. At least 11 Caribbean countries are already developing digital policy frameworks to address these challenges.

Foster social inclusion and strengthen social protection systems

Well-being has improved, yet poverty, inequality and food security are enduring challenges

Over the last three decades, the Caribbean has experienced an increase in the Human Development Index (HDI), similar to that of the Latin American region. In 2022, the average Caribbean person could expect to live 72.6 years (an increase of 4.2 years since 1990), the average child could expect to complete 14.1 years of education (an increase of 2.9 years) and the mean gross national income (GNI) per capita stood at 17 280 constant 2021 international USD (66% increase in that period) (UNDP, 2024[13]). Although social protection systems are far from universal in the Caribbean, they show better coverage and adequacy than in Latin American countries (IDB, 2021[14]).

Despite this, important and lasting gaps remain across socio-economic groups, territories and genders. For instance, poverty and inequality are persistent challenges. Almost one in four people are poor in the Caribbean, according to the latest data available. Within this broader picture there is large heterogeneity: poverty levels range from 11% to 58.5% among those countries with available data. Inequality is also relatively high in the Caribbean. The average Gini coefficient in the region was 0.40, slightly below the average of 0.45 in LAC. In this context, there is also heterogeneity across Caribbean countries, ranging from 0.48 in Antigua and Barbuda to 0.32 in Barbados (ECLAC, 2023[15]). The most recent Gini coefficient for the OECD average was 0.33 (World Bank, 2024[16]).

The share of people living in moderate or severe food insecurity in the Caribbean – 37% on average – is high. This is more than the Latin American average of 33%, ranging from 20% in The Bahamas, Grenada and Saint Lucia to around 50% in the Dominican Republic and Jamaica and more than 80% in Haiti (Figure 3). The region is unique in having a generally high cost of food. Around 57% of the Caribbean population does not have access to a healthy diet due to its high cost, which is 42% higher than the OECD average (FAO, 2023[17]). This is largely because of the high dependency on food imports: 80-90% of all food consumed in the region is imported, mostly from outside the Caribbean region (IICA, 2018[18]; Turnbull, 2021[19]). In fact, intra-regional food trade accounts for only 16.6% of total food imports.

Figure 3. Prevalence of moderate or severe food insecurity in Caribbean countries, 2022

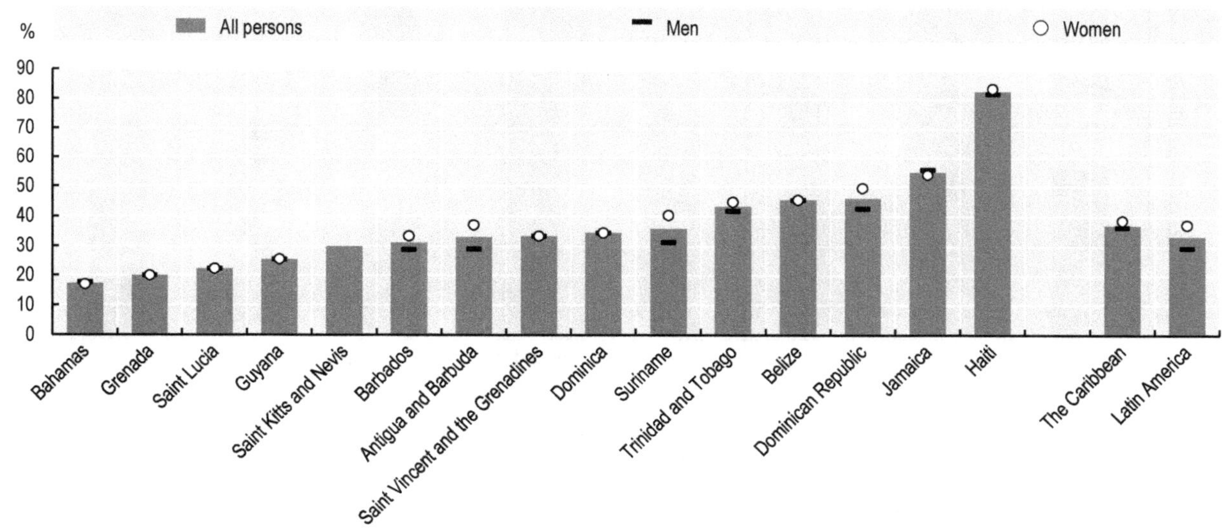

Note: The indicator measures the percentage of the population that has experienced food insecurity at moderate or severe levels during the reference period. Food insecurity at moderate levels of severity is associated with the inability to regularly eat healthy, balanced diets. Severe levels of food insecurity imply a high probability of reduced food intake and therefore can lead to more severe forms of undernutrition, including hunger. Comparable data by gender was not available for Saint Kitts and Nevis.
Source: Authors' elaboration based on the United Nations SDG Indicators Database (2024[20]).

StatLink https://stat.link/p5i0ua

Fostering formalisation will improve working conditions and extend the coverage of social protection to vulnerable groups

Labour market outcomes in the Caribbean have room for improvement. In 2022, less than 6 out of 10 of the working-age population (57.5%) were employed, slightly lower than the Latin America average (58.2%) (ECLAC, 2024[21]; ILO, 2024[22]). Women and youth are especially vulnerable. Women are less likely to be employed (50.1% held a job in 2022) than men (65.1%). In 2022, the employment rate among youth (15-24 years old) was 33.4%, compared to 39.6% in Latin America. In addition, 22.9% of the youth labour force was unemployed in 2020 (25.6% for women and 21.6% for men) (ILO, 2024[22]). Similarly, in 2020, and for 6 countries with available data, almost one-third of young people (31%) were not engaged in education, employment, or training compared to 19% in Latin America (ECLAC, 2024[21]; ILO, 2024[22]).

Labour informality is widespread in the Caribbean. On average, in the latest year with available data, almost 1 worker in 2 in the region held an informal job (47.2%), a rate of informality lower than across Latin America (57%). At the household level, for 6 countries with available data, 6 out of 10 people in the Caribbean (59.6%) on average lived in a household that depended solely or partially on informal work (below the Latin American mean of 67.3%). There was high heterogeneity across countries (Figure 4). On average, more than a third (34.1%) of the total population lived in households where all workers were informal.

Figure 4. Distribution of population by household informality, latest available year

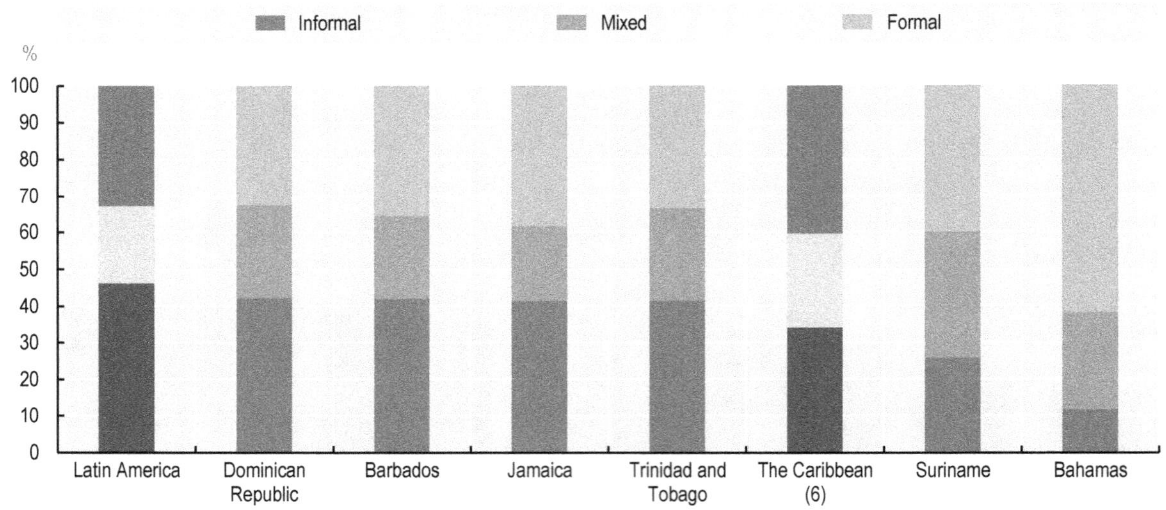

Note: Household types are defined according to the formality status of a household's principal earners. If all the earners are formal or informal, the household is defined as completely formal or informal, respectively. If at least one earner is informal while the other is formal, the household is defined as mixed.

Source: Authors' elaboration based on The Household Expenditure Survey (HES) 2013 for The Bahamas, the Barbados Survey of Living Conditions (BSLC) 2016, the OECD KIIbIH database (OECD, 2024[23]) for the Dominican Republic, the Jamaica Survey of Living Conditions (JSLC) 2019, the Suriname Survey of Living Conditions (SSLC) 2022, and the Trinidad and Tobago Survey of Living Conditions (TT-SLC) 2014.

StatLink https://stat.link/v9ncxg

Informality in the Caribbean affects younger and older workers disproportionately. More than 6 out of 10 children under 15 and 6 out of 10 people older than 65 lived in completely informal or mixed households. Informality is also deeply entangled with poverty and income inequality. On average, 17.9% of informal workers in the Caribbean lived under the national poverty line in the latest period with available data, while 8.4% of formal workers were poor.

Social protection, health care and education systems must be strengthened and adapted to emerging challenges

The Caribbean need stronger social protection systems to address and mitigate the pervasive effects of informality and support vulnerable groups, including women, youth, and the elderly. Regarding old age pensions, the active coverage rate of the population (i.e. the share of people who contribute to the pension system) was 63% in the Caribbean around 2018. This was almost 20 percentage points higher than the average of Latin American countries around the same year, with important differences across Caribbean countries (Arena De Mesa, 2019[24]; IDB, 2021[14]; OECD et al., 2024[25]).

Labour and social protection policies must consider the implications of a changing population structure and the accelerating pace of population ageing. The Caribbean's old-age dependency ratio (i.e. the number of people over 65 years relative to the working-age population) was 13.5% in 2021. It is expected to increase to 26.1% by 2050 (United Nations, 2022[26]). This means that many Caribbean countries will complete their demographic bonus in the coming years, underscoring the importance of promoting access to decent, formal jobs with adequate pay and social protection coverage.

Access to – and quality of – health and education must be improved. Health status in the Caribbean is highly heterogeneous. Life expectancy at birth varies from 80 years in Barbados to 64 years in Haiti. On average, infant mortality improved from 20 for 1 000 live births in 2000 to 24 in 2020. Educational attainment has progressed in the Caribbean. On average, in 2022, Caribbean people aged 25 or more had spent more time in education (9.6 years) than their Latin American peers (8.9), adding 1.4 additional years of education between 2002 and 2022 (UIS, 2024[27]). However, in many countries of the region, young people entering upper secondary education have unsatisfactory completion outcomes due to high dropout rates (UIS, 2024[27]). Evaluating learning outcomes, possibly through internationally comparable mechanisms like the Programme for International Student Assessment (PISA), can inform education policy making in the region.

Boost productivity, strengthen macroeconomic stability, and upgrade production

Caribbean economies show modest potential growth and are highly exposed to shocks in the global economy

Potential growth in Caribbean economies is relatively low and has been declining in recent years. Potential GDP per capita growth in the region is estimated at around 1.4%. This is slightly above the Latin American average (1.1%) and below the 1.8% estimated for the average of advanced economies (Figure 5). With these modest potential growth levels, Caribbean economies will not be able to converge with the per capita income levels of advanced economies. Historically, the region has experienced greater GDP growth volatility than Latin America and advanced economies.

Relatively low productivity levels are at the core of modest potential growth. Average labour productivity in the Caribbean was almost 50% of the OECD's in the early 1990s, but this level declined to around 38.3% in 2021. There was improvement in 2022 and 2023 to 42% and 46%, respectively, largely driven by Guyana's extraordinary economic growth due to a surge in oil production.

Several factors explain such low productivity levels: an economic structure highly dependent on external demand, inadequate infrastructure limiting market access and knowledge spillovers, limited access to finance for innovative and productive activities, high informality in the labour market, and significant vulnerability to natural disasters (ILO, 2023[28]; Rosenblatt et al., 2023[29]; Ianchovichina, 2024[30]). However, structural heterogeneity is a significant feature in the region, with low-productivity economies co-existing with higher-productivity ones.

Figure 5. Potential GDP per capita growth in the Caribbean, Latin America and advanced economies

As estimated by different methods since 1980

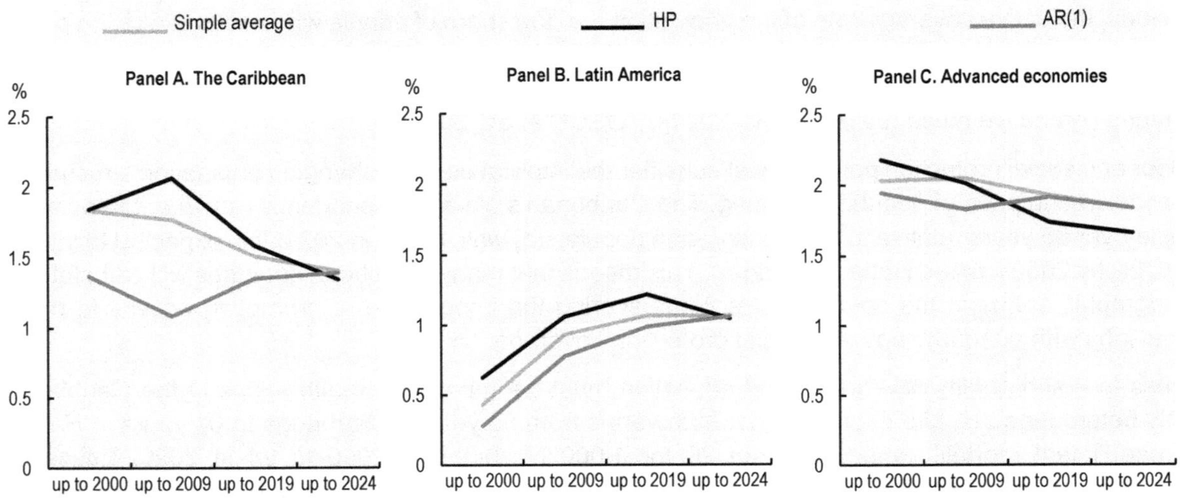

Note: Potential GDP growth is the growth rate that the economy can sustain over the long run, excluding short-term effects linked to a difference between demand and the potential level of supply. The variable refers to the growth in potential output, which is the maximum output level an economy can reach without putting strain on production factors that translate into inflationary pressures. Average growth is a simple average of growth in all countries for each region, over the period analysed. Caribbean countries included are: HP=the Hodrick-Prescott filter, which was used as an alternative model due to its resilience to short-term shocks to create a smoothed curve (lambda 100); AR=autoregressive model, which uses GDP per capita growth data. The number of lags (one) was determined by analysing the autocorrelation function and choosing the model that maximised the log-likelihood.
Source: Authors' elaboration based on IMF (2024[31]).

StatLink https://stat.link/5kycfg

Sound economic policies are needed to ensure macroeconomic stability in a region markedly exposed to the variation of global economic conditions. Effective fiscal policies are crucial for overcoming high deficits and public debt while building resilience to economic shocks and fostering macroeconomic stability. Though still high in several countries, fiscal deficits are being reduced. They narrowed on average from 2.4% in 2022 to 1.6% of GDP in 2023.

On the monetary front, as Caribbean economies are generally small, poorly diversified and highly dependent on imports, they are particularly vulnerable to inflation driven by the pass-through of international prices. Credible monetary regimes committed to anchoring inflation expectations and keeping inflation rates low are fundamental to ensuring macroeconomic stability in these countries.

High public debt levels remain a challenge in many Caribbean economies

In 2022, central government total public debt remained high, averaging 78.8% of GDP (Figure 6). This was well above the average for Latin America (52.9%). It was also higher than central government public debt 10 years before (69.2% of GDP in 2012).

Substantial heterogeneity is evident across countries, both in the level of public debt and in recent trends. In 2022, Barbados and Suriname showed levels of public debt higher than 100% of GDP, but both countries have made important efforts to improve fiscal conditions. For its part, Suriname's public debt fell to 93% in 2023 following debt restructuring agreements. Meanwhile, debt in Barbados fell to 116.5% in 2023, in line with pre-pandemic levels, and with a commitment to bring it down to 60% for the financial year 2035/36. This followed its 2018-19 sovereign debt restructuring and fiscal consolidation under the Economic

Recovery and Transformation Plan (IMF, 2024[32]; IMF, 2024[33]). Trinidad and Tobago, the Dominican Republic, and Saint Kitts and Nevis showed public debt levels below 60%, the latter being, together with Jamaica, two notable cases of public debt reduction in the region.

Figure 6. Central government total public debt, selected Caribbean countries and regional averages, 2012 and 2022

As a percentage of GDP

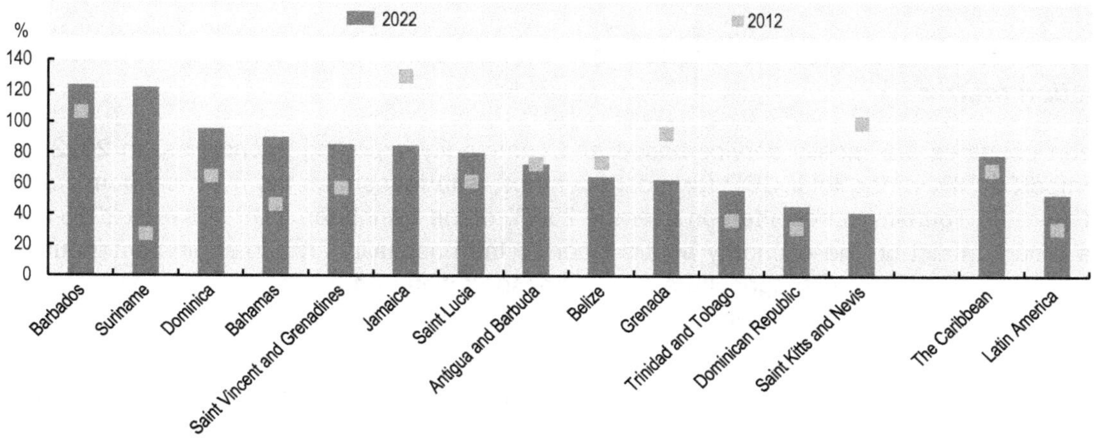

Source: Authors' elaboration based on CEPALSTAT (ECLAC, 2023[34]).

StatLink https://stat.link/jqiyem

High debt principal and interest payments constrain fiscal space for public investment and social spending. In 2022, the Caribbean's average debt service-to-tax revenue ratio reached 12.9%, above Latin America (11.5%) and much higher than the OECD average (4.8%) (Figure 7). Some Caribbean countries have significantly reduced their debt burden, including Jamaica, Saint Kitts and Nevis, Grenada, Barbados and Guyana. However, the burden of debt service as a share of tax revenues has increased in several Caribbean economies in the context of higher interest rates internationally.

Figure 7. Debt service-to-tax revenues ratio, 2012 and 2022

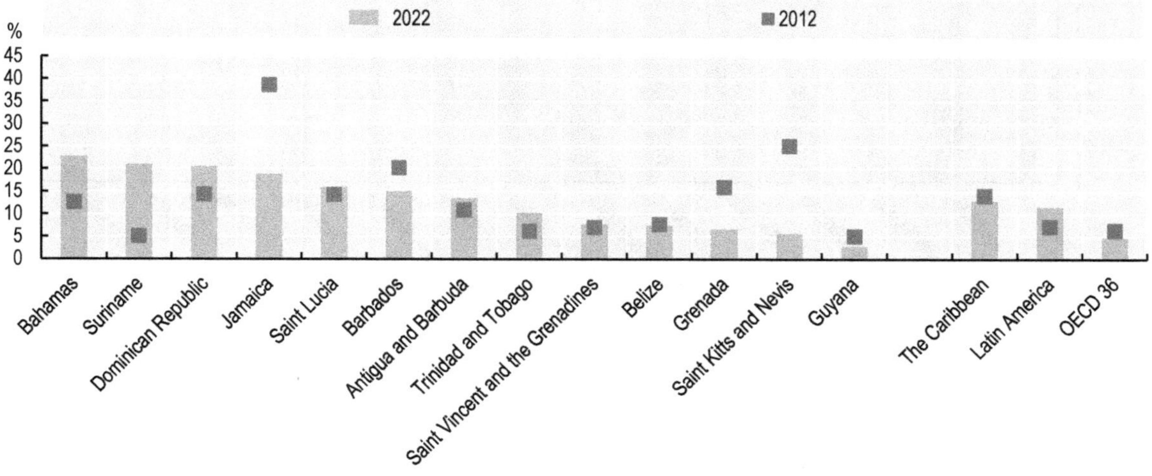

Source: Authors' elaboration based on WEO (IMF, 2023[35]).

StatLink https://stat.link/4itq6x

Fiscal frameworks are an essential tool to preserve medium- and long-term stability. They establish regulations, such as fiscal rules, that can help fiscal policy to be countercyclical, reducing discretionary public spending and guaranteeing debt sustainability. They can also help protect public investments that are essential for production transformation. In the Caribbean, countries have adopted various fiscal rules to enhance economic stability and manage public debt. Jamaica's Fiscal Responsibility Framework includes balanced budget and debt rules, and an escape clause for emergencies like natural disasters and economic downturns. Grenada's Fiscal Responsibility Act targets a primary surplus and debt-to-GDP ratio, allowing for rule suspensions during economic shocks. Similarly, The Bahamas' Fiscal Responsibility Act sets deficit and debt ceilings, with provisions for unexpected external shocks.

The economic structure reflects limited levels of diversification and sophistication of the production matrix

Caribbean countries are mostly service-based and commodity-exporting economies. In 2022, services represented 55-78% of the total GDP for most countries, with tourism as the main economic activity for many (Figure 8). Tourism represented on average 25.4% of the Caribbean GDP between 2015 and 2019. It had a broad impact on the economy as it supported the hospitality and entertainment industries and created backward linkages with agriculture, trade, transportation and construction (Gomez Garcia et al., 2021[36]). Nevertheless, tourism depends highly on external economies. It is also seasonal and vulnerable to climate shocks.

Tourism in the Caribbean has experienced significant growth. Between 1995 and 2018, tourist arrivals in the Caribbean increased from 10 million to 27 million per year. This growth was followed by a major decline due to the pandemic, although pre-pandemic levels have almost been recovered, with 22 million tourists arriving in the Caribbean in 2022. The main recipients of tourists are The Bahamas, the Dominican Republic, Jamaica and Barbados, which collectively account for 75% of arrivals during this period. Moreover, financial services play an important role, accounting for between 8% and 27% of GDP for countries in the region. The highest shares are observed in The Bahamas (27%), Barbados (26%) and Saint Lucia (21%) (ECLAC, 2023[34]).

Figure 8. Contribution of economic sectors to total GDP, 2022

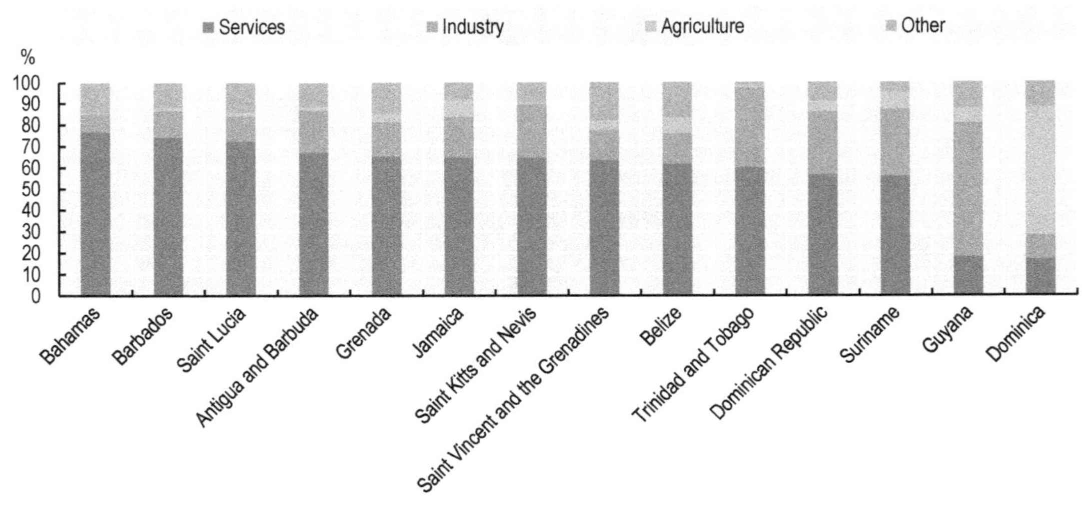

Note: Calculations based on GDP at constant dollar prices. "Other" includes taxes on products minus subsidies on products and statistical discrepancy of GDP by sector of origin.
Source: Authors' elaboration based on CEPALSTAT (ECLAC, 2023[34]).

StatLink https://stat.link/7scxho

Natural resources also play a significant role in Caribbean economies. The oil and gas exploration and production sector in Guyana contributed markedly to the 62% real GDP growth in 2022. The economy of Trinidad and Tobago is also driven by oil and gas production and the associated petrochemical sector. For its part, Suriname relies on mining but has a large potential to develop the oil and gas industry following the successful recent exploration of offshore reserves. Agriculture remains important for Belize, the Dominican Republic, Guyana and, most notably, Dominica. Historically focused on sugar and banana exports, the sector now faces slow productivity growth due to high trade costs and limited capacity to meet modern food safety standards. This has led to a higher reliance on imports to meet the growing demand from tourism, processing and retail industries. Challenges within the food sector include inadequate technology, low credit availability, high labour costs and insufficient infrastructure (FAO, 2019[37]).

Most Caribbean countries experience current account deficits. Limited domestic production results in significant dependence on imports to meet internal demand and support manufacturing and services like tourism. In terms of trade in goods, the region is a net importer. Exports are concentrated in primary products and resource-based manufactures, such as crude and refined petroleum, alcoholic beverages, cereals, food preparations, chemical elements, minerals, and tobacco. These accounted for 57% of total goods exports in 2022. Imports are dominated by resource-based manufactures (29%) and medium-technology manufactures (27%), including processed food, automotive vehicles, and machinery and equipment (UNCTAD, 2022[38]; ECLAC, 2023[39]).

Strengthening investment and connecting it to development goals are fundamental to drive production transformation, build resilience, and adapt to climate change impacts. Investment levels in the Caribbean increased between 2015 and 2023, on average, from around 23% to almost 27% of GDP, with important variation across countries. This compares to averages ranging from 20-22% in Latin America and 23-24% in OECD countries in the same period. The region has been successful in attracting foreign direct investment (FDI), mainly towards the energy and services sectors. Between 2013 and 2021, FDI net inflows were on average above 6% of GDP; in 2022, they represented close to 4.2% of GDP, similar to the level in 2023 of 4.3% (excluding Guyana, which saw an extraordinary increase of FDI in 2023, reaching 42.8% of GDP). FDI flows to the Caribbean in 2023 were higher than in Latin America (2.7% of GDP), the OECD (0.1% weighted average) and the world (0.7% weighted average) (OECD et al., 2023[40]; World Bank, 2024[16]).

Relatively low levels of diversification and sophistication are also observed at the level of firms in the Caribbean. Such firms show limited levels of internationalisation and innovation and face persistent barriers to doing business. Caribbean firms identify important obstacles to their business operations, including access to finance (69.3% of firms report this as a major or severe obstacle), navigating customs and trade procedures (63.3%), and finding workers with adequate skills (59.8%). In parallel, Caribbean firms' innovation activities are limited. Only one firm out of ten reported having introduced at least one innovation in the major areas of their operations between 2018 and 2021.

Build trust, improve evidence-based policy making and public services

Citizen satisfaction with democracy and with the quality of key public services has fallen in the last decade

In 2023, more than 65% of people in the Caribbean, on average (for eight countries with available and comparable data), expressed low levels of satisfaction with the democratic system, an increase of 22.6 percentage points in the last decade (LAPOP Lab, 2023[41]). The satisfaction of Caribbean citizens with the quality of key public services has fallen in the last decade. In 2023, only 40% of Caribbean people were satisfied or very satisfied, on average, with health services, a decline of 15.4 percentage points in the last decade. Moreover, this decline was almost 3 times more than in Latin American countries, where satisfaction decreased 5.6 percentage points in the same period (from 55.6% to 50%). Satisfaction with the quality of education is higher (65.2%, on average, in 2023), although it has been declining in the last decade, falling 9.5 percentage points (LAPOP Lab, 2023[41]).

Strengthening citizen security is paramount as crime and violence represent an important challenge in some Caribbean countries

Caribbean countries exhibit per capita average murder rates amongst the highest globally, with significant levels of homicidal violence associated with organised crime (Figure 9). This situation varies across countries but poses a common challenge in the region. The average cost of crime in the Caribbean is estimated at 3.7% of GDP (IDB, 2017[42]). Young people, particularly men aged 15-29, are disproportionately affected by and involved in violent crime, both as victims and perpetrators. Meanwhile, women are more affected by homicides linked to domestic violence and intimate partner violence.

Figure 9. Intentional homicides rate in the Caribbean, 2022

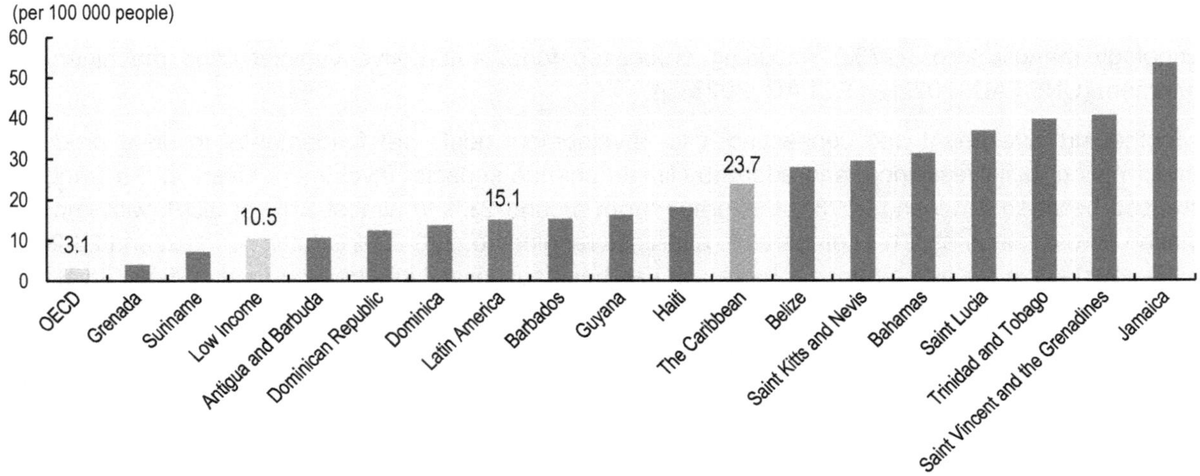

Note: The OECD average considers all OECD member states except Finland, New Zealand and the United Kingdom. The Latin American average considers: Argentina, the Plurinational State of Bolivia, Brazil (2021), Chile, Colombia, Costa Rica, Ecuador, El Salvador, Guatemala (2021), Honduras, Mexico, Nicaragua, Panama, Paraguay, Peru (2020) and Uruguay. The Caribbean average considers Antigua and Barbuda, The Bahamas, Barbados, Belize, Dominica (2021), the Dominican Republic, Grenada (2021), Guyana (2021), Haiti, Jamaica, Saint Kitts and Nevis (2021), Saint Lucia, Saint Vincent and the Grenadines, Suriname, and Trinidad and Tobago.
Source: Authors' elaboration based on UNODC (2022[43]).

StatLink https://stat.link/4uhp61

Citizens' perception of security risks in the Caribbean shows similar levels to those in LAC (5.7 compared to 5.4, respectively, based on a 0-10 index where 0 refers to an absence of security risks). However, this is more than double the rate of OECD countries (2.4). Trinidad and Tobago (7.3), Jamaica (7), Haiti (6.8), Belize (6.8) and Guyana (6.5) show perceptions of security risks above the Caribbean average (5.7). Moreover, on average, in 2022, 37% of Caribbean firms considered crime, theft and disorder as severe or very severe obstacles to their operations, on average (IDB, 2021[44]).

Women are largely under-represented in political and business life

Women in the Caribbean region face different obstacles – from gender-based violence to unequal pay and limited access to education and health care. Women's representation in politics in the Caribbean is also low. In 2022, women held only 23.7% of parliamentary seats compared to 33.8% in Latin America, on average (Figure 10). Guyana (35.4%) and Dominica (34.4%) show the highest female parliamentary representation, surpassing Latin America's average. At the firm level, respondents in 6 Caribbean countries[2] consider that, on average, 70.3% of the owners and shareholders of the firms where they work are all male or predominantly male. This ranges from 60% in Jamaica to 76% in Trinidad and Tobago and 78% in Barbados (IDB, 2021[44]). Moreover, only 18.5% of Caribbean firms actively seek to employ, retain, train and promote women, ranging from 8% in Barbados to 28% in Guyana (IDB, 2021[44]).

Figure 10. Women's political representation in Caribbean countries, 2022

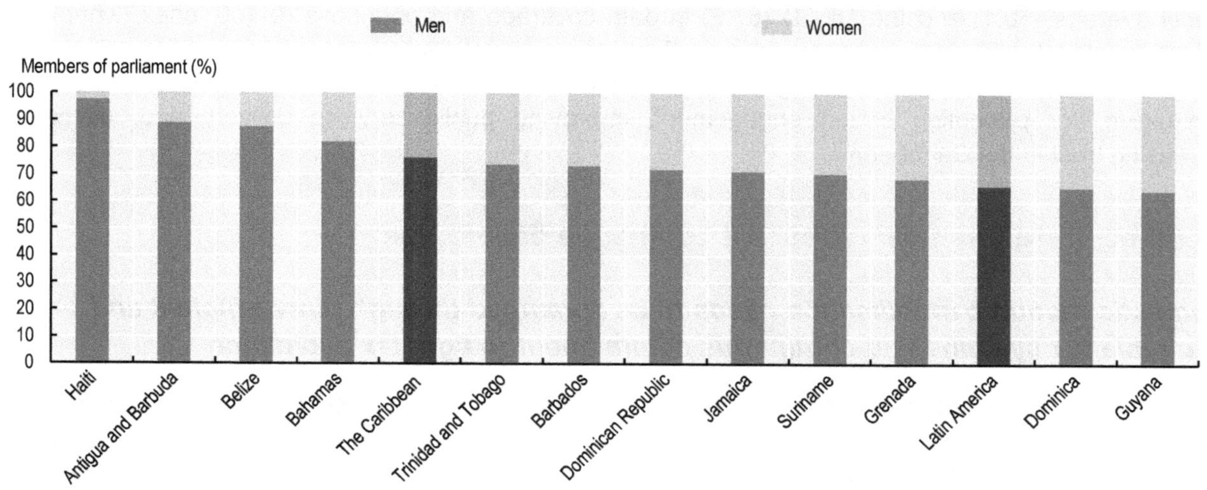

The Latin American average considers Argentina, the Plurinational State of Bolivia, Brazil, Chile, Colombia, Costa Rica, Ecuador, El Salvador, Guatemala, Honduras, Mexico, Nicaragua, Panama, Paraguay, Peru, Uruguay and Venezuela. The Caribbean average considers Antigua and Barbuda, The Bahamas, Barbados, Belize, Dominica, Dominican Republic, Grenada, Guyana, Haiti, Jamaica, Suriname, and Trinidad and Tobago.
Source: Authors' elaboration based on OECD (2023[45]).

StatLink https://stat.link/j6i2gx

Stronger and more inclusive public institutions, coupled with more evidence-based public policies, can contribute to advancing a new social contract

Caribbean countries face a range of socio-economic and environmental challenges in their pursuit of sustainable development. High poverty levels, informal employment, and inequalities across socio-economic and age groups, territories and genders, combined with low social protection and high violence and homicide rates, pose significant social and political challenges to Caribbean societies. In this context, Caribbean countries should consider whether and how to rethink their social contracts to address these intertwined challenges.

Strengthening institutions is essential to improve policy effectiveness, enhance public services and foster a legitimate social contract. Public institutions must strategically balance economic, social and environmental objectives while ensuring consistent implementation of long-term strategies. A Centre of Government (CoG) Approach will be crucial in aligning policy planning, budgeting, stakeholder engagement and performance management with citizens' needs and expectations. Inclusive public policy requires active participation from the private sector, academia, civil society and local communities in every phase of the public policy cycle. National Development Plans (NDPs), already adopted by 13 Caribbean countries, provide a useful existent tool for fostering consensus on a renewed social contract. While NDPs differ in structure, common priorities include governance, human capital development, environmental sustainability, social equality and cultural identity.

A new social contract will require broad political consensus and a rebalancing of the roles of the state, market, society, and environment. Sustainable development must be central, along with welfare systems and financing models, putting citizen well-being at the centre. As policies will affect socio-economic groups and territories differently, an intersectional approach is essential to balancing costs and benefits fairly and building support for the sustainable agenda.

Improving the quality and availability of data is paramount for informed policy design, implementation, and monitoring. In 2021, only half of the Caribbean countries with data available were implementing a statistical plan.[3] The Open Data Inventory reveals Caribbean countries (40.9) lag behind Latin America (48.5), the global average (50.1) and the OECD (67.8) in data coverage and openness (0-100 index, where 100 means total data coverage and openness). Strengthening national statistical offices, adopting open government practices, and embracing digital transformation will be instrumental actions, although non-exhaustive, for promoting citizen engagement, improving public services delivery and, ultimately, increasing trust in the Caribbean.

Mobilise more financial resources to finance development

Domestic resource mobilisation needs to be revamped through more efficient and equitable tax systems and continuous commitment to fight tax avoidance

Tax revenues in the Caribbean can be strengthened to enhance domestic resource mobilisation and better finance the development agenda. In 2022, average tax revenues in the Caribbean amounted to 21% of GDP – slightly below the Latin American average of 22.4% and significantly lower than the OECD average of 34% – with significant variation across nations (Figure 11).

Figure 11. Tax structure in selected Caribbean economies and Latin America and OECD averages, 2022

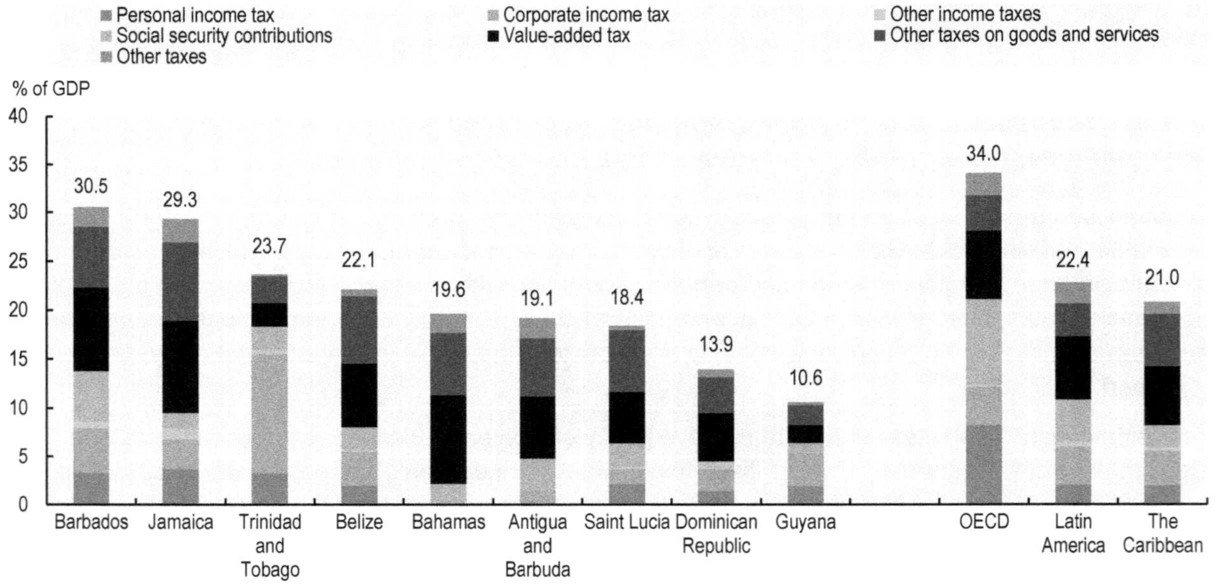

Note: The Latin America average excludes Venezuela due to data issues. Due to data quality issues, Ecuador is excluded from the Latin America average for PIT and CIT revenues. The OECD average represents the unweighted average of the 38 OECD member countries. Chile, Colombia, Costa Rica and Mexico are also part of the OECD (38).
Source: Authors' elaboration based on OECD (2024[46]).

StatLink https://stat.link/3l48or

Tax collection and efficiency can be improved by rendering tax structures more equitable. Currently, tax revenues rely heavily on indirect taxes, often with a regressive impact. Indirect taxes (VAT plus other taxes on goods and services) accounted for an average of 55% in the Caribbean. This was higher than the Latin American average of 48%. It was also significantly above the OECD average of 32%. Corporate income tax (CIT) represented a larger share for the Caribbean than for the OECD, although with heterogeneity across countries. On average, CIT revenues represented 17.5% of total tax revenues in the Caribbean, compared to 12% in the OECD average.

To enhance revenue generation and equity, Caribbean countries could focus on improving the progressivity of the taxation system by enhancing, for instance, revenues from direct taxes, particularly personal income taxes, and rethinking inefficient tax exemptions that place a greater burden on lower-income groups. Additionally, to further strengthen their fiscal capacity, some countries can rationalise tax expenditures, carefully explore non-tax revenue sources, such as citizenship-by-investment programmes with enhanced oversight, and implement environmentally related taxes, including carbon pricing mechanisms.

Strengthening tax systems in the Caribbean will also require continuing efforts to address tax avoidance issues through greater international co-operation and implementation of global tax standards. Caribbean nations are increasingly engaging with frameworks such as the OECD's Base Erosion and Profit Shifting (BEPS) measures and the Global Forum on Transparency and Exchange of Information for Tax Purposes. These frameworks aim to enhance tax transparency and ensure that multinational corporations pay taxes where their profits are earned. Improving tax administration, increasing participation in international tax initiatives and building regional co-operation are essential for modernising Caribbean tax systems, improving compliance, and fostering economic development.

Several Caribbean countries have pioneered the use of innovative financing instruments

Innovative debt instruments being developed in the Caribbean can effectively channel resources towards social, green and blue development goals. Notably, green, social, sustainability, sustainability-linked and blue (GSSSB) bonds collectively amassed a cumulative value of USD 1.5 billion in the region from 2019 to November 2024 (Figure 12). In 2019, Williams Caribbean Capital, based in Barbados, issued the first certified green bond in the Caribbean region, valued at USD 2 million. This was followed by another issuance in 2021, amounting to USD 7 million. Both bonds were earmarked for solar energy projects and certified under the Climate Bonds Standard Solar Energy Criteria (Climate Bonds Initiative, 2022[47]; Climate Bonds Initiative, 2019[48]).

Blue bonds are crucial for marine conservation and the development of sustainable "blue economies". In 2022, The Bahamas issued two blue bonds for a total of USD 385 million to support marine-focused businesses. The bonds were oversubscribed, indicating high investor interest (Ministry of Finance of The Bahamas, 2022[49]). Other blue bonds have been issued in the context of debt-for-nature swaps, for instance in Barbados. Corporates or quasi-sovereign entities are also issuing sustainability-linked bonds and social bonds. This is demonstrated by the USD 44.2 million social bond issued by Trinidad and Tobago in 2020 and the USD 300 million sustainability-linked bond issued by EGE Haina, an energy company in the Dominican Republic.

Other important financial tools can help address pressing needs. For example, catastrophe (CAT) bonds offer a strategic means for managing natural disaster risks and enhancing borrowing capacity. In 2021, the World Bank issued Jamaica a USD 185 million CAT bond, providing coverage for 3 hurricane seasons. In addition, natural disaster clauses in debt contracts also provide critical fiscal resilience by allowing for payment deferrals following disasters. The IDB was the first to offer one of these to three Caribbean countries – Belize, The Bahamas and Barbados. These countries have activated the option for loans totalling over USD 1.1 billion (IDB, 2024[54]). Subsequently, in 2024, in a world first, Grenada was able to pause debt repayment due to a hurricane debt suspension clause after Hurricane Beryl, saving the country USD 28 million.

Debt-for-nature swaps present an opportunity to advance environmental goals while reducing debt. These swaps involve issuing a guaranteed instrument (loan or bond) at more favourable terms and using the proceeds to repurchase more expensive sovereign debt. Such a swap thus generates savings on interest rates and/or principal, which are then used to finance nature conservation and climate change mitigation or adaptation activities. To maximise the effectiveness of these mechanisms, it is crucial to enhance regulatory frameworks and develop comprehensive sustainable finance taxonomies (OECD, 2024[50]). These measures should ensure transparency, attract investment and foster regional financial stability.

To date, the Caribbean region has executed four debt-for-nature swaps amounting to more than USD 400 million destined for marine conservation. In 2021, Belize conducted a debt-for-nature conversion, retiring USD 580 million in debt for Belize (8.7% of GDP) and generating an estimated USD 178 million for marine conservation. In late 2022, Barbados completed a debt-for-nature conversion backed by a USD 100 million guarantee from the IDB and a USD 50 million guarantee from The Nature Conservancy (TNC), resulting in USD 50 million allocated to marine conservation initiatives. In November 2024, the Bahamas launched a new debt conversion project that is expected to save an estimated USD 124 million over the next 15 years and enable improvements in ocean conservation and the management of the Bahamas Protected Areas System. Finally, in July 2024, the European Investment Bank and the IDB approved USD 300 million in guarantees for an innovative debt-for-climate-resilience swap, structured as a sovereign sustainability-linked loan. This initiative will save USD 125 million for new resilience investments and marks the first such loan tied to a sovereign water security project. It features an innovative design in which, if the sustainability targets are not achieved, the government will incur a financial penalty.

Figure 12. International GSSSB bond issuance in the Caribbean by type and issuer, 2019 - August 2024

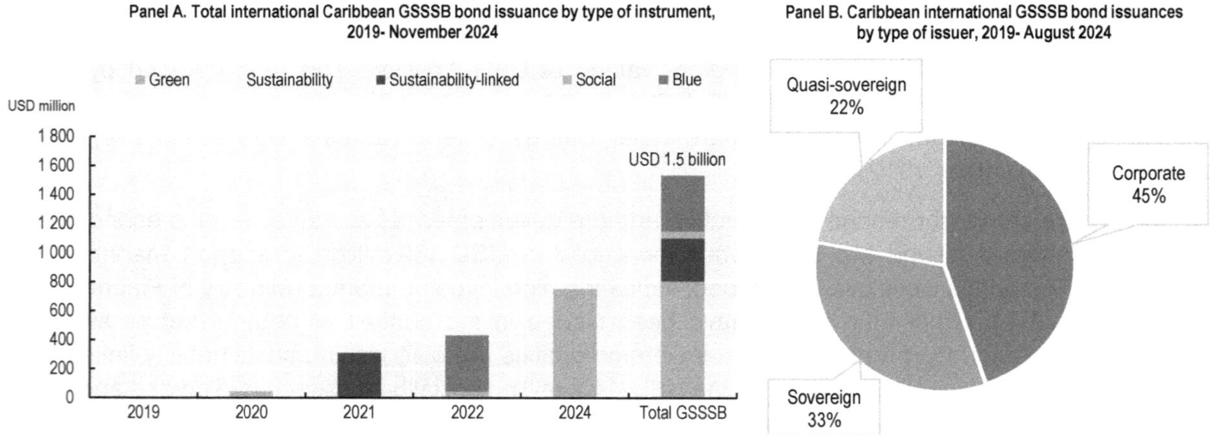

Note: GSSSB=Green, social, sustainability, sustainability-linked and blue bonds. Quasi-sovereign issuers are defined as companies with full or partial government ownership.
Source: Authors' elaboration based on official figures and Núñez, G., H. Velloso and F. Da Silva (2022[51]); ECLAC (2023[52]); and OECD (2023[40]).

StatLink https://stat.link/m7vsdy

Financial markets require further development to channel resources towards sustainable and inclusive development effectively

Financial depth in the Caribbean has been historically low, constraining households and business participation in the financial system. Domestic credit to the private sector as a percentage of GDP stood at an average of 42% for the Caribbean in 2022, lagging behind the averages in Latin America (55%) and OECD countries (149%) (Figure 13). Efficiency in the banking sector is characterised by high profitability. The sector boasts a net interest margin (NIM) of 4.8%, above the OECD average of 1.7%. A high NIM also signals costly credit due to various factors that vary between countries, such as high market concentration, high risks, and inadequate regulatory frameworks. Stability is reinforced by strong capitalisation and liquidity levels in most Caribbean banking systems. However, asset quality remains a potential risk in some countries.

Figure 13. Domestic credit to private sector by region 2000-22 and domestic bank credit and deposits as percentage of GDP in the Caribbean, 2022

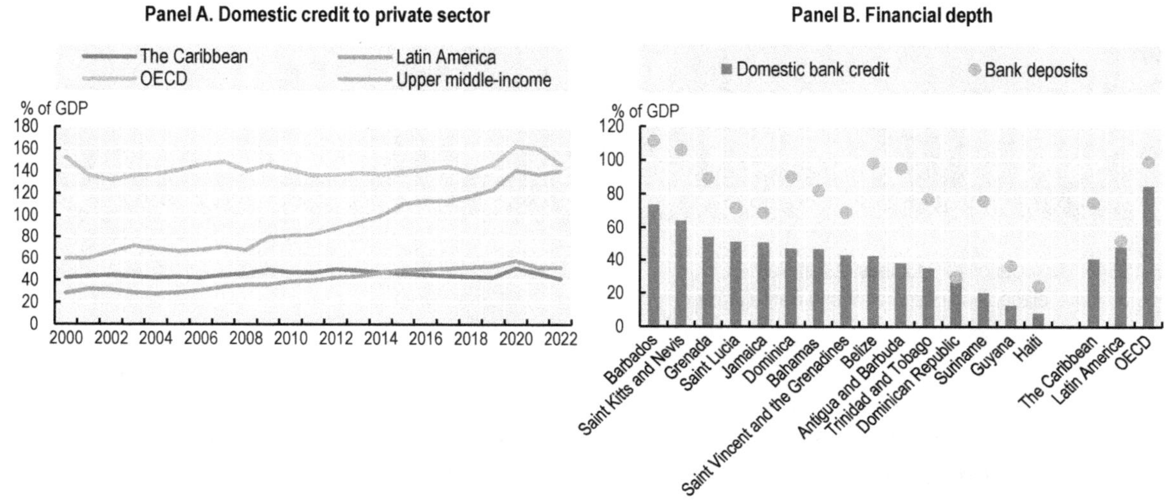

Note: Panel A – OECD and upper middle-income belong to World Bank data classification. Panel B – Figures for bank deposits as a percentage of GDP correspond to 2021 due to data availability.
Source: Authors' elaboration based on World Development Indicators (World Bank, 2022[53]).

StatLink https://stat.link/5zhbdl

Deepen regional integration and expand international partnerships

Caribbean countries have room to improve intra- and extra-regional trade

Despite progress in liberalising trade within the region, intra-regional trade represented 6.7% of total trade in 2015-18, which is low compared to other trade blocs, in part due to limited diversification and complementarity among Caribbean economies. The region has a relatively high Export Concentration Index score of 0.432, with 52.5% of exports comprising primary products and resource-based manufactures, while only 4.1% are high-technology goods. Simultaneously, the Caribbean relies heavily on the import of essential goods, with 80-90% of food sourced from abroad. Non-tariff barriers (NTBs) continue to affect intra- and extra-regional trade, reflected in the region's low average score in the OECD's Trade Facilitation Indicators. Existent trade agreements have not yielded the expected benefits, as many countries still show a concentration of export destinations, particularly to the United States. Overall, the Caribbean's participation in world exports has been decreasing, representing 0.23% of total in 2022 (Figure 14). Meanwhile, despite geographic proximity and potential complementarities, trade with Latin America remains an under-exploited opportunity. The Caribbean can improve its trade performance by developing regional value chains in strategic sectors, integrating into global value chains where it holds comparative advantages, reducing NTBs, improving trade facilitation, deepening market penetration with existing partners and expanding into new international markets.

Figure 14. Participation in world exports (percentage) of the Caribbean, Latin America and ASEAN, 1981-2022

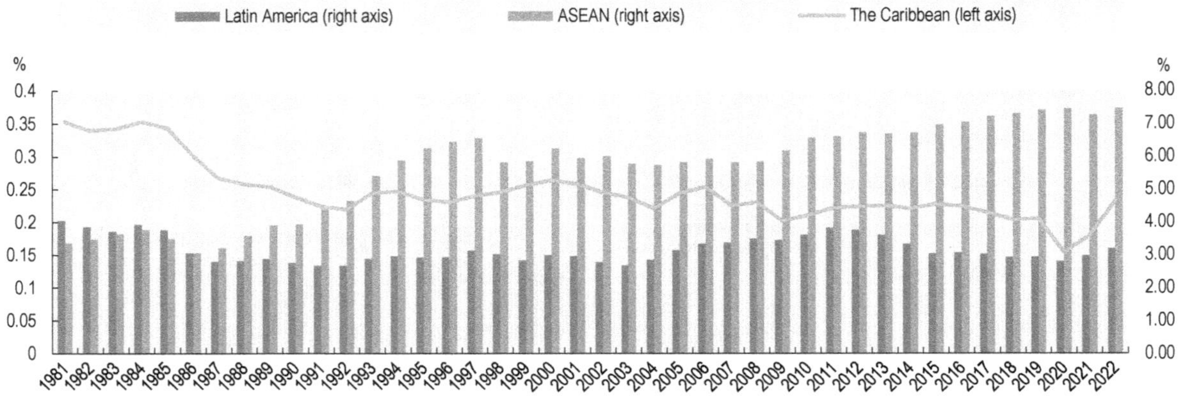

Note: ASEAN=Association of Southeast Asian Nations.
Source: Authors' elaboration based on World Bank (2023[54]).

StatLink https://stat.link/ptj4c8

Regional co-operation can support the region in addressing outstanding challenges like transport and digital connectivity and disaster risk reduction

Transport connectivity continues to be a major obstacle to the development of Caribbean countries. Transport cost intensity is relatively high compared to other regions (Figure 15), with logistics costs representing 16-26% of GDP, significantly above the OECD average of roughly 9%. This is primarily due to regulatory hurdles, including the tax structure, limited competition in the transport sector, and insufficient airport and port infrastructure. Furthermore, the region's geographic isolation, dis-economies of scale, inefficient shipping routes, and poor inter-island connectivity increase transportation costs and reduce trade efficiency. Further initiatives based on public-private partnerships are needed to enhance intra- and extra-regional trade through market integration and higher efficiency. New efforts could include enabling a financially sustainable regional airline, developing a fast-ferry service between Caribbean islands or designing new regulations that promote more effective competition among private transport providers.

Figure 15. Transport cost intensity, selected regions and country groups (2016-21)

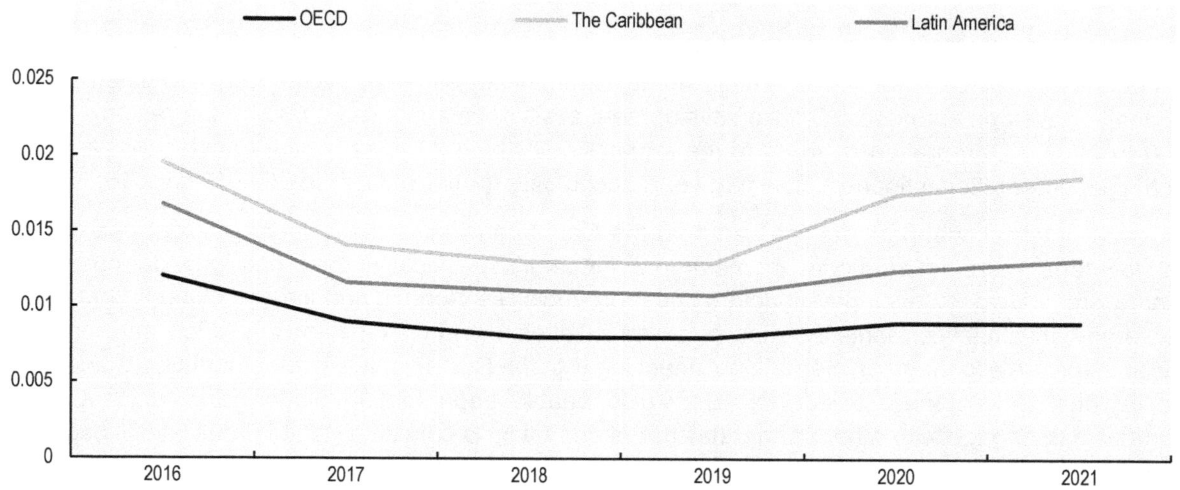

Note: Average transport expenditure in USD per 1 000 km as a ratio to their Free on Board (FOB) value of the traded goods. Formula ([transport expenditure] / [transport work in terms of value]) x 1 000. This dataset is experimental.
Source: Authors' elaboration based on UNCTADStat (2024[55]).

StatLink https://stat.link/a4bpyz

The region has made significant strides in co-operation on EWS and disaster recovery efforts through the Caribbean Disaster Emergency Management Agency. To that end, it has generated economies of scale and facilitated logistics throughout all phases of the disaster management cycle. However, additional regional initiatives are required to tackle other urgent environmental challenges and capitalise on the opportunities of the just green transition. For instance, co-ordinated efforts are necessary to establish region-wide environmental policies, regulations and standards aimed at reducing marine pollution caused by the shipping industry or for creating incentives for investments in renewable energies.

Caribbean nations have strong incentives to develop a more integrated and resilient green energy network. Energy imports make up nearly 7% of the region's GDP, which restricts public sector investment in climate adaptation and social services. The Caribbean is already taking concrete steps towards an energy transition through a Regional Energy Policy prioritising renewable energy. Further efforts should focus on advancing harmonised regulatory frameworks and scaling up energy interconnection projects to encourage investment in resilient and renewable energy systems.

Digital technologies offer a significant opportunity to enhance connectivity in the Caribbean, where physical connectivity is complex and costly. In 2021, 78% of the Caribbean population used the Internet, compared to 72% in Latin America and 89.3% in the OECD. A region-wide digital transition can spur substantial development by boosting productivity, supporting industry diversification and fostering economic integration. Digitalisation lowers transaction costs, improves information flows, and increases competition, helping micro, small and medium-sized enterprises compete and integrate into global value chains. Further, digital tools can improve climate resilience through better disaster preparedness and response. Caribbean nations are advancing digital initiatives, including through regional projects like CARICOM's "Single ICT Space" and the work of the Association of Caribbean States to digitalise the transport sector, as well as through the support of international partners like the Inter-American Development Bank (IDB) which has invested USD 480 million over the last decade. Improving regional co-operation regulatory dialogue, infrastructure investments, improved connectivity, and enhanced cybersecurity would assist the region in fully benefiting from the digital transition.

Renewed international partnerships can help channel financing for development towards the region and raise the Caribbean's voice globally

Most Caribbean countries depend on external flows to finance development. This reliance is due to several factors, including their limited size, limited domestic financial resources, vulnerability to external shocks and major development needs. Official development assistance averaged 2.53% of the region's GNI from 2000 to 2022. FDI represented 4.3% of the region's GDP in 2023. Meanwhile, remittances represented the biggest international financial flow that year, accounting for 6% of GDP in 2023 (Figure 16).

Innovative international partnerships can help the Caribbean region make more efficient use of finance and leverage more international development funding. Specifically, they can provide co-ordination mechanisms between development actors and more tools like blended finance and blue and green bonds to leverage private investments. Further, following a Development in Transition approach, partnerships are crucial to ensure alignment of international financing with the Sustainable Development Goals and national and regional development objectives. They also enable equal-footing platforms in which Caribbean countries can engage with other partners as peers and foster a cohesive voice in multilateral negotiations towards transforming the international financial architecture. This will help the region seize the global momentum for rethinking international finance, including in the discussions around the Paris Pact for People and the Planet and the 2025 4th UN Conference on Financing for Development in Spain.

Figure 16. Main external financial flows to the Caribbean, 2000-23

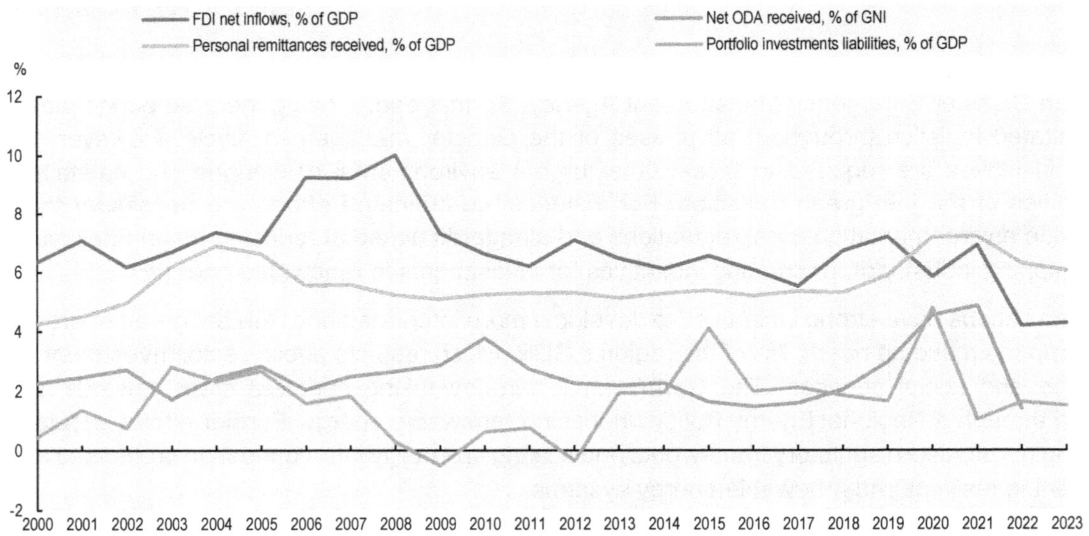

Note: FDI=foreign direct investment; GDP=gross domestic product; GNI=gross national income; ODA=official development assistance. Graduation out of ODA recipient status for Barbados and Trinidad and Tobago after 2010, Saint Kitts and Nevis after 2013, and Antigua and Barbuda after 2022. Portfolio investment liabilities based on authors' calculations. In 2023, Guyana was excluded from the FDI average calculation due to its significantly higher FDI inflows as a share of GDP, making it an outlier. Including Guyana in the calculations, the regional average FDI net inflows in 2023 amount to 6.8% of GDP.
Source: Authors' elaboration based on (IMF, 2024[56]; World Bank, 2024[57]; World Bank, 2024[3]; World Bank, 2023[58]).

StatLink https://stat.link/jck8h4

The IDB's *One Caribbean* initiative encapsulates this approach, leveraging resources, encouraging co-operation and exploiting economies of scale to tackle shared challenges across the region. *One Caribbean* represents a multi-year, multi-sector approach to promoting sustainable and inclusive development. The initiative is organised around four pillars: (1) climate resilience, adaptation and disaster risk management; (2) citizen security; (3) private sector development; and (4) food security. Two cross-cutting areas complement the initiative: strengthening institutions and digital transformation. As such, this partnership tackles the critical regional challenges and opportunities set out in this report.

Notes

[1] Transition risks refer more specifically to the financial risks that could arise from the transition to a lower-carbon economy. For insurance firms, this risk factor is mainly about the potential repricing of carbon-intensive financial assets, and the speed at which any such repricing might occur. To a lesser extent, insurers may also need to adapt to potential impacts on the liability side resulting from reductions in insurance premiums in carbon-intensive sectors (Caldecott et al., 2016[59]).

[2] The Bahamas, Barbados, Guyana, Jamaica, Suriname, and Trinidad and Tobago.

[3] Antigua and Barbuda, Belize, the Dominican Republic, Grenada, Jamaica, Saint Kitts and Nevis, and Suriname.

References

Arena De Mesa, A. (2019), “Los sistemas de pensiones en la encrucijada, Desafíos para la sostenibilidad en América Latina”, [English Translation], United Nations Economic Commission for Latin America and the Caribbean, Santiago, Chile, https://repositorio.cepal.org/server/api/core/bitstreams/ef2286b9-b700-45e9-ac66-e343faa75211/content. [24]

Caldecott, B. et al. (2016), *Stranded Assets: A Climate Risk Challenge*, Inter-American Development Bank, Washington, DC, https://doi.org/10.18235/0012646. [59]

Climate Bonds Initiative (2022), *Latin America and the Caribbean Sustainable Debt: State of the Market 2022*, Climate Bonds Initiative, London, https://www.climatebonds.net/files/reports/cbi_lac_sotm_2022_en__0.pdf. [47]

Climate Bonds Initiative (2019), “Williams Caribbean Capital”, webpage, https://www.climatebonds.net/certification/williams-caribbean-capital#:~:text=The%20Climate%20Bonds%20Standard%20Board,limit%20in%20the%20Paris%20Agreement (accessed on 1 October 2024). [48]

CSGM/UWI (2020), *The State of the Caribbean Climate*, The University of West Indies, http://socc.mona.uwi.edu/sites/default/files/The%20State%20of%20the%20Caribbean%20Climate%20Report.pdf. [1]

ECLAC (2024), “Ratio of employed population to total population by sex, age group and geographic area”, *CEPALSTAT*, (database), https://statistics.cepal.org/portal/cepalstat/dashboard.html?theme=1&lang=en (accessed on 31 July 2024). [21]

ECLAC (2023), *Capital Flows to Latin America and the Caribbean: First 10 months of 2023*, United Nations Economic Commission for Africa and the Caribbean, Washington, DC, https://www.cepal.org/en/publications/68745-capital-flows-latin-america-and-caribbean-first-10-months-2023#:~:text=Latin%20American%20and%20Caribbean%20bond,higher%20than%20the%20annual%20volume. [52]

ECLAC (2023), *CEPALSTAT*, (database), https://statistics.cepal.org/portal/cepalstat/index.html?lang=es (accessed on 1 October 2024). [34]

ECLAC (2023), *International Trade Outlook for Latin America and the Caribbean 2023. Structural change and trends in global and regional trade: Challenges and opportunities*, United Nations Economic Commission for Latin America and the Caribbean, Santiago, https://www.cepal.org/en/publications/68664-international-trade-outlook-latin-america-and-caribbean-2023-structural-change. [39]

ECLAC (2023), *Social Panorama of Latin America 2023*, United Nations Economic Commission for Latin America and the Caribbean, Santiago, Chile, https://repositorio.cepal.org/server/api/core/bitstreams/7ddf434a-6073-4f1e-8b71-a6639e4586d5/content. [15]

EIB (2021), "Assessing climate change risks at the country level: The EIB scoring model", *EIB Working Paper*, No. 2021/03, European Investment Bank, Luxembourg, https://www.eib.org/attachments/efs/economics_working_paper_2021_03_en.pdf. [5]

EM-DAT (2024), *EM-DAT*, (database), https://doc.emdat.be/ (accessed on 10 September 2024). [2]

FAO (2023), *Regional Overview of Food Security and Nutrition in Latin America and the Caribbean*, Food and Agriculture Organization of the United Nations, Rome, https://openknowledge.fao.org/server/api/core/bitstreams/f6d5a32f-c6f5-476c-bcc4-c72c74be3b8d/content. [17]

FAO (2019), "Current status of agriculture in the Caribbean and implications for agriculture policy and strategy", *Food, Agriculture and Rural Development in Latin America and the Caribbean*, No. 14, Food and Agriculture Organization of the United Nations, Santiago, http://www.fao.org/3/ca5527en/ca5527en.pdf. [37]

GCF (2022), *Annual Results Report 2021*, Green Climate Fund, Incheon City, Korea, https://www.greenclimate.fund/annual-results-report-2021. [11]

Gomez Garcia, O. et al. (2021), *Caribbean Quarterly Bulletin, Volume 10, Number 1*, Inter-American Development Bank, Washington, DC, https://doi.org/10.18235/0003265. [36]

Ianchovichina, E. (2024), "Why is productivity growth so low in Latin America and the Caribbean?", *World Bank blogs*, 26 February, https://blogs.worldbank.org/en/latinamerica/low-productivity-growth-latin-america-caribbean. [30]

IDB (2021), *Compete Caribbean. Innovation, Firm Performance and Gender Survey*, (database), https://www.competecaribbean.org/docs/ifpg-survey/index.html (accessed on 31 July 2024). [44]

IDB (2021), *Economic Institutions for a Resilient Caribbean*, Inter-American Development Bank, Washington, DC, https://doi.org/10.18235/0003053. [14]

IDB (2017), *Restoring Paradise in the Caribbean: Combatting Violence with Numbers*, Inter-American Development Bank, Washington, DC. [42]

IICA (2018), *Annual Report*, Inter-American Institute for Cooperation on Agriculture, Turrialba, Costa Rica, http://apps.iica.int/SReunionesOG/Content/Documents/CE2019/en/7acc1088-9aa0-4818-8b18-392e8318a7a5_wd699_2018_iica_annual_report.pdf. [18]

ILO (2024), *ILOSAT*, (database), https://ilostat.ilo.org/data/ (accessed on 31 July 2024). [22]

ILO (2023), *Employment Situation in Latin America and the Caribbean: Towards the Creation of Better Jobs in the Post-Pandemic Era*, International Labour Organization, Geneva, https://www.ilo.org/publications/employment-situation-latin-america-and-caribbean-number-28-towards-creation. [28]

IMF (2024), *Balance of Payments Analytic Presentation by Indicator: Supplementary Items, Portfolio Investment, Net Incurrence of Liabilities (Excluding Exceptional Financing), US Dollars*, (database), https://data.imf.org/?sk=7a51304b-6426-40c0-83dd-ca473ca1fd52&sid=1542633711584 (accessed on 10 October 2024). [56]

IMF (2024), *Barbados: Third Reviews Under the Arrangement Under the Extended Fund Facility, Arrangement Under the Resilience and Sustainability Facility, and Request for Modification of Performance Criteria-Press Release; and Staff Report*, International Monetary Fund, Washington, DC, https://www.imf.org/en/Publications/CR/Issues/2024/06/28/Barbados-Third-Reviews-Under-the-Arrangement-Under-the-Extended-Fund-Facility-Arrangement-551173. [33]

IMF (2024), *Suriname: Sixth Review Under the Extended Arrangement Under the Extended Fund Facility-Press Release; Staff Report; and Statement by the Executive Director for Suriname*, International Monetary Fund, Washington, DC, https://www.imf.org/en/Publications/CR/Issues/2024/07/30/Suriname-Sixth-Review-Under-the-Extended-Arrangement-Under-the-Extended-Fund-Facility-Press-552783. [32]

IMF (2024), *World Economic Outlook*, (database), https://www.imf.org/en/Publications/WEO/weo-database/2024/April (accessed on 1 October 2024). [31]

IMF (2023), *World Economic Outlook*, (database), https://www.imf.org/en/Publications/WEO/weo-database/2023/October (accessed on 1 October 2024). [35]

IOM (2023), *Data Report: Trends in Caribbean Migration and Mobility*, International Organization for Migration, Grand-Saconnex, Switzerland. [7]

LAPOP Lab (2023), "The AmericasBarometer", webpage, https://www.vanderbilt.edu/lapop/about-americasbarometer.php (accessed on 1 October 2024). [41]

Masson, M., D. Ehrhardt and V. Lizzio (2020), *Sustainable Energy Paths for the Caribbean*, Inter-American Development Bank, Washington, DC, https://doi.org/10.18235/0002236. [9]

Ministry of Finance of The Bahamas (2022), "The Commonwealth of The Bahamas successfully prices US$385 million notes: Offering takes advantage of IDB US$200 million guarantee", 10 July, Press Release, Government of The Bahamas, https://www.bahamas.gov.bs/wps/portal/public/gov/government/news/the%20commonwealth%20of%20the%20bahamas%20successfully%20prices%20us385%20million%20notes/!ut/p/b1/vZPJsps4FlafJQ_giwQlwVIGzDwPttlQ2HgAAwZjm-Hpm9vVi5tUdbJJlq0k_Tqf6lMdKqF2VNJk7-KSPYt7k1Wf64R. [49]

ND-GAIN (2021), *ND-GAIN*, (database), https://gain.nd.edu/our-work/country-index/rankings/ (accessed on 1 October 2024). [4]

Núñez, G., H. Velloso and F. Da Silva (2022), *Corporate Governance in Latin America and the Caribbean: Using ESG Debt Instruments to Fiinance Sustainable Investment Projects*, United Nations Economic Commission for Latin America and the Caribbean, Santiago, https://repositorio.cepal.org/handle/11362/47778. [51]

OECD (2024), "Key indicators of Informality based on Individuals and their Households (KIIbIH)", *OECD Data Explorer*, (database), https://shorturl.at/lZXl5 (accessed on 1 October 2024). [23]

OECD (2024), "The surge of Green, Social, Sustainability and Sustainability-linked (GSSS) bonds in Latin America and the Caribbean: Facts and policy implications", *OECD Development Policy Papers*, No. 56, OECD Publishing, Paris, https://doi.org/10.1787/f1c893a3-en. [50]

OECD (2023), *Social Institutions & Gender Index*, (database), https://www.oecd.org/en/data/dashboards/social-institutions-gender-index.html (accessed on 1 October 2024). [45]

OECD (2023), *Towards Climate Resilience and Neutrality in Latin America and the Caribbean: Key Policy Priorities*, OECD Publishing, Paris, https://doi.org/10.1787/278e52e8-en. [6]

OECD et al. (2024), *Latin American Economic Outlook 2024: Financing Sustainable Development*, OECD Publishing, Paris, https://doi.org/10.1787/c437947f-en. [25]

OECD et al. (2023), *Latin American Economic Outlook 2023: Investing in Sustainable Development*, OECD Publishing, Paris, https://doi.org/10.1787/8c93ff6e-en. [40]

OECD et al. (2024), *Revenue Statistics in Latin America and the Caribbean 2024*, OECD Publishing, Paris, https://doi.org/10.1787/33e226ae-en. [46]

Rosenblatt, D. et al. (2023), *Caribbean Economics Quarterly: Reflections on Innovation and Productivity as Caribbean Businesses Emerge from the Pandemic*, Inter-American Development Bank, Washington, DC, https://doi.org/10.18235/0004902. [29]

Turnbull, D. (2021), "Food security in the Caribbean", *IICA blog*, 23 April, https://blog.iica.int/blog/food-security-caribbean. [19]

UIS (2024), "Data for the Sustainable Development Goals", (database), https://uis.unesco.org/ (accessed on 18 June 2024). [27]

UNCTAD (2022), *UNCTADstat*, (database), https://unctadstat.unctad.org/datacentre/ (accessed on 1 July 2024). [38]

UNCTADStat (2024), *Data Centre*, (database), https://unctadstat.unctad.org/datacentre/ (accessed on 1 July 2024). [55]

UNDP (2024), *Human Development Index (HDI)*, (database), https://hdr.undp.org/data-center/human-development-index#/indicies/HDI (accessed on 1 October 2024). [13]

UNDRR (2022), "The Caribbean is at the forefront of early warning systems", 13 October, United Nations Office for Disaster Risk Reduction, Geneva, https://www.undrr.org/news/caribbean-forefront-early-warning-systems. [8]

UNEP (2019), *The Caribbean – Keeping it Real*, 29 May, UN Environment Programme, Nairobi. [10]

United Nations (2024), *SDG Indicators Database*, https://unstats.un.org/sdgs/dataportal/database. [20]

United Nations (2022), "World Populations Prospects 2022", webpage, https://population.un.org/wpp/Publications/. [26]

UNODC (2022), "International Homicide Statistics", *dataUNODC*, (database), https://dataunodc.un.org/dp-intentional-homicide-victims. [43]

World Bank (2024), "Foreign direct investment, net inflows (% of GDP)", *World Bank Group Data*, (database), https://data.worldbank.org/indicator/BX.KLT.DINV.WD.GD.ZS (accessed on 1 July 2024). [57]

World Bank (2024), "GDP Current US$", *World Development Indicators*, (database), https://databank.worldbank.org/reports.aspx?source=2&series=NY.GDP.MKTP.CD&country=# (accessed on 1 July 2024). [3]

World Bank (2024), *World Development Indicators*, https://data.worldbank.org/indicator/SI.POV.GINI. [16]

World Bank (2023), "Exports of goods and services (BoP, current US$)", *World Bank Group Data*, (database), https://data.worldbank.org/indicator/BX.GSR.GNFS.CD (accessed on 1 July 2024). [54]

World Bank (2023), "Net ODA received (% of GNI)", *World Bank Group Data*, (database), https://data.worldbank.org/indicator/DT.ODA.ODAT.GN.ZS (accessed on 1 July 2024). [58]

World Bank (2022), *Global Financial Development Database*, (database), https://www.worldbank.org/en/publication/gfdr/gfdr-2016/data/global-financial-development-database (accessed on 1 July 2024). [53]

WTTC (2022), *Travel and Tourism in the Caribbean: Prospects for Growth*, World Travel and Tourism Council, London, https://wttc.org/Portals/0/Documents/Reports/2022/Travel-and-tourism-in-the-caribbean.pdf. [12]

1 Understanding macro-structural conditions

This chapter analyses the Caribbean's macroeconomic and structural conditions in the context of modest potential economic growth. It examines the role of low productivity in constraining economic activity and assesses the relevance of fiscal and monetary policy in promoting sustained economic growth. It also emphasises the importance of enhancing quality investment and aligning it with development goals. Then, the chapter delves into the region's economic structure, focusing on the limited diversification of service-based and commodity-exporting economies, and examines how these characteristics influence their external balances and trade dynamics. Finally, the chapter addresses the low levels of internationalisation and innovation among Caribbean firms and the persistent barriers to business growth.

Introduction

Macro-structural conditions in the Caribbean are strongly influenced by the global context. The relatively small size of most Caribbean economies, coupled with their dependence on external markets, makes economic conditions in these countries volatile and highly susceptible to global downturns. In this context, strengthening macro-structural conditions in the Caribbean is vital to ensuring sustainable and inclusive growth, reducing vulnerabilities, attracting quality investments, and creating formal jobs, among other objectives.

This chapter analyses macro-structural conditions in Caribbean countries. The first section explores the importance of boosting productivity, strengthening fiscal and monetary policies, managing public debt sustainably, and establishing the conditions necessary to attract investments, which are all key drivers of sustained and higher long-term potential growth. The second section examines the economic structure of Caribbean countries, which are predominantly service-based and commodity-exporting economies. This section highlights the importance of upgrading production structures, improving diversification, enhancing integration into regional and global value chains, and fostering an environment where firms can innovate, expand, and better connect with global markets.

Macroeconomic conditions are characterised by modest potential growth, coupled with volatility and vulnerability to external shocks

The Caribbean's economic trajectory exhibits volatility and heterogeneity, posing a challenge for long-term growth

Potential growth in Caribbean economies is relatively low and has declined in recent years. The region's average potential gross domestic product (GDP) per capita growth is estimated at 1.4%. This is slightly above the Latin American average (1.1%) and below the 1.8% estimated for the average of advanced economies (Figure 1.1). Modest potential growth implies that Caribbean economies will find it challenging to converge with the per capita income levels of advanced economies and thus must develop new engines of economic growth.

Figure 1.1. Potential GDP per capita growth in the Caribbean, Latin America and advanced economies (as estimated by different methods since 1980)

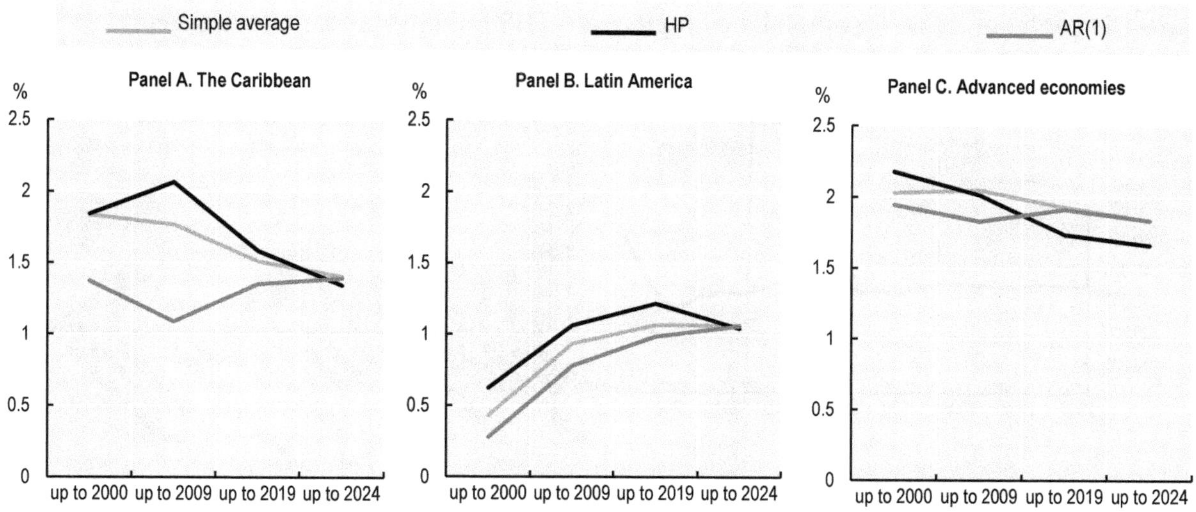

Note: Potential GDP growth is the growth rate the economy can sustain over the long run, excluding short-term effects linked to a difference between demand and the potential supply level. The variable refers to the growth in potential output, which is the maximum output level an economy can reach without putting strain on production factors that translate into inflationary pressures.
Average growth is a simple average of growth in all countries for each group over the period analysed. HP=the Hodrick-Prescott filter, which was used as an alternative model due to its resilience to short-term shocks to create a smoothed curve (lambda 100); AR=autoregressive model, which uses GDP per capita growth data. The number of lags (one) was determined by analysing the autocorrelation function and choosing the model that maximised the log-likelihood.
Source: Authors' calculations based on IMF (2024[1]).

StatLink https://stat.link/5kycfg

Over the last decades, GDP and GDP per capita growth in the Caribbean have been modest and heterogeneous. Average annual real GDP growth between 2000 and 2023 was 2.5% in the Caribbean, similar to the Latin American average for the same period. The average GDP per capita in the Caribbean increased from constant USD 15 000 to USD 21 800 between 2000 and 2023. While this was a larger relative increase than what was observed in OECD countries, in absolute terms, this was smaller than the increase in the OECD (from USD 40 000 to USD 53 000), hence widening the income gap between both regions (Figure 1.2, Panel A).

The average GDP per capita in the Caribbean has remained higher than that of Latin America over the same period, although there is significant heterogeneity across countries (Figure 1.2, Panel A). In 2023, individual country figures ranged from USD 2 934 to USD 49 811 per capita, highlighting the economic disparities within the Caribbean. Indeed, the Caribbean has economies ranging from lower middle-income levels (Haiti) to upper middle-income (Belize, Dominica, the Dominican Republic, Grenada, Jamaica, Saint Lucia, Saint Vincent and the Grenadines, and Suriname) and to high-income (Antigua and Barbuda, the Bahamas, Barbados, Guyana, Saint Kitts and Nevis, and Trinidad and Tobago) (World Bank, 2023[2]).

Historically, the region has experienced greater annual GDP growth volatility than Latin America and advanced economies. From 2000 to 2023, the standard deviation of GDP growth in the Caribbean averaged 6%, in contrast to 4% in Latin America and 2% in advanced economies. Moreover, disparities among countries in the Caribbean are significant. For instance, Guyana exhibited a GDP growth standard deviation of 15% over the same period – mostly related to positive developments linked to oil discoveries and increased oil production – while the figure for Saint Vincent and the Grenadines was 3% (Figure 1.2, Panel B). This heightened volatility in the Caribbean is primarily attributed to small market sizes, heavy reliance on tourism and external financing, limited economic diversification and high exposure to climate threats. These factors make the region more vulnerable to external shocks and prone to fluctuations.

Figure 1.2. Evolution of GDP per capita by region and GDP growth standard deviations in the Caribbean, 2000-23

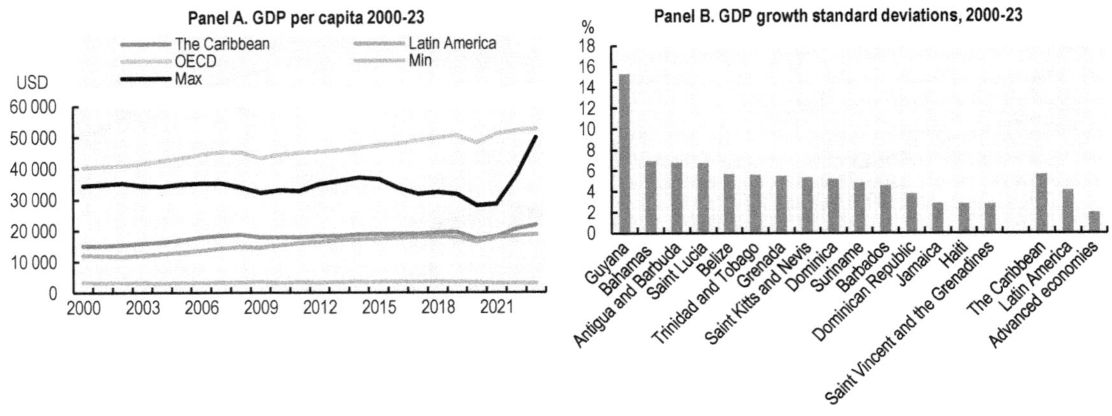

Note: Panel A. GDP per capita is expressed in constant 2021 international USD per person. Max = maximum value among the Caribbean countries per year. Min = minimum value among the Caribbean countries per year.
Source: Authors' elaboration based on IMF (2024[1]) and World Bank (2023[3]).

StatLink https://stat.link/9b5wxp

Low productivity is at the core of low potential growth

The region has historically exhibited low productivity, constraining the potential for sustained high economic growth. Relative to OECD countries, Caribbean economies show a widening gap: average labour productivity in the Caribbean represented almost 50% of that of the OECD in the early 90s, and this level declined to around 38.3% in 2021, with an improvement in 2022 (42%) and 2023 (46%) (Figure 1.3). Structural heterogeneity is a significant feature in the region, with low-productivity economies coexisting alongside higher-productivity ones.

Several factors explain such low productivity levels, including an economic structure highly dependent on external demand, inadequate infrastructure limiting market access and knowledge spillovers, limited access to finance for innovative and productive activities, a high level of informality in the labour market, and significant vulnerability to natural disasters (ILO, 2023[4]; Rosenblatt et al., 2023[5]; Ianchovichina, 2024[6]).

Given these factors, accurately measuring productivity is complex. Economic events tend to affect small economies disproportionately. For example, Guyana's recent productivity surge reflected oil discoveries and increased production and has, in turn, positively affected the region’s average productivity since 2021 (Figure 1.3). Moreover, aggregate productivity figures can be biased by sectors that generate low employment, profits and value-added. Finally, standard productivity metrics fail to account for changes in external demand, commodity prices, or the impact of natural disasters, which all play an important role in shaping the region’s development dynamics (Rosenblatt et al., 2023[5]).

Figure 1.3. Labour productivity in the Caribbean and Latin America as a share of the OECD, 1991-2023

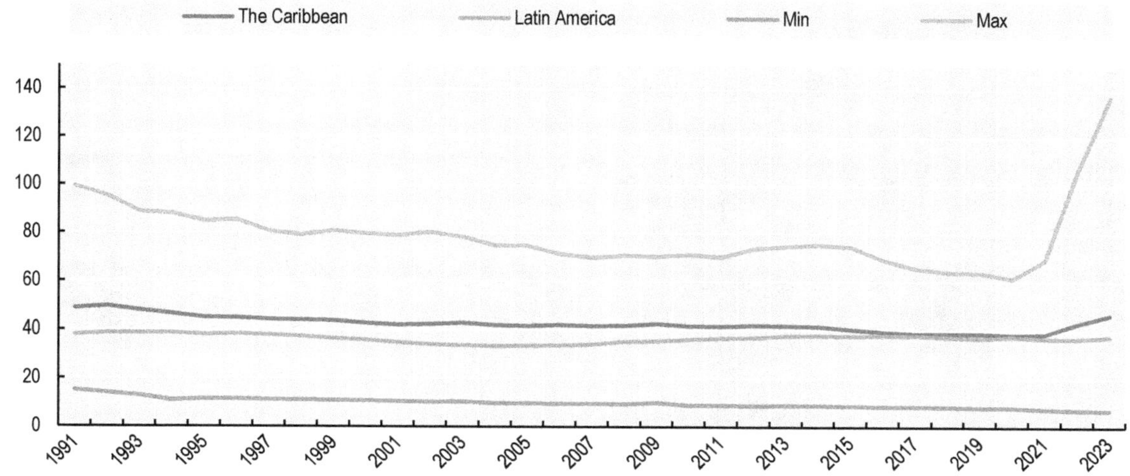

Note: Productivity is measured by GDP per person employed (constant 2021 PPP USD). Max = maximum value among the Caribbean countries per year. Min = minimum value among the Caribbean countries per year.
Source: Authors' elaboration based on World Bank (2023[3]).

StatLink https://stat.link/myj4ie

Fiscal policy is a fundamental ingredient for sustained growth

Many Caribbean economies face persistent challenges associated with high deficit and debt levels. This situation is largely the result of macroeconomic vulnerabilities, costly financial crises, and frequent natural disasters that disrupt economic activity and erode fiscal buffers (Acevedo, LaFramboise and Wong, 2017[7]). Effective fiscal policy is therefore crucial for sustained growth. Governments need to be able to invest in development objectives while building resilience to economic shocks without compromising financial stability.

Fiscal balances vary considerably across countries. In 2023, the region's overall fiscal deficit narrowed to 1.6% of GDP, from 2.4% in 2022. This was largely due to reduced primary expenditure following the end of COVID-19 emergency programmes and anti-inflationary measures in 2022, alongside decreased capital expenditure (ECLAC, 2024[8]). This progress is particularly pronounced in service-exporting nations benefiting from strengthened international tourism. By 2023, several countries improved their fiscal positions: Grenada recorded a surplus of 8.4% of GDP, and Saint Kitts and Nevis maintained a positive balance of 0.9%. In addition, countries such as Suriname are achieving substantial primary surpluses under programmes supported by the International Monetary Fund, which require fiscal consolidation efforts (ECLAC, 2024[8]). In contrast, some countries like Dominica and Saint Vincent and the Grenadines still faced significant challenges, with deficits of -7.3% and -8.4% of GDP, respectively (Figure 1.4, Panel A). Over the period 2013 and 2023, many Caribbean countries experienced fiscal deficits, with Suriname, the Bahamas, and Guyana averaging overall deficits of -6.7%, -5.1%, and -4.2% of GDP, respectively (Figure 1.4, Panel B). Jamaica's high primary balance over the period is noteworthy, with this consistent performance supported by important reforms to fiscal institutions.

Figure 1.4. Central government fiscal balance as percentage of GDP, 2013-23 average

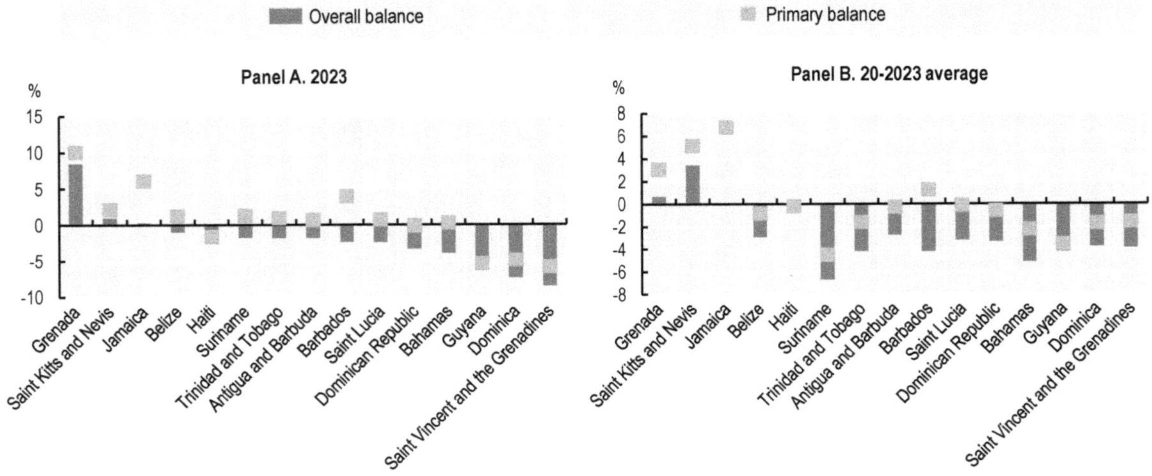

Note: Data is from 2022 for Dominica and 2018 for Haiti due to data availability.
Source: Authors' elaboration based on CEPALSTAT (ECLAC, 2023[9]).

StatLink https://stat.link/rxl5k3

High public debt levels remain a challenge in many Caribbean economies

Public debt levels grew significantly in most Caribbean economies in the last decade, but heterogeneity exists across countries. In 2022, the central government's total public debt remained high, averaging 78.8% of GDP. This was well above the average for Latin America (52.9%). It was also higher than central government public debt ten years before: in 2012, this stood at 69.2% (Figure 1.5).

Substantial heterogeneity is evident across countries, both in the level of public debt and in recent trends. In 2022, Barbados and Suriname showed public debt levels higher than 100% of GDP. However, Suriname's public debt fell to 93% in 2023 following debt restructuring agreements. Similarly, Barbados' debt fell to 116.5% in 2023, in line with pre-pandemic levels, following its 2018–19 sovereign debt restructuring and fiscal consolidation under the Economic Recovery and Transformation Plan, which includes a commitment to bring debt down to 60% of GDP for the financial year 2035/36 (IMF, 2024[10]; IMF, 2024[11]). On the other hand, Trinidad and Tobago, and Saint Kitts and Nevis have figures below 60%. While public debt levels have risen in most countries since 2012, Jamaica, Belize, Grenada and Saint Kitts and Nevis managed to reduce public debt in this period. Jamaica is a notable case of debt reduction through the adoption of well-designed fiscal rules and a partnership agreement with the government, the private sector and civil society that ensures an equitable distribution of adjustment burdens (Arslanalp, Eichengreen and Blair, 2024[12]).

Figure 1.5. Central government total public debt as a percentage of GDP, selected Caribbean countries and regional averages, 2012 and 2022

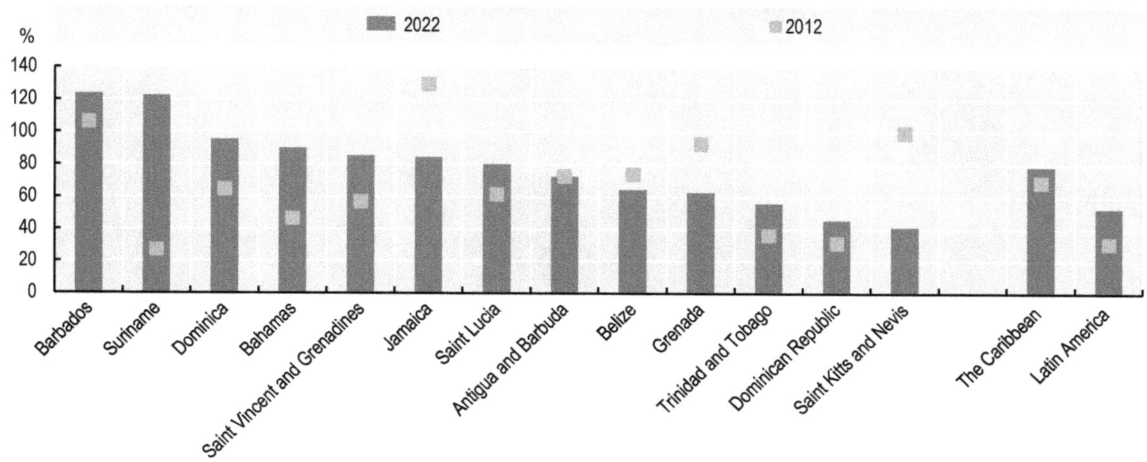

Source: Authors' elaboration based on CEPALSTATS (ECLAC, 2023[9]).

StatLink https://stat.link/jqiyem

Exposure to international price levels underscores the importance of sound monetary policy

After a spike in 2022, inflation is converging towards lower levels for some countries in the region. Food and energy prices drove higher inflation, which impacted the overall economy and then decreased in 2023 (Galindo and Izquierdo, 2024[13]). Caribbean economies, which are generally small, low diversified and highly dependent on imports, are particularly vulnerable to inflation driven by the pass-through of international prices.

The different monetary and exchange rate regimes in the region partly explain the different ability to tame inflation after the food and energy price shock. Countries with fixed exchange rate regimes, which peg their currencies to the US dollar, have exhibited the lowest inflation rates, averaging around 2% between 2012-23 (Figure 1.6). This stability is due to the outsourcing of monetary policy to the United States, which provides an external anchor but limits countries' flexibility to respond to shocks. Countries with inflation-targeting regimes, which allow central banks to adjust interest rates for price stability, experienced slightly higher inflation, averaging about 4% in the same period. Central bank independence and inflation targeting are associated with lower inflation and anchored inflation expectations (Beuermann et al., 2021[14]). Intermediate regimes, which use a combination of policies, show the highest volatility, with inflation reaching 33.4% in 2023. Suriname mainly drives this group's figures due to currency depreciation, government fiscal consolidation measures and external macroeconomic shocks (ECLAC, 2024[15]), while Haiti faces profound social and political instability.

Figure 1.6. Average inflation rate by monetary regimes in the Caribbean, 2000-23

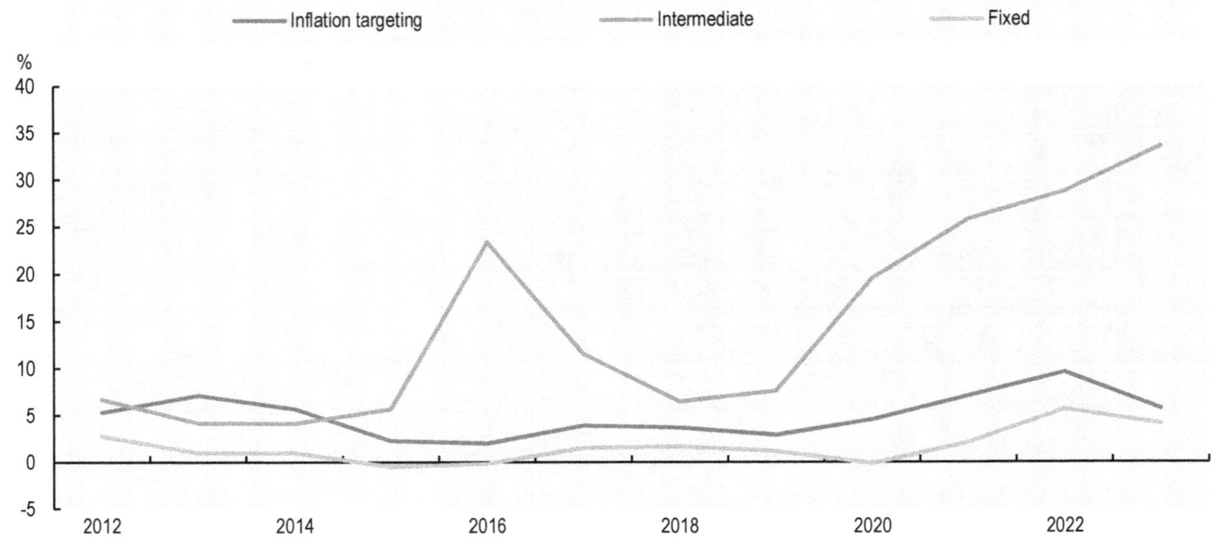

Note: Inflation-targeting regimes: the Dominican Republic and Jamaica. Intermediate: Haiti, Trinidad and Tobago, and Suriname. Fixed: Antigua and Barbuda, the Bahamas, Barbados, Belize, Dominica, Grenada, Guyana, Saint Kitts and Nevis, Saint Lucia, and Saint Vincent and the Grenadines.

Source: Authors' elaboration based on WEO database (IMF, 2024[1]).

Strengthening investment and connecting it to development goals is fundamental to drive inclusive and sustainable growth

Investment levels have shown an increasing trend in recent years. Between 2015 and 2023, average investment in the Caribbean increased from around 23% to almost 27% of GDP, compared to averages ranging from 20% to 22% in Latin America and from 23% to 24% in OECD countries in the same period (Figure 1.7). Investment is crucial for driving economic growth and development as it increases productive capacity, fosters job creation, enhances productivity, and has a positive multiplier effect throughout the economy. In small economies like those in the Caribbean, large investments can have an outsized impact due to their relative size. Significant investments in sectors such as tourism or natural resources can influence overall investment levels, rendering them particularly sensitive to large-scale projects.

Investment levels vary considerably within the region. In 2023, they ranged from more than 40% of GDP in Suriname and Grenada to less than 20% in Barbados, Guyana and Haiti (Figure 1.7). In Suriname, investment is primarily driven by the exploration of offshore oil and gas reserves (IMF, 2024[16]). In Grenada, the Disaster Resiliency Strategy, which focuses on building resilient infrastructure, and the Citizenship-by-Investment (CBI) program, which supported public and private investments, mainly in real estate, played a key role (IMF, 2023[17]). The private sector is the main driver of investment in the region. In Antigua and Barbuda, the Bahamas and the Dominican Republic, private investment represented more than 89% of total investment in 2019 (OECD et al., 2023[18]).

Figure 1.7. Total investment as a percentage of GDP, 2015-23

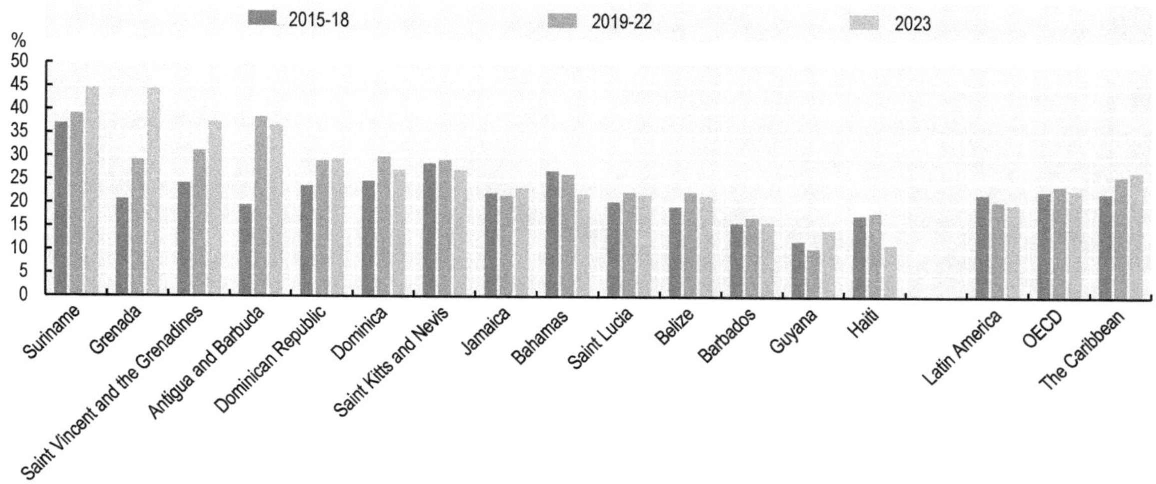

Source: Authors' elaboration based on IMF (2024[1]).

StatLink https://stat.link/crhu1t

Public investment in infrastructure for some countries in the region remains low. Between 2015 and 2021, average public investment in infrastructure in Belize, the Dominican Republic, Guyana and Trinidad and Tobago was 1.3% of GDP, below the Latin American average of 1.9%. Belize invested 4.7% of its GDP in water, energy, telecommunications, and transport sectors, Guyana, Trinidad and Tobago, and the Dominican Republic invested around 1% of their GDP, focusing mainly on transport and water. (Figure 1.8).

Quality public infrastructure is crucial for sustainable and inclusive development as it can attract private investment and promote growth and connectivity (OECD et al., 2023[18]). Investing in resilient infrastructure is essential for integrating national and international markets and adapting to climate change impacts. However, Caribbean countries face significant challenges in developing infrastructure. As small states, they struggle to achieve economies of scale and have limited access to concessional financing and global capital markets. Additionally, high public debt burdens, frequent natural disasters and exposure to climate change create uncertainties and necessitate innovative and resilient infrastructure solutions (Queyranne, Daal and Funke, 2019[19]).

Figure 1.8. Public investment in infrastructure in selected Caribbean countries as a percentage of GDP, 2015-21

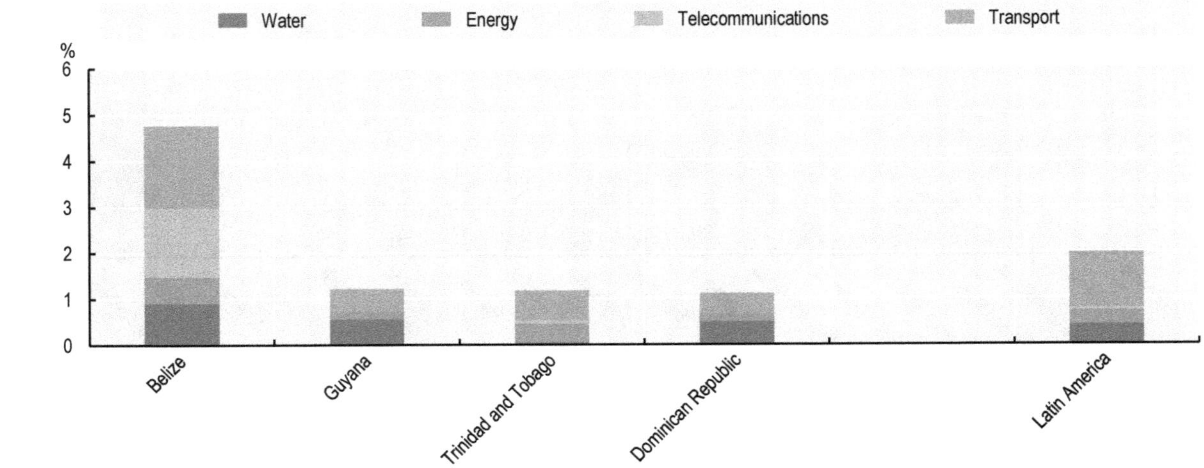

Source: Authors' elaboration based on Infralatam (2021[20]).

StatLink https://stat.link/r9yn17

The region has attracted foreign direct investment (FDI), mainly towards the energy and services sectors. Between 2013 and 2021, FDI net inflows as a percentage of GDP were on average above 6%; in 2022 they represented 4.18%, similar to the level in 2023 of 4.3% (excluding Guyana, which saw an extraordinary increase of FDI in 2023, reaching 42.8%). FDI flows to the Caribbean in 2023 were higher than in Latin America (2.7%) and the OECD (0.1%) (Figure 1.9).

FDI inflows show varied trends across different economies. Guyana has experienced a significant surge in FDI, primarily driven by investments associated with oil discoveries. The Bahamas and Jamaica attract FDI mainly in financial services and tourism. Meanwhile, flows to the Dominican Republic are channelled to tourism, natural resources and building capacity to generate renewable energy. Conversely, Trinidad and Tobago has seen a decline due to a slowdown in the energy sector caused by the maintenance of facilities and the shutdown of some petrochemical plants (UNCTAD, 2022[21]; ECLAC, 2023[22]; ECLAC, 2022[23]).

Figure 1.9. Foreign direct investment net inflows (percentage of GDP), 2013-23

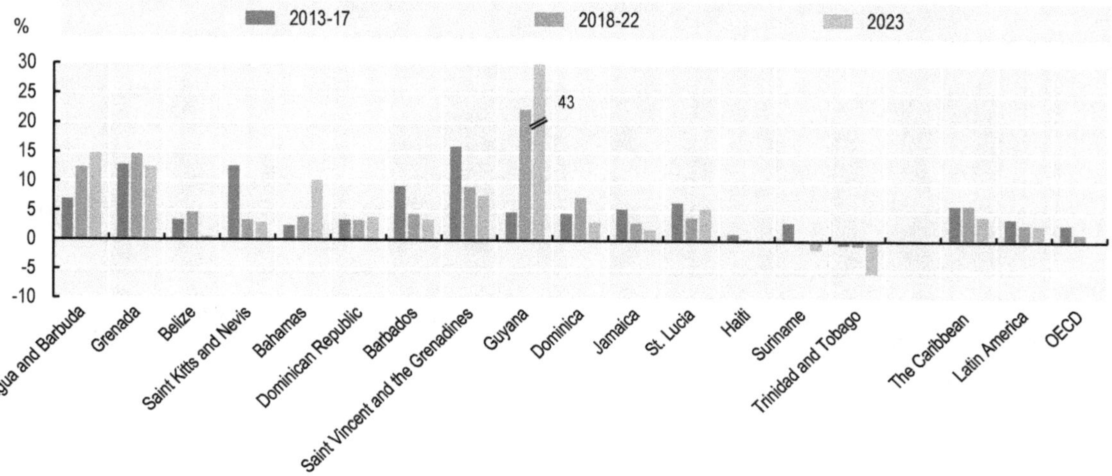

Source: Authors' elaboration based on World Bank (2023[3]).

StatLink https://stat.link/o8jnuq

The economic structure reflects low levels of productivity and limited diversification and upgrading of the production matrix

Caribbean countries are mostly service-based and commodity-exporting economies

In 2022, services accounted for 55-78% of total GDP for most countries, with tourism as the main economic activity for many of them (Figure 1.10). Tourism supports hospitality and entertainment industries and creates backward linkages with agriculture, trade, transportation and construction. Between 2015 and 2019, tourism accounted on average for 25.4% of Caribbean countries GDP (Gomez Garcia et al., 2021[24]). Nevertheless, tourism depends highly on external conditions. It is seasonal and also vulnerable to climate shocks (Acevedo, LaFramboise and Wong, 2017[7]; CDB, 2017[25]). For instance, 46% of tourists come from the United States and 20% from Europe. This makes the region highly susceptible to external shocks, as evidenced by the impact of the 2008 financial crisis and the COVID-19 pandemic. It is equally vulnerable to natural disasters such as hurricanes, which have destroyed buildings, roads and infrastructure in the past (Mooney et al., 2021[26]). In addition to tourism, financial services play an important role, accounting for between 8% and 27% of GDP for countries in the region, with the highest shares observed in the Bahamas (27%), Barbados (26%), and Saint Lucia (21%) (ECLAC, 2023[9]).

Figure 1.10. Contribution of economic sectors to total GDP, 2022

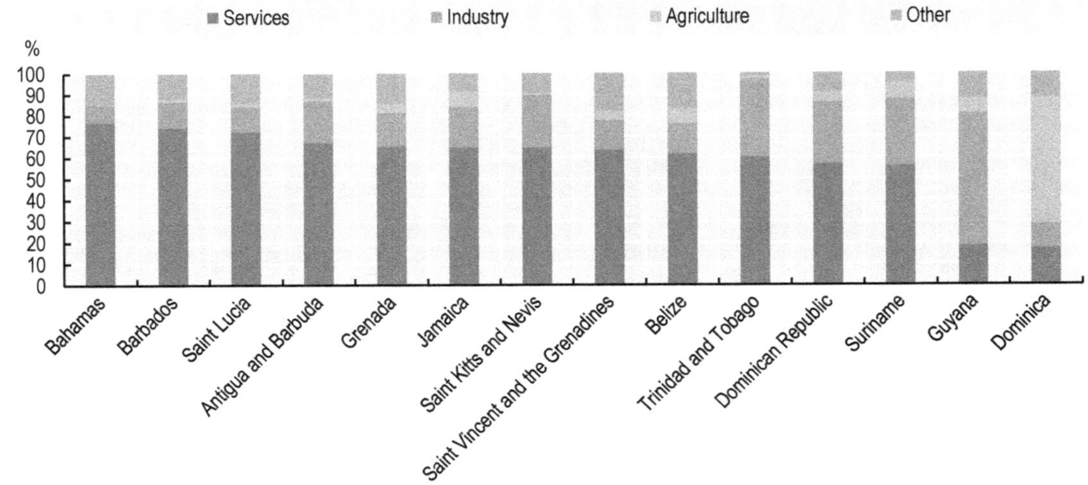

Note: Calculations based on GDP at constant 2018 USD prices. "Other" includes taxes on products minus subsidies on products and statistical discrepancy of GDP by sector of origin.
Source: Authors' elaboration based on CEPALSTAT (ECLAC, 2023[9]).

StatLink https://stat.link/7scxho

Tourism in the Caribbean has experienced significant growth. Between 1995 and 2018, tourist arrivals in the Caribbean increased from 10 million to 27 million per year. However, the COVID-19 pandemic caused a significant drop in 2020 and 2021. In 2022, tourist arrivals rebounded to 22 million, although they remained below pre-pandemic levels (Figure 1.11, Panel A). The primary recipients of tourists are the Bahamas, the Dominican Republic, Jamaica and Barbados, which collectively account for 75% of arrivals during this period. Tourism expenditure contributes significantly to the regional economy, reaching 32% of GDP in 2022 (Figure 1.11, Panel B).

Figure 1.11. Tourist arrivals and tourism expenditure as percentage of GDP, 1995-2022

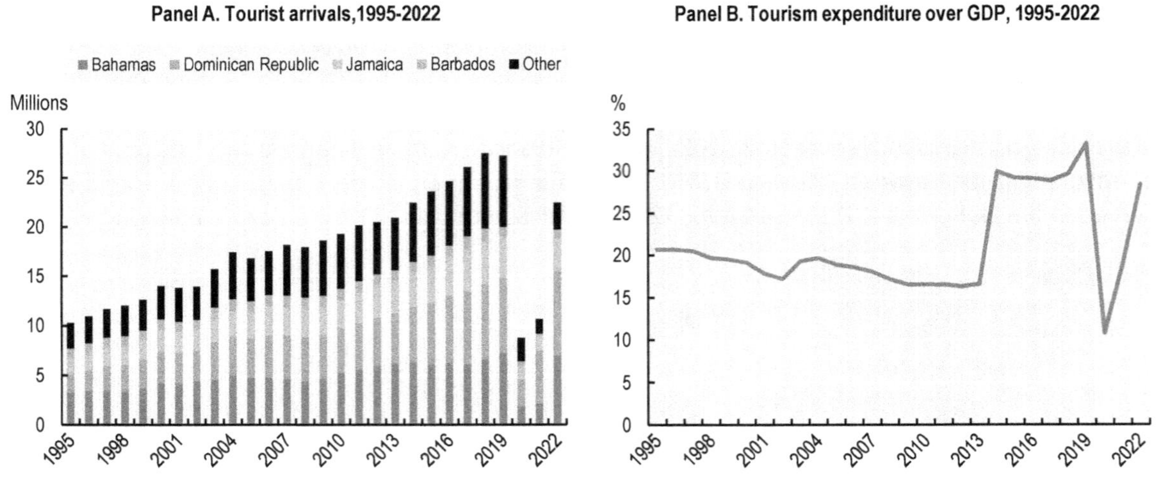

Note: Panel A. "Other" includes Antigua and Barbuda, Belize, Dominica, Grenada, Haiti, Saint Lucia, and Saint Vincent and the Grenadines.
Source: Authors' elaboration based on ECLAC (2023[9]) and UNWTO (2024[27]).

StatLink https://stat.link/n3me76

Natural resources also play a significant role in Caribbean economies. Guyana's oil and gas exploration and production sector contributed to the country's 62% real GDP growth in 2022. Since 2019, oil production has been the country's primary driver of economic growth (IMF, 2023[28]). The economy of Trinidad and Tobago is also driven by oil and gas production and the associated petrochemical sector, while Suriname relies on mining and has a large potential to develop the oil and gas industry following the successful recent exploration of offshore reserves. Agriculture remains important for countries like Belize, Guyana and Dominica. Historically focused on sugar and banana exports, the sector now faces slow productivity growth due to high trade costs and limited capacity to meet modern food safety standards. This has led to a higher reliance on imports to meet the growing demand from tourism, processing and retail industries. Challenges within the sector include inadequate technology, low credit availability, high labour costs and insufficient infrastructure (FAO, 2019[29]).

Countries in the region face current account deficits associated with their external dependencies

Most Caribbean countries experience current account deficits as limited domestic production results in significant import dependence. Between 2012 and 2022, Dominica, and Saint Vincent and the Grenadines, exhibited average deficits accounting for 23% and 17% of GDP, respectively. In Dominica, the current account deficit has been narrowing since 2019 but widened to 33.7% of GDP in 2023, as higher imports for the construction of strategic infrastructure projects outweighed higher tourism receipts (IMF, 2024[30]). In Saint Vincent and the Grenadines, current account deficits have narrowed representing 5.4% of GDP in 2023 – and are expected to fall over the medium term, supported by lower fossil fuel imports (IMF, 2024[31]). For its part, Trinidad and Tobago held a surplus of 8% (Figure 1.12). In 2022, Saint Lucia, Dominica, the Bahamas and Grenada saw improvements in their current account balances thanks to tourism recovery after the COVID-19 pandemic (ECLAC, 2022[32]).

Oil exports and rising prices boosted the balances of Trinidad and Tobago, Guyana, Jamaica and the Bahamas. Meanwhile, Grenada, Saint Lucia, Dominica, and Antigua and Barbuda increased exports in agricultural products, prepared foods, beverages and tobacco (ECLAC, 2023[33]).

Figure 1.12. Current account balance in the Caribbean, 2012-22

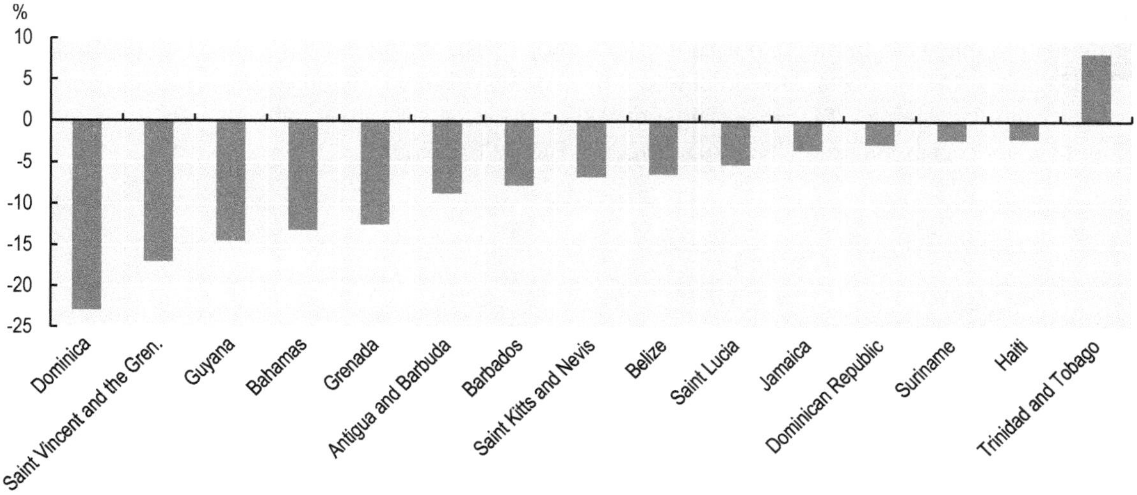

Source: Authors' elaboration based on World Bank (2023[3]).

StatLink https://stat.link/pbjqt7

The export basket reflects low value added and limited diversification

Caribbean economies rely significantly on international trade. Given their small size, they depend on imports to meet internal demand and support manufacturing and services like tourism. At the same time, they export a limited range of services and commodities. Services constitute the primary component of the export basket for many Caribbean countries. This sector accounts for 60% of total exports in Belize and up to 97% in Antigua and Barbuda. It is driven by tourism and financial, computer and information services (Giordano and Ortiz de Mendívil, 2021[34]) (Figure 1.13).

Figure 1.13. Share of services exports in total exports, 2022

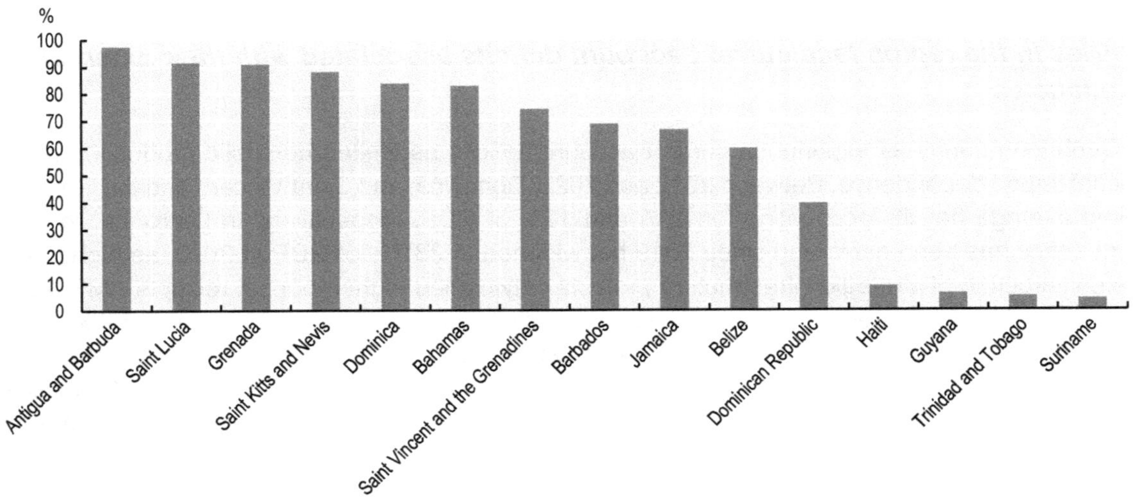

Source: Authors' elaboration based on UNCTADstat (2022[35]).

StatLink https://stat.link/rhi5q0

In terms of trade in goods, the region is a net importer. Exports are concentrated in primary products and resource-based manufactures, such as crude and refined petroleum, alcoholic beverages, cereals, food preparations, chemical elements, minerals and tobacco. These accounted for 57% of total goods exports in 2022 (Figure 1.14). Imports are dominated by resource-based manufactures (29%) and medium technology manufactures (27%), including processed food, automotive vehicles, and machinery and equipment for various industries (UNCTAD, 2022[35]; ECLAC, 2023[33]).

Figure 1.14. Goods trade structure by technology intensity in the Caribbean, 2022

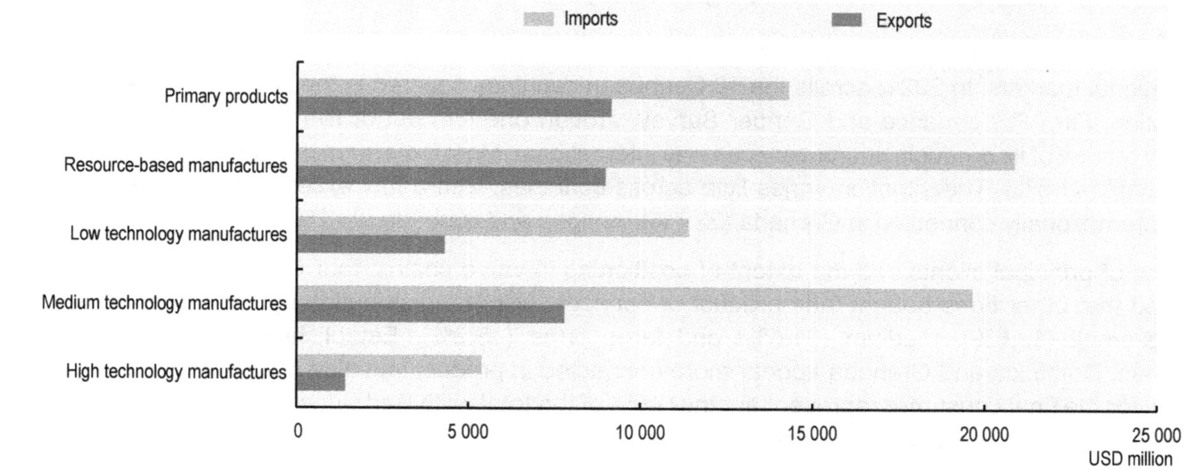

Note: Values are USD million in current prices.
Source: Authors' elaboration based on UNCTADstat (2022[35]).

StatLink https://stat.link/e0lc4x

Caribbean economies engage with various trade partners to enhance market access and co-operation. Many islands are members of trade blocs like the Caribbean Community (CARICOM) and the Organisation of Eastern Caribbean States (OECS), which help facilitate trade integration (see Chapter 6). Country members from these blocs also participate in Economic Partnership Agreements (EPA) with the European Union and the United Kingdom through the CARIFORUM-EU and CARIFORUM-UK EPA. These agreements remove all tariffs and export quotas and cover various trade issues, including services, intellectual property rights and public procurement. They aim to promote sustainable development and regional integration (Grieger, 2023[36]).

Additionally, the Caribbean Basin Initiative, a programme by the United States, promotes economic development and export diversification in the region by allowing duty-free and quota-free treatment for goods (USTR, 2023[37]). In 2022, CARICOM's main export destinations were Europe (35%, mainly the Netherlands, Germany, Italy and the United Kingdom), the United States (27%), and Latin America (20%). Imports primarily came from the United States (45%), the People's Republic of China (10%) and Europe (16%, mainly from Italy, the Netherlands, Germany and the United Kingdom) (OEC, 2022[38]).

Deeper economic integration, trade diversification and upgrading are vital strategies to support economic dynamism in Caribbean economies (see Chapter 6). Caribbean countries need to diversify their trade partners, manage complex trade networks, strengthen regional ties, and brand themselves as quality trade and manufacturing partners to harness their productive potential (OECD/UNCTAD/ECLAC, 2020[39]). Strengthening the potential of current lead sectors will also be important. For instance, by expanding services provided to tourists and increasing linkages of tourism to domestic producers or by engaging in more processing and transformation of existing raw material exports.

Firms in the Caribbean show low levels of internationalisation and innovation, partly as a result of persistent barriers to doing business

Levels of internationalisation of Caribbean firms seem to be limited, as firms tend to operate mainly in local and national markets. In 2021, across the 13 Caribbean countries covered in the 2021 Compete Caribbean Innovation, Firm Performance and Gender Survey, around one firm out of five (19.6%) reported that the primary market of its products and/or services was international. Most firms' primary market was local (38.9%) or national (41.5%). The situation varies little across countries, with a few exceptions: firms appear to be more internationally connected in Grenada (22.7%), Antigua and Barbuda (24.7%) and Belize (58.7%).

In terms of principal clients and the extent of positioning in value chains, four Caribbean firms out of ten reported that other firms bought their product or services, with the distribution by client size being equal among small (13.6%), medium (11.6%) and large firms (15.2%). Establishments in Suriname, the Bahamas, Dominica and Grenada appear more connected in production value chains. Firms that operate directly for the final consumer represent another 40% of the total, with Barbados (47.3%), Guyana (55.8%) and Belize (69%) well above the regional average.

Across the region, most establishments compete with informal firms (56.8% of the total), with particularly high levels in Belize (73.6%), Guyana and Grenada (66%), or with firms that do not register receipts or formal records (48.2%).

Regarding innovation, only 10% of firms reported introducing at least one innovation in the major areas of their operations in the three years preceding the survey (2018-21) (Figure 1.15). Among those firms, most innovations were linked to marketing, packaging, and pricing of products and services (16.5% of establishments), new or improved goods (15.8%) and new methods for producing goods or providing services (15.1%). Conversely, less than 8% of Caribbean firms introduced innovations in business organisational practices, work responsibility, decision-making and human resources, accounting and other administrative operations, or information processing and communication. Establishments operating in services appear generally more innovative than those in manufacturing.

Figure 1.15. Areas of innovation at the firm level in the Caribbean

Areas of innovation across establishments having introduced innovations in the past three years (2018-21)

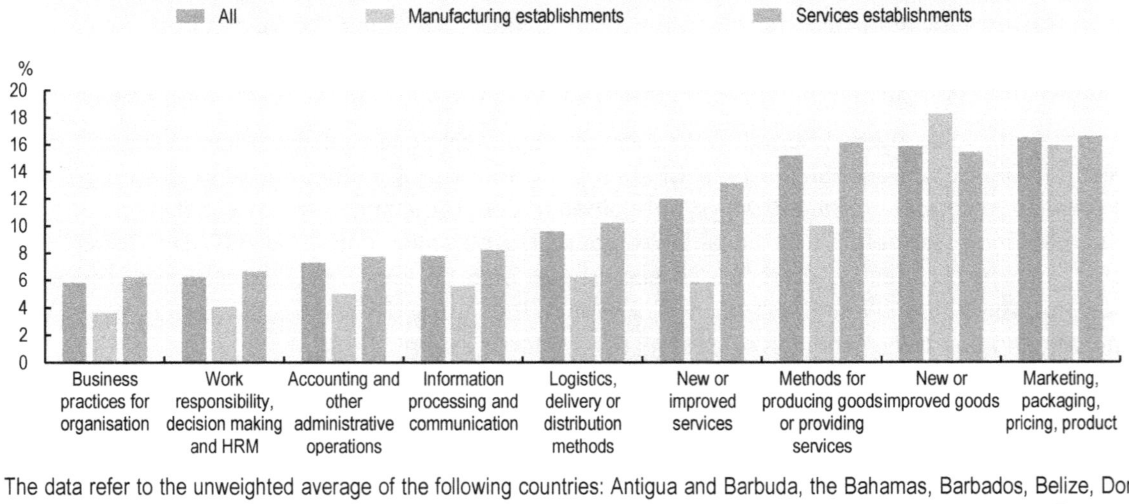

Note: The data refer to the unweighted average of the following countries: Antigua and Barbuda, the Bahamas, Barbados, Belize, Dominica, Grenada, Guyana, Jamaica, Saint Kitts and Nevis, Saint Lucia, Saint Vincent and the Grenadines, Suriname, and Trinidad and Tobago.
Source: Authors' elaborations based on the Compete Caribbean Innovation, Firm Performance and Gender Survey, 2021.

StatLink https://stat.link/5x1obk

Among the firms that introduced at least one innovation in the reported areas, most (52.7%) affirmed that the innovation process was critical or important for accessing new markets. A smaller percentage (43.3%) affirmed it increased production capacity or improved the quality of their products or services (33.4%). Only a few firms reported innovating to reduce unit production costs (26.4%), improving working conditions (18.5%) or improving supervision in the production processes (15.9%). In most cases, firms reported having financed innovations with capital of private shareholders and other stakeholders (55% of total establishments) or bank loans (30.5%). Meanwhile, public funding was reported to fund innovations in only 3.1% of firms.

Innovations are particularly important for achieving environmental and biodiversity goals and reducing pollution and the economy's carbon footprint (see Chapter 3). In the Caribbean, less than one establishment out of five has introduced innovations leading to environmental improvements. Green innovations were more likely to be introduced in areas such as recycling waste, water or materials and reducing energy or material use per output unit. They were less likely for broader green policies such as reducing overall carbon footprint or air, soil and air pollution (Figure 1.16).

Figure 1.16. Green innovation at the firm level in Caribbean countries

Percentage of establishments that introduced innovations in the past three years

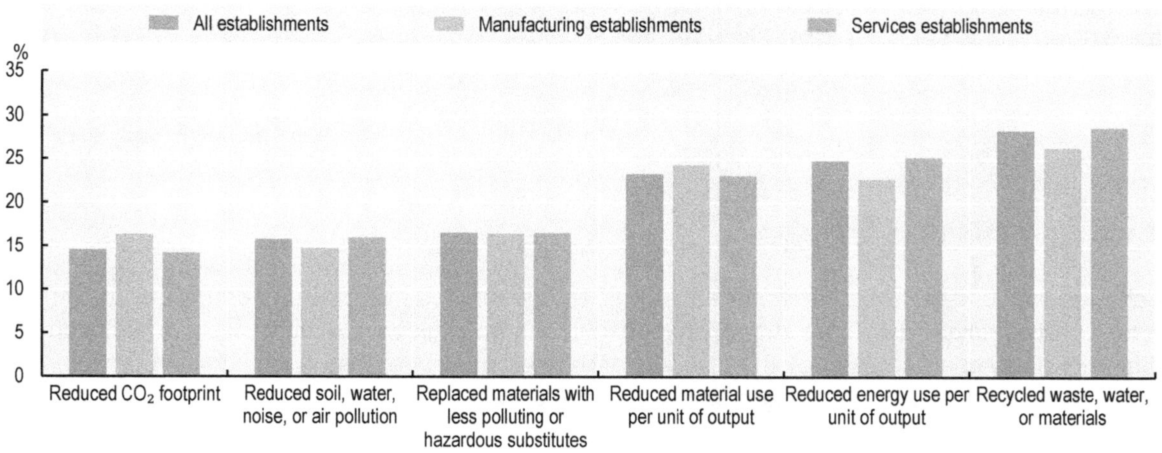

Note: The data refer to the unweighted average of the following countries: Antigua and Barbuda, the Bahamas, Barbados, Belize, Dominica, Grenada, Guyana, Jamaica, Saint Kitts and Nevis, Saint Lucia, Saint Vincent, Suriname, and Trinidad and Tobago.
Source: Authors' elaboration based on the Compete Caribbean Innovation, Firm Performance and Gender Survey, 2021.

StatLink https://stat.link/3sxfa8

Caribbean firms identified various obstacles to their business operations. The major obstacles to production operations in the region are access to finance (69.3% of firms report this as a major or severe obstacle), customs and trade operations (63.3%), an inadequately educated workforce (59.8%) and tax rates (52.7%). Fewer than three out of ten Caribbean firms indicate aspects like labour regulations, access to telecommunications networks, practices of informal competitors, the political environment, business licensing and permits as significant obstacles to doing business (Figure 1.17).

Figure 1.17. Main obstacles affecting firms' operation in Caribbean economies

Percentage of establishments reporting the severity of each item affecting their operations

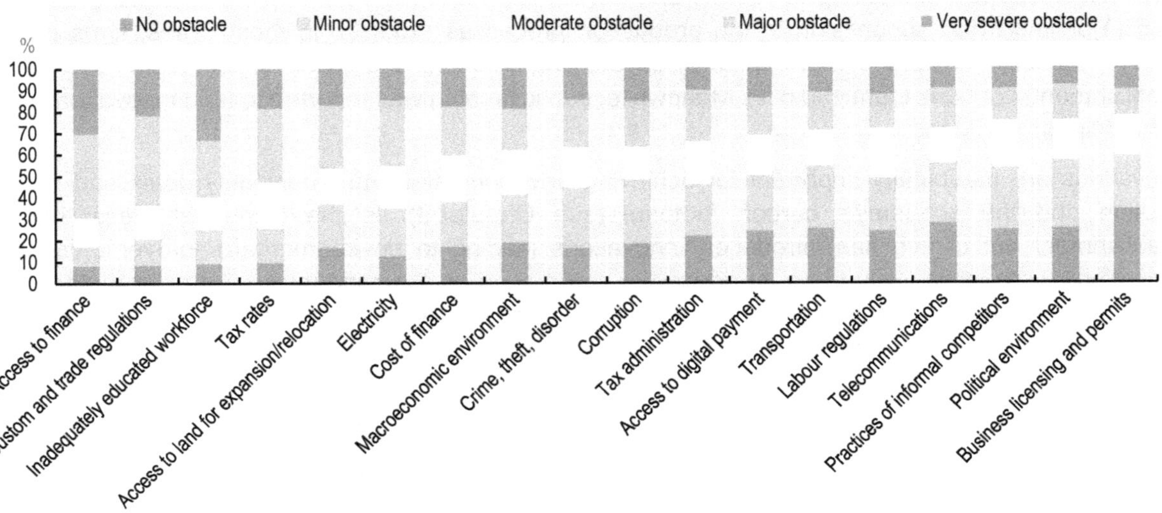

Note: The data refer to the unweighted average of the following countries: Antigua and Barbuda, the Bahamas, Barbados, Belize, Dominica, Grenada, Guyana, Jamaica, Saint Kitts and Nevis, Saint Lucia, Saint Vincent and the Grenadines, Suriname, and Trinidad and Tobago.
Source: Authors' elaborations based on Compete Caribbean's Innovation, Firm Performance and Gender Survey, 2021.

StatLink https://stat.link/ublw5v

Key policy messages

This chapter has underscored the importance of strengthening macro-structural conditions in Caribbean countries, particularly as these are strongly exposed to changing global circumstances. While countries in the Caribbean are characterised by the diversity and heterogeneity across them, Box 1.1 includes some common challenges and overarching considerations that can guide national, regional and international policy action in the region in the medium-term.

Box 1.1. Key policy messages

Strengthening macroeconomic conditions and boosting potential growth

- Implement a broad agenda to boost productivity in the region. Due to the multi-dimensional nature of productivity, this would involve putting in place a horizontal strategy encompassing actions to raise skills, accelerate innovation and invest in infrastructure, among others.
- Maintain fiscal consolidation efforts, with a key role for sustainable fiscal frameworks and improved debt management strategies (see Chapter 5).
- Underpin credible monetary regimes committed to anchoring inflation expectations and keeping inflation rates low.
- Enable conditions for investment mobilisation, with an increased role for the public sector and for public-private partnerships (e.g. for key infrastructure), while attracting quality FDI with an impact on key dimensions of development.

Upgrading the production structure, together with deeper economic integration and an enabling environment for the internationalisation of firms

- Strengthen the potential of current lead sectors in the region, for instance by expanding services provided to tourists and increasing linkages of tourism to domestic producers, or by engaging in more processing and transformation of existing raw material exports.
- Manage large capital inflows associated to natural resource exploration and exploitation, so that these can have a trickle-down effect in the rest of the economy in terms of creation of jobs, environmental sustainability, and upgrading of the production structure.
- Explore and invest in new opportunity sectors, especially those associated with rich biodiversity and natural endowments of Caribbean countries (see Chapter 3).
- Consider possibilities for the diversification in terms of products or services and in terms of trade partners, strengthening regional ties within the Caribbean and with other Latin American countries (see Chapter 6).
- Foster an environment where firms can innovate, expand, and better connect with global markets.

References

Acevedo, S., N. LaFramboise and J. Wong (2017), "Caribbean tourism in the global marketplace: Trends, drivers and challenges", in *Unleashing Growth and Strengthening Resilience in the Caribbean*, International Monetary Fund, Washington, DC, https://doi.org/10.5089/9781484315194.071. [7]

Arslanalp, S., B. Eichengreen and P. Blair (2024), "Sustained debt reduction: The Jamaica exception", *Brooking Papers on Economic Activity*, Brookings Institution, Washington, DC, https://www.brookings.edu/articles/sustained-debt-reduction-the-jamaica-exception/. [12]

Beuermann, D. et al. (2021), *Economic Institutions for a Resilient Caribbean*, Inter-American Development Bank, Washington, DC, https://doi.org/10.18235/0003053. [14]

CDB (2017), *Tourism Industry Reform: Strategies for Enhanced Economic Impact*, Caribbean Development Bank, St. Michael, Barbados, https://www.caribank.org/sites/default/files/publication-resources/CDB_Tourism_Industry_Reform_Web_FINAL.pdf. [25]

ECLAC (2024), *Fiscal Panorama of Latin America and the Caribbean, 2024: Fiscal Policy for Addressing the Challenges of Climate Change*, United Nations Economic Commission for Latin America and the Caribbean, Santiago, https://www.cepal.org/en/publications/69217-fiscal-panorama-latin-america-and-caribbean-2024-fiscal-policy-addressing. [8]

ECLAC (2024), *Preliminary Overview of the Economies of the Caribbean 2022-2023*, United Nations Economic Commission for Latin America and the Caribbean, Santiago, https://repositorio.cepal.org/server/api/core/bitstreams/d3cd47a5-bc9a-435a-b329-e6f1691c54c6/content. [15]

ECLAC (2023), *CEPALSTAT*, (database), https://statistics.cepal.org/portal/cepalstat/index.html?lang=es (accessed on 1 October 2024). [9]

ECLAC (2023), *Foreign Direct Investment in Latin America and the Caribbean 2023*, United Nations Economic Commission for Latin America and the Caribbean, Santiago, https://www.cepal.org/en/publications/48979-foreign-direct-investment-latin-america-and-caribbean-2023. [22]

ECLAC (2023), *International Trade Outlook for Latin America and the Caribbean 2023. Structural change and trends in global and regional trade: Challenges and opportunities*, United Nations Economic Commission for Latin America and the Caribbean, Santiago, https://www.cepal.org/en/publications/68664-international-trade-outlook-latin-america-and-caribbean-2023-structural-change. [33]

ECLAC (2022), *Economic Survey of Latin America and the Caribbean: Trends and Challenges of Investing for a Sustainable and Inclusive Recovery*, United Nations Economic Commission for Latin America and the Caribbean, Santiago, https://repositorio.cepal.org/server/api/core/bitstreams/e77f282a-c7cb-42bc-9045-d58e955e6504/content. [32]

ECLAC (2022), *Foreign Direct Investment in Latin America and the Caribbean 2022*, United Nations Economic Commission for Latin America and the Caribbean, Santiago, https://www.cepal.org/en/publications/48521-foreign-direct-investment-latin-america-and-caribbean-2022. [23]

FAO (2019), "Current status of agriculture in the Caribbean and implications for agriculture policy and strategy", *Food, Agriculture and Rural Development in Latin America and the Caribbean*, No. 14, Food and Agriculture Organization of the United Nations, Santiago, http://www.fao.org/3/ca5527en/ca5527en.pdf. [29]

Galindo, A. and A. Izquierdo (2024), *2024 Latin American and Caribbean Macroeconomic Report: Ready for Take-Off? Building on Macroeconomic Stability for Growth*, Inter-American Development Bank, Washington, DC, https://doi.org/10.18235/0005667. [13]

Giordano, P. and C. Ortiz de Mendívil (2021), *Trade in Services in Latin America and the Caribbean: An Overview of Trends, Costs, and Policies*, Inter-American Development Bank, Washington, DC, https://doi.org/10.18235/0003801. [34]

Gomez Garcia, O. et al. (2021), *Caribbean Quarterly Bulletin: Volume 10: Issue 1*, Inter-American Development Bank, Washington, DC, https://doi.org/10.18235/0003265. [24]

Grieger, G. (2023), *EU Trade with Latin America and the Caribbean: Overview and Figures*, European Parliamentary Research Service, Brussels, https://www.europarl.europa.eu/RegData/etudes/STUD/2023/751413/EPRS_STU(2023)751413_EN.pdf. [36]

Ianchovichina, E. (2024), "Why is productivity growth so low in Latin America and the Caribbean?", World Bank blogs, 26 February, https://blogs.worldbank.org/en/latinamerica/low-productivity-growth-latin-america-caribbean. [6]

ILO (2023), *Employment Situation in Latin America and the Caribbean: Towards the Creation of Better Jobs in the Post-Pandemic Era*, International Labour Organization, Geneva, https://www.ilo.org/publications/employment-situation-latin-america-and-caribbean-number-28-towards-creation. [4]

IMF (2024), *Barbados: Third Reviews Under the Arrangement Under the Extended Fund Facility, Arrangement Under the Resilience and Sustainability Facility, and Request for Modification of Performance Criteria-Press Release; and Staff Report*, International Monetary Fund, Washington, DC, https://www.imf.org/en/Publications/CR/Issues/2024/06/28/Barbados-Third-Reviews-Under-the-Arrangement-Under-the-Extended-Fund-Facility-Arrangement-551173. [11]

IMF (2024), "Dominica: 2024 Article IV Consultation-Press Release; Staff Report; and Statement by the Executive Director for Dominica", *Country Report*, No. 2024/192, International Monetary Fund, Washington, DC, https://www.imf.org/en/Publications/CR/Issues/2024/06/27/Dominica-2024-Article-IV-Consultation-Press-Release-Staff-Report-and-Statement-by-the-551143. [30]

IMF (2024), *St. Kitts and Nevis: 2024 Article IV Consultation-Press Release and Staff Report*, International Monetary Fund, Washington, DC, https://www.imf.org/en/Publications/CR/Issues/2024/05/15/St-549018. [31]

IMF (2024), *Suriname. Country Report No. 24/97*, International Monetary Fund, Washington, DC, https://www.imf.org/en/Publications/CR/Issues/2024/04/25/Suriname-Fifth-Review-Under-the-Extended-Arrangement-Under-the-Extended-Fund-Facility-548310. [16]

IMF (2024), "Suriname: Sixth Review Under the Extended Arrangement Under the Extended Fund Facility-Press Release; Staff Report; and Statement by the Executive Director for Suriname", *Country Report*, No. 2024/254, International Monetary Fund, https://www.imf.org/en/Publications/CR/Issues/2024/07/30/Suriname-Sixth-Review-Under-the-Extended-Arrangement-Under-the-Extended-Fund-Facility-Press-552783. [10]

IMF (2024), *World Economic Outlook*, (database), https://www.imf.org/en/Publications/WEO/weo-database/2024/April (accessed on 3 June 2024). [1]

IMF (2023), *Grenada: 2023 Article IV Consultation-Press Release and Staff Report*, International Monetary Fund, Washington, DC, https://www.imf.org/en/Publications/CR/Issues/2023/07/18/Grenada-2023-Article-IV-Consultation-Press-Release-and-Staff-Report-536521. [17]

IMF (2023), *Guyana: 2023 Article IV Consultation-Press Release; and Staff Report*, International Monetary Fund, Washington, DC, https://doi.org/10.5089/9798400260384.002. [28]

Infralatam (2021), *Data on Public Investment in Economic Infrastructure in Latin America and the Caribbean*, (database), https://www.infralatam.info/home/ (accessed on 1 October 2024). [20]

Mooney, H. et al. (2021), *Caribbean Quarterly Bulletin*, Inter-American Development Bank, Washington, DC, https://doi.org/10.18235/0003573. [26]

OEC (2022), *The Observatory of Economic Complexity*, (database), https://oec.world/en/profile/international_organization/caribbean-community?tradeBetweenYearSelector=2022&tradeBetweenFlowSelector=flow0&depthSelector5=HS4Depth&historicalDataFlowSelector=flow1&yearSelector1=2022&extraTradeFlowSelector=flow1&yearSelector5 (accessed on 1 October 2024). [38]

OECD et al. (2023), *Latin American Economic Outlook 2023: Investing in Sustainable Development*, OECD Publishing, Paris, https://doi.org/10.1787/8c93ff6e-en. [18]

OECD/UNCTAD/ECLAC (2020), *Production Transformation Policy Review of the Dominican Republic: Preserving Growth, Achieving Resilience*, OECD Development Pathways, OECD Publishing, Paris, https://doi.org/10.1787/1201cfea-en. [39]

Queyranne, M., W. Daal and K. Funke (2019), "Public-private partnerships in the Caribbean region: Reaping the benefits while managing fiscal risks", *Departmental Paper*, No. 2019/007, International Monetary Fund, Washington, DC, https://www.imf.org/en/Publications/Departmental-Papers-Policy-Papers/Issues/2019/05/08/Public-Private-Partnerships-in-the-Caribbean-Region-Reaping-the-Benefits-while-Managing-46239. [19]

Rosenblatt, D. et al. (2023), *Caribbean Economics Quarterly: Reflections on Innovation and Productivity as Caribbean Businesses Emerge from the Pandemic*, Inter-American Development Bank, Washington, DC, https://doi.org/10.18235/0004902. [5]

UNCTAD (2022), *UNCTADstat*, (database), https://unctadstat.unctad.org/datacentre/ (accessed on 1 October 2024). [35]

UNCTAD (2022), *World Investment Report: Regional Trends, Latin America and the Caribbean*, United Nations Conference on Trade and Development, Geneva, https://unctad.org/system/files/non-official-document/WIR2022-Regional_trends_LAC_en.pdf. [21]

UNWTO (2024), *Tourism Statistics*, (database), https://www.unwto.org/tourism-statistics/key-tourism-statistics (accessed on 1 October 2024). [27]

USTR (2023), *Fifteenth Report to Congress on the Operation of the Caribbean Basin Economic Recovery Act*, Office of the United States Trade Representative, Washington, DC, https://ustr.gov/issue-areas/trade-development/preference-programs/caribbean-basin-initiative-cbi. [37]

World Bank (2023), "World Bank Country and Lending Groups (website)", https://datahelpdesk.worldbank.org/knowledgebase/articles/906519-world-bank-country-and-lending-groups. [2]

World Bank (2023), *World Development Indicators*, (database), https://databank.worldbank.org/source/world-development-indicators (accessed on 1 October 2024). [3]

2 Improving social conditions

Social inclusion remains a significant challenge in the Caribbean region. Many Caribbean countries experience relatively high levels of poverty, and important inequalities exist across socio-economic groups, territories, and genders. Labour markets are characterised by relatively high informality, resulting in low levels of social protection and high vulnerability across some segments of the population. Moreover, access to quality public services for all is also a pending challenge in most Caribbean economies.

Introduction

Social conditions have significantly improved in most Caribbean countries in recent decades. However, important challenges remain, particularly in relation to poverty and food insecurity, which are high for certain groups and countries. Vulnerabilities and inequalities persist among specific socioeconomic groups, territories, and genders, for instance in terms of modest levels of social protection coverage, which are directly linked to the prevalence of labour informality. Improving the quality of key public services and strengthening social protection systems will be fundamental for enhancing social inclusion in the region. Furthermore, limited data availability to measure social conditions highlights a critical area requiring attention to support evidence-based social policies.

This chapter analyses social conditions in Caribbean countries and is structured into four sections. The first section examines poverty, inequality and food insecurity as key areas requiring improvements to strengthen social inclusion. The second sections analyses labour market dynamics, highlighting the need to foster formalisation across the region. The third section focuses on social protection and healthcare systems, and on the need to improve coverage and efficiency to reduce vulnerabilities among certain groups. Finally, the fourth section analyses education systems in the region, examining progress and pending challenges related to access, retention, learning outcomes and the need to improve the quality of education.

Poverty and inequality remain high, although with large disparities across countries and significant information gaps

Poverty and inequality are a persistent challenge in the Caribbean, but there are major disparities across countries. The share of the total population living under the national poverty line ranges from 11% to 58.5%, according to available data (Figure 2.1). The extreme poverty rate is close to 3%, substantially lower than in the average for Latin America and the Caribbean (LAC) (OECD et al., 2023[1]; OECD et al., 2024[2]). Due to data limitations, it is difficult to identify clear trends in the evolution of poverty over time, except for a few countries. In a decade, poverty has dropped in the Dominican Republic by 12.5 percentage points, reaching 20.4% of the population in 2022; in Grenada by 12.7 percentage points, reaching 25% of the population in 2018; by 6.6 percentage points in Jamaica, reaching 11% in 2019; and by 3.8 percentage points in Saint Lucia, reaching 25% in 2016. Conversely, poverty has increased substantially in Barbados – by 6.4 percentage points in six years.

Average poverty figures in the Caribbean should be analysed with caution. First, poverty and income inequalities are difficult to track due to low coverage of household income or living conditions surveys in the region (ECLAC, 2023[3]). Some countries, including Barbados, Jamaica, the Dominican Republic, Suriname, and Trinidad and Tobago, have developed more up-to-date and granular statistics through living conditions or household surveys. However, many Caribbean economies still rely on outdated data. This hampers the ability to accurately assess poverty levels and the effectiveness of policies aimed at reducing poverty. Strengthening statistical systems is a priority (see Chapter 5).

Figure 2.1. Monetary poverty in Caribbean countries, latest year available

Headcounts poverty, percentages of total population

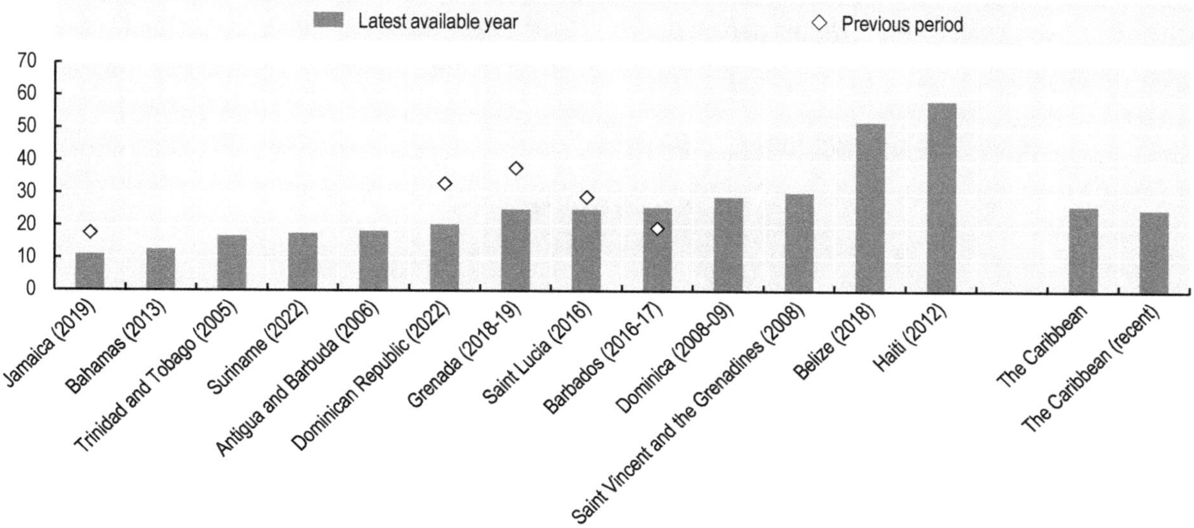

Note: The average for the Caribbean refers to the simple mean of the latest available years of reference for the whole sample of countries. The recent average for the region refers to simple mean for the sub-sample of countries with years of reference dating not earlier than 2016. The previous period is 2010 for Barbados, 2014 for the Dominican Republic, 2008 for Grenada, 2010 for Jamaica and 2006 for Saint Lucia.
Source: (SIB, 2018[4]; ECLAC, 2023[3]; World Bank, 2024[5]).

StatLink https://stat.link/tmc2p3

Second, poverty is a multi-dimensional phenomenon, as is social inclusion in a broader sense. To fully understand the evolution of poverty and social inclusion, it is necessary to consider factors beyond income. Labour conditions, access to health care, education and other basic public services, and broader socio-economic inequalities all contribute to the overall picture of social inclusion.

Multi-dimensional socio-economic conditions have improved, although the pandemic left an impact

Over the last three decades, the Caribbean has experienced an upward trend in the Human Development Index (HDI), similar to the Latin American region (Figure 2.2, Panel A).[1] However, important and lasting gaps remain if compared to the level of human development of, for example, OECD countries.

After a period of strong growth throughout the 1990s and early 2000s, progress in human development slowed down in the region afterwards, with a negative impact of the 2008 global financial crisis and the COVID-19 crisis. All the determinants of the HDI have improved since 1990. In 2022, the average Caribbean person could expect to live 72.6 years (an increase of 4.2 years since 1990), the average child could expect to study 14.1 years (an increase of 2.9 years) and the mean gross national income (GNI) per capita stood at 17 280 constant 2021 international USD (66% increase).

These advances are similar to those observed in Latin America (Figure 2.2, Panels A and B). In 2022, the average Latin American could expect to live 73.5 years (an increase of 5.5 years since 1990), the average child could expect to study 14.3 years (an increase of 3.8 years) and the mean GNI per capita stood at 14 300 constant 2021 international USD (70% increase) (UNDP, 2024[6]).

Socio-economic multi-dimensional conditions are quite diverse across the Caribbean. In 2022, the HDI ranged from 0.55 in Haiti to 0.84 in Saint Kitts and Nevis (Figure 2.2, Panel B). The latter is ranked globally among those with a very high HDI (51st), together with Antigua and Barbuda (54th), the Bahamas (57th), Trinidad and Tobago (60th), and Barbados (62nd). Seven Caribbean countries are categorised as having a high HDI: Dominica, the Dominican Republic, Grenada, Guyana, Jamaica, Saint Lucia, and Saint Vincent and the Grenadines. Meanwhile, Haiti and Suriname are among the medium HDI countries.

Figure 2.2. Human Development Index, 1990-2022

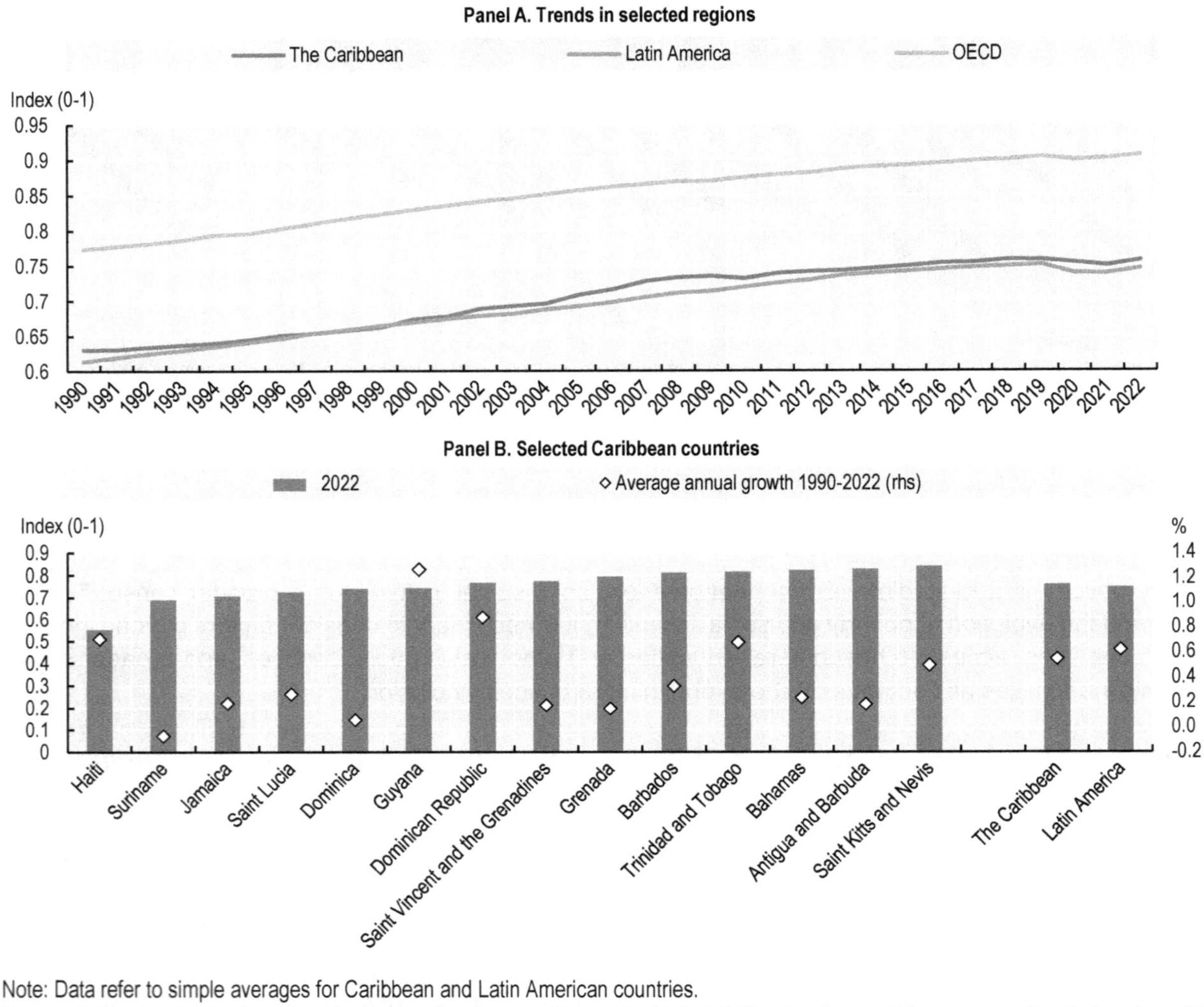

Note: Data refer to simple averages for Caribbean and Latin American countries.
Source: Authors' estimates based on the Human Development Data of the United Nation Development Programme, https://hdr.undp.org/data-center/documentation-and-downloads.

StatLink https://stat.link/1gl0ps

The pace of improvement in HDI has been different across Caribbean countries. In six countries, the average yearly growth rates of the HDI have been close to or lower than 0.2%. Guyana, the Dominican Republic, Trinidad and Tobago, and Saint Kitts and Nevis have experienced yearly rates of growth close to or higher than 0.5%. Meanwhile, at 0.5% on average per year, the improvement of the HDI in the Caribbean region has been slightly more modest than in Latin America (0.6%).

Inequalities and food insecurity remain high

Inequality is high in the Caribbean region, as it is in LAC (OECD et al., 2024[2]), largely above levels in OECD countries. In the latest year for which surveys of living conditions are available, the average of Gini coefficients in the Caribbean was 0.4 (the higher the value, the more unequal the distribution). This ranged between 0.48 in Antigua and Barbuda and 0.32 in Barbados, compared to a simple average of 0.45 in LAC (ECLAC, 2023[3]).

Food insecurity is high across the region (Figure 2.3). The share of people living in moderate or severe food insecurity in the Caribbean represented 37% on average in 2022 (33% in Latin America), ranging from 20% in the Bahamas, Grenada and Saint Lucia to around 50% in the Dominican Republic and Jamaica, and more than 80% in Haiti. The Caribbean is unique in having a generally high cost of food compared to other regions. Around 57% of the Caribbean population does not have access to a healthy diet due to its high cost (FAO, 2023[7]).The average cost of a healthy diet in Caribbean countries was estimated at USD 4.4 per person per day in 2021 in purchasing power parity terms. This is 42% higher than the OECD average. Although many Caribbean economies produce and export agricultural products, between 80% and 90% of all food consumed in the region is imported, mostly from outside the region itself. In fact, intraregional food trade accounts for only 16.6% of total food imports (IICA, 2018[8]; Turnbull, 2021[9]).

Several structural factors present a challenge to reducing food prices. While Caribbean countries aim to increase food production and diversification, domestic production volumes and productivity remain low. The cost and transport time related to intraregional food trade are high (see Chapter 6). The small size of markets reduces the options for achieving economies of scale, leading to higher per-unit production, logistics and transportation costs.

Figure 2.3. Prevalence of moderate or severe food insecurity (%) in Caribbean countries, 2022

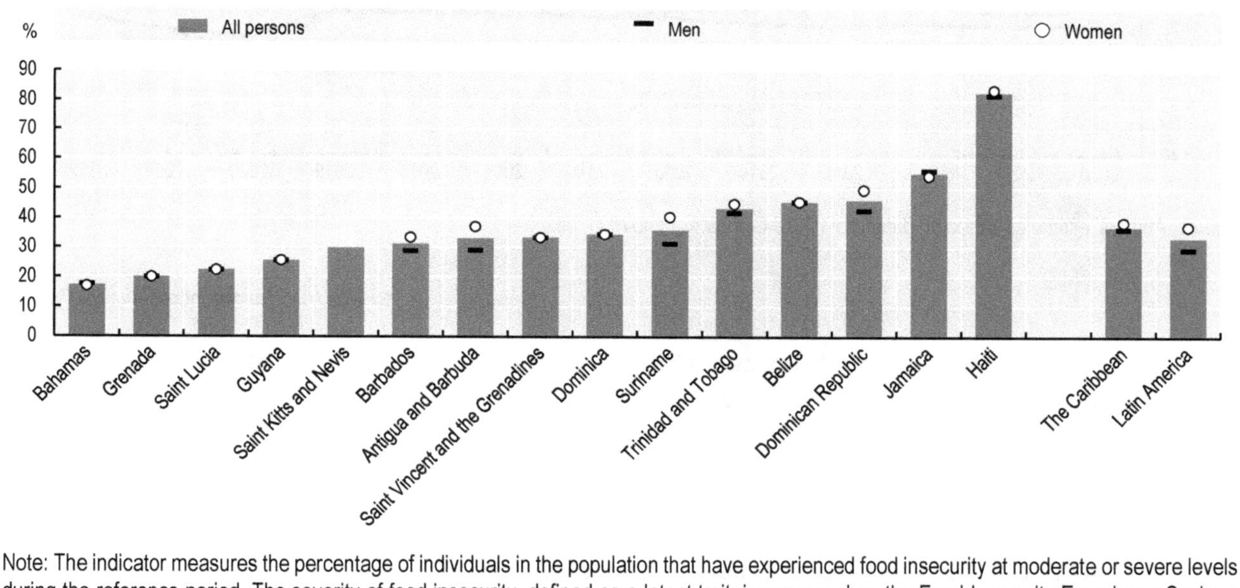

Note: The indicator measures the percentage of individuals in the population that have experienced food insecurity at moderate or severe levels during the reference period. The severity of food insecurity, defined as a latent trait, is measured on the Food Insecurity Experience Scale, a measurement standard started in 2014 by the Food and Agriculture Organization of the United Nations (FAO) in more than 140 countries worldwide. Data are collected using the Food Insecurity Experience Scale survey module (FIES-SM) developed by FAO, or other experience-based food security scale questionnaires. Food insecurity at moderate levels of severity is typically associated with the inability to regularly eat healthy, balanced diets. Severe levels of food insecurity, on the other hand, imply a high probability of reduced food intake and therefore can lead to more severe forms of undernutrition, including hunger.
Source: Authors' calculations based on the United Nations SDG Indicators Database, https://unstats.un.org/sdgs/dataportal/database.

StatLink https://stat.link/p5i0ua

Labour markets remain largely informal, resulting in poor working conditions and heightened social vulnerability for many

Employment opportunities are limited in Caribbean countries

Employment levels are relatively low in the Caribbean. In 2022, almost six out of ten in the working-age population (57.5%) were employed (Figure 2.4). This is slightly lower than the Latin America average (58.2%) and still 0.3 percentage points below the pre-pandemic level of 2019 (58.5%). Heterogeneity in employment levels is high across the region. In 2022, the employment rate ranged from 65% in the Bahamas and Jamaica to less than 53% in Saint Vincent and the Grenadines, and Trinidad and Tobago. In 2022, the unemployment rate was 9.8% for the region, after reaching a peak of 10.8% in 2020. This was well above the average of Latin America (7%), which experienced a more sustained recovery after the peak of the COVID-19 pandemic in 2020 (10.3%).

Figure 2.4. Employment to population rate, by gender, Caribbean countries

Percentage of the population in each group

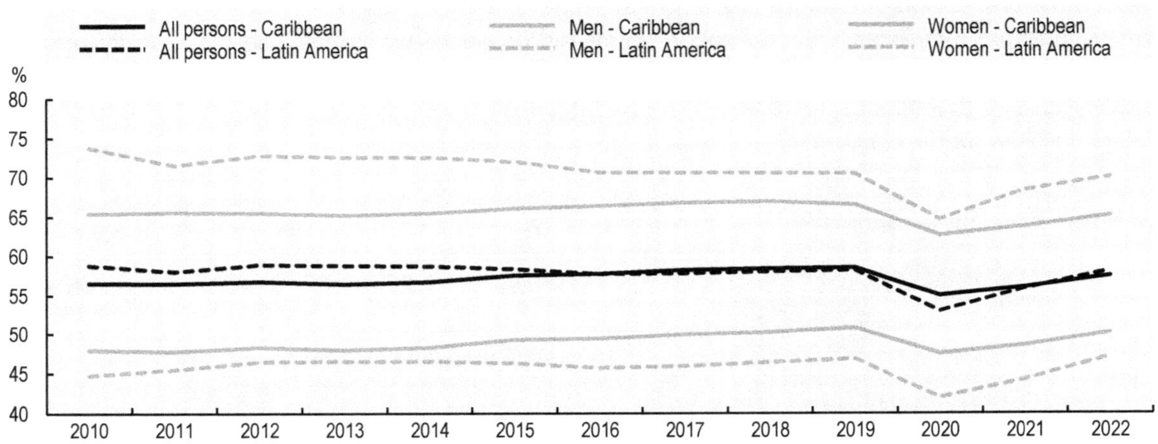

Source: Authors' estimates based on data from (ECLAC, 2024[10]) and (ILO, 2024[11]).

StatLink https://stat.link/60hm8r

Caribbean labour markets are highly concentrated in services, reflecting the specialisation of economies linked directly or indirectly to tourism and financial services (see Chapter 1). In 2022, the share of employment in services was higher in the Caribbean (69.5%) than in Latin America (62.8%). Employment in agriculture and in industry was 13% and 17.5% of total employment, respectively, compared to 17% and 20.1% in Latin America (ILO, 2024[11]).

Women and youth have poorer employment prospects

The gender gap in employment has narrowed, but women are still more likely to be out of the labour market than men. In 2022, one out of two working-age women (50.1%) were employed compared to more than six out of ten men (65.1%). Still, the gender gap in employment rates shifted from 22.5 to 15 percentage points between 2000 and 2022, indicating a better integration of women into labour markets in recent years, as well as a quicker post-pandemic recovery of levels of employment for women than for men

(Figure 2.4). This is above the employment rate for women in Latin America (47.2%), while Latin American men are much more likely to be employed (70%).

Women are also more at risk of being unemployed. In 2022, the female unemployment rate was 10.9%, two percentage points higher than the one for men. The gender gap in unemployment has only slightly improved over time. In the early 2000s, it stood at 3.7 percentage points.

In 2022, the youth employment rate was 33.4%, after reaching the record low level of 30% in 2020. Youth are much less likely to be employed in the Caribbean than in Latin America, where the employment rate for this group was 39.6% in 2022 (ILO, 2024[11]).

Both young men and women are at high risk of not finding a job, but the latter are particularly vulnerable. The rate of unemployment for young women in 2022 was 25.6% compared to 21.6% for men. The poor prospects for Caribbean youth in the labour market are also reflected in the large share of those not engaged in education, employment or training (NEET). In 2020, at the peak of the pandemic, young people in NEET represented 31% of the population aged 15-24 compared to 19% in Latin America (Figure 2.5). Women were more likely than men to be neither employed nor in education. The gender gap in NEET rates was more than two percentage points in the same year.

Figure 2.5. Young people not in education, employment or training by gender, in selected Caribbean countries, 2020

As a percentage of the population aged 15-24, in each group

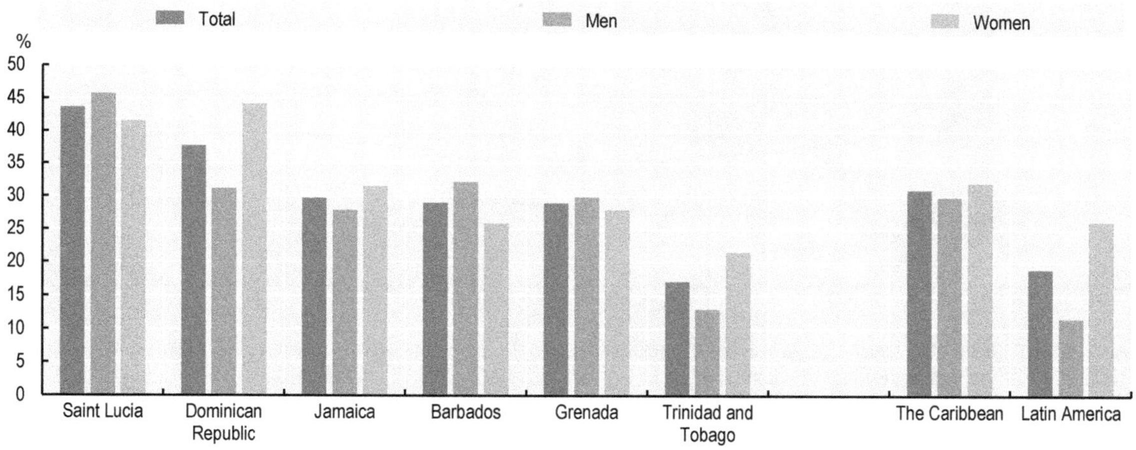

Source: Authors' calculations based on data from (ECLAC, 2024[10]) and (ILO, 2024[11]).

StatLink https://stat.link/65df8p

Informality in the Caribbean remains high and particularly affects young and older workers

Labour informality is widespread in the Caribbean, as it is in Latin America. On average, using the latest years and countries for which comparable data are available, one worker in two held an informal job in the region (Figure 2.6, Panel A). This was lower than the rate of informality across Latin America (57%).

Informality affects particularly younger and older workers (Figure 2.6, Panel B). In Caribbean countries, the informality rate of workers aged 15-24 is above the average rate of all workers, with the notable exceptions of Jamaica and the Bahamas. The same is true for the rate of informality for older workers aged 65 or plus, with only Trinidad and Tobago being the exception.

Figure 2.6. Informality rates in selected Caribbean countries, latest available year

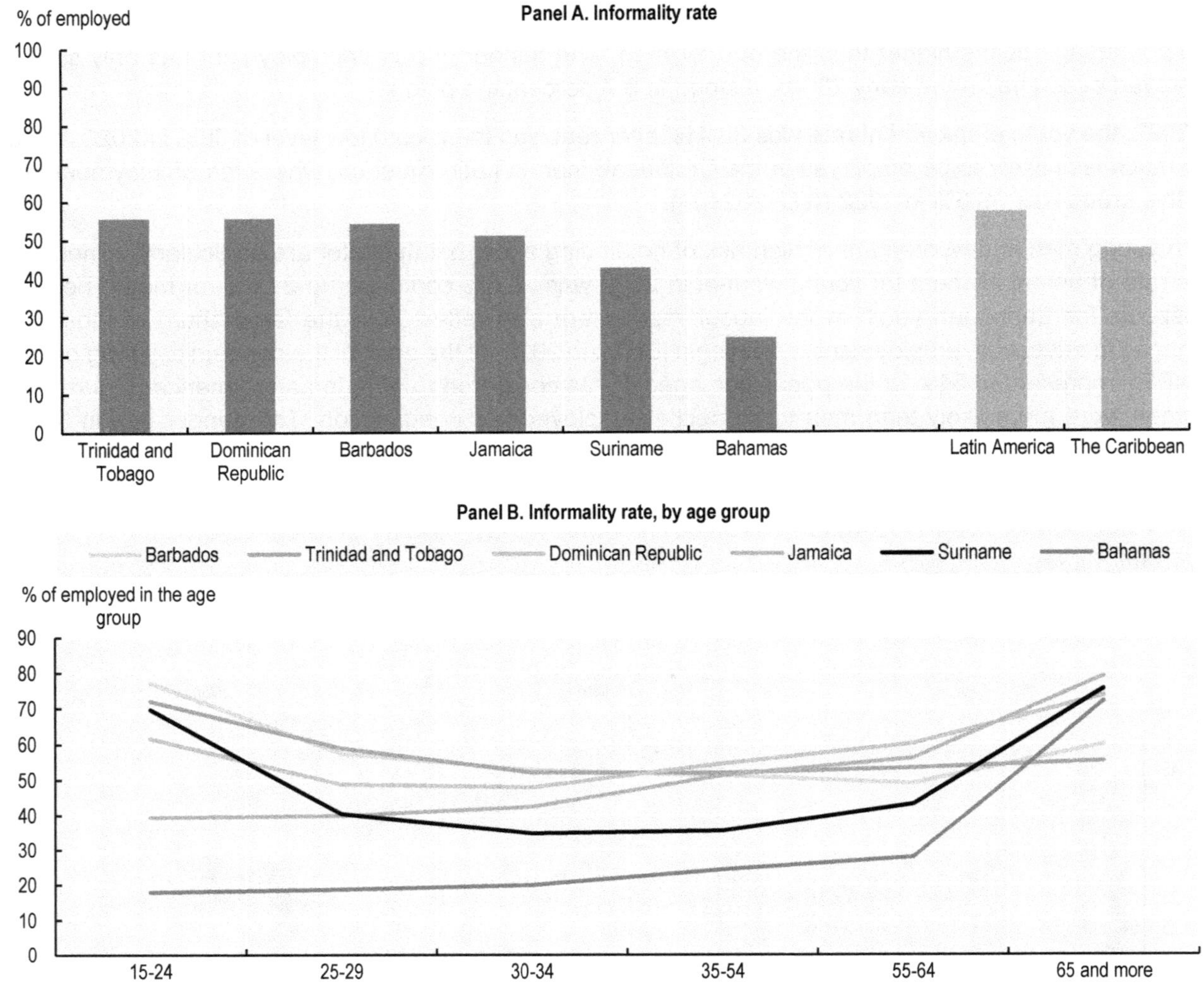

Source: Authors' elaboration based on the OECD KIIbIH database (OECD, 2024[12]). Authors' calculations based on The Household Expenditure Survey (HES) 2013 for the Bahamas, the Barbados Survey of Living Conditions (BSLC) 2016, on the OECD KIIbIH database (OECD, 2024[12]) for the Dominican Republic, the Jamaica Survey of Living Conditions (JSLC) 2019, the Suriname Survey of Living Conditions (SSLC) 2022, and the Trinidad and Tobago Survey of Living Conditions (TT-SLC) 2014.

StatLink https://stat.link/cf30jh

Almost 60% of the Caribbean population lives in households depending solely or partially on informal work

Informality negatively affects people's lives in multiple ways. Beyond being associated with low wages and poor occupational conditions for workers, it is also a major driver of low income and low living standards for households and their members. The formal or informal status of working members within a household has important implications for dependents and for the design of social policies.

In Caribbean countries for which data are available, around six out of ten people lived in a household depending solely or partially on informal work (Figure 2.7). More than a third (34.1%) of the population lives in completely informal households (i.e. households where all workers are informal), while 25.5% live in mixed households and around 40% live in completely formal ones.

There is heterogeneity within the region, and the prevalence of informal work does not completely correlate with income per capita. For instance, in the Dominican Republic and Suriname, both upper middle-income countries, the share of people living in completely informal households is 42.3% and 25.8%, respectively.

The most vulnerable dependents of Caribbean households – children and elders – rely heavily, or exclusively, on the income of family members working in the informal economy. More than 6 out of 10 children under the age of 15, and 6 out of 10 people older than 65 lived in completely informal or mixed households. This is slightly less than the LAC average, where more than 65% of these age groups depended totally or partially on the income of informal workers. This situation highlights the partial or complete absence of social safety nets for large shares of the population.

Figure 2.7. Distribution of population by household informality, latest available year

Percentage of the population

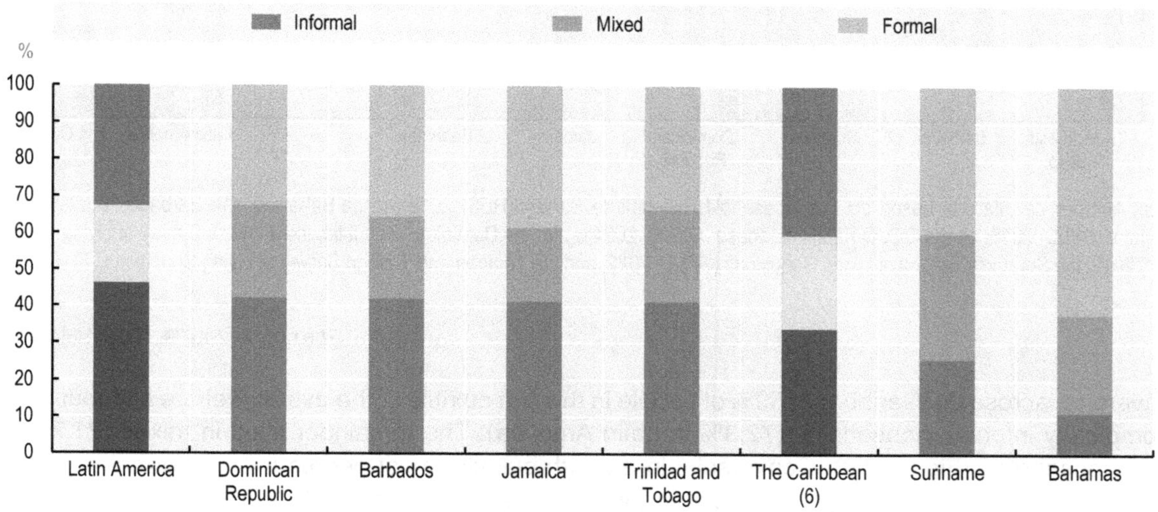

Note: Household types are defined according to the formality status of a household's principal earners. If all the earners are formal or informal, the household is defined as completely formal or informal, respectively. If at least one earner is informal, while the other is formal, the household is defined as mixed.
Source: Authors' calculations based on The Household Expenditure Survey (HES) 2013 for the Bahamas, the Barbados Survey of Living Conditions (BSLC) 2016, on the OECD KIIbIH database (OECD, 2024[12]) for the Dominican Republic, the Jamaica Survey of Living Conditions (JSLC) 2019, the Suriname Survey of Living Conditions (SSLC) 2022, and the Trinidad and Tobago Survey of Living Conditions (TT-SLC) 2014.

StatLink https://stat.link/v9ncxg

Informality is closely linked to households' economic conditions

Informality is deeply entangled with poverty. On average, 17.9% of informal workers in the Caribbean lived under the national poverty line in the latest period for which data are available, while 8.4% of formal workers were poor (Figure 2.8).

Figure 2.8. Workers living under the national poverty line, by informality status, selected Caribbean countries, latest available year

Percentages of workers in each group

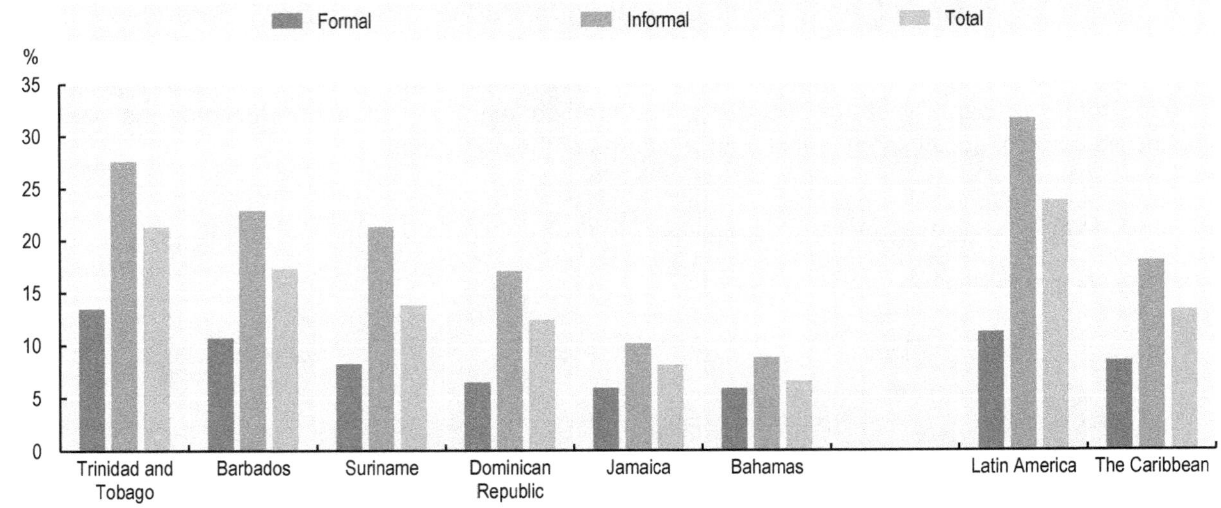

Source: Authors' calculations based on The Household Expenditure Survey (HES) 2013 for the Bahamas, the Barbados Survey of Living Conditions (BSLC) 2016, on the OECD KIIbIH database (OECD, 2024[12]) for the Dominican Republic, the Jamaica Survey of Living Conditions (JSLC) 2019, the Suriname Survey of Living Conditions (SSLC) 2022, and the Trinidad and Tobago Survey of Living Conditions (TT-SLC) 2014.

StatLink https://stat.link/6sqolk

On average, across the Caribbean, 50% of people in the first quintile of the overall welfare distribution lived in completely informal households (72.3% in Latin America). The remainder lived in mixed (21.7%) and formal households (Figure 2.9). Conversely, in the fifth quintile, most people lived in formal households (52.4%), while the rest of the population was almost equally likely to live in mixed (21.4%) or informal households (26.1%).

Regional averages hide considerable variability across countries. In the Dominican Republic, the share of people living in informal households in the first quintile was close to or higher than 70%, whereas in Suriname and the Bahamas those shares were significantly lower.

Figure 2.9. Distribution of the population by household informality and welfare quintile, latest available year

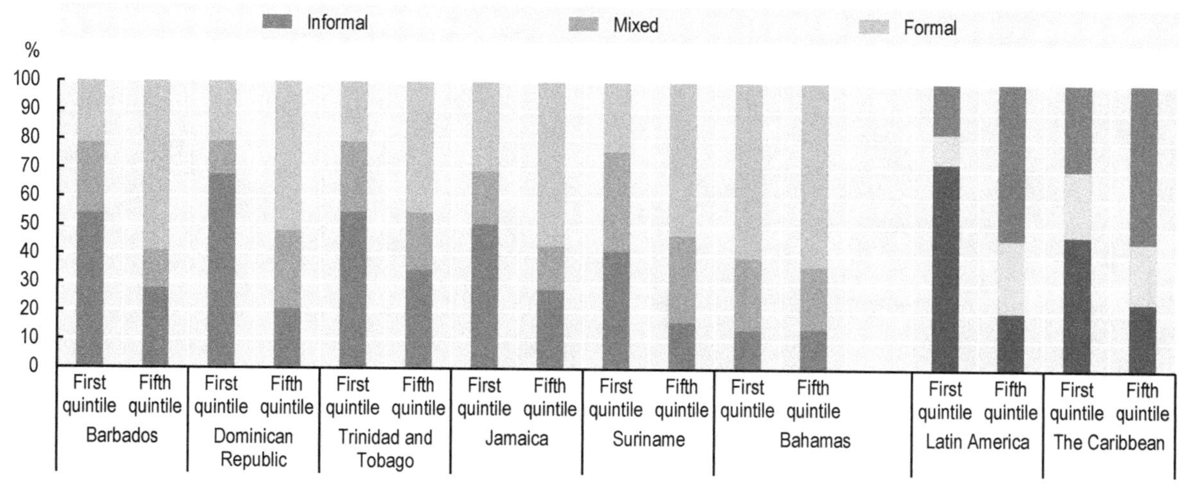

Note: Household types are defined according to the formality status of a household's principal earners. If all the earners are respectively formal or informal, the household is defined as completely formal or informal. If at least one earner is informal while the other is formal, the household is defined as mixed. The welfare distribution refers to the distribution of either household per capita income or consumption.

Source: Authors' calculations based on The Household Expenditure Survey (HES) 2013 for the Bahamas, the Barbados Survey of Living Conditions (BSLC) 2016, on the OECD KIIbIH database (OECD, 2024[12]) for the Dominican Republic, the Jamaica Survey of Living Conditions (JSLC) 2019, the Suriname Survey of Living Conditions (SSLC) 2022, and the Trinidad and Tobago Survey of Living Conditions (TT-SLC) 2014.

StatLink https://stat.link/rmpxf2

Social protection and healthcare systems must be strengthened and adapted to climate vulnerabilities and emerging challenges

In the Caribbean region, as in other parts of the world, the pandemic and a uncertain global context have exacerbated social and environmental problems. This situation continues to put pressure on fiscal policy to respond with sustainable, inclusive programmes. Public social spending – comprising spending on social protection, education, health, housing and community services, recreation, culture and religion, and environmental protection – has returned to levels attained before the COVID-19 pandemic in the six Caribbean countries for which comparable data are available. Relative to GDP, social spending in the Caribbean dropped to 11.1% from the peak of 13.8% in 2021 during the pandemic. Latin America experienced a similar drop during the same period – from 13.7% of GDP to 11.5% (Figure 2.10) (ECLAC, 2023[3]).

Social protection systems are far from universal in the Caribbean. However, they show better outcomes in terms of coverage and adequacy compared to Latin American countries (IDB, 2021[13]).

Figure 2.10. Central government social spending in selected Caribbean economies, 2008-22

Percentage of GDP

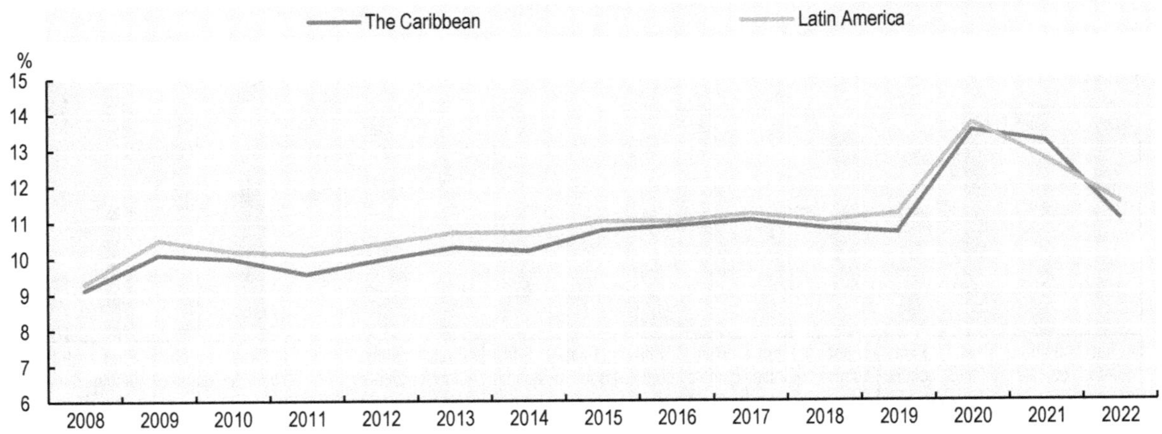

Note: Data for the Caribbean refer to the arithmetic mean of the following Caribbean countries: the Bahamas, Barbados, the Dominican Republic, Guyana, Jamaica, and Trinidad and Tobago. The fiscal calendar of some Caribbean countries differs from that of Latin American countries: the Bahamas (July–June), Barbados, Jamaica (April–March), and Trinidad and Tobago (October–September). The published reference period corresponds to the calendar year of the closing month. Data for Latin America refer to the arithmetic mean of the following countries: Argentina, Brazil, Chile, Colombia, Costa Rica, the Dominican Republic, Ecuador, El Salvador, Guatemala, Honduras, Mexico, Nicaragua, Panama, Paraguay, Peru, Plurinational State of Bolivia (hereafter "Bolivia") and Uruguay. Coverage in Bolivia corresponds to central administration and that of Peru to general government. Data for Panama and Bolivia refer to 2021.
Source: Authors' elaborations based on (ECLAC, 2023[3]).

StatLink https://stat.link/654ov2

Public expenditures on pensions were close to 4.7% of GDP around 2018 (Figure 2.11). Almost three-quarters of these expenditures (3.4% of GDP) were provided through contributory insurance programmes. The remainder (1.3% of GDP) was provided from social assistance programmes to those not meeting the contribution requirements and thus not qualifying for social insurance pensions.

Three of the countries for which estimates are available – Guyana, Trinidad and Tobago, and Barbados – are well above the region's average, with the latter spending more than 8% of GDP in pensions. On the other hand, in the other three – Jamaica, the Bahamas and Suriname – public expenditures on pensions as a percentage of GDP are close to or well below the average.

The active coverage rate of the population (i.e. the share of people who contribute to the pension system) was 63% in the Caribbean around 2018. This was almost 20 percentage points higher than the average of Latin American countries around the same year (Arena De Mesa, 2019[14]; IDB, 2021[13]; OECD et al., 2024[2]). However, this hides important differences across Caribbean countries. Barbados has the highest ratio of contributors as a percentage of the labour force (79%), followed by Trinidad and Tobago (77.5%), the Bahamas (72%), Guyana (63.1%), Jamaica (53.7%), and Suriname (45.1%). Men are just slightly more likely to contribute to the pension system (51.8% of contributors are men) than women in Caribbean countries. This suggests that gender disparity in active coverage is not significant.

Figure 2.11. Public expenditures on pensions in selected Caribbean countries, latest available year

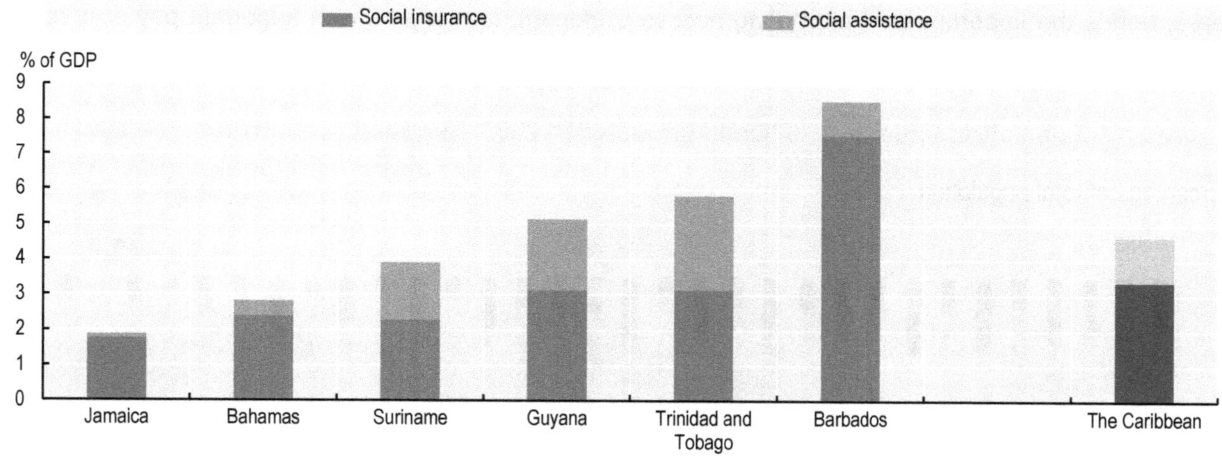

Note: Social insurance schemes include contributory pensions paid to private and public employed persons who have contributed and reached the minimum requirements needed to qualify for a pension. Social assistance programmes included social pensions for all people not having reached the minimum contribution requirements, as well as disability and survivors' pensions. Data exclude administrative costs. Data for the Bahamas refer to 2017, for Barbados to 2019, for Guyana to 2016-17, for Jamaica to 2018, for Suriname to 2017, and for Trinidad and Tobago to 2017.
Source: Authors' calculations based on (IDB, 2021[13]).

StatLink https://stat.link/5980xd

All member states of the Organisation of Eastern Caribbean States (OECS) have limited social protection systems. The OECS lacks permanent unemployment schemes, and existing social assistance programmes are fragmented and not well co-ordinated, often funded by donors and multilateral organisations, such as the Pan American Health Organization (PAHO) and the World Bank. Streamlining existing programmes can reduce fragmentation and improve efficiency in social protection. A framework for developing social programmes can be organised at a regional level to facilitate adoption across the different member states. In addition to establishing the OECS Economic Union, the Revised Treaty of Basseterre also envisaged the development and adoption of a harmonised common policy framework for human and social development (OECS, 2020[15]).

Social protection systems must be adapted to an ageing population and a growing exposure to climate threats

Caribbean countries have a predominance of young population, yet they are undergoing an important demographic transition. In 2022, 20-24 year-olds were the largest age group in the Caribbean, and in 2050, the share of the population older than 55 years is forecasted to be 31.5% versus 18.8% in 2021 (Figure 2.12). This demographic transition is characterised by a shift from high to lower levels of fertility and mortality, and a considerable increase in life expectancy. Between 1950 and 2021, the total fertility rate in the region dropped from 5.71 to 1.85 live births per woman and is expected to drop to 1.71 live births in 2050. Meanwhile, life expectancy rose from 51.2 to 71.6 years, and is predicted to be 81.9 years in 2050. These two main factors caused the age structure of the population to change significantly. The median age rose from 18.8 years in 1950 to 30.9 in 2021 and is expected to reach 43.2 in 2050 (United Nations, 2022[16]).

Labour and social protection policies must take into account the implications of a changing population structure and the accelerating pace of population ageing. The old-age dependency ratio (i.e. the number of people over 65 years relative to the working-age population) is a crucial aspect to consider. In the

Caribbean, this ratio was 9.8% in 2021 and is expected to be 20.2% in 2050 (United Nations, 2022[16]). This involves that many Caribbean countries will be completing their demographic bonus in the coming years, hence the importance of promoting access to decent, formal jobs with adequate pay and social protection coverage.

Figure 2.12. Population structure, 2021 and projected in 2050, Caribbean countries

Percentage of total population

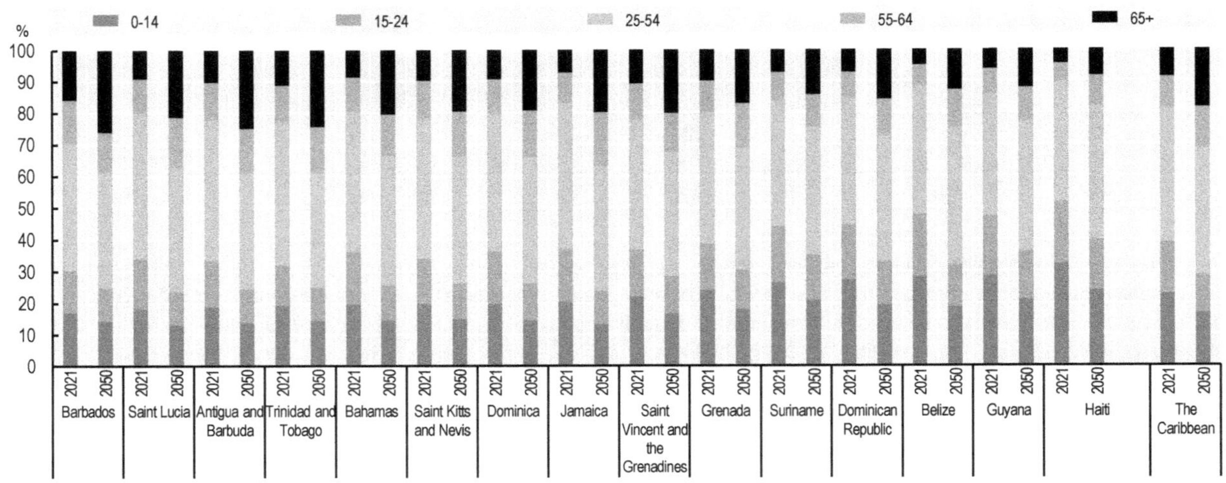

Note: Medium scenario projection: in projecting future levels of fertility and mortality, probabilistic methods were used to reflect the uncertainty of the projections based on the historical variability of changes in each variable. The method considers the past experience of each country, while also reflecting uncertainty about future changes based on past experience of other countries under similar conditions. The projection corresponds to the median of several thousand distinct trajectories of each demographic component derived using the probabilistic model of the variability in changes over time. Prediction intervals reflect the spread in the distribution of outcomes across the projected trajectories and thus provide an assessment of the uncertainty inherent in the projection.
Source: Authors' calculations based on data from (United Nations, 2022[16]), https://population.un.org/wpp/ .

StatLink https://stat.link/8f5g96

Social protection is also a crucial tool for addressing environmental risks. This is particularly relevant in the Caribbean, a region highly prone to regular natural hazards (see Chapter 3). Those shocks severely affect people's lives and livelihoods, undermining development and poverty reduction efforts. Effective social protection systems and adaptive social protection schemes are essential for providing timely and appropriate assistance, especially to those living in poverty and to populations that are highly vulnerable to natural hazards.

A shock-responsive social protection system should ensure continuity during widespread shocks, absorb additional demand for benefits and services, and mitigate negative impacts, particularly for the poor and vulnerable (Beazley, Ciardi and Bailey, 2020[17]). Efforts are underway to strengthen these systems, including policy loans from international financial institutions aimed at making social protection more adaptive (WFP, 2021[18]).

Ministries responsible for social protection are essential for managing emergency operations, conducting assessments and implementing assistance. It is important to continue strengthening the capacity of social protection systems in the Caribbean to identify beneficiaries, manage data, deliver aid and provide services. At the regional level, organisations like CARICOM and OECS are spearheading initiatives to ensure social protection benefits and equal treatment across states. They do this through agreements and strategies like CARICOM's Agreement on Social Security (CARICOM, 1996[19]) and Protocol on Contingent Rights (CARICOM, 2018[20]) and the OECS Development Strategy (OECD, 2018[21]) (Chapter 6).

Healthcare systems should be improved to address persistent health challenges

Public expenditures and compulsory insurance-financed health expenditures are generally lower than in Latin American countries. In 2021, among the 14 Caribbean countries for which comparable data are available, the average expenditure per capita in the region was USD 644 in purchasing power parities (PPP), representing 3.5% of the GDP, compared to USD 830 in Latin America (4.9% of GDP). In per capita terms, only Trinidad and Tobago (USD 839), Saint Kitts and Nevis (USD 1 031), and the Bahamas (USD 1 031) spent more than the Latin American average. Meanwhile, relative to GDP, the situation is more heterogeneous, also due to the very different stages of economic development of Caribbean countries (Figure 2.13).

OECS region has high out-of-pocket costs for patients. The increasing prevalence of Non-Communicable Diseases (NCDs) contributes to high out-of-pocket expenditure. On average, out-of-pocket expenditure accounted for 39% of total health spending in the OECS region in 2019, almost twice the WHO-suggested limit of 20% and nearly three times the OECD average of 13.9%. This indicates the low overall health spending, with underfunded health systems which provide insufficient care. However, out-of-pocket expenditure has been on a slow downward trend over the past decade, and public-to-private expenditure ratios are increasing in the region (OECD, 2022[22]).

Figure 2.13. Health expenditure per capita and as a percentage of GDP, 2021

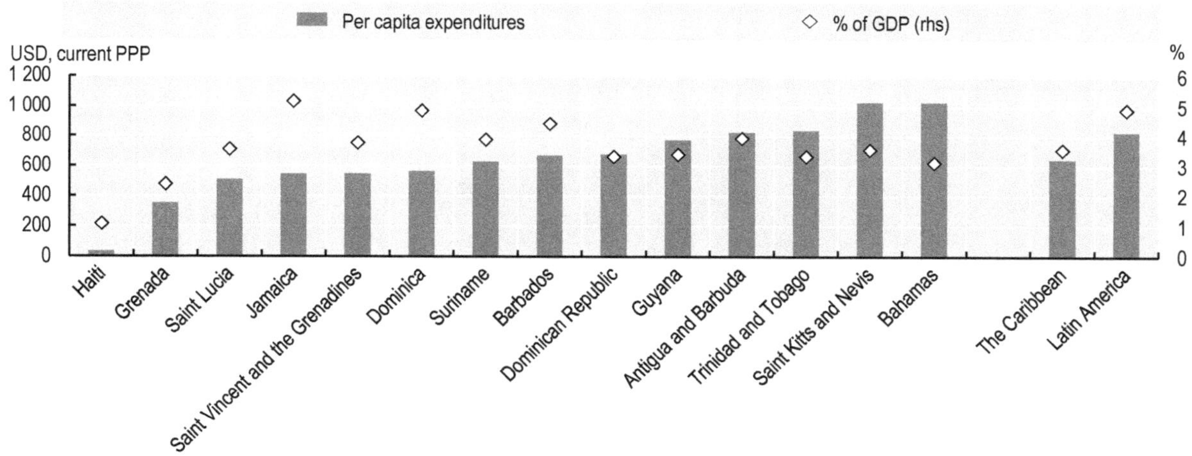

Source: Authors' calculations based on data from (ECLAC, 2023[3]).

StatLink https://stat.link/3sl48u

Health status in the Caribbean is highly heterogeneous, with several countries showing worse results than Latin America. For instance, life expectancy at birth was 75.1 years for the LAC average in 2021, and some Caribbean countries performed above that average, including Barbados (80 years), Antigua and Barbuda (77), and Saint Lucia (76). In contrast, life expectancy at birth was particularly low for Haiti (64), Guyana (70), Suriname (72), Grenada (72), and Saint Vincent and the Grenadines (73). Similarly, in 2020, infant mortality rates were close to or below 20 for 1 000 live births in most Caribbean countries, while in 2000, it was 24 for 1 000, improving less than in Latin America, where infant mortality was 14 in 2020 and 26 in 2000 (Figure 2.14).

Caribbean countries face extreme environmental and climate conditions that affect health status. Climate-resilient health systems, along with other social determinants of health, play an important role in mitigating the impacts of climate change on population health and well-being. Climate-informed health-related early warning systems are essential tools for anticipating and preparing for climate hazards affecting health. However, only Saint Kitts and Nevis has an early warning system for heat-related illness (OECD/The World Bank, 2023[23]).

Figure 2.14. Infant mortality rates, 2020 and 2000

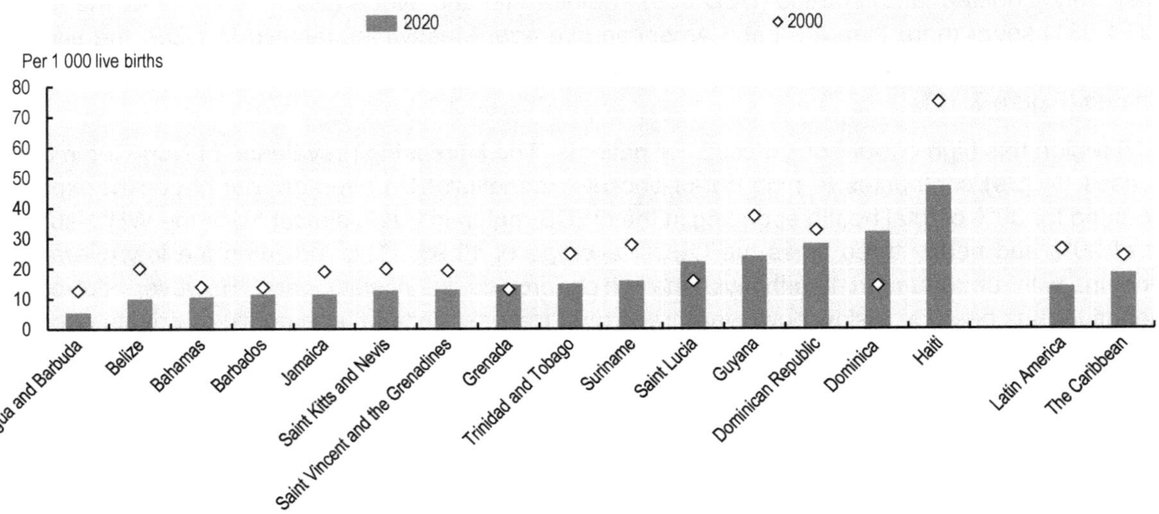

Source: Authors' calculations based on (OECD/The World Bank, 2023[23]).

StatLink https://stat.link/f0blsc

Education systems have improved in recent decades, yet with challenges in access and completion after lower secondary and in overall learning outcomes

Public expenditure in education in some Caribbean countries remains modest

In 2022, average public spending on education in the Caribbean stood at 3.9% of GDP, 0.9 percentage points lower than the Latin American average (Figure 2.15). This average has not improved significantly in the last decade. Only Jamaica and Saint Vincent and the Grenadines showed levels of public spending on education as a share of GDP higher than the Latin American average and close to the OECD average of 5.1% of GDP (OECD, 2023[24]).

Figure 2.15. Government expenditures on education in the Caribbean as a percentage of GDP, 2013-22

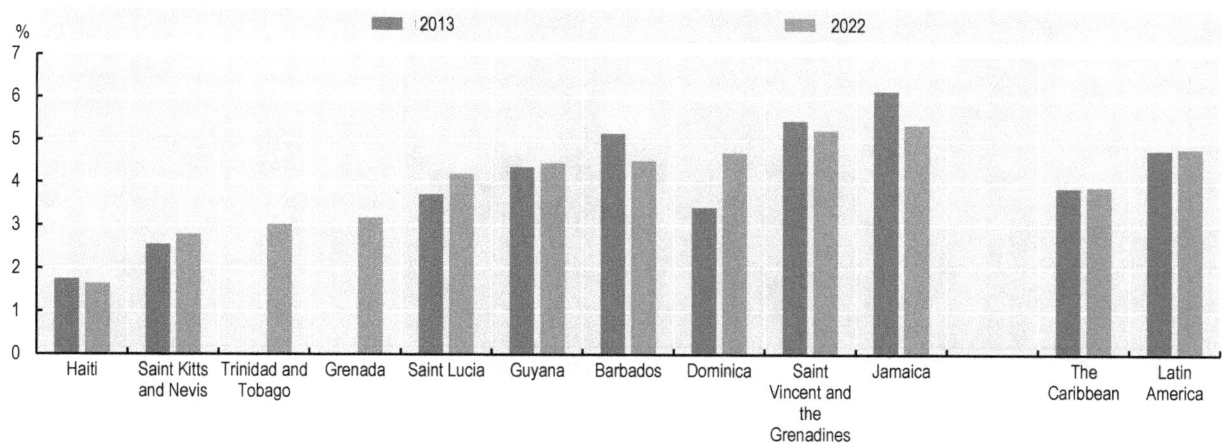

Note: Data for Dominica refer to 2020; for Guyana, Haiti, and Saint Vincent and the Grenadines to 2018; for Trinidad and Tobago to 2021.
Source: Authors' estimates based on data of the UNESCO Institute for Statistics, https://data.uis.unesco.org/.

StatLink https://stat.link/9ioe4a

As in Latin America, most spending on public education in the Caribbean was allocated to teachers' salaries. For instance, in 2019, spending on teachers' salaries represented more than half of total public education spending in Jamaica (66.9% of the total) and Barbados (55.8%), higher than the OECD average (53.7%). The share was lower in Trinidad and Tobago (40%) (Arias et al., 2024[25]).

Educational attainment has improved, but dropout rates are still high for many in upper secondary

Educational attainment has positively progressed in the Caribbean. On average, in 2022, Caribbean people aged 25 or more had spent more time in education (9.6 years) than their Latin American peers (8.9), although the Caribbean experienced a lower progression between 2002 and 2022 (1.5 additional years of education), than Latin America (1.9 years) (Figure 2.16). Educational attainment, however, is heterogeneous across Caribbean countries. Barbados and the Bahamas have the largest proportion of 25-65 year-olds who have attained at least secondary education (87% and 82% of the total population, respectively) (Thailinger et al., 2023[26]). Barbados has the highest proportion of adults 25-65 years old with a post-secondary or university degree, followed again by the Bahamas (39% and 31%). Meanwhile, in Trinidad and Tobago, Jamaica and Guyana, this proportion stands at 23%, 18% and 9%, respectively.

Figure 2.16. Mean years of schooling of people aged 25 or more, Caribbean countries, 2002-22

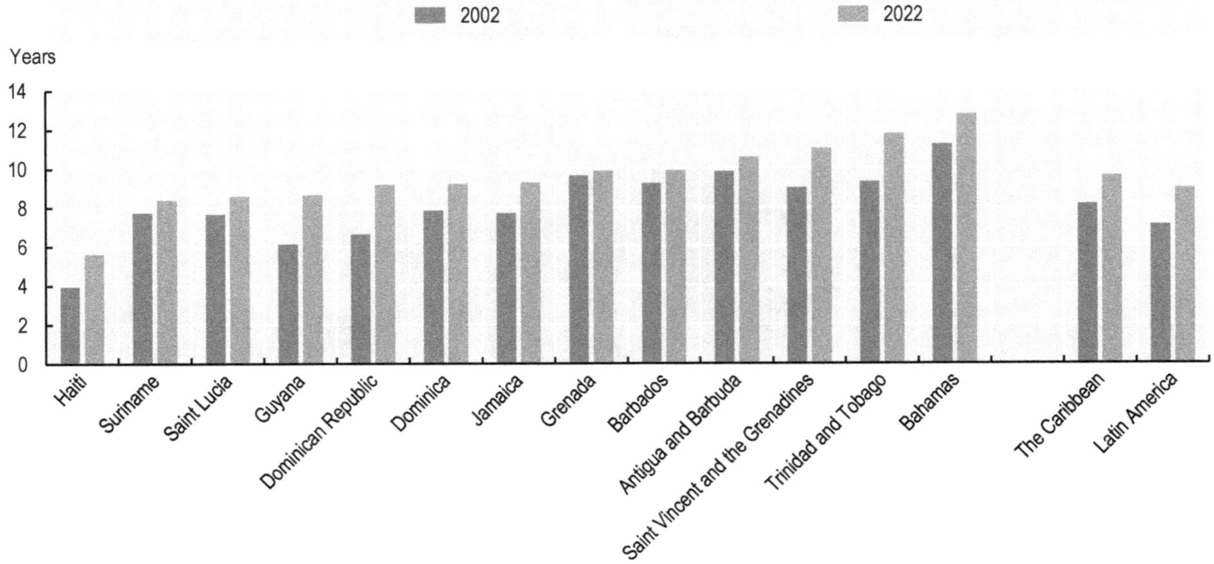

Note: Data for Suriname refer to 2004 instead of 2002. Mean years of schooling are defined as the average number of years of education received by people aged 25 and older, converted from education attainment levels using official durations of each level.
Source: Authors' estimates based on data of the UNESCO Institute for Statistics, https://data.uis.unesco.org/.

StatLink https://stat.link/yd873v

One of the reasons behind progress in educational attainment is the improvement in completion rates, particularly in primary education. In the early 2020s, completion rates for primary school were close to 99% in Barbados, the Dominican Republic, Guyana, Jamaica, Saint Lucia, and Trinidad and Tobago. In 2013, countries' completion rates close to 99% were only recorded in Barbados, Jamaica and Saint Lucia (UIS, 2024[27]). However, in many countries of the region, young people entering upper secondary education have unsatisfactory completion outcomes due to high dropout rates (UIS, 2024[27]). In the early 2020s, the completion rate in upper secondary education was 66.7% across the region, albeit slightly increasing over a decade (61%% in 2013).

Moreover, in 2022 (the latest year available), the share of young people out of school at upper secondary school age varied from 40% in Suriname to close to 5% in Barbados, Antigua and Barbuda, and Saint Vincent and the Grenadines (Figure 2.17). Out-of-school rates are ten or more percentage points higher than the Caribbean average (23%) in the Dominican Republic, Trinidad and Tobago, the Bahamas, and Guyana. The Caribbean average out-of-school rate (23%) was only slightly lower than the Latin American average (24.7%). Girls (22%) are less likely to be out of upper secondary school than boys (24%) (Figure 2.17). This is especially the case in Grenada (an 11.1 percentage-point difference in favour of girls in out-of-school rates), the Dominican Republic (6.4), Guyana (5.6), and Suriname (4.3). Conversely, Dominica is the only country where boys attend upper secondary school significantly more than girls (a 6.6 percentage-point difference).

Regarding tertiary education, the Caribbean has one of the lowest rates of enrolment (less than 25%) (Beckles and Richards-Kennedy, 2021[28]). Tertiary enrolment rates in the Eastern Caribbean are lower than in the rest of the sub-region. Only 15% of upper secondary graduates in the Eastern Caribbean are enrolled in tertiary education, and less than 10% of adults successfully attain a tertiary degree. Gender disparities and unequal access to tertiary education for the most vulnerable are also unresolved (OECS Secretariat, 2012[29]).

Figure 2.17. Out-of-school rate for youth of upper secondary school age, 2022 or latest available year

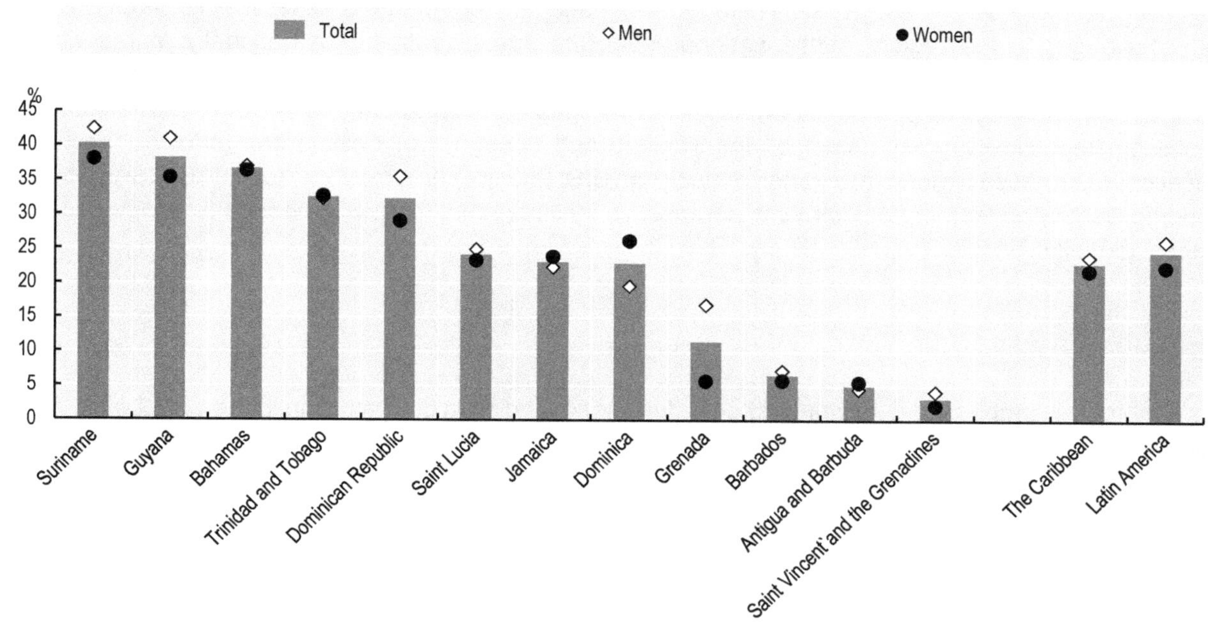

Note: Data for Antigua and Barbuda refer to 2019, for the Bahamas, Guyana, and Saint Kitts and Nevis to 2021, for Grenada to 2016, for Guyana to 2021 and for Suriname to 2015.
Source: Authors' estimates based on data of the UNESCO Institute for Statistics, https://data.uis.unesco.org/.

StatLink https://stat.link/jfcsiu

Learning outcomes are modest in most Caribbean countries, and internationally comparable assessments can inform policies aimed at improving the quality of education

Despite broad improvements in access and participation in the education system (i.e. the quantity of education), learning outcomes (i.e. the quality of education) are modest in most Caribbean countries. Based on available data from the OECD Programme for International Student Assessment (PISA), the two Caribbean countries participating in this assessment – the Dominican Republic and Jamaica – stood at the lower end of the overall cross-country distribution in 2022. Compared to Latin American countries covered by PISA, Jamaica performs slightly above the average in the three tests (mathematics, science and reading). The Dominican Republic was among the least successful performers in the Latin American region, although it has made clear improvements since the previous PISA round (2018) (OECD, 2023[30]).

The Caribbean Secondary Examination Certificate (CSEC), taken at the end of secondary school in English-speaking Caribbean countries, has relatively low passing rates. Moreover, performance in the CSEC exams has deteriorated since 2015, with a significant drop in the percentage of students passing key subjects (OECD, 2022[22]).

Learning outcomes tend to be higher for girls than for boys in the Caribbean, although these results depend largely on the type of subject. Girls outperform boys in most subjects, especially reading in English and literature (De Lisle, 2022[31]). However, boys sometimes outperform girls in subjects like mathematics and physics (Ellis, 2018[32]; Figueroa, 2000[33]). Despite the advantages in school attendance and educational outcomes, young women in the Caribbean usually perform worse in the labour market (see sections above). This can be the result of an education mismatch in the field of study compared to labour demand, discriminatory practices or the uneven burden of non-paid work (such as caring- or household-related activities) on women (Thailinger et al., 2023[26]).

Evaluating learning outcomes, possibly through internationally comparable assessments, is one of the main challenges in the region. At the national level, the administration of a nationally representative learning assessment of reading and mathematics performances at the end of the primary cycle of education is well developed in countries like Antigua and Barbuda, Barbados, Dominica, the Dominican Republic, Guyana, Jamaica, and Trinidad and Tobago, while at the end of lower secondary education, those assessments are generally lacking (UIS, 2024[27]). International tests like PISA can help in putting Caribbean learning outcomes in perspective by comparing them with best performing education systems globally.

Key policy messages

This chapter has emphasised the importance of further advancing social inclusion in the Caribbean. While countries in the region are characterised by the diversity and heterogeneity across them, Box 2.1 includes some common challenges and overarching considerations that can guide national, regional and international policy action in the region in the medium term.

Box 2.1. Key policy messages

Addressing the persistent challenges of poverty, food insecurity and inequality

- Continue efforts to reduce poverty, taking into consideration the multiple dimensions it entails and enhancing the effectiveness of targeted actions to support vulnerable groups.
- Adopt an ambitious strategy to tackle the challenge of high food insecurity, encompassing issues like agricultural productivity and resilience and reducing dependence on imports.
- Improving data availability to support evidence-based social policies.

Fostering a labour formalisation agenda and strengthening social protection systems

- Advance a comprehensive labour formalisation agenda, including efforts to improve skills, facilitate the transition from school to formal jobs, formalise MSMEs, and drive production transformation to create new formal jobs.
- Integrate the household dimension into efforts to improve coverage and effectiveness of social protection systems, with a view to i) targeting social assistance measures at households where all members are informal; ii) strengthening the coverage of social protection to dependents in households where there is at least one formal worker.

Strengthening healthcare and education systems

- Increase spending in healthcare, reducing the burden on citizens, who face high out-of-pocket costs, and address the increasing prevalence of non-communicable diseases.
- Implement measures to improve access and retention in the education systems, as well as to improve learning outcomes, notably by investing in teachers' training and participating in international assessments.

Notes

[1] The HDI comprises three main areas of human well-being, which are evaluated through specific statistical indicators. "A long and healthy life" is measured through life expectancy at birth. "Being knowledgeable" is measured by the mean years of schooling for adults aged 25 years and more, as well as the expected number of years of schooling for children of school-entering age. "Having a decent standard of living" is measured by gross national income per capita (GNI). The HDI uses the logarithm of income to reflect the diminishing importance of income with increasing GNI (UNDP, 2024[6]).

References

Arena De Mesa, A. (2019), "Los sistemas de pensiones en la encrucijada, Desafíos para la sostenibilidad en América Latina", [English Translation], United Nations Economic Commission for Latin America and the Caribbean, Santiago, Chile, https://repositorio.cepal.org/server/api/core/bitstreams/ef2286b9-b700-45e9-ac66-e343faa75211/content. [14]

Arias, E. et al. (2024), "The state of education in Latin America and the Caribbean 2023", *Technical Note*, No. IDB-TN-02708, Inter-American Development Bank, Washington, DC, https://doi.org/10.18235/0005515. [25]

Beazley, R., F. Ciardi and S. Bailey (2020), *Shock-Responsive Social Protection in the Caribbean, Synthesis Report*, World Food Programme, https://docs.wfp.org/api/documents/WFP-0000122075/download/?_ga=2.111899332.1339332319.1726208878-78902515.1726208878. [17]

Beckles, H. and S. Richards-Kennedy (2021), "Accelerating the future into the present: Re-imagining higher education in the Caribbean", in van't Land, H., A. Corcoran and D. Iancu (eds.), *The Promise of Higher Education*, Springer, Cham, https://doi.org/10.1007/978-3-030-67245-4_54. [28]

CARICOM (2018), *Protocol on Contingent Rights*, CARICOM, Georgetown, Guyana, https://caricom.org/documents/16422-protocol_on_contingent_rights_-_july_2018.pdf. [20]

CARICOM (1996), "Social security in CARICOM", 22 May, CARICOM, Georgetown, Guyana, https://caricom.org/social-security-in-caricom/. [19]

De Lisle, J. (2022), "Theorizing on the marginalization of boys and girls in Caribbean schooling: Recurring myths and emerging realities", in Blackman, S. (ed.), *Equitable Education for Marginalized Youth in Latin America and the Caribbean*, Routledge, https://doi.org/10.4324/9780429276866-1. [31]

ECLAC (2024), *Ratio of employed population to total population by sex, age group and geographic area*, (database), https://statistics.cepal.org/portal/cepalstat/dashboard.html?theme=1&lang=en (accessed on July 2024). [10]

ECLAC (2023), *Social Panorama of Latin America 2023*, United Nations Economic Commission for Latin America and the Caribbean, Santiago, Chile, https://repositorio.cepal.org/server/api/core/bitstreams/7ddf434a-6073-4f1e-8b71-a6639e4586d5/content. [3]

Ellis, E. (2018), "Gender complexities in Jamaican secondary education: Class culture and the 'elephant' in the room", *Gender and Education*, Vol. 30/8, pp. 1019-1031, https://doi.org/10.1080/09540253.2017.1290218. [32]

FAO (2023), *Regional Overview of Food Security and Nutrition in Latin America and the Caribbean*, Food and Agriculture Organization of the United Nations, Rome, https://openknowledge.fao.org/server/api/core/bitstreams/f6d5a32f-c6f5-476c-bcc4-c72c74be3b8d/content. [7]

Figueroa, M. (2000), "Making sense of male experience: The case of academic underachievement in the English-speaking Caribbean", *IDS Bulletin*, Vol. 31/2, pp. 68-74, https://doi.org/10.1111/j.1759-5436.2000.mp31002009.x. [33]

IDB (2021), *Economic Institutions for a Resilient Caribbean*, Inter-American Development Bank, Washington, DC, https://doi.org/10.18235/0003053. [13]

IICA (2018), *Annual Report*, Inter-American Institute for Cooperation on Agriculture, Turrialba, Costa Rica, http://apps.iica.int/SReunionesOG/Content/Documents/CE2019/en/7acc1088-9aa0-4818-8b18-392e8318a7a5_wd699_2018_iica_annual_report.pdf. [8]

ILO (2024), *ILOSAT*, (database), https://ilostat.ilo.org/data/ (accessed on July 2024). [11]

OECD (2024), *Key indicators of Informality based on Individuals and their Households (KIIbIH)*, https://shorturl.at/IZXI5. [12]

OECD (2023), *Education at a Glance 2023: OECD Indicators*, OECD Publishing, Paris, https://doi.org/10.1787/e13bef63-en. [24]

OECD (2023), *PISA 2022 Results (Volume I): The State of Learning and Equity in Education*, OECD Publishing, Paris, https://doi.org/10.1787/53f23881-en. [30]

OECD (2022), *Development Strategy Assessment of the Eastern Caribbean*, OECD Publishing, https://doi.org/10.1787/f1566c7a-en. [22]

OECD (2018), "OECD support to Organisation of Eastern Caribbean States (OECS) strategy implementation", OECD Publishing, Paris, https://www.oecd-ilibrary.org/sites/f1566c7a-en/index.html?itemId=/content/publication/f1566c7a-en#:~:text=This%20strategy%20runs%20from%202019,Sustainable%20Use%20of%20Natural%20Endowments. [21]

OECD et al. (2024), *Latin American Economic Outlook 2024: Financing Sustainable Development*, OECD Publishing, Paris, https://doi.org/10.1787/c437947f-en. [2]

OECD et al. (2023), *Latin American Economic Outlook 2023: Investing in Sustainable Development*, OECD Publishing, Paris, https://doi.org/10.1787/8c93ff6e-en. [1]

OECD/The World Bank (2023), *Health at a Glance: Latin America and the Caribbean 2023*, OECD Publishing, Paris, https://doi.org/10.1787/532b0e2d-en. [23]

OECS (2020), *Social inclusion and social protection strategic framework*, https://oecs.int/en/our-work/knowledge/library/social-development/social-inclusion-and-social-protection-strategic-framework-july21-2020#:~:text=The%20Social%20Inclusion%20and%20Social%20Protection%20Strategy%20. [15]

OECS Secretariat (2012), *OECS Education Sector Strategy 2012-2021*, Organisation of Eastern Caribbean States, Castries, Saint Lucia, https://www.globalpartnership.org/sites/default/files/2012-2021-oecs-education-sector-strategy_0.pdf. [29]

SIB (2018), "Poverty Analysis Main Findings, 2018", (infographic), Statistical Institute of Belize, Belomopan, Belize, https://sib.org.bz/wp-content/uploads/PovertyInfographic.pdf. [4]

Thailinger, A. et al. (2023), "Gender gaps in the English-speaking Caribbean: Education, skills, and wages", *Technical Note*, No. IDB-TN-02718, Inter-American Development Bank, Washington, DC, http://file:///C:/Users/Manfredi_t/Downloads/Gender-Gaps-in-the-English-speaking-Caribbean-Education-Skills-and-Wages%20(1).pdf. [26]

Turnbull, D. (2021), "Food security in the Caribbean", *IICA blog*, 23 April, https://blog.iica.int/blog/food-security-caribbean. [9]

UIS (2024), "Data for the Sustainable Development Goals", (database), https://uis.unesco.org/ (accessed on 18 June 2024). [27]

UNDP (2024), *Human Development Index (HDI)*, (database), https://hdr.undp.org/data-center/human-development-index#/indicies/HDI. [6]

United Nations (2022), "World Populations Prospects 2022", webpage, https://population.un.org/wpp/Publications/ (accessed on July 2024). [16]

WFP (2021), *Research Programme on Shock-Responsive Social Protection in the Caribbean*, World Food Programme, Rome, https://www.wfp.org/publications/research-programme-shock-responsive-social-protection-caribbean. [18]

World Bank (2024), *World Development Indicators*, (database), https://data.worldbank.org/ (accessed on July 2024). [5]

3 Environmental challenges and opportunities for sustainable development

Caribbean countries are highly vulnerable to climate change due to their geographical location, highly populated low-coastal zones and gaps in infrastructure, making them susceptible to climate-related extreme weather events that generate significant socio-economic impacts. Planning and implementing adaptation policies to enhance preparedness and resilience are crucial for safeguarding livelihoods and well-being. This chapter is structured into four sections. First, it presents key environmental challenges, including exposure to extreme weather events and their socio-economic and spatial impacts. Second, it highlights the importance of adopting comprehensive, long-term adaptation policies and specific instruments for resilience. Third, it advocates for transitioning from vulnerability analysis to identifying strategic opportunities in economic sectors with potential for promoting sustainable and resilient development in the Caribbean. Finally, the chapter presents key policy messages.

Introduction

The Caribbean stands out as one of the most at-risk regions for climate-related issues. Its geographical location, topographical characteristics, densely populated low-coastal zones, and infrastructure gaps contribute to its high susceptibility to extreme weather events and natural disasters. Storms and flooding, including tropical cyclones, are a major hazard for the region which has been hit by over 200 such events in the past two decades. Caribbean countries have experienced the highest temperature increases in Latin America and the Caribbean (LAC) in the last three decades, exacerbating risks from rising sea levels, considering that more than half of Caribbeans live within 1.5 m of the coastline and one-third live in low elevation zones. Natural disasters associated with climate change have high socioeconomic and spatial impacts in the region and the most vulnerable populations are disproportionally affected.

These risks underscore the urgent need for adaptation policies to address climate vulnerabilities and enhance climate resilience in the Caribbean. Three key dimensions to promote climate resilient economies are: investing in resilient infrastructure; implementing early warning systems (EWS) and aligning national adaptation commitments with international targets while examining trade-offs with sectoral and non-climate policies.

Despite the significant challenges and risks, this chapter highlights the need to advance from a vulnerability-focused perspective to identifying strategic areas of opportunity that a green and just transition can bring to the Caribbean while advancing climate-resilience. Areas such as energy transition, the blue economy, the circular economy, sustainable tourism, sustainable transport, nature-based solutions and digital transformation can promote the transformation of the region's production matrix, making it more sustainable while creating quality jobs, enhancing well-being and addressing climate-related challenges.

This chapter is divided into four main sections. First, it outlines the key environmental challenges faced by Caribbean countries, including exposure to climate-related extreme weather events and their socio-economic and spatial impacts. Second, it emphasises the importance of adopting comprehensive, long-term adaptation policies to increase climate resilience. Third it advocates for a shift from vulnerability analysis to identifying strategic areas of opportunity to promote sustainable and resilient development in the Caribbean. Finally, the chapter concludes with key policy messages.

Caribbean countries face unique challenges linked to their geographical location and the vulnerabilities associated with Small Island Developing States

Caribbean countries are highly vulnerable to extreme climate events and the effects of climate change

Countries in the Caribbean show higher vulnerability levels to climate change than Latin American (+2) and OECD countries (+11), on average, as illustrated by the Notre Dame Adaptation Initiative (ND-GAIN) vulnerability index (Figure 3.1) They tend to be more exposed (due to their geographical location), more sensitive (given the magnitude of population and sectors affected) and have less adaptive capacity (institutional and infrastructural) to respond to climate change and climate hazards.

Figure 3.1. Vulnerability Index: Caribbean, Latin American, and OECD selected countries, 2021

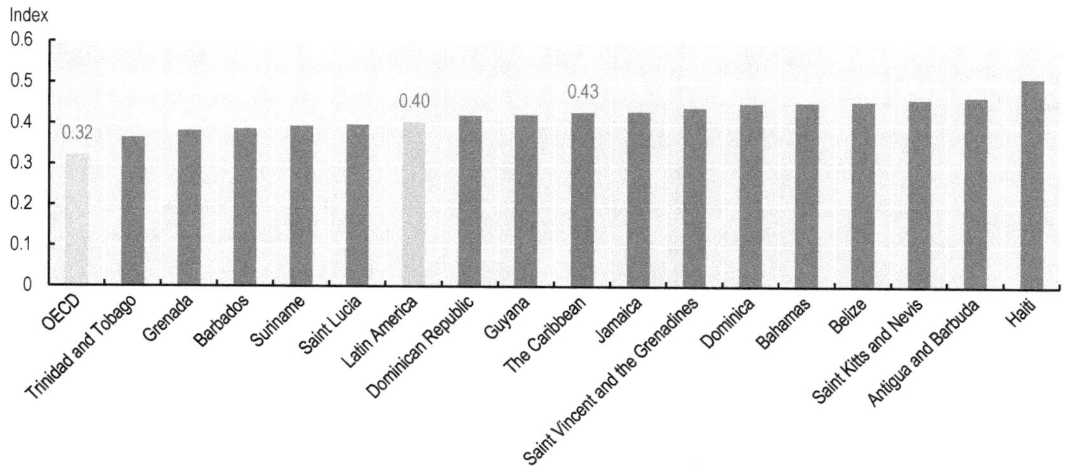

Note: The Vulnerability Index expresses the propensity or predisposition of human societies to be negatively affected by climate hazards by measuring countries' exposure, sensitivity, and adaptive capacity to climate events and climate change. Scores range from 0 to 1, the lower the score, the lower the vulnerability, and the higher the score, the higher the vulnerability. Exposure: the degree to which a system is exposed to significant climate change, independent of socioeconomic context. Indicators are projected impacts for future decades, remaining constant over time in ND-GAIN. Sensitivity: The extent of a country's dependence on sectors negatively affected by climate hazards or the proportion of the population particularly vulnerable to such hazards. This can vary over time. Adaptive capacity: The availability of social resources for sector-specific adaptation, including both sustainable solutions and the capacity to implement new adaptations. This varies over time in all countries. The Latin America country average includes 17 countries: Argentina, the Plurinational State of Bolivia, Brazil, Chile, Colombia, Costa Rica, Ecuador, El Salvador, Guatemala, Honduras, Mexico, Nicaragua, Panama, Paraguay, Peru, Uruguay and Venezuela. The Caribbean average includes 14 countries: Antigua and Barbuda, The Bahamas, Barbados, Belize, Dominica, Dominican Republic, Grenada, Guyana, Haiti, Jamaica, Saint Lucia, Saint Vincent and the Grenadines, Suriname, and Trinidad and Tobago. The OECD group includes all 38 OECD member states.
Source: Authors' elaboration based on data from Notre Dame Adaptation Initiative (2021[1]).

StatLink https://stat.link/48bkez

The Caribbean is increasingly exposed to different extreme weather events linked to climate change effects, including extreme heat, droughts, storms and hurricanes, sea level rise, and excessive flooding (CSGM/UWI, 2020[2]). The region is also particularly vulnerable to biodiversity loss, as many of the main economic drivers such as tourism, agriculture and mineral extraction, are linked to natural resources and the quality of ecosystems (OECD, 2023[3]). From 1980 to 2020, Caribbean countries suffered 322 climate-related extreme weather events triggered by natural hazards. Haiti (100), Dominican Republic (63) and Jamaica (31) experienced 60.2% of total climate hazard events in the region (Figure 3.2). The number of such events in the Caribbean in the period 2001-20 was 85% higher than in 1980-2000 (EM-DAT, 2024[4]).

Figure 3.2. Climate-related extreme weather events by type, selected Caribbean countries (1980-2020)

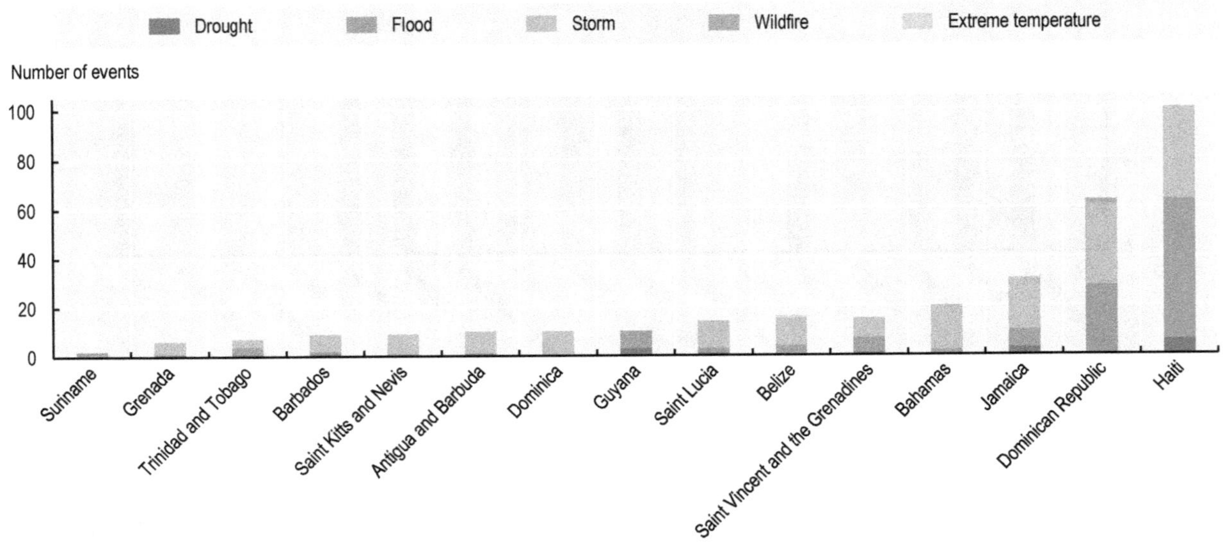

Note: Disasters are considered here as situations or events that overwhelm local capacity, necessitating a request to the national or international level for external assistance, or an unforeseen and often sudden event that causes great damage, destruction and human suffering. The graph considers only climate-related events like droughts, floods, storms, extreme temperatures, and wildfires. Geophysical events (earthquakes and volcanoes), technological events (industrial accidents) and biological events (from epidemics, insects or animals) are recorded in EM-DAT but excluded from the scores as they are not directly associated with climate change.
Source: Authors' elaboration based on data from EM-DAT (2024[4]).

StatLink https://stat.link/qxflsr

Caribbean countries experienced the highest temperature increases in the last three decades in Latin America and the Caribbean

The last 30 years have been the warmest on record in nearly all Caribbean countries and average temperatures are expected to rise further by 2030 (Figure 3.3). The average temperature recorded for the period 2000 to 2023 is more than 1°C higher than the average for 1910-1930. Temperatures were warmer than average especially in The Bahamas, Belize and Jamaica

The year 2020 was one of the warmest in Latin America and the Caribbean (LAC)'s history, one of the three warmest in the Caribbean and Central America, and the second-warmest in South America. The Caribbean recorded the largest temperature increases in LAC, confirming its greater vulnerability to climate change (WMO, 2021[5]). Temperature increases can augment the frequency of extreme heatwaves, extreme rainfall events and droughts; reduce ice sheets, sea ice and glaciers; accelerate sea level rise; and ocean heating (WMO, 2024[6]). According to the IPCC, at a 1.5°C global warming above pre-industrial (1861–1900) levels scenario, the Caribbean region will experience a 0.5°C–1.5°C mean surface temperature increase compared to a 1971-2000 baseline. At 2.0°C and 2.5°C scenarios, the warming ranges in the Caribbean increase to 1.08–2.58°C and 1.58–3.08°C, respectively (Taylor et al., 2018[7]). Impact studies increasingly highlight the adverse effects of surpassing global warming pre-industrial levels will have on key socioeconomic sectors critical to the Caribbean's quality of life, including water availability, agriculture and food production, health, natural resources and biodiversity, and tourism (Rhiney, 2015[8]; Taylor, M. A., 2015[9]; Taylor, Jones and Stephenson, 2016[10]).

Figure 3.3. Annual mean temperature anomalies in the Caribbean, 1960-2023

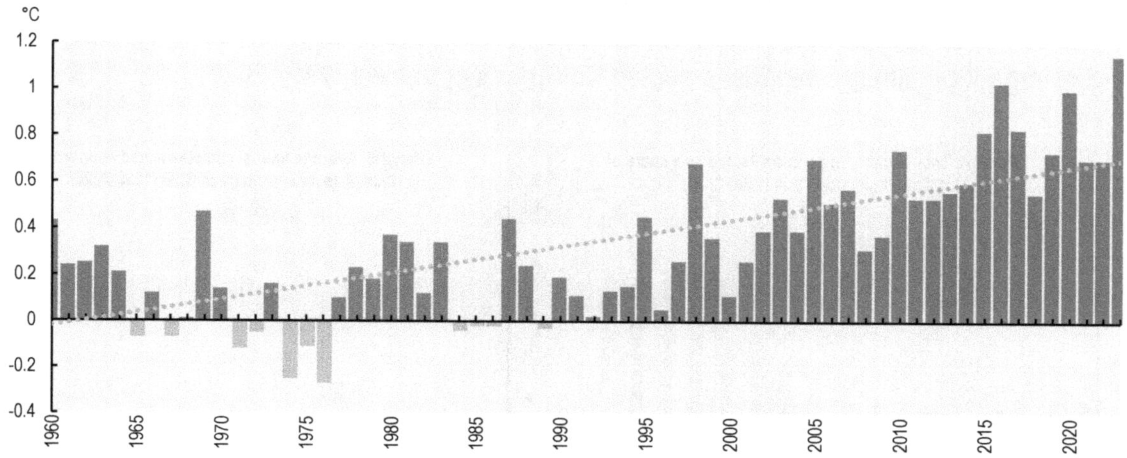

Note: This chart illustrates annual temperature anomalies relative to the 1910-2000 baseline average for both ocean and land surfaces in the Caribbean Islands. The y-axis displays the average temperature anomaly in degrees Celsius, calculated from January to December of each year presented in the x-axis. The average was computed based on monthly data for the islands and regions of the Caribbean Sea located south of Florida, excluding most continental shelf regions from the southern coast of Mexico to Venezuela.
Source: Authors' elaboration based on Climate at a Glance (NOAA, 2024).

StatLink https://stat.link/fp8zw9

Rising sea levels are a major threat for the region

More than half of Caribbeans live within 1.5 km of the coastline and one-third live in low-elevation zones, increasing their exposure to the effects of climate change. Many Caribbean coastal areas comprise reclaimed land that houses critical infrastructure such as air and seaports, hotels, energy generation, transmission and distribution networks and road networks. Rising sea levels mean a higher risk of damage to this infrastructure, freshwater resources, local economies and livelihoods and coastal communities.

Given the region's proximity to the equator, rising sea levels generated by higher temperatures will continue to erode coasts and damage ecosystems. This, in turn, can lead to land loss, household damage, relocations, and business closures (Bleeker et al., 2021[11]). Sea levels in the Caribbean could rise by approximately 2.5 ± 0.4 mm/year, which, for example, could affect 49-60% of Belize's tourist resort properties (Walker, 2022[12]). Moreover, the Caribbean also has the highest population density in the Americas, three times bigger than Latin America, making relocation even more challenging, especially given the limited land space in some of the smaller islands.

Natural disasters have high economic impacts on the region

In the last four decades, climate hazards in the Caribbean affected over 24 million people. The amount of people affected by natural disasters in the Caribbean represents more than the region's average population between 1980 and 2020 (Figure 3.4. Panel A) and had an economic cost of over USD 22 billion in damages in that period (EM-DAT, 2024[4]). This vulnerability is heightened by the region's limited capacity to adapt to and recover from such impacts, necessitating robust climate resilience and disaster risk management strategies (Roy, 2023[13]).

Over the last four decades, annual climate-related damages have accounted for an average of 2.13% of GDP across Caribbean countries (Figure 3.4, Panel B). For example, the economic cost of Hurricane Ivan in 2004 in Grenada represented 148% of the country's GDP (EM-DAT, 2024[4]) and damaged 90% of its physical infrastructure and housing stock, respectively (IMF, 2005[14]). Most economic damages from climate hazards in the Caribbean between 1980 and 2020 were generated by storms (94%), including tropical cyclones, followed by floods (5%) and droughts (1%).

Figure 3.4. Impact of climate hazards, selected Caribbean countries (1980-2020)

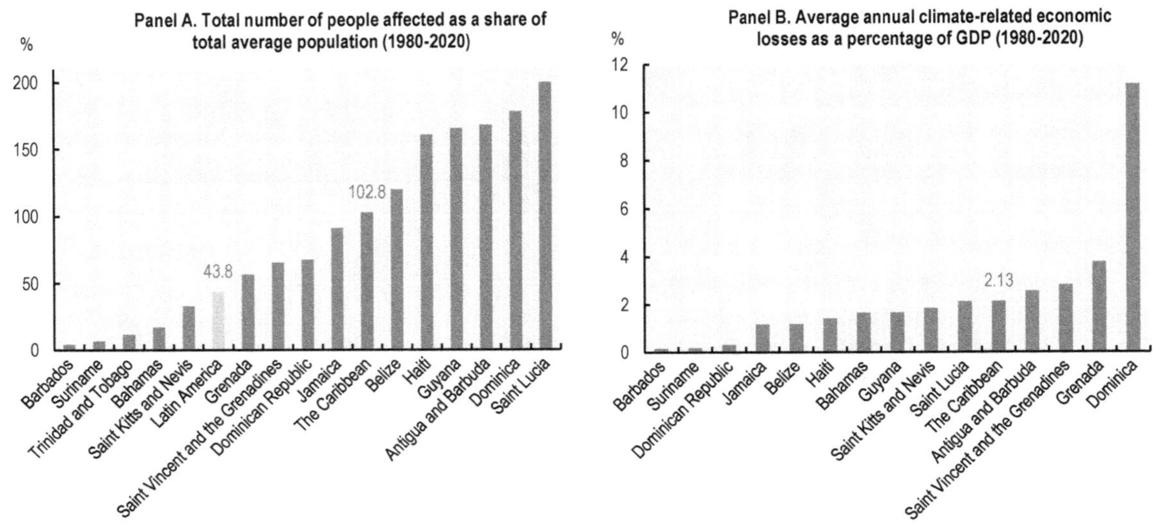

Note: Panel A illustrates the relative impact of natural disasters on different countries by showing the ratio between affected people and average population size in the Caribbean from 1980 to 2020. The number of affected people is determined by multiplying the number of affected families or damaged houses by the average family size for the area (×5 for developing countries, ×3 for industrialised countries, per UNDP classification); if a range is provided, the average of the range is used, and estimates like thousands affected are taken at face value despite likely underestimation. Panel B shows the average annual total damage caused by natural disasters as a percentage of GDP on average from 1980 to 2020. The Caribbean average includes 15 countries: Antigua and Barbuda, The Bahamas, Barbados, Belize, Dominica, Dominican Republic, Grenada, Guyana, Haiti, Jamaica, Saint Kitts and Nevis, Saint Lucia, Saint Vincent and the Grenadines, Suriname, and Trinidad and Tobago. The Latin America Average comprises 17 countries: Argentina, Bolivia, Brazil, Chile, Colombia, Costa Rica, Ecuador, El Salvador, Guatemala, Honduras, Mexico, Nicaragua, Panama, Paraguay, Peru, Uruguay and Venezuela.
Source: Authors' elaboration based on data from EM-DAT (2024[4]); United Nations (2022[15]); World Bank (2024[16]).

StatLink https://stat.link/ru8bkp

Barbados experienced a relatively low incidence of climate events with the lowest financial impact and the fewest people affected in the last four decades. This was supported by a comprehensive disaster management strategy, which relies on improved regulations, funding mobilisation, resilient infrastructure and community resilience initiatives through EWS, and research-backed planning (Parliament of Barbados, 2022[17]).

Vulnerable populations are the most affected by climate change consequences

The effects of global warming are expected to intensify in the coming years. In so doing, they will continue affecting disproportionately the most vulnerable countries and their most exposed socio-economic groups. Climate change impacts could drive an additional 5.8 million people into extreme poverty in LAC by 2030 (Jafino et al., 2020[18]). Disproportionate impacts of climate change on most vulnerable populations in the Caribbean will reinforce forced migration trends and spatial and gender inequalities, among other relevant dimensions. A total of 17 million citizens in LAC are projected to migrate by 2050 due to climate change (World Bank, 2021[19]). Between 2012 and 2022, environmental disasters in the Caribbean caused 5.3 million new internal displacements (IOM, 2023[20]). Moreover, during the 2017 Atlantic hurricane season alone, 3 million Caribbean people were displaced in a single month, with the most vulnerable populations disproportionately affected (Bleeker et al., 2021[11]). Relocation programmes co-ordinated at a regional level would help anticipate and contain forced migration due to climate change and reduce unnecessary exposure to risk (Chapter 6).

Socio-economic inequalities in the Caribbean are concentrated in urban areas disconnected from each other. Wealth accumulates in a few privileged locations, distinct from the rest of the urban landscape. High urbanisation rates, unregulated urban expansion, and socio-economic residential segregation have forced vulnerable groups into high-risk zones, such as floodplains and landslide-prone slopes, without adequate infrastructure. This situates them at heightened risk to climate change impacts and other phenomena, such as heatwaves, amplifying health risks and vulnerability to extreme weather events based on their socio-economic status (OECD et al., 2021[21]).

Lower-income households in the Caribbean who tend to live in areas highly vulnerable to the effects of climate change, might not receive enough financial help to rebuild their houses. Consequently, they have a greater chance of suffering longer periods of displacement after a natural disaster (Bleeker et al., 2021[11]). These households often face significant financial burdens due to loss of income, as the widespread damage in the region frequently burdens the local economy during the recovery process.

Climate change also exacerbates the socio-economic divide between rural and urban areas in the Caribbean by increasing the effects of droughts on agricultural areas and driving migration from rural to urban regions. This movement will further strain urban areas, highlighting the need for urban renewal policies that foster the inclusion of marginalised populations and social cohesion. This is particularly significant in regions with large indigenous populations, such as Belize, Guyana and Suriname, where rural-to-urban migration could significantly alter the socio-economic landscape. In Guyana, for example, indigenous people remain the most economically disadvantaged and vulnerable ethnic group comprising around 10% of the population and residing mostly in rural areas. Addressing these challenges requires comprehensive strategies that account for both urban and rural socio-economic dynamics. To effectively integrate climate change mitigation and adaptation into urban planning, these efforts must include urban development and land use reforms, improved data collection and climate risk assessments, community involvement in sustainable infrastructure planning, and securing adequate financing.

Women are disproportionately affected by natural disasters. Women and children are 14 times more likely to die than men during a disaster globally. Moreover, unequal access to resources and decision-making power between women and men in pre- and post-disaster contexts affects their capacity to prepare for and respond to disasters (OECD, 2023[22]). There is a higher concentration of impoverished people living in households led by women, and, in the Caribbean, women mostly work in sectors highly vulnerable to such events (Bleeker et al., 2021[11]). In The Bahamas, for instance, at least one-third of women are employed in the tourism sector, which typically collapses or experiences temporary shutdowns following natural disasters (Bleeker et al., 2021[11]). Furthermore, women are often the last to evacuate during extreme weather events due to caregiving responsibilities for children and the elderly. They also tend to have less training in preparedness and response to such events. Additionally, women may face barriers to accessing and acting on early warnings, often due to lower levels of education, illiteracy, or insufficient technical training (OECD, 2023[3]). Caribbean countries are working on making their climate-related policies more gender-responsive. For example, Grenada is including women in the discussions at the stages of design, implementation and evaluation of climate mitigation and adaptation strategies, while Jamaica includes women in identifying high-risk areas and critical infrastructure that could be affected by climate disasters (OECD, 2023[3]).

High vulnerability comes in combination with Caribbean countries' minimal contribution to global greenhouse gas emissions

The Caribbean contribution to global greenhouse gas (GHG) emissions from 1990-2015 is minimal compared to the consequences they have on the region. The Caribbean has contributed only 0.23% to total GHG global emissions in 2021, a figure that is closely aligned with the region's share of global GDP, approximately 0.22%, in that same year (World Bank, 2024[16]). However, total emissions have increased from 73 Mt Co2e in 1990 to 109 Mt Co2e in 2020, which reflects a 49.3% increase in emissions for the Caribbean region (Figure 3.5) (Climate Watch, 2024[23]).

The occurrence of natural disasters will continue to increase as a consequence of climate change. Investment in climate adaptation strategies is needed to allow the most vulnerable countries to prepare and create resilient strategies and resources. In doing so, they can avoid human suffering and economic losses, and build a resilient path towards development. To advance a sustainable and just green transition in line with the Paris Agreement commitments, Caribbean countries will need to address the transitional risks associated with meeting their emissions targets under a common but differentiated responsibility. Transition risk refers to the climate risk resulting from mitigation policies as economies move towards a greener, less polluting society, leading to changes in the energy system and throughout the economy.[1] For example, firms involved in fossil fuels and those with a high emission intensity could face large shifts in asset values or higher costs of doing business (EIB, 2021[24]).

Figure 3.5. Total GHG emissions by subregions, 1990-2020

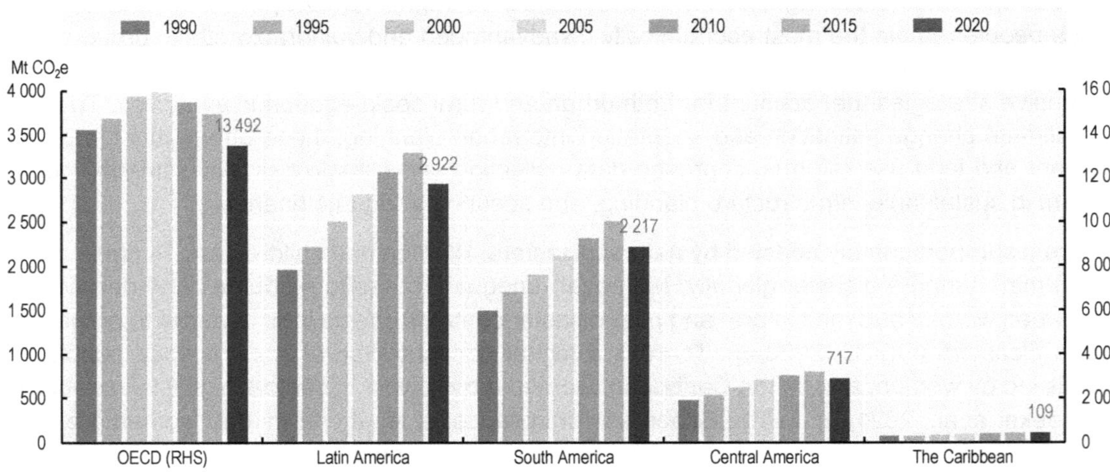

Note: Total GHG emissions excluding land-use change and forestry (LUCF). The OECD total represents the sum of GHG emissions for all member countries. The Caribbean total includes 15 countries: Antigua and Barbuda, The Bahamas, Barbados, Belize, Dominica, Dominican Republic, Grenada, Guyana, Haiti, Jamaica, Saint Kitts and Nevis, Saint Lucia, Saint Vincent and the Grenadines, Suriname, and Trinidad and Tobago. The Central America total consists of eight countries: Belize, Costa Rica, El Salvador, Guatemala, Honduras, Nicaragua, Panama and Mexico. The South America total comprises 12 countries: Argentina, Bolivia, Brazil, Chile, Colombia, Ecuador, Guyana, Paraguay, Peru Suriname, Uruguay and Venezuela. The Latin America total comprises 17 countries: Argentina, Bolivia, Brazil, Chile, Colombia, Costa Rica, Ecuador, El Salvador, Guatemala, Honduras, Mexico, Nicaragua, Panama, Paraguay, Peru, Uruguay and Venezuela. The OECD total includes all 38 member states. OECD is represented on the right axis (RHS).
Source: Authors' elaboration based on (Climate Watch, 2024[23]).

StatLink https://stat.link/3dk8x7

Adaptation measures are central to tackling climate vulnerabilities and fostering climate resilience in the Caribbean

Vulnerability to climate change is multifaceted, encompassing social, spatial and institutional factors. These factors include high poverty and inequality, high population density in risk-prone areas, inadequate infrastructure, and risk of natural disasters. Thus, adopting climate adaptation policies is essential to address the underlying vulnerabilities in all dimensions and increase climate resilience and preparedness. Comprehensive strategies combine immediate disaster preparedness with long-term vulnerability reduction. Such strategies are needed to enable Caribbean nations to better protect their populations and economies from the adverse effects of climate change and natural disasters (World Bank, 2023[25]).

Caribbean countries vary significantly in their vulnerability to climate change and readiness to address it. Stronger governance, economic stability and more developed social protection systems can enhance the adaptive capacity of countries to natural disasters. The analysis of vulnerability and readiness indexes at the regional level shows that Caribbean countries, on average, are more vulnerable than Latin American countries. However, Caribbean countries have been more active in designing policies to increase readiness to address the effects of climate change. OECD countries, on average, have lower levels of vulnerability and significantly higher levels of preparedness than Caribbean and Latin American countries, respectively. This positions them in a relatively more secure situation with fewer challenges.

Building climate resilience entails different types of climate risk management interventions that comprise climate risk and vulnerability assessments and monitoring actions, the development of EWS, effective governance to manage climate risks accompanied by human and institutional capacity-building; nature-based solutions (NbS) used to reduce risks; climate-proofing of infrastructure and services; insurance and social protection instruments to reduce investment and social risks; increased access and quality of public and private finance to invest in resilience (Global Climate Action and the Marrakech Partnership, 2022). Promoting international co-operation among Caribbean countries to exchange best practices and collaboration is also key for a more resilient Caribbean (Chapter 6). The following section highlights three areas of action that are particularly relevant to advance climate resiliency in the Caribbean: i) resilient infrastructure; ii) EWS and iii) climate adaptation policy instruments. Resilient infrastructure is crucial for economic stability, as it significantly reduces GDP losses by minimising the destruction of capital during natural disasters. By prioritising climate-resilient infrastructure, countries can enhance the reliability of service provision and extend the lifespan of assets. Saint Lucia, Dominica, and Barbados offer interesting examples of resilient infrastructure experiences (Box 3.1).

Integrating climate change adaptation with disaster risk reduction measures – such as early warning systems (EWS) and civil protection systems – can enhance countries' capacity to mitigate the economic, environmental, and social impacts of extreme climate events. EWS are a key element of disaster risk reduction, and Caribbean countries were frontrunners in developing their EWS.

National Adaptation Plans (NAPs) and other policy instruments, including Nationally Determined Contributions (NDCs) and Long-Term Strategies (LTS), can help integrate adaptation into national planning while collecting, developing, adopting, and implementing adaptation actions. They also serve as a framework under which countries can reduce vulnerability derived from climate change, strengthen their resilience and increase their adaptive capacity (OECD, 2024[26]).

Investing in resilient infrastructure

Infrastructure plays a key role in shaping a country's vulnerability to climate change and natural disasters and its ability to respond to them. Latin American countries perform better than the Caribbean in terms of infrastructure vulnerabilities, with Antigua and Barbuda, Jamaica and Saint Vincent and the Grenadines presenting the highest infrastructure vulnerabilities in the Caribbean (Figure 3.6). Vulnerabilities are also closely related to physical location. Over half of Jamaica's economic assets and tourism infrastructure are located in coastal areas, which poses a huge risk given natural disasters and climate change. Integrating climate considerations into long-term strategic infrastructure planning is a priority for the region, also in light of its significant investment needs in climate-resilient infrastructure.

Figure 3.6. Infrastructure Vulnerability Index 2021: Caribbean, Latin American, and OECD selected countries, 2021

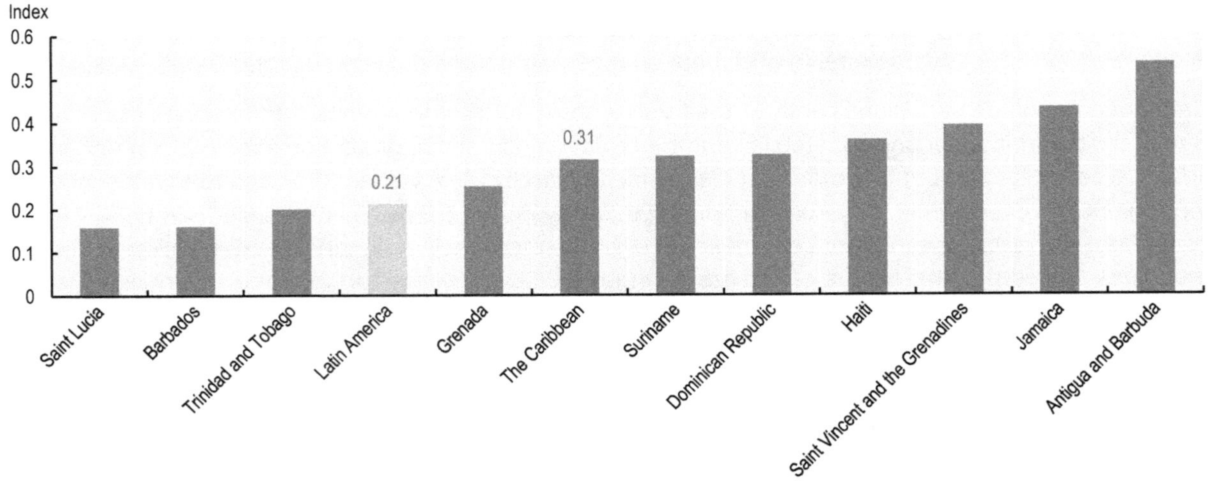

Note: The ND Gain Infrastructure Vulnerability Country Index captures the vulnerability of coastal and energy infrastructure to climate change. This relates primarily to general preparedness for climate-related natural disasters, coastal hazards, and energy supply challenges. It considers six indicators: projected change of hydropower generation capacity; impacts of projected change of rising sea levels; dependency on imported energy; population living under 5m above sea level; electricity access; and disaster preparedness. The Latin America average comprises 18 countries: Argentina, the Plurinational State of Bolivia, Brazil, Chile, Colombia, Costa Rica, Ecuador, El Salvador, Guatemala, Honduras, Mexico, Nicaragua, Panama, Paraguay, Peru, Uruguay and Venezuela. The Caribbean average contains ten countries: Antigua and Barbuda, Barbados, Dominican Republic, Grenada, Haiti, Jamaica, Saint Kitts and Nevis, Saint Lucia, Suriname, and Trinidad and Tobago. The OECD group includes all OECD member states.
Source: Authors' elaboration based on ND-GAIN (2021[1]).

StatLink https://stat.link/nsjm3g

New infrastructure should be developed in a resilient way that considers climate risks. Development finance institutions play a key role in helping to finance this kind of infrastructure in the Caribbean (Chapter 5). Box 3.1 presents some examples of Caribbean countries that use a resilient infrastructure approach to increase climate resilience.

Box 3.1. Resilient infrastructure in the Caribbean

In **Saint Lucia**, strategic long-term infrastructure planning is crucial to enhance resilience in the face of significant climate challenges. The island uses several key tools for maximising climate-resilient infrastructure development: i) a national infrastructure assessment ensures future projects meet economic, environmental, and social needs; ii) strategic planning focuses on critical sectors like energy, water supply, wastewater, and solid waste management, integrating future demand changes and tourism impacts; iii) aligning assessment and planning with the SDGs and the Paris Agreement ensures priorities in the National Adaptation Plan (NAP) are integrated into the national infrastructure assessment; and iv) the National Integrated Planning and Programme Unit, facilitates cross-ministerial co-ordination guiding the island's infrastructure strategy. These efforts aim to build resilient infrastructure that can withstand and adapt to climate change impacts, promoting sustainable development and enhancing residents' quality of life (UNOPS, 2020[27]).

Since 2014, **Dominica** has implemented the Disaster Vulnerability Reduction Project (DVRP). The DVRP aims to bolster resilience to climate hazards through investments in robust infrastructure and enhanced hazard data collection and monitoring systems. In 2017, for example, Hurricane Maria caused more than USD 1 billion in damages. However, Dominica's airport resumed operations within days, demonstrating the effectiveness of resilient infrastructure rebuilt after Tropical Storm Erika in 2015 (IMF, 2021[28]). In 2018, Dominica enacted the Climate Resilience Act, reaffirming its commitment to becoming a climate-resilient nation after recovery. As part of its 2030 Development Plan, the country aims to make 90% of all homes resilient. To achieve this, it introduced new building standards and fiscal incentives. The Housing Recovery Project pledged to deliver 5 000 resilient homes for vulnerable populations by 2030, having achieved 36% of this goal by the end of 2023 (Government of Commonwealth of Dominica, 2022[29]; Business View, 2023[30]).

The Richard Haynes Boardwalk in **Barbados** is a key project under the Government's Coastal Infrastructural Programme, aimed at mitigating hurricane impacts on shorelines and beaches. Located in a densely populated coastal area, its goals include promoting shore protection and stabilising beaches during severe climate events. The structure was designed with considerations for climate change, including storm surges and projected sea level rise, ensuring resilience against intense waves while safeguarding the local population now and in the future (Cashman and Nagdee, 2017[31]).

Grenada recently secured USD 15 million to invest in transportation infrastructure resilient to the impacts of climate change and natural hazards. The Grenada Resilience Improvement Project will finance interventions to protect principal transport corridors against coastal erosion fuelled by sea level rise and flooding at the crossing of the country's largest river (World Bank, 2022[32]; NEMO, 2024[33]).

Developing effective early warning systems

Climate change adaptation and disaster risk reduction interventions aim at increasing resilience by protecting communities and infrastructure from natural hazards by minimising disaster losses (OECD, 2023[3]). Enhanced coherence between policies through co-ordinated action among stakeholders can improve interventions and support local development informed by climate change. For example, integrating EWS with disaster risk reduction strategies can significantly boost resilience. Successful EWS require people-centred technology development, robust data management, forecasting capabilities, innovation, and sustainable funding to ensure their success.

Caribbean countries have been frontrunners in developing EWS. Antigua and Barbuda, Dominica, Dominican Republic, Saint Lucia and Saint Vincent and Grenadines have implemented projects to create

EWS national assessments and roadmaps, with support from the United Nations Development Programme (UNDP), the International Federation of Red Cross (IFRC), and the Caribbean Disaster Emergency Management Agency (CDEMA). These involve the sharing of best practices and tools that can improve risk knowledge, monitoring, and response capacities (CDEMA, 2024[34]). The World Meteorological Organisation (WMO) multi-hazard EWS checklist has been instrumental in helping countries identify gaps in their EWS systems and provide a roadmap for improvement (WMO, 2018[35]). Other efforts include technical training, test runs for new meteorological products, and regional tools for improving adaptation policy monitoring. Moreover, the Climate Risk Early Warning Systems (CREWS) Caribbean project prioritises investments that support EWS developed with the participation of local communities (OECD, 2023[3]).

In addition to EWS, effective management of extreme weather events requires robust disaster preparedness at both national and local levels, including healthcare, shelter, and essential relief supplies. Long-term strategies, such as constructing resilient infrastructure and investing in ecosystem preservation, are equally critical for strengthening overall resilience to natural hazards (OECD, 2023[3]).

Investing in the development of capacities in public institutions is key to making this possible (see Chapter 4). For instance, the Department of Emergency Management of Barbados has been working on EWS projects for several years. The leading programme focused on tsunami preparedness and includes multi-hazard warning systems. These measure canals to indicate the risk of flooding, set up automatised sirens throughout the city and establish shelter areas. They also promote involvement of the community with annual drills for natural disasters, involving the local population in a community-based approach to disaster management (UNDRR, 2022[36]).

Climate adaptation planning instruments

National Adaptation Plans (NAPs) serve as a comprehensive framework under which countries aim to reduce vulnerability derived from climate change, strengthen resilience, and increase their adaptive capacity. The development of a NAP has also become an accepted process through which countries align their adaptation actions with other international frameworks and goals. These include the specific Sendai Framework for Disaster Risk Reduction, or more generally the SDGs.

While most Caribbean countries have adopted national legislation or policy frameworks on climate adaptation or resilience, Grenada (2009), Haiti (2023), Saint Lucia (2018), Saint Vincent and the Grenadines (2019), Suriname (2020) and Trinidad and Tobago (2023) have submitted their NAPs under the United Nations Framework Convention on Climate Change (UNFCCC). Other countries are including adaptation considerations in sectoral or specialised legislation, but there remains a gap between the introduction and effective implementation of national climate adaptation plans. Major challenges include aligning NAPs with sectoral plans, securing implementation budgets, and obtaining detailed climate impact information (OECD, 2023[3]).

Only Saint Lucia and Grenada have submitted sectoral NAPs (Annex Table 3.A.2). In the case of Saint Lucia, the sectoral approach includes specific adaptation actions for sectors such as tourism, water, agriculture, fisheries, infrastructure, natural resource management, education, and health (Government of Saint Lucia, 2018[37]). NAPs are not the only tool available for countries wishing to advance with setting and implementing climate adaptation policy measures and actions.

Adaptation is also addressed in the NDCs that countries use to make plans for reducing greenhouse gas emissions, adapting to climate change, and recording the reduction in their emissions. All Caribbean countries have submitted their NDCs including adaptation goals. A total of 60% of Caribbean countries have covered all sectors within their NDCs commitments (Annex Table 3.A.1). Belize was the only Caribbean country to submit a Long-term Strategy (LTS), which lays out policies to achieve carbon neutrality by 2050 (Annex Table 3.A.1). Belize's LTS elaborates on different scenarios for lowering emissions for each sector, dividing it by sectors: forestry, electricity and energy use, transport, agriculture, and waste (UNFCC, 2023[38]).

To ensure policies align with international targets and national environmental commitments, countries should update NAPs regularly. This process should use evidence-based analyses and examine trade-offs and synergies with sectoral and non-climate policies while aligning adaptation goals with mitigation efforts (OECD, 2023[3]).

Harnessing the potential of unique biodiversity and natural endowments: From vulnerabilities to opportunities in the Caribbean

Caribbean countries need to implement adaptation, readiness and resilience policies, which can turn challenges into opportunities. This section highlights some strategic sectors that can provide opportunities to increase resilience while advancing the diversification of Caribbean economies and achieving higher well-being for their people: i) energy transition; ii) blue economy; iii) the circular economy; iv) sustainable tourism; v) sustainable transport; vi) nature-based solutions (NbS); and vii) digital transformation.

The energy transition can drive sustainable economic growth while increasing resilience

Transitioning towards a more diversified and sustainable energy mix in the Caribbean can help the region to increase resilience and economic growth. Increasing renewable energy production, improving energy efficiency, and developing more reliable and efficient electrical systems in the Caribbean is key. For instance, the IDB estimates that an investment of USD 11 billion in this area could generate up to USD 6.1 billion in net economic benefits, reduce fuel oil imports by 260 million barrels and save up to 41 million tonnes of CO_2 emissions by 2040 (IDB, 2020[39]).

The Caribbean's shift to a low-carbon energy system faces relevant challenges, including high implementation costs, small energy grids ill-equipped to incorporate renewables, limited space for large-scale solar or onshore wind farms, and vulnerability to climate events that threaten energy infrastructure. Additionally, the top-down, vertically integrated utility companies, limited access to affordable financing for governments and clean energy developers, and weak public administrative capacities contribute to slowing progress.

A successful energy transition should address transitional risks to guarantee a just transition while transforming energy infrastructures to a low-carbon economy, reducing the risks of stranded assets, particularly in Caribbean oil-producing countries, and the impacts on workers in brown sectors by providing retraining opportunities and compensation measures (IDB, 2016[40]; EIB, 2021[24]; OECD et al., 2022[41]). The transition could adopt a hybrid energy approach, integrating clean energy sources alongside low-carbon fossil fuels, such as natural gas, to replace bunker fuel and diesel, and supporting the region's energy transformation (Atlantic Council, 2023[42]). This transition also requires a new business model for utilities while ensuring that electricity costs remain low for consumers and profitable for governments and the private sector. Finally, national action will not be enough. International partners have a key role in advancing the transition and helping guarantee energy security in the region (Chapter 6).

Caribbean tourism-dependent economies rely heavily on imported fossil fuels. Nine Caribbean countries with data available produce over 80% of their electricity from imported fossil fuels, except for oil-producing Trinidad and Tobago, Suriname and Guyana (World Bank, 2022[43]). This heavy reliance on fossil fuel imports translates into some of the highest average electricity prices globally. According to the World Bank, in 2019 the average price for a kWh in the Caribbean stood at USD 0.26, surpassing the European Union (USD 0.21 kWh) and the United States (USD 0.18 kWh) (World Bank, 2022[43]).

The energy mix of oil-producing Caribbean countries is also heavily dependent on fossil fuel sources. Diversifying energy sources would help enhance energy security in the region. This, in turn, makes it less vulnerable to global oil price fluctuations, fostering resilience and reducing energy costs at the household level.

Many Caribbean countries have already made significant efforts towards the adoption of renewable energy technologies, deploying geothermal energy projects (Dominica); solar water heating (Barbados) and windfarms (Jamaica). Barbados has implemented a comprehensive National Energy Policy framework aimed at transitioning to 100% renewable energy by 2030 (Table 3.1). The Caribbean Community (CARICOM) has set a regional target of 47% renewable energy in total electricity generation by 2027. Nonetheless, in most Caribbean economies renewable energies are still limited. In 2022, on average, renewable energy production in the Caribbean (17%) lagged compared to Latin America (63%). Hydropower (15%) is the most widespread renewable electricity source in the Caribbean followed by solar (2.5%) and eolic (1.3%) (Figure 3.7). Belize, Suriname, and Haiti stand out based on their hydropower capacity. The Dominican Republic and Jamaica show a more diversified electricity generation combining hydropower, eolic and solar, while Barbados has prioritised solar energy (Figure 3.7).

Figure 3.7. Renewable electricity generation, selected Caribbean countries, 2010 and 2022

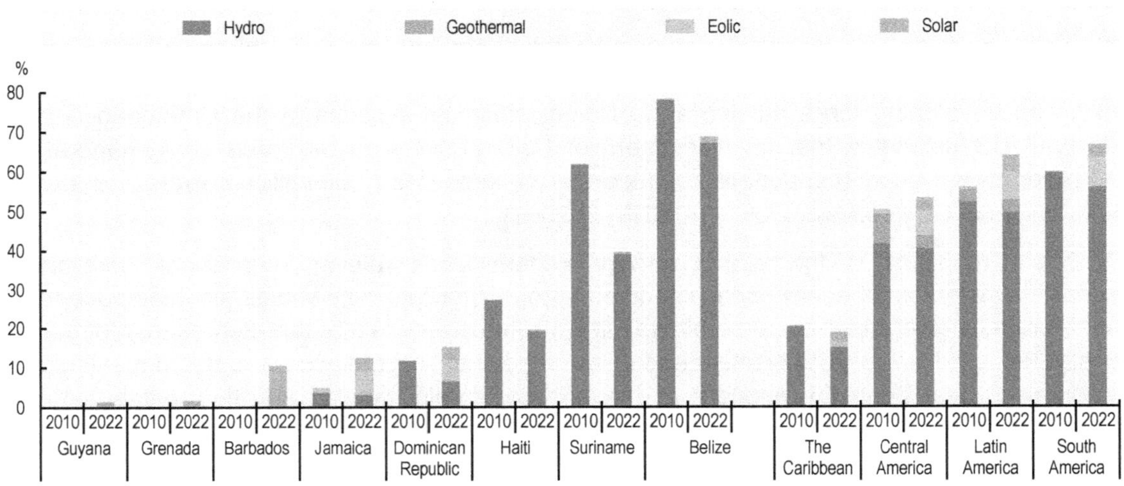

Note: Total renewable electricity generation for selected countries. The Caribbean average included Barbados, Belize, Dominican Republic, Grenada, Guyana, Haiti, Jamaica, and Suriname. The Central America average includes Costa Rica, El Salvador, Guatemala, Honduras, Mexico, Nicaragua and Panama. The Latin America average includes Argentina, the Plurinational State of Bolivia, Brazil, Chile, Colombia, Costa Rica, Ecuador, El Salvador, Guatemala, Honduras, Mexico, Nicaragua, Panama, Paraguay, Peru, Uruguay and Venezuela. The South America average includes Argentina, Bolivia, Brazil, Chile, Colombia, Ecuador, Paraguay, Peru, Uruguay and Venezuela.
Source: Authors' elaboration based on SieLAC (2024[44]).

StatLink https://stat.link/mukjwv

Offshore wind energy represents an opportunity to diversify the energy matrix in the Caribbean. It could generate additional 473 GW or about 97.5 times the electricity currently generated from all sources in the Caribbean (4.85 GW in 2022) based on the Caribbean countries with available data on electricity production installed capacity (Figure 3.8). Offshore wind energy could help reduce dependence on fossil fuels and enable the possibility of exporting energy (World Bank/ESMAP, 2020[45]). If this potential is fully achieved, offshore wind would multiply by 100 times the current electricity generated from renewable and non-renewable sources in Jamaica (from 0.5 GW to 50 GW), and by 26 times the electricity currently produced in the Dominican Republic (reaching 65 GW). Trinidad and Tobago is undertaking an offshore Wind Resource

Assessment Programme to realise the activities required to support offshore wind development in the country. Of all the renewable energy sources available in Trinidad and Tobago, offshore wind offers the largest potential for the island (GASCO, 2022[46]). A combination of policies entailing financial incentives and international co-operation actions will be needed to overcome investment, regulatory and logistical challenges and unlock the region's offshore wind potential. IDB estimates show that by 2040, energy generation from solar PV will reach an estimated 179GW annually under the sustainable energy pathway, compared to only 9 MW (0.009 GW) in a business-as-usual scenario (IDB, 2020[39]).

Figure 3.8. Technical potential for offshore wind generation, selected Caribbean countries by 2020

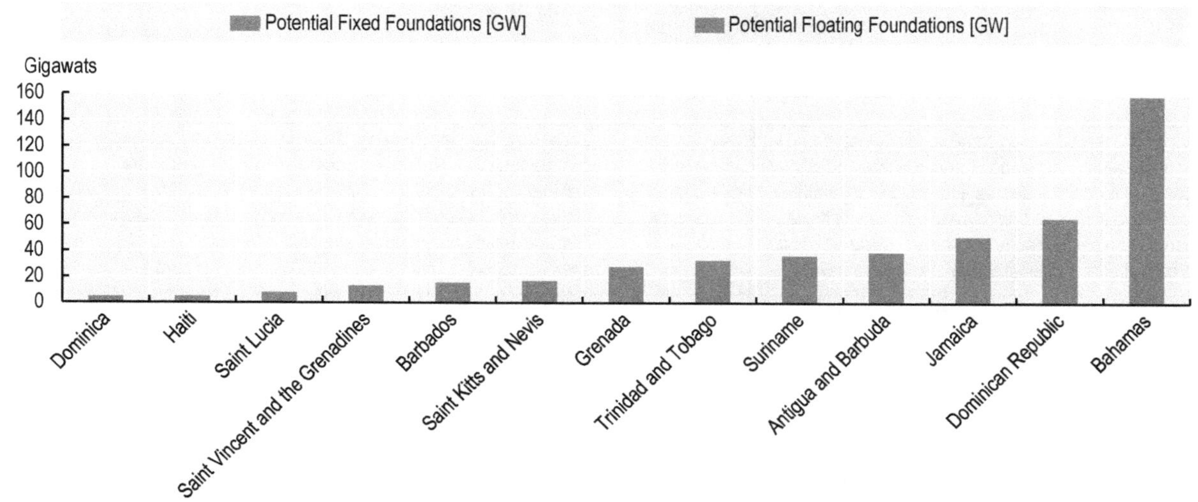

Notes: The offshore wind technical potential is an estimate of the amount of generation capacity that could be technically feasible with current technology, considering only wind speed and water depth, and it is expressed in terms of installed power capacity in gigawatts (GW) within 200 kilometres of the shoreline. Results report the total fixed foundations potential and the total floating foundations potential. Above 50 m depth is considered optimal for fixed foundations and, 50-1 000 m depth is where floating wind can be considered. The Caribbean region includes Antigua and Barbuda, Barbados, The Bahamas, Dominica, Dominican Republic, Grenada, Jamaica, Haiti, Saint Kitts and Nevis, Saint Vincent and the Grenadines, Saint Lucia, Suriname, and Trinidad and Tobago.
Source: Authors' calculations based on World Bank/ESMAP (2020[45]).

StatLink https://stat.link/zy248k

A successful energy transition strategy for the Caribbean should pursue multiple objectives simultaneously. These include modernising the electric grid, enhancing distributed generation, improving energy service quality and efficiency, and advancing towards vertically integrated systems while exploring decentralised power generation as a climate adaptation measure. Mobilising finance and reducing risks to scale up energy projects is crucial, supported by innovative financing mechanisms (Chapter 5) and international partnerships (Chapter 6). These partnerships can bolster regional energy security and resilience, such as through electricity integration via submarine cables for geothermal energy (e.g. in Saint Lucia, Saint Vincent and the Grenadines, Saint Kitts and Nevis, and Dominica) and maximising distributed generation from solar and wind sources (ECLAC, 2020[47]).

Table 3.1. Energy transition

Key facts	Relevance for sustainable development
• Nine Caribbean countries generate more than 80% of their electricity needs from fuel imports while five import 90% of their energy (CCREEE, 2024[48]). • Caribbean countries have one of the highest prices for electricity in the world, more than 30% higher than prices in the European Union (EUROSTAT, 2024[49]; CCREEE, 2024[48]). • Combined benefits of transitioning to renewable energy sources, reducing electricity use and more reliable and efficient electrical systems could reach USD 16 billion in net economic benefits in CARICOM countries by 2040. Investments of USD 11 billion are needed over the next ten years to reach this scenario (IDB, 2020[39]).	• **Reducing carbon emissions**: Transitioning to renewable energy sources and the application of energy efficiency policies can help mitigate 55% of global GHG emissions (UNEP, 2023[50]). • **Energy security:** Diversifying energy sources enhances energy security and resilience against global oil price fluctuations and natural disasters (UNEP, 2021[51]). • **Economic growth**: Renewable energy projects can drive sustainable economic growth and create employment opportunities (UNEP, 2021[51]).
Relevant policy instruments	**Relevant experiences**
• National Energy Policy Frameworks: These frameworks set targets for renewable energy adoption and energy efficiency improvements, providing a roadmap for transitioning to sustainable energy systems. They support regulatory measures, incentives, and strategic planning to enhance energy security and sustainability (e.g. Barbados National Energy Policy Framework). • Renewable Energy Incentive Programs: These programmes offer financial incentives, such as tax credits, subsidies and grants, to encourage the development and adoption of renewable energy technologies. They aim to reduce the cost barriers associated with renewable energy projects. • Public-private partnerships (PPPs): PPPs aim to help governments and private sector entities collaborate on the development and financing of renewable energy projects. These partnerships could leverage private investment and expertise to advance energy transition goals.	• **Barbados National Energy Policy:** Barbados has implemented a comprehensive National Energy Policy framework aimed at transitioning to 100% renewable energy by 2030. The framework sets targets for renewable energy adoption and energy efficiency improvements, providing a strategic roadmap. In 2023, renewable energy production increased by 400%, and the total fuel burned was reduced by 25% compared with 2021 (Government of Barbados, 2024[52]). • **Barbados Solar Water Heating Project:** Barbados has become a world leader in solar water heating (SWH), with over 50 000 installations. Two out of five households in the country have SWH. This initiative saves 100 000 thermal megawatts of electricity per year. A series of incentives for SWH adopters has been established including tax reductions for products used to build solar heating machinery, and extended loan periods to finance the equipment (Smart Energy Barbados, 2024[53]). • Dominica's Geothermal Risk Mitigation Project: Dominica is developing its geothermal resources through a PPP to provide a stable, renewable energy source. The project aims to reduce the island's reliance on imported fossil fuels and lower energy costs and involves the construction of a 7 MW geothermal powerplant by 2026 (World Bank, 2024[54]) • **Jamaica's Wigton Windfarm**: This wind farm produces 6% of the renewable energy supply in Jamaica (3.7% of total energy). It has helped diversify Jamaica's energy mix while reducing carbon emissions and energy costs. Tax breaks and subsidies were given to incentivise the project. The company sells its production to the public utility, responsible for powering the national power grid (Development Bank of Jamaica Limited, 2024[55]).

The blue economy offers a pathway to sustainable growth with employment creation and higher well-being

Defined by the OECD as the sum of the economic activities of ocean-based industries, and the assets, goods and services of marine ecosystems, the blue economy can boost economic diversification, providing sustainable growth opportunities and reducing economic vulnerabilities, if pursued sustainably (OECD, 2024[56]).[2] The goal of applying the blue economy concept as a lens is to emphasise the connection between the ocean's ecological systems and the human activity that takes place in the ocean economy. The concept recognises that some activities in the ocean economy depend on the underlying ecological systems (the natural capital), while all have the potential to degrade them. Blue carbon ecosystems protect coasts from flooding, buffer ocean acidification, enhance water filtration, promote biodiversity conservation, help carbon sequestration, and boost sustainability in fishery productivity, which in turn creates jobs and increases economic returns (IPCC, 2019[57]). So far, the region's ocean economy is not well-measured or sufficiently understood. According to the World Bank, the blue economy generated revenues of USD 407 billion in the Caribbean in 2012, mainly from ocean transport, tourism, and oil and gas production, in an area that contains just 1% of the global ocean (World Bank, 2016[58]). The fishing industry alone employed over 350 000 people in 2019, producing more than USD 500 million of revenues in the Caribbean (CAF, 2021[59]).

The Caribbean is particularly well-placed to benefit from the blue economy due to its rich marine biodiversity and reliance on ocean-based industries like tourism and fisheries. The region hosts almost 10% of the world's coral reefs, approximately 45% of its fish species and 25% of its coral species (UNEP, 2019[60]). However, the region faces significant challenges in pursuing a blue economy. First, coral coverage is declining drastically with 75% of reefs at risk due to human activities (World Bank, 2016[58]). Second, the region needs to preserve biodiversity and ensure the health of marine environments. Third, it must address marine pollution, as 320 tonnes of plastic waste remain uncollected annually in the region (World Bank, 2023[61]). Fourth, after more than a decade since the first mass stranding of sargassum in the region, sargassum has become a major threat to local ecosystems and tourism and fishery economic activities contributing to major negative economic, environmental and health impacts.

Developing new opportunities from an expanding global ocean economy, such as renewable energy and aquaculture, is key to advancing sustainable development in Caribbean countries (OECD, 2020[62]). Some key actions to confront these challenges and realising the opportunities of the blue economy are: i) adopting a sustainable marine resource management approach to preserve the ecosystems that underpin key sectors like tourism and fisheries; ii) enhancing coastal resilience against natural disasters for maintaining economic stability and protecting people leaving in those areas (World Bank, 2016[58]); iii) implementing holistic policy frameworks with a spatial perspective; iv) implementing policies to promote investment in existing and new blue economy enterprises. Significant opportunities for value addition and job creation in the Caribbean lie within small and medium-sized enterprises (SMEs) operating across blue economy value chains. To support the growth of these firms, securing finance for start-ups, capacity building, and technological advancement will be key.

Examples of the responses mentioned above are the development of a blue economy strategy in Grenada ("Blue Growth Master Plan"); the adoption of integrated coastal zone management (ICZM) strategies in Belize; and Marine Spatial Plans (MSP) to integrate environmental, economic, and social policies to protect marine resources and biodiversity in The Bahamas. The Seychelles ("2018 Blue Economy Strategic Framework and Roadmap") and Mauritius' ("Oceans economy road map") provide other relevant blue economy examples in Small Island Developing Stated (SIDS) (OECD, 2020[62]). Some Caribbean countries have created blue economy ministries, for example, the Maritime Affairs and Blue Economy Ministry in Barbados, or the Ministry of Economic Development, Planning, Tourism, Creative Economy, Culture, Agriculture and Lands, Forestry, Marine Resources and Cooperatives in Grenada.

Other relevant instruments focus on finance, insurance and regional co-operation. Financial and conservation tools, for example, include using Blue Bonds like the Caribbean Blue Economy Financing (BLUEfin) or the Caribbean Biodiversity Fund (Chapter 5). Insurance instruments such as the Caribbean Catastrophe Risk Insurance Facility provide financial safety nets to mitigate natural disaster impacts Finally, processes such as the Caribbean Regional Fisheries Mechanism – which promotes responsible use of fishery resources – strengthen regional co-operation (Table 3.2).

Table 3.2. Blue economy

Key facts	Relevance for sustainable development
• The region hosts almost 10% of the world's coral reefs, approximately 45% of the fish species and 25% of the coral species (UNEP, 2019[60]). Nonetheless, coral coverage in the region has dropped significantly in recent decades, with 75% of all Caribbean reefs considered to be at risk from anthropogenic impacts (World Bank, 2016[58]). • The blue economy generated revenues of USD 407 billion in the Caribbean in 2012, mainly from ocean transport, tourism, and oil and gas production, in an area that contains just 1% of the global ocean (World Bank, 2016[58]). • In 2019, the fishing sector in the Caribbean employed more than 350 000 people, producing more than USD 500 million, and accounting for up to 8% of GDP (CAF, 2021[59]; Shortte, 2013[63]). • Nearly 60% of all commercially exploited fish stocks in the Caribbean Sea are either overexploited or at risk of collapse (World Bank, 2016[58]). • On average, 3% of the Caribbean total territorial waters were protected in 2021, compared to 19.4% in LAC, and 20.3% in the OECD (2018) (OECD, 2022[64]; World Bank, 2022[65]). • Each year, 320 tonnes of plastic waste remain uncollected in the Caribbean (World Bank, 2023[61]); total economic damage to the world's marine ecosystems from plastics is well over USD 15.5 billion every year (UNEP-CEP, 2019[66]). • One third of the Caribbean population lives in low-elevation coastal zones which are highly vulnerable to rising sea levels (Mycoo and Wairiu, 2022[67]).	• Economic diversification through the blue economy can provide sustainable growth pathways and reduce economic vulnerabilities (World Bank, 2016[58]). • Sustainable marine resource management is crucial to protecting the ecosystems that underpin key sectors like tourism and fisheries (United Nations, 2024[68]). • Addressing marine pollution is essential for preserving biodiversity and ensuring the health of marine environments (World Bank, 2024[69]). • Enhancing coastal resilience against natural disasters is vital for sustaining economic stability and protecting livelihoods (World Bank, 2016[58]). • SDG 1 (No Poverty) and SDG 2 (Zero Hunger): Sustainable aquaculture and mariculture can help feed a growing and wealthier global population, advancing progress on poverty reduction and food security by 2030. • SDG 8 (Decent Work and Economic Growth) and SDG 13 (Climate Action): Marine-based renewable energy offers new job opportunities and can shift the global energy mix toward clean energy, contributing to economic growth and climate action goals. • SDG 13 (Climate Action) and SDG 16 (Peace, Justice, and Strong Institutions): Preserving the ocean's capacity to regulate the climate and support biodiversity can further advance climate action, while also having a positive impact on climate migration, peace, and stability.
Relevant policy instruments	**Relevant experiences**
• **Holistic Policy Frameworks with a Spatial Perspective:** These frameworks integrate environmental, economic, and social policies to ensure sustainable use of marine resources. They often include coastal master plans or Marine Spatial Plans (MSP) and integrated coastal zone management (ICZM) instruments for ecosystem-based adaptation (Muñoz, 2020[70]). • **Financing and conservation tools:** These tools support the development and conservation of marine and coastal resources through funding mechanisms that encourage sustainable practices. They include grants, loans, and investments to enhance the blue economy's infrastructure and capabilities (e.g. the Caribbean Biodiversity Fund -CBF- and the Caribbean Blue Economy Financing -BLUEfin- aimed to finance conservation efforts and sustainable development) (CBD, 2024[71]; CBF, 2023[72]). • **Regional co-operation and governance:** These mechanisms involve collaborative efforts among Caribbean states to manage shared challenges such as marine resources management (including overfishing, pollution, and habitat destruction). They often include regional treaties and collaborative projects. (e.g. the Eastern Caribbean Regional Ocean Policy).	• **Grenada:** The "Blue Growth Master Plan" is a global first, identifying blue growth opportunities in fisheries, aquaculture, blue biotechnology, renewable energy, research and innovation, including the creation of a Ministry (on Economic Development, Planning, Tourism, Creative Economy, Culture, Agriculture and Lands, Forestry, Marine Resources and Cooperatives) and the "Blue Innovation Institute". It includes improving airport infrastructure, maritime transport, small-scale hotels, marine research, new Marina Communities, and relocating ports to boost shipping (Patil and Dlez, 2016[73]). • **The Bahamas:** The Protected Plan aims to protect near-shore marine resources and has advanced the country's MSP, protecting 17% of its marine area as of 2023 (CBF, 2024[74]). • **Belize:** The ICZM co-ordinates development and conservation across Belize's coastal zone, enhancing ecosystem protection and supporting sustainable activities like eco-tourism and responsible fisheries. It includes data management, coastal planning, water quality monitoring, and sport fishing programs, dividing the coast into nine planning regions (Coastal Zone Belize, 2024[75]). • The **Caribbean Regional Fisheries Mechanism (CRFM)** promotes the responsible use of regional fishery resources for economic sustainability. It facilitates collaboration among 17 member states on overfishing and marine resource management. In 2020, CRFM initiated research on Sargassum seaweed influxes, resulting in a promising liquid-fertilizer prototype now in field trials (CRFM, 2024[76]).

The circular economy can contribute to mitigation and adaptation objectives

Promoting the circular economy is particularly relevant for the service-based economies of the Caribbean. A circular economy approach aims to extend the lifespan of materials, reduce waste by design, enhance resource efficiency, promote innovative sustainable business models and create a balanced relationship between economic activity, environmental stewardship, and social well-being (Circle Economy, 2023[77]). In the Caribbean, the circular economy could contribute to more sustainable tourism, and create quality formal jobs, while reducing emissions and negative externalities (OECD et al., 2022[41]). This model provides a viable alternative to current development strategies and directly addresses the threefold environmental crisis (UNEP, 2023[50]). Table 3.3 provides an overview of policy instruments and relevant experiences to advance the circular economy in the region.

The development of supportive financial mechanisms is crucial. Leveraging environmental, social, and governance funding can attract investments in circular economy projects. Such financial models have proven successful in enhancing corporate profitability and reputation, as well as reducing the cost of debt and financing for circular initiatives.

Clear regulatory frameworks and economic incentives, such as tax benefits and subsidies for businesses adopting sustainable practices, can further stimulate the transition to a circular economy. These measures, combined with comprehensive educational campaigns to raise awareness and build capacity among stakeholders, can create a robust foundation for a thriving circular economy in the Caribbean (Van Hoof, Núñez Reyes and De Miguel, 2023[78]).

Regional co-operation and the establishment of a unified framework can boost the acceleration of a circular economy. Platforms like the Latin American and Caribbean Circular Economy Coalition, facilitate the sharing of best practices and resources among member states. By fostering collaboration, these kinds of initiatives can help streamline efforts and ensure consistency in the implementation of circular economy principles across the region (Van Hoof, Núñez Reyes and De Miguel, 2023[78]; Circular Economy Coalition, 2022[79]).

Table 3.3. The circular economy

Key facts	Relevance for sustainable development
• Transitioning to a circular economy can transform the way societies produce and use goods contributing to mitigating 45% of global GHG emissions (Circular Economy Coalition, 2022[79]). • Caribbean countries produce 13 million tonnes of solid waste every year (AFD, 2023[80]). • Plastics account for 12.4% of municipal solid waste – the fourth largest waste stream in the LAC region (Kaza et al., 2018[81]). The average amount of mismanaged plastic in LAC is 19%, ranging from 2% in the Cayman Islands to 49% in Haiti (Brooks et al., 2020[82]).	• The circular economy can foster sustainable and responsible production and consumption patterns (SDG 12); on water (SDG 6); on energy (SDG 7); on infrastructure, industrialisation and innovation (SDG 9); on sustainable cities and communities (SDG 11); on climate action (SDG 13); and on life on land (SDG 15) (OECD et al., 2022[41]). • The circular economy can generate jobs while reducing dependency on fuel, minerals and metals exports, mitigating exposure to exchange rate fluctuation (UNEP, 2023[50]; Circle Economy, 2023[77]). • The circular economy can help increase adaptation in the Caribbean by enabling communities to adjust to and mitigate the adverse impacts of climate by implementing circular business models (Circular Economy Coalition, 2022[79]).
Relevant policy instruments	**Relevant experiences**
• **Economic and financial incentives** can help boost local entrepreneurship and circular innovation by providing: o **Economic incentives** could include favourable tax or extended producer responsibility schemes, subsidies, tradeable permits or deposit-refund systems. o **Financing incentives** could entail public contests to finance circular business model initiatives or dedicated public budgets. • **Green public procurement**: The public sector can use this strategic tool to purchase goods, services, and works incorporating circular economy principles into the procurement process. Tools include encouraging circular business models, promoting circular construction developments, incorporating secondary materials, and encouraging repair and reuse. Incorporating lifecycle thinking and resource efficiency can significantly reduce waste and environmental impact (OECD et al., 2022[41]).	• **The Latin American and the Caribbean Circular Economy Coalition:** The coalition serves as a platform for regional co-operation, promoting the exchange of best practices and fostering collaboration between governments, businesses, and civil society. It aims to create a shared vision of circular development between all sectors of society. Suriname, the Dominican Republic, and Trinidad and Tobago are taking part (Circular Economy Coalition, 2022[79]). • **Barbados Cleantech Cluster (BLOOM):** As part of its broader work promoting a cleantech industry, the cluster has incubated different start-ups working on the circular economy. In Biotech, BLOOM has explored the creation of bio-resource circularity centres to serve as a role model for other SIDS. Regarding the conception of waste as a resource, BLOOM has developed an app to promote waste minimisation and convert waste into new products (e.g. waste to energy and waste to product approach). BLOOM has also supported the conversion of

- **Regulatory instruments:** These foster legislation and regulation (e.g. adapting waste regulations) to remove potential barriers. They can limit or ban polluting activities (e.g. introducing plastic bans or setting waste reduction targets). They can also promote circular production and consumption (e.g. introducing standards and certification for reused, remanufactured or recycled products).
- **Development of circular data and monitoring tools:** The production, sharing and monitoring of data (e.g. on energy consumption, air quality or waste production) is key to developing circular economy strategies and monitoring their advancements.
- **Promotion of public-private initiatives:** Such partnerships foster close collaborations between the public and private sectors and academia to fund, research and implement circular economy projects. This includes creating a favourable financial and innovation ecosystem that supports circular businesses at different stages of maturity, giving micro, small and medium-sized enterprises an important role.
- **Co-operation and knowledge sharing:** These initiatives promote education and research through training programs, circular economy observatories, and knowledge networks. They also provide information instruments such as eco-labelling to aid responsible purchasing and facilitate co-operation via public-private partnerships, circular hotspots, and collaboration across value chains (OECD et al., 2022[41]).

organic waste materials into biological soil treatment and crop protection solutions (Red Diamond Compost) and the use of local waste streams (e.g. Sargassum seaweed, cassava and sweet potato peels) as a raw material for biodegradable plastics (*EcoMycö*) (Bloom, 2024[83]).

- **Dominican Republic Comprehensive Management of Solid Waste Law**: This legislation, passed in 2020, addresses the environmental challenges of improper waste management by promoting reduction at the source, prioritising reuse, recycling, valuation of waste, and ensuring the principle of "polluter pays". The law also emphasises the need for collaboration between government and stakeholders, development of adequate waste management infrastructure and formalisation of informal waste collectors. Mechanisms should be in place to guarantee these objectives are fulfilled (Osaka Blue Ocean Vision, 2024[84]).
- **Project Caribe Circular:** This aims to prevent plastic waste from entering the Caribbean Sea and promote a circular economy through regional co-operation. Funded by the European Union and Germany's Federal Ministry of Economic Cooperation and Development (BMZ), it gathers several Central American and Caribbean countries, including the Dominican Republic and Belize. The project aligns with the G20 Marine Litter Action Plan and focuses on sustainable environmental practices, economic recovery, and job creation (SICA, 2024[85]).

Sustainable tourism is vital to balance economic growth with environmental preservation

Tourism is a cornerstone of the Caribbean economy, accounting on average for 25.4% of Caribbean countries' GDP between 2015-19, and employing 2.35 million (13.4% of total jobs) in 2021 (WTTC, 2022[86]; ECLAC, 2023[87]) (Figure 3.9). The sector's contribution to GDP varies significantly across Caribbean countries, ranging from 3.2% (Suriname) to 42.8% (Grenada). Over the next decade, the sector is expected to grow at an average annual rate of 5.5%, more than double the projected growth rate of the overall economy at 2.4% (WTTC, 2022[86]) This presents a significant opportunity for the Caribbean to leverage sustainable tourism, which can attract higher-spending tourists and add greater value to the local economy. The Caribbean's unique natural beauty and commitment to environmental preservation make it well-positioned to become a leading destination for sustainable tourism, enhancing the sector's long-term viability and resilience.

Figure 3.9. Tourism sector contribution to GDP, average 2015-19

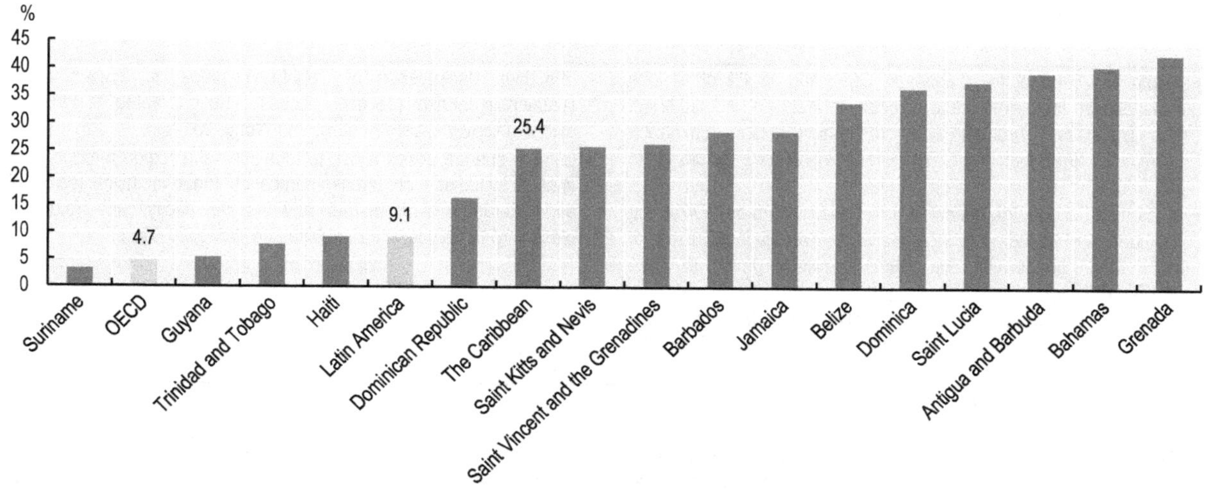

Note: The Latin American average includes 16 countries: Argentina, the Plurinational State of Bolivia, Brazil, Chile, Colombia, Costa Rica, Ecuador, El Salvador, Guatemala, Honduras, Nicaragua, Panama, Paraguay, Peru, Uruguay and Venezuela. The OECD average includes Australia, Austria, Chile, Czechia, France, Iceland, Japan, Kora, Luxembourg, Mexico, Norway, Slovak Republic, Slovenia, Spain and Sweden.
Source: Authors' elaboration based on (Gomez Garcia et al., 2021[88]; OECD, 2020[89]).

StatLink https://stat.link/vgjcta

Several policy instruments and strategic initiatives can help advance sustainable tourism development in the Caribbean. National sustainable tourism policies can set a vision and outline objectives to achieve sustainability (CTO, 2020[90]). Legislation can support sustainable tourism and climate strategies. Finally, promoting a supportive tax and incentive environment can encourage investments and optimise public spending to ensure future tourism investments are sustainable. Some examples of the latter include simplifying tax compliance; providing tax benefits; and expanding incentives for sustainable practices and climate responsiveness, such as mandatory Environmental Impact Statements for all tourism projects (CTO, 2020[90]).

Several Caribbean nations have made significant strides in sustainable tourism (Table 3.4). The Sustainable Development Master Plan of Andros Island in The Bahamas aims to transform the island into a model for sustainable ecotourism. To that end, it would leverage its natural assets, such as national parks and unique attractions like blue holes and underwater caves. Ultimately, the master plan would guide sustainable tourism investment and decision making over the next 25 years (CTO, 2020[90]). In Belize, the National Tourism Council Act establishes an autonomous council to enhance tourism management, ensuring collaborative public-private sector efforts to sustain tourism practices (CTO, 2020[90]). In Saint Kitts and Nevis, the Sustainable Destination Council (SDC), established in 2013, fosters public-private partnerships (PPPs) to enhance sustainable tourism. The SDC engages stakeholders to support initiatives like water conservation and plastic waste reduction. It was instrumental in creating the Heart of Saint Kitts Foundation, which collaborates with local businesses to promote sustainability and protect the island's natural and cultural assets (CTO, 2020[90]).

Table 3.4. Sustainable tourism

Key facts	Relevance for sustainable development
• A total of 25.4% of the Caribbean GDP, and 13.4% of all jobs depended on tourism in the Caribbean, in 2021 (WTTC, 2022[86]). The Travel and Tourism GDP contribution varies from 3.2% (Suriname) to as high as 42.8% (Grenada) (Gomez Garcia et al., 2021[88]). • In the next decade, the impact of travel and tourism on GDP in the Caribbean is forecasted to increase at an average annual rate of 5.5%, more than double the overall economic growth of 2.4% (WTTC, 2022[86]). • Caribbean reef-building corals have declined by 50% since the late 1970s (when systematic reef monitoring was introduced) (Cramer et al., 2020[91]).	• The high dependence of Caribbean states on tourism makes sustainable tourism practices necessary to guarantee its long-term viability (Acevedo, LaFramboise and Wong, 2017[92]). • Climate change poses a risk to tourism in the region through direct impacts including more intense hurricanes, droughts, rising sea- levels and alteration of terrestrial and marine ecosystems (e.g. coral bleaching) (Acevedo, LaFramboise and Wong, 2017[92]).
Relevant policy instruments	**Relevant experiences**
• **National Sustainable Tourism Policy:** These frameworks outline a vision that recognises the national significance of tourism and states the commitment to sustainable tourism development (CTO, 2020[90]). • **Legislative support for tourism growth:** Updated laws support sustainable tourism and climate strategies, streamlining frameworks to encourage investment, and monitoring public spending to optimise future investments in tourism (CTO, 2020[90]). • **Promoting supportive taxes and incentives to promote a good business environment:** Key measures include simplifying tax compliance, enhancing tax benefits awareness, and expanding incentives for sustainable practices and climate responsiveness. It advocates for incentives for energy-efficient technologies and mandates environmental impact statements for all tourism projects. The policy aims to balance direct and national investment in tourism, ensuring it aligns with sustainable development principles. (CTO, 2020[90]).	• **Bahamas Sustainable Development Master Plan for Andros Island:** The plan aims to transform Andros Island into a model for sustainable ecotourism by utilising its natural and recreational assets, including national parks and other attractions like blue holes, underwater caves, and birding opportunities. It provides a framework to guide investment and decision making in sustainable tourism on the island for the next 25 years (CTO, 2020[90]). • **The Belize National Tourism Council Act:** This autonomous council in Belize, chaired by the Minister of Tourism, aims to enhance tourism management and development. Including members from key governmental ministries and various tourism industry sectors, the council develops, co-ordinates, and monitors policies and strategies for efficient tourism practices, aligning public and private sector efforts to support and sustain the nation's tourism industry. (CTO, 2020[90]). • **Saint Kitts and Nevis' Sustainable Destination Council (SDC):** Established in 2013, the SDC promotes sustainable tourism through public-private partnerships. It protects the environment, culture, and local livelihoods by engaging stakeholders and supporting initiatives like water conservation and plastic waste reduction. The SDC also founded the Heart of St. Kitts Foundation to collaborate with local businesses on sustainability projects to safeguard natural and cultural assets (CTO, 2020[90]).

Sustainable transport can enhance accessibility, connectivity, and economic growth

The transition to sustainable transport is another important objective for the economic and environmental future of the Caribbean. Fuel imports account for approximately 10% of the region's GDP on average, with the transport sector consuming 30% of these imports (CCREEE, 2024[93]). Sustainable transportation can reduce the dependency on fuel imports, promote energy diversification and efficiency, increase air quality, improve daily commutes to enhance the quality of life in the Caribbean and reduce GHG emissions (CCREEE, 2024[93]).

Successful strategies to promote sustainable transport would improve the efficiency and resilience of transport systems, accessibility, and connectivity (United Nations, 2021[94]). They require the design and implementation of strategic policy frameworks, at the national and regional level; the broader adoption of digital technologies and digital transformation (e.g. using the Internet of Things, artificial intelligence, and blockchain) to enhance efficiency and integration (United Nations, 2021[94]); and higher investment in multimodal and modern transport solutions. The harmonisation of regulatory standards at the regional level encourages cross-border co-ordination and facilitates smoother transport and logistics (Monios and Wilmsmeier, 2020[95]) (Chapter 6). Table 3.5 provides an overview of relevant policy instruments and experiences to advance sustainable transport in the region.

Table 3.5. Sustainable transport

Key facts	Relevance for sustainable development
• Fuel imports account for roughly 10% of GDP, with 30% of total fuel consumed by the transport sector (CCREEE, 2024[93]). • Transportation accounted for 23% of global GHG emissions in 2019 (Jaramillo et al., 2022[96]).	• **Reducing fuel import dependency**: This promotes energy diversification and efficiency, improving the quality of life in the Caribbean (CCREEE, 2024[93]). • **Digital transformation in transport**: Digital transformation (Internet of things, artificial intelligence, blockchain) in transport can enhance efficiency and integration, supporting sustainable development (United Nations, 2021[94]). • **Multimodal transport solutions and infrastructure investments**: These can enhance accessibility, connectivity, and economic growth (United Nations, 2021[94]). • **Modernisation of maritime transport:** This boosts operational efficiency and resilience against environmental and economic shocks (United Nations, 2021[94]). • **Improved transport systems:** These contribute to reducing GHG emissions, aligning with SDGs (United Nations, 2021[94]).
Relevant policy instruments	**Relevant experiences**
• **National Transportation Comprehensive Plans:** These can provide strategic frameworks for the development and management of a country's transport infrastructure and services. They address current and future transportation needs, promoting economic growth, and enhancing connectivity. The plans are important to monitor and develop transportation in alignment with other infrastructure. • **Tax incentives:** Offering tax incentives can support investments in multimodal transport solutions, to link maritime, air and land transport, enhancing accessibility and connectivity (Gillingham and Stock, 2018[97]). • **Regional policy harmonisation:** Developing regional policies to harmonise regulatory standards, which encourages cross-border co-ordination and facilitates smoother transport and logistics operations (Monios and Wilmsmeier, 2020[95]).	• **IMO Carib-Smart**: This is a regional initiative by the International Maritime Organisation for safe, secure, efficient and reliable transport of goods across the region, while minimising pollution, maximising energy efficiency and ensuring resource conservation (IMO, 2022[98]). • **Belize National Transportation Master Plan:** The Department of Public/Private-sector Dialogue in the Office of the Prime Minister of Belize launched this master plan in 2018. Funded by the Inter-American Development Bank, it aims to establish current and future transportation demands, while aligning its goals with the development and sustainability goals of the country, and setting strategies and policies for all transportation sectors (Department of Public-Private Sector Dialogue, 2018[99]).

Nature-based solutions as a policy tool for climate adaptation and local economic development

The Caribbean region is progressively incorporating Nature-based Solutions (NbS) to address climate change, enhance sustainable development, and increase resilience to environmental challenges. NbS such as wetland restoration and forest conservation, are increasingly acknowledged for their ability to offer robust natural defenses against climate risks (OECD, 2024[26]). These strategies play a crucial role in mitigating the impacts of climate change and addressing associated threats.

NbS contribute to biodiversity conservation, climate adaptation, and local economic development while helping to solve issues such as flooding, lack of access to water, and land sliding (WRI, 2021[100]; UNDP, 2021[101]). Integrating NbS into national and regional development plans can ensure these solutions are considered in infrastructure and urban planning. For example, NbS in the water and sanitation sectors can improve water quality and supply while mitigating flood risks. The Bahamas' National Biodiversity and Strategy Plan has successfully restored mangroves and seagrasses, augmenting the number of fish stock available while reducing the risks of coastal flooding during storms (CBD, 2024[102]). Moreover, international biodiversity funds, such as the Green Climate Fund (GCF), are financing NbS projects in Saint Lucia, helping to reforest degraded land and restore wetlands, improving the access to water while transferring knowledge on sustainable agriculture practices (GCF, 2022[103]). NbS should be considered alongside other solutions due to their ability to provide multiple benefits, such as enhancing biodiversity, supporting livelihoods, and offering cost-effective and sustainable protection against climate risks, especially in urban contexts. NbS and circular economy principles could help transform sargassum, a major threat to local ecosystems and the tourism and fishery sectors, into an economic opportunity. Sargassum transformed into different by-products such as fertilisers, raw material for biodegradable plastics, cosmetics, electricity and biomass could become a resource to boost local economies' resilience. Table 3.6 provides an overview of relevant policy instruments and experiences to advance the use of NbS in the region.

Table 3.6. Nature-based Solutions

Key facts	Relevance for sustainable development
• By 2030, nature-based solutions (NbS) can mitigate up to 37% of the CO_2 needed to keep global temperature rise under 2°C (Griscom et al., 2017[104]). • Coastal ecosystems, such as mangroves and coral reefs, can reduce wave energy by 71%, protecting coastal communities from storm surges (Narayan et al., 2016[105]). • NbS could generate an estimated USD 10 trillion of business opportunities and could create 395 million jobs globally in 2030 (WEF, 2020[106]).	• **Enhancing biodiversity:** NbS can help preserve and restore biodiversity, ensuring ecosystem health and resilience. • **Climate adaptation:** NbS help communities adapt to climate change by protecting against floods, stabilising shorelines, and maintaining water quality. • **Economic benefits:** NbS provide economic benefits through tourism, fisheries, and reduced disaster recovery costs (WEF, 2020[106]).
Relevant policy instruments	**Relevant experiences**
• **Integration of green and grey infrastructures:** This involves integrating the urban areas' infrastructure with natural resources. • **Regional Frameworks for Ecosystem Management:** These are common guidelines for implementing climate resilience projects, including NbS (CCCCC, 2019[107]). • **National Biodiversity Strategies and Action Plans:** These are national strategies to protect and enhance biodiversity, incorporating NbS (CBD, 2024[71]). • **Financial instruments to support ecosystem protection and resilience:** Funding and support for Caribbean countries to implement NbS projects for climate resilience and sustainable development (GCF, 2022[103]).	• Urban green spaces: Jamaica has used green infrastructure for the redevelopment of urban parks applying an Ecosystem-based Adaptation (EbA) approach and introducing multifunctional green spaces such as recreational areas, community gardens and flood management systems (City Adapt Jamaica, 2024[108]). • **Mangrove restoration and coastal resilience:** The Caribbean Community Climate Change Centre (CCCCC) has implemented NbS projects, including artificial reef installations in Barbados, enhancing marine habitats and coastal protection. Similarly, national biodiversity strategies and action plans in The Bahamas focus on mangrove and seagrass restoration, boosting fish populations and mitigating coastal flooding (CBD, 2024[102]; CCCCC, 2024[109]). • **Reforestation and wetland restoration:** The G-CREWS project in Grenada focuses on reforestation and wetland restoration to enhance water resources and reduce climate vulnerability. Similarly, the Green Climate Fund supports reforestation and wetland restoration in Saint Lucia, aiming to improve water security, mitigate landslides, and boost agricultural productivity (GCF, 2022[103]; GIZ, 2019[110]).

Digital transformation is a pivotal element in the region's sustainable development agenda

Digital transformation can drive economic growth, improve governance, and enhance resilience against natural disasters, ultimately leading to a more prosperous and sustainable future for the Caribbean. In 2021, the Caribbean had 78% of internet users, compared to 72% in Latin America and 89.3% in the OECD.

The relevance of digital transformation is particularly significant for the Caribbean due to its unique geographic and economic context. As a region composed largely of SIDS, digital connectivity can help overcome physical barriers, providing access to global markets, education, and services that their geographic isolation would otherwise limit. However, the cost of digital infrastructure can be high particularly for small countries, posing a challenge that requires innovative solutions.

Targeted policy instruments and strategic initiatives are essential to drive digital transformation effectively. At least 11 Caribbean countries have already developed policy frameworks for digital development (Alexander, Døhl Diouf and Prescod, 2023[111]). Digital skills and training programmes help improve digital literacy and skills among the population. In Barbados, digital literacy programmes contribute to bridging the digital divide and equip the workforce with the necessary skills to thrive in a digital economy. Table 3.7

provides an overview of relevant policy instruments and experiences to advance the digital transformation in the region.

Table 3.7. Digital transformation

Key facts	Relevance for sustainable development
• In 2023, the Caribbean had 78% of internet users (ECLAC, 2024[112]). • At least 11 Caribbean countries have already developed policy frameworks for digital development (Alexander, Døhl Diouf and Prescod, 2023[111]).	• **Economic growth:** Digitalisation can significantly boost economic productivity and create new job opportunities. Due to the high reliability on tourism, it is important to keep up with consumer trends and the use of online tools. • **Governance**: Digital government services can enhance transparency, reduce corruption, and improve public service efficiency. • **Resilience:** Due to the high vulnerability to natural disasters of the region, it is important to have reliable ICT infrastructures, both for maintaining access to communication services, and having access to emergency awareness tools.
Relevant policy instruments	**Relevant experiences**
• Digital skills training programmes: These programmes aim to improve digital literacy and skills among the population to support the digital economy. • Public-private partnerships (PPPs): PPPs in digitalisation projects can leverage private sector expertise and investment to accelerate digital transformation. • **Regulations**: Development and enforcement of regulations can facilitate e-commerce, data protection, cybersecurity, and electronic transactions. • **Innovation incentives**: These offer tax incentives, grants or subsidies for start-ups and businesses focusing on digital innovation and technology. • Metrics and benchmarks: Establish clear metrics and benchmarks to monitor the progress and impact of digital transformation initiatives.	• Barbados' Digital Literacy Programme: Barbados has implemented comprehensive digital skills training programmes targeting young people and professionals to enhance their digital capabilities and support the growing tech industry (TVET, 2024[113]). • CARCIP Project: The Caribbean Regional Communications Infrastructure Program implemented broadband infrastructure in Saint Lucia, Grenada, and Saint Vincent and the Grenadines through a pioneering PPP. It leveraged approximately USD 45 million to increase high-quality Internet for 22 500 residents (45% female) in Saint Lucia, 25 200 people (54% female) in Grenada, and 20 586 individuals (53.7% female) in Saint Vincent and the Grenadines, providing fibre optic connections to residences and businesses. The three countries collaborated to enhance digital public services and internet access for education, including Government Wide Area Networks (GWANs) and a subsea cable. This joint tender approach helped achieve economies of scale, resulting in lower costs and improved service quality (World Bank, 2022[114]). • **Antigua and Barbuda's** Digital Transformation Strategy: The government has adopted a strategy to digitise all public services, enhance cybersecurity measures, and promote ICT education by 2030. Initiatives include the establishment of ICT centres and digital skills training programmes (UNDP, 2024[115]).

Key policy messages

This chapter has underscored the Caribbean's unique vulnerabilities to climate change. However, it also highlights opportunities for transformation through proactive adaptation and sustainable development strategies. Context-specific socioeconomic characteristics, challenges and possible solutions call for tailored approaches across Caribbean countries. However, some overarching considerations as those presented in Box 3.2 can help countries establish effective "policy menus" and achieve a good policy mix.

Box 3.2. Key policy messages

Build resilience to address high exposure to climate threats

- Design and implement adaptation measures to tackling climate vulnerabilities and fostering climate resilience.
- Invest in resilient infrastructure to protect people and promote economic stability, as it significantly reduces GDP losses by minimising the destruction of capital during natural disasters.
- Integrate climate change adaptation with disaster risk reduction measures, such as EWS and civil protection systems, to enhance countries' capacity to mitigate the economic, environmental, and social impacts of extreme climate events.
- Implement NAPs and other policy instruments, including NDCs and LTS to help integrate adaptation into national planning while collecting, developing, adopting, and implementing adaptation actions.

Harness the potential of rich biodiversity and unique natural endowments

- Advance from a vulnerability-focused perspective to identifying strategic areas of opportunity that a green and just transition can bring to the Caribbean while advancing climate-resilience.
- Transform the region's production matrix to foster sustainability, create quality jobs, enhance well-being and address climate-related challenges.
- Foster opportunities in strategic areas such as energy transition, the blue economy, the circular economy, sustainable tourism, sustainable transport, nature-based solutions and digital transformation.

Notes

[1] Transition risks refers more specifically to the financial risks that could arise from the transition to a lower-carbon economy. For insurance firms, this risk factor is mainly about the potential repricing of carbon-intensive financial assets, and the speed at which any such repricing might occur. To a lesser extent, insurers may also need to adapt to potential impacts on the liability side resulting from reductions in insurance premiums in carbon-intensive sectors (IDB, 2016[40]).

[2] There is still no single accepted definition of the blue economy. Four selected definitions conceive the blue economy as: i) the sum of the economic activities of ocean-based industries, and the assets, goods and services of marine ecosystems (OECD, 2024[56]); ii) the sustainable use of ocean resources for economic growth, improved livelihoods, and jobs while preserving the health of ocean ecosystem (World Bank,

2016[58]); iii) all economic activities related to oceans, seas and coasts covering a wide range of interlinked established and emerging sectors (EU, 2023[117]); and iv) a range of economic sectors and related policies that together determine whether the use of ocean resources is sustainable (UNDESA, 2019[118]).

References

AFD (2023), *Plagued by plastic, Caribbean countries team up with partners to forge a greener future*, Agence Françaice de Dévelopment, https://www.afd.fr/en/actualites/plagued-plastic-caribbean-countries-team-partners-forge-greener-future. [80]

Alexander, D., L. Døhl Diouf and K. Prescod (2023), *Digital Inclusion in the Caribbean Digital Transformation Frameworks and Initiatives*, Economic Commission for Latin America and the Caribbean, https://repositorio.cepal.org/server/api/core/bitstreams/1528cfb4-dec8-4655-9497-1467dfd4f14e/content. [111]

Alleyne, T. (ed.) (2017), *Caribbean Tourism in the Global Marketplace: Trends, Drivers, and Challenges*, International Monetary Fund, https://doi.org/10.5089/9781484315194.071. [92]

Atlantic Council (2023), *A roadmap for the Caribbean's energy transition*, https://www.atlanticcouncil.org/in-depth-research-reports/issue-brief/a-roadmap-for-the-caribbeans-energy-transition/#challenges. [42]

Bleeker, A. et al. (2021), *Advancing gender equality in environmental migration and disaster*, United Nations, https://kmhub.iom.int/sites/default/files/publicaciones/advancing_gender_equality_in_environmental_migration_and_disaster_displacement_in_the_caribbean.pdf. [11]

Bloom (2024), *Homepage*, Barbados Cleantech Cluster, https://bloomcluster.com/. [83]

Brooks et al. (2020), *Plastic Waste Management and Leakage in Latin America and the Caribbean*, Inter-American Development Bank, https://doi.org/10.18235/0002873. [82]

Business View (2023), *Dominica Reaches 35% of its total target of 5,000 resilient homes by 2030*, Business View Caribbean, https://businessviewcaribbean.com/category/best-practices-in-business-economic-development/. [30]

CAF (2021), *Blue Economy Opportunities for Revival in the Caribbean*, Development Bank of Latin America and the Caribbean, https://www.caf.com/en/knowledge/views/2021/10/blue-economy-opportunities-for-revival-in-the-caribbean/. [59]

Cashman, A. and M. Nagdee (2017), "Impacts of Climate Change on Settlements and Infrastructure in the Coastal and Marine Environments of Caribbean Small Island Development States (SIDS)", *Science Review*, pp. 155-173, https://assets.publishing.service.gov.uk/media/5a82c330ed915d74e623781c/11._Settlements_and_Infrastructure_combined.docx.pdf. [31]

CBD (2024), *Bahamas Country Profile*, Convention on Biological Diversity, https://www.cbd.int/countries/profile?country=bs. [102]

CBD (2024), *National Biodiversity Strategies and Action Plans*, Convention on Biological Diversity, https://www.cbd.int/nbsap. [71]

CBF (2024), *Bahamas Protected Area Fund (BPAF)*, Caribbean Biodiversity Fund, https://caribbeanbiodiversityfund.org/wp-content/uploads/2023/03/BPAF-NCTF-fact-sheet_Mar2024.pdf. [74]

CBF (2023), *Caribbean Blue Economy Finance*, Caribbean Biodiversity Fund, https://caribbeanbiodiversityfund.org/wp-content/uploads/2023/10/Caribbean-BLUEFin-Fact-Sheet_Oct2023.pdf. [72]

CCCCC (2024), *Ongoing Projects*, Caribbean Community Climate Change Center, https://www.caribbeanclimate.bz/blog/category/on-going-projects/. [109]

CCCCC (2019), *CCCCC Launches Climate Risk Management Framework Project*, Caribbean Community Climate Change Centre, https://www.caribbeanclimate.bz/blog/2019/09/16/ccccc-launches-climate-risk-management-framework-project/. [107]

CCREEE (2024), *Making the Transition: Challenges and Opportunities*, Carribean Centre for Renewable Energy and Energy Efficiency, https://www.ccreee.org/blog/making-the-transition/#:~:text=Available%20data%20shows%20that%20nine,import%2090%25%20of%20their%20energy. [48]

CCREEE (2024), *Sustainable Transport Programme*, Caribbean Centre for Renewable Energy and Energy Efficiency, https://www.ccreee.org/our-work/sustainable-transport-programme/. [93]

CDEMA (2024), *Early Warning Systems (EWS) Project*, Caribbean Disaster Emergency Management Agency, https://www.cdema.org/index.php/early-warning-systems-ews-project. [34]

Circle Economy (2023), *Circularity gap report Latin America and the Caribbean*, Commissioned by ECLAC, IDB, IDB Invest, UNEP and UNIDO. Circle Economy, Amsterdam, https://circularity-gap.world/lac. [77]

Circular Economy Coalition (2022), *Circular Economy in Latin America and The Caribbean: A Shared Vision*, Circular Economy Coalition, https://coalicioneconomiacircular.org/wp-content/uploads/2022/02/ENGLISH-Circular-economy-in-Latin-America-and-the-Caribbean.pdf. [79]

City Adapt Jamaica (2024), *Guidelines on urban and peri-urban Forestry in Jamaica*, Jamaica's Forestry Department, https://www.forestry.gov.jm/resourcedocs/Guidelines_on_Urban_and_Peri-urban_Forestry_in_Jamaica_CityAdapt_Guidelines.pdf. [108]

Climate Watch (2024), *Climate Watch [database]*, https://www.climatewatchdata.org/ghg-emissions?end_year=2021&regions=ATG%2CBHS%2CBRB%2CDOM%2CGRD%2CGUY%2CHTI%2CJAM%2CKNA%2CLCA%2CVCT%2CSUR%2CTTO%2CDMA&start_year=1990. [23]

Coastal Zone Belize (2024), *Belize Coastal Zone*, Coastal Zone Belize, https://www.coastalzonebelize.org/. [75]

Cramer et al. (2020), "Widespread loss of Caribbean acroporid corals was underway before coral bleaching and disease outbreaks", *Sciences Advances*, https://doi.org/10.1126/sciadv.aax9395. [91]

CRFM (2024), “Field trials on the horizon for Sargassum-derived fertilizer”, Press Release, 12 April, Caribbean Regional Fisheries Mechanism, https://www.crfm.int/index.php?option=com_k2&view=itemlist&task=tag&tag=sargassum%20products%20for%20climate%20resilience%20project. [76]

CSGM/UWI (2020), *The State of the Caribbean Climate*, The University of West Indies, http://socc.mona.uwi.edu/sites/default/files/The%20State%20of%20the%20Caribbean%20Climate%20Report.pdf . [2]

CTO (2020), *Caribbean Sustainable Tourism Policy and Development Framework*, Caribbean Tourism Organization, https://www.onecaribbean.org/wp-content/uploads/2020-CSTPF-Final-for-Design-and-Translation-July-31-2020.pdf. [90]

Department of Public-Private Sector Dialogue (2018), *Comprehensive National Transportation Master Plan for Belize*, Government of Belize, https://edc.gov.bz/wp-content/uploads/2020/12/5.-CNTMP-Final-Report-April-201807220714.pdf. [99]

Development Bank of Jamaica Limited (2024), *Jamaica Wigton Windfarm*, Jamaica Development Bank, https://dbankjm.com/wigton-wind-farm/. [55]

ECLAC (2024), *Observatorio de Desarrollo Digital (ODD) based on World Telecommunication/ICT Indicators Database July 2023 and the Bank of Household Surveys (BADEHOG), International Telecommunication Union (ITU) and ECLAC, 2000 to 2022*, http://www.eclac.org/. [112]

ECLAC (2023), *CEPALSTAT*, (database), https://statistics.cepal.org/portal/cepalstat/index.html?lang=es (accessed on 1 October 2024). [87]

ECLAC (2020), *Building a New Future: Transformative Recovery with Equality and Sustainability*, United Nations, https://www.cepal.org/sites/default/files/publication/files/46226/S2000665_en.pdf. [47]

EIB (2021), *Assessing climate change risks at the country level: the EIB scoring model*, European Investment Bank, https://www.eib.org/attachments/efs/economics_working_paper_2021_03_en.pdf. [24]

EM-DAT (2024), *EM-DAT Database*, EM-DAT, https://doc.emdat.be/. [4]

EU (2023), *The EU blue economy report 2023, Publications Office of the European Union, 2023*, European Commission: Directorate-General for Maritime Affairs and Fisheries, Joint Research Centre, https://data.europa.eu/doi/10.2771/7151. [117]

EUROSTAT (2024), *Electricity Price Statistics [database]*, EUROSTAT, https://ec.europa.eu/eurostat/statistics-explained/index.php?title=Electricity_price_statistics. [49]

GASCO (2022), *Green infrastructure: how building with nature can help human habitats*, https://ngc.co.tt/wp-content/uploads/2023/02/Green-Infrastructure.pdf. [46]

GCF (2022), *Annual Results Report 2021*, Green Climate Fund, https://www.greenclimate.fund/annual-results-report-2021. [103]

Gillingham, K. and J. Stock (2018), “The Cost of Reducing Greenhouse Gas Emissions”, *Journal of Economic Perspectives*, Vol. 32/4, pp. 53-72, https://www.aeaweb.org/articles?id=10.1257/jep.32.4.53. [97]

GIZ (2019), *Making water management and use in Grenada climate-resilient*, GIZ, https://www.giz.de/en/worldwide/120411.html. [110]

Gomez Garcia, O. et al. (2021), *Caribbean Quarterly Bulletin: Volume 10: Issue 1*, Inter-American Development Bank, Washington, DC, https://doi.org/10.18235/0003265. [88]

Government of Barbados (2024), *Barbados Clean Energy Dashboard*, Government of Barbados, https://energy.gov.bb/dashboard/. [52]

Government of Commonwealth of Dominica (2022), *Dominica Climate Resilience and Recovery Plan 2020-2030*, Government of Commonwealth of Dominica, https://odm.gov.dm/wp-content/uploads/2022/02/CRRP-Final-042020.pdf. [29]

Government of Saint Lucia (2018), *Saint Lucia's Sectoral*, Government of Saint Lucia, https://www.undp.org/latin-america/publications/saint-lucias-sectoral-adaptation-strategy-and-action-plan-water-sector-water-sasap-2018-2028. [37]

Griscom et al. (2017), *Nature Climate Solutions*, PNAS, https://doi.org/10.1073/pnas.1710465114. [104]

IDB (2020), *Sustainable Energy Paths for the Caribbean*, Inter-American Development Bank, https://doi.org/10.18235/0002236. [39]

IDB (2016), *Stranded Assets: A Climate Risk Challenge*, https://doi.org/10.18235/0012646. [40]

IMF (2021), *Dominica: Disaster Resilience Strategy*, https://www.imf.org/-/media/Files/Publications/CR/2021/English/1DMAEA2021001.ashx. [28]

IMF (2005), *Transcript of an IMF Economic Forum - Tracking Grenada's Recovery: Six Months after Hurricane Ivan*, https://www.imf.org/en/News/Articles/2015/09/28/04/54/tr052505. [14]

IMO (2022), *Sustainable Maritime Transport in Caribbean: Carib-Smart*, International Maritime Organization, https://www.imo.org/en/MediaCentre/PressBriefings/pages/CaribSMARTPreparatoryPhase.aspx. [98]

IOM (2023), *Data Report: Trends in Caribbean Migration and Mobility*, https://rosanjose.iom.int/sites/g/files/tmzbdl1446/files/documents/2023-07/data-report-trends-in-caribbean-migration-and-mobility.pdf. [20]

IPCC (2019), *IPCC Special Report on the Ocean and Cryosphere in a Changing Climate*, Cambridge University Press, https://doi.org/10.1017/9781009157964. [57]

Jafino, B. et al. (2020), *Revised Estimates of the Impact of Climate Change on Extreme Poverty by 2030*, World Bank, https://doi.org/10.1596/1813-9450-9417. [18]

Jaramillo, P. et al. (2022), *Transport*, Cambridge University Press, https://doi.org/10.1017/9781009157926.012. [96]

Kaza, S. et al. (2018), *What a Waste 2.0: A Global Snapshot of Solid Waste Management to 2050*, World Bank, https://doi.org/10.1596/978-1-4648-1329-0. [81]

Monios, J. and G. Wilmsmeier (2020), "Deep adaptation to climate change in the maritime transport sector – a new paradigm for maritime economics?", *Maritime Policy and Management*, pp. 1-20, https://doi.org/10.1080/03088839.2020.1752947. [95]

Muñoz, J. (2020), "Progress of coastal management in Latin America and the Caribbean", *Ocean and Coastal Management*, Vol. 184/105009, https://doi.org/10.1016/j.ocecoaman.2019.105009. [70]

Mycoo, M. and M. Wairiu (2022), *Small Islands*, IPCC, https://www.ipcc.ch/report/ar6/wg2/downloads/report/IPCC_AR6_WGII_Chapter15.pdf. [67]

Narayan et al. (2016), "The Effectiveness, Costs and Coastal Protection Benefits of Natural and Nature-Based Defences", *Plos One*, https://doi.org/10.1371/journal.pone.0154735. [105]

ND-GAIN (2021), *ND-GAIN [database]*, University of Notre Dame, https://gain.nd.edu/our-work/country-index/rankings/. [1]

NEMO (2024), *National Emergency Development Plan*, Saint Lucia National Emergency Development Plan, https://nemo.gov.lc/Disaster-Management/National-Emergency-Management-Plan/National-Plans. [33]

OECD (2024), *Nature-based solutions and climate-resilient infrastructure*, OECD, https://www.oecd.org/en/topics/sub-issues/nature-based-solutions-and-climate-resilient-infrastructure.html. [26]

OECD (2024), *The Blue Economy in CIties and Regions*, OECD Urban Studies, OECD Publishing, Paris, https://doi.org/10.1787/bd929b7d-en. [56]

OECD (2023), *SIGI 2023 Global Report: Gender Equality in Times of Crisis*, Social Institutions and Gender Index, OECD Publishing, Paris, https://doi.org/10.1787/4607b7c7-en. [22]

OECD (2023), *Towards Climate Resilience and Neutrality in Latin America and the Caribbean: Key Policy Priorities*, OECD Publishing, Paris, https://doi.org/10.1787/278e52e8-en. [3]

OECD (2022), *Development Strategy Assessment of the Eastern Caribbean*, OECD Publishing, Paris, https://doi.org/10.1787/f1566c7a-en. [64]

OECD (2020), *OECD Tourism Trends and Policies 2020*, OECD Publishing, Paris, https://doi.org/10.1787/6b47b985-en. [89]

OECD (2020), *Sustainable Ocean for All: Harnessing the Benefits of Sustainable Ocean Economies for Developing Countries*, The Development Dimension, OECD Publishing, Paris, https://doi.org/10.1787/bede6513-en. [62]

OECD et al. (2022), *Latin American Economic Outlook 2022: Towards a Green and Just Transition*, OECD Publishing, Paris, https://doi.org/10.1787/3d5554fc-en. [41]

OECD et al. (2021), *Latin American Economic Outlook 2021: Working Together for a Better Recovery*, OECD Publishing, Paris, https://doi.org/10.1787/5fedabe5-en. [21]

Osaka Blue Ocean Vision (2024), *Dominican Republic: Actions and progress on marine plastic litter*, Osaka Blue Ocean VIsion, https://g20mpl.org/partners/dominican-republic. [84]

Parliament of Barbados (2022), *Comprehensive Disaster Management Policy for Barbados*, Parliament of Barbados, https://www.barbadosparliament.com/uploads/sittings/attachments/8c199056cbd882f5ac61c3cb71cec944.pdf. [17]

Patil, P. and S. Dlez (2016), *Grenada - Blue growth coastal master plan*, World Bank Group, https://documents.worldbank.org/en/publication/documents-reports/documentdetail/358651480931239134/grenada-blue-growth-coastal-master-plan. [73]

Rhiney, K. (2015), *Geographies of Caribbean vulnerability in a challenging climate: Issues and trends.*, https://doi.org/10.1111/gec3.12199. [8]

Roy, D. (ed.) (2023), *How the Caribbean Is Building Climate Resilience*, Council on Foreign Relations, https://www.cfr.org/backgrounder/how-caribbean-building-climate-resilience. [13]

Shortte, F. (2013), *Promoting Sustainable Fish Trade between CARICOM States and their Trading Partners the Eu and US: The Case of St. Vincent and the Grenadines*, United Nations - Nippon Foundation Fellowship, https://www.un.org/depts/los/nippon/unnff_programme_home/fellows_pages/fellows_papers/Shortte_1314_StVin.pdf. [63]

SICA (2024), *Proyecto Caribe Circular*, Sisteman de la Integración Centroamericana, https://www.sica.int/caribecircular/que-es-caribe-circular. [85]

SieLAC (2024), *Siestema de Información Energética de Latinoamérica y el Caribe*. [44]

Smart Energy Barbados (2024), *Smart Energy 2030*, Barbados National Energy Policy, https://smartenergybarbados.com/smart-products/solar-water-heaters/. [53]

Taylor, M. A. (2015), *Why Climate Demands Change*, The Grace Kennedy Foundation Lecture, 97 pp., http://www.gracekennedy. com/images/lecture/GKL2015-Climate.pdf. [9]

Taylor, M. et al. (2018), "Future Caribbean Climates in a World of Rising Temperatures: The 1.5 vs 2.0 Dilemma", *Journal of Climate*, Vol. 31/7, pp. 2907-2926, https://doi.org/10.1175/JCLI-D-17-0074.1. [7]

Taylor, M., J. Jones and T. Stephenson (2016), "Climate change and the Caribbean: Trends and implications", in *Climate Change and Food Security: Africa and the Caribbean*, Routledge. [10]

TVET (2024), *TVET Council Barbados (website)*, https://www.tvetcouncil.com.bb/about-us/#what-is-the-tvet-council. [113]

UNDESA (ed.) (2019), *Diving into the blue economy*, https://www.un.org/development/desa/en/news/sustainable/blue-economy.html. [118]

UNDP (2024), *Antigua and Barbuda targets complete digitalization of its public services by 2030*, United Nations Development Programme, https://www.undp.org/news/antigua-and-barbuda-targets-complete-digitalization-its-public-services-2030. [115]

UNDP (2021), *Nature-based Solutions in Latin America and the Caribbean*, United Nations Development Programme, https://cssh.northeastern.edu/policyschool/wp-content/uploads/sites/2/2021/07/Northeastern-NbS-report-final.pdf. [101]

UNDRR (2022), *The Caribbean is at the forefront of early warning systems*, United Nations for Disaster Risk Reduction, https://www.undrr.org/news/caribbean-forefront-early-warning-systems. [36]

UNEP (2023), *Unlocking Circular Economy Finance in Latin America and the Caribbean: The Catalyst for a Positive Change*, UN Environment Programme Finance Initiative, https://idbinvest.org/en/publications/unlocking-circular-economy-finance-latin-america-and-caribbean-catalyst-positive. [50]

UNEP (2021), *Theme report on Energy Transition: Towards the achievement of SDG 7 and Net-Zero Emissions*, United Nations Environment Programme, https://www.un.org/sites/un2.un.org/files/2021/11/2021-twg_2.pdf. [51]

UNEP (2019), *The Caribbean - Keeping it Real*, https://www.unep.org/cep/fr/node/132?%2Fnews%2Feditorial%2Fcaribbean-keeping-it-real=#:~:text=Almost%2010%20per%20cent%20of,nowhere%20else%20in%20the%20world. [60]

UNEP-CEP (2019), *State Of the Cartagena Convention Area: An Assessment of Marine Pollution from Land-Based Sources and Activities in the Wider Caribbean Region*, UNEP-CEP, https://wedocs.unep.org/handle/20.500.11822/36346. [66]

UNFCC (2023), *Low Emissions Strategy and Action Plan: Belize*, United Nations Framework Convention on Climate Change, Geneva, https://unfccc.int/documents/628056. [38]

UNFCCC (2024), *National Adaptation Plans*, UNFCCC, https://unfccc.int/topics/adaptation-and-resilience/workstreams/national-adaptation-plans. [116]

United Nations (2024), *UN Sustainable Development Goals*, United Nations, https://sdgs.un.org/fr/goals. [68]

United Nations (2022), *2022 Revision of World Population Prospects*, https://population.un.org/wpp/. [15]

United Nations (2021), *Sustainable Transport, Sustainable Development*, United Nations, https://sdgs.un.org/sites/default/files/2021-10/Transportation%20Report%202021_FullReport_Digital.pdf. [94]

UNOPS (2020), *Saint Lucia National Infrastructure Assessment*, United Nations Office for Project Services, https://content.unops.org/publications/Saint-Lucia-National-Infrastructure-Assessment.pdf. [27]

Van Hoof, B., G. Núñez Reyes and C. De Miguel (2023), *Scaling up circular economy initiatives in Latin America and the Caribbean*, ECLAC, https://www.cepal.org/en/publications/48835-scaling-circular-economy-initiatives-latin-america-and-caribbean. [78]

Walker, L. (2022), "Climate Change, The Caribbean Sea, and the Ocean Economy: Securing Livelihoods of Caribbean People", *ECLAC - FOCUS CDCC* 3, pp. 4-13, https://repositorio.cepal.org/server/api/core/bitstreams/c94d4b38-7867-4049-b500-e2ca09f21e1e/content. [12]

WEF (2020), *The Future of Nature and Business*, World Economic Forum, https://www3.weforum.org/docs/WEF_The_Future_Of_Nature_And_Business_2020.pdf. [106]

WMO (2024), *State of the Climate in Latin America and the Caribbean 2023*, World Meteorological Organization, https://library.wmo.int/idurl/4/68891. [6]

WMO (2021), *State of the Climate in Latin America and the Caribbean 2020*, World Meteorological Organization, https://library.wmo.int/doc_num.php?explnum_id=10876. [5]

WMO (2018), *Multi-hazard Early Warning Systems: A Checklist*, World Metereological Organization, https://library.wmo.int/idurl/4/55893. [35]

World Bank (2024), *Blue Economy*, World Bank, https://www.worldbank.org/en/topic/oceans-fisheries-and-coastal-economies. [69]

World Bank (2024), *Dominica Geothermal Risk Mitigation Policy*, World Bank, https://projects.worldbank.org/en/projects-operations/project-detail/P162149. [54]

World Bank (2024), *GDP (current US$) [database]*, World Bank, https://data.worldbank.org/indicator/NY.GDP.MKTP.CD. [16]

World Bank (2023), *Addressing Plastic Polution in the Caribbean*, World Bank, https://www.worldbank.org/en/news/infographic/2023/06/05/addressing-plastic-pollution-in-the-caribbean#:~:text=Over%20320%2C000%20tons%20of%20plastic,kilometer%2C%20compared%20to%20573%20worldwide. [61]

World Bank (2023), *Dominica's Journey to become the World's First Climate Resilient Country*, World Bank, https://www.worldbank.org/en/news/feature/2023/09/26/dominica-s-journey-to-become-the-world-s-first-climate-resilient-country. [25]

World Bank (2022), *Building the Caribbean Digital Economy Bit by Bit*, World Bank, https://www.worldbank.org/en/results/2022/05/11/building-the-caribbean-digital-economy-bit-by-bit. [114]

World Bank (2022), "Clean energy in the Caribbean: A triple win", World Bank blogs, https://blogs.worldbank.org/en/latinamerica/clean-energy-caribbean-triple-win. [43]

World Bank (2022), *Grenada secures $15 million to improve the resilience of the country's infrastructure*, World Bank, https://www.worldbank.org/en/news/press-release/2022/05/23/grenada-secures-15-million-to-improve-the-resilience-of-the-country-s-infrastructure. [32]

World Bank (2022), *World Development Indicators [database]*, World Bank, https://databank.worldbank.org/source/world-development-indicators/Series/ER.MRN.PTMR.ZS. [65]

World Bank (2021), *Climate Change Could Force 216 Million People to Migrate Within Their Own Countries by 2050*, World Bank, https://www.worldbank.org/en/news/press-release/2021/09/13/climate-change-could-force-216-million-people-to-migrate-within-their-own-countries-by-2050. [19]

World Bank (2016), *Toward a Blue Economy: A Promise for Sustainable Growth in the Caribbean*, World Bank, https://www.cbd.int/financial/doc/wb-blueeconomy.pdf. [58]

World Bank/ESMAP (2020), *Offshore Wind Technichal Potential [database]*, World Bank/Energy Sector Management Assistance Program, https://energydata.info/dataset/offshore-wind-technical-potential. [45]

WRI (2021), *Nature-Based Solutions in Latin America and The Caribbean: Regional Status and Priorities for Growth*, World Resources Institute, http://Nature-Based Solutions in Latin America and The Caribbean: Regional Status and Priorities for Growth. [100]

WTTC (2022), *Travel and Tourism in the Caribbean: Prospects for Growth*, World Travel and Tourism Council, https://wttc.org/Portals/0/Documents/Reports/2022/Travel-and-tourism-in-the-caribbean.pdf. [86]

Annex 3.A.

Annex Table 3.A.1. Nationally determined contributions, selected Caribbean countries

Country	NDC submission	Relevant targets	Conditionality	Covers all sectors
Antigua and Barbuda	Sep21	Net zero by 2040; 86% renewable energy generation from local resources in the electricity sector by 2030; 100% of all new vehicle sales to be electric vehicles by 2030	Conditional	Yes
Bahamas	Nov-22	-30% GHGBAU by 2030	Conditional	Yes
Barbados	Jul-21	Carbon neutrality by 2030; -35% GHGBAU by 2030 (unconditional); -70% GHGBAU by 2030 (conditional)		Yes
Belize	Sep-21	Promise of net zero by 2050; Sectoral Targets	Unconditional	Yes
Dominica	Jul-22	-45% GHGBAU2014 by 2030	Conditional	Yes
Dominican Republic	Dec-20	Carbon neutrality by 2050; -27% GHGBAU by 2030 (conditional); -7% GHGBAU by 2030 (unconditional); -6% BCBAU by 2030		Yes
Grenada	Nov-20	CO2 neutrality only by 2050; -40 GHG2010 by 2030	Conditional	Yes
Guyana	May-16	Already CO2 neutral; sectoral targets	Unconditional	No
Haiti	Jun-22	-31.8% GHGBAU by 2030 (conditional); -6.32% GHGBAU by 2030 (unconditional)		
Jamaica	Jul-22	Net zero by 2050 (conditional); -28.5% GHGBAU by 2030 (conditional); -25.4% GHGBAU by 2030 (unconditional)		No
Saint Kitts and Nevis	Oct-21	Net zero by 2050; -61% GHGBAU2010 by 2030	Conditional	Yes
Saint Lucia	Jan-21	-7% GHG 2010 by 2030	Conditional	Energy
Saint Vincent and the Grenadines	Feb-16	-22% GHGBAU by 2025	Unconditional	Yes
Suriname	Dec-19	Already CO2 neutral; sectoral targets	Conditional	Yes
Trinidad and Tobago	Feb-18	-20% GHGBAU by 2030	Conditional	Energy

Note: NDC=National Determined Contribution; GHGBAU=Greenhouse gas emissions/business-as-usual.
Source: Authors' elaboration based on OECD (2023[3]) and UNFCCC (2024[116]).

Annex Table 3.A.2. Climate adaptation in national adaptation plans and long-term strategies, selected Caribbean countries

Country	National Adaptation Plan	Sectoral NAPs and other outputs	Adaptation within NDCs	Long-term strategy (LTS)	National adaptation legislation and policies (general framework)	Adaptation in other national plans and strategies
Antigua and Barbuda	No	No	Yes (conditional targets on buildings, renewable energy, water, gender and finance)	No	Antigua and Barbuda's 2015-20 National Action Plan: Combatting Desertification, Land Degradation & Drought	
Bahamas	No	No	Yes (target on reducing vulnerability, with components on preparedness, funding, food and water security, ecosystems' management, energy, education, information and monitoring)	No	2005 National Policy for the Adaptation to Climate Change	Climate Change and Carbon Market Initiatives Act 2022

Barbados	No	No	Yes (though no explicit targets)	No	Proclamation of the Planning and Development Act (2021); 2021 Physical Development Plan (PDP)	Barbados Comprehensive Disaster Management Country Work Programme (CWP) 2019-23; other policies on tourism, coastal zone management, storm water management, and other sectoral plans (agriculture, fisheries, water and health)
Belize	No	No	Yes (with sectoral targets on coastal zone and marine resources, agriculture, fisheries and aquaculture, human health, tourism, forestry and biodiversity, land use, human settlements and infrastructure and water resources)	Yes	2014 National Climate Change Policy, Strategy and Action Plan (with focus on priority sectors including agriculture, tourism, energy, forestry and fisheries)	
Dominica	No	No	Yes (ecosystems, coastal and marine resources, health, agriculture)	No	Climate Resilience Act 2018; National Resilience Development Strategy 2018-30; Climate Resilience and Recovery Plan 2020-30	National Forest Policy 2022
Dominican Republic	No	No	Yes	No	Law 1-12: National Development Strategy 2030; National Adaptation Plan for Climate Change Adaptation 2015-2030 (PNACC DR)	National Adaptation Strategy for the Agricultural Sector 2014-20; Climate Change and Gender Action Plan (PAGCC-RD) 2018
Grenada	06-Nov-19	Yes (National Climate Change Policy)	Only reference to co-benefits and NAP	No	National Climate Change Policy; National Sustainable Development Plan 2020-35	
Guyana	No	No	Yes (agriculture, water)	No		
Haiti	05-Jan-23	No	Yes (agriculture, fishing, water resources, road infrastructure, coastal zones, health and habitat)	No		
Jamaica	No	No	Yes (co-benefits)	No		
Saint Kitts and Nevis	No	No	Yes	No	National Climate Change Adaptation Strategy 2018	Food and Nutrition Security Policy and Plan of Action 2019

Saint Lucia	21-Sep-18	Yes (agriculture, fisheries, water, communication strategy, monitoring and evaluation)	Yes (link to NAP)	No	National Environment Policy and National Environmental Management Strategy (2004; Revised 2014)	
Saint Vincent and the Grenadines	14-Nov-19	No	Yes (coastal zones, water resources, health, agriculture)	No		
Suriname	02-Jun-20	No	Yes (agriculture)	No	Policy Development Plan 2017-21; Multi-Annual Development Plan 2022-26	Suriname National REDD+ Strategy
Trinidad and Tobago	15-May-24	No	Yes (co-benefits)	No		

Source: Authors' elaboration based on OECD (2023[3]) and UNFCCC (2024[116]).

4 Stronger institutions for a renewed social contract

Strengthening public institutions is crucial for enhancing policy effectiveness and delivering better public services. These efforts are vital for advancing towards a new social contract that can help align public policy agendas with citizens' priorities. This chapter begins with an overview of citizen perceptions on areas such as trust in democracy, satisfaction with public services, citizen security and climate change, highlighting unmet social aspirations. The second section explores strategies to build more effective and inclusive institutions that meet citizen expectations and help restore trust. The third section argues that these two dimensions should unite around a renewed social contract, establishing a shared vision for Caribbean development priorities agreed upon with citizens. The chapter concludes with key policy messages.

Introduction

Caribbean countries face enduring socio-economic and environmental challenges to advance sustainable development. These are compounded by declining levels of satisfaction with public institutions and the quality of public services, which underscore the unmet aspirations of many Caribbeans. To address these challenges, public institutions must become more effective and inclusive, fostering a renewed social contract that crafts a Caribbean development vision shaped in partnership with citizens.

This chapter examines these elements in detail. The first section presents an overview of citizens' perceptions on key topics, including trust in democracy, satisfaction with public services, citizen security, and climate change. The second section focuses on the need for more effective and inclusive institutions to restore trust and address citizens' unmet demands. The third section argues for the need to foster a renewed social contract that reconnects citizens and public institutions around a shared vision of long-term development. Finally, the chapter concludes with key messages for policy action.

Understanding citizens' perceptions to improve policy outcomes

Understanding citizens' perceptions is key to aligning development strategies' objectives with the actual needs and aspirations of Caribbean societies. By incorporating citizens' views into policy making, governments can create more inclusive and effective strategies, thereby fostering public support and participation. This enhances transparency, accountability, and resilience (Keefer and Scartascini, 2022[1]; Beuermann et al., 2018[2]). This is important in a region where overall levels of satisfaction with democracy and key public services have been falling over time, as this section shows.

Citizen satisfaction with democracy has declined in the last decade

In 2023, more than 65% of people in the Caribbean (8 countries with comparable available data), on average, expressed low satisfaction with the democratic system, an increase of 22.6 percentage points (p.p.) in the last decade (Figure 4.1). Dissatisfaction with democracy in Latin America increased by 12.6 p.p. in the same period (from 45.6% to 58.1%). There are important differences across Caribbean countries: from Haiti (87.9%) and Suriname (86.6%) in the higher-end, to the Dominican Republic (50.8%) and Grenada (45.3%) in the lower-end, but still with around half of the population showing low satisfaction (Figure 4.1).

Trust in elections is also low in the Caribbean, putting their legitimacy at stake. In 2023, on average, 42% of Caribbean citizens had low confidence in the election results in their countries, slightly lower than in 2014 (44.9%). This was also 2 p.p. less than the average in Latin America (44.3%) (LAPOP Lab, 2023[3]). Moreover, only 25% of Caribbean citizens thought that votes were always correctly and fairly counted, while 15% believed this never happened. Latin American countries show similar trends with slightly higher values (30.4% and 21.9%) (LAPOP Lab, 2023[3]).

Figure 4.1. Satisfaction with democracy in the Caribbean and Latin America, 2014-23

Share of citizens by level of satisfaction with democracy in their country

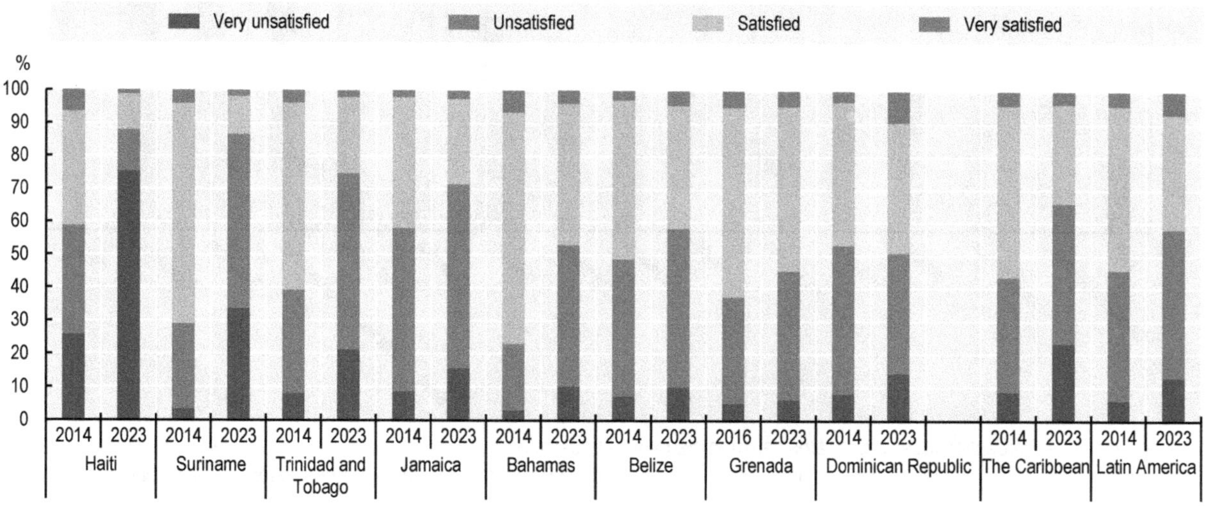

Note: The question featured in the figure is: "In general, would you say that you are very satisfied, satisfied, dissatisfied or very dissatisfied with the way democracy works in (country)?" The Latin America average considers Argentina, Plurinational State of Bolivia, Brazil, Chile, Colombia, Costa Rica, Ecuador, El Salvador, Guatemala, Honduras, Mexico, Nicaragua, Panama, Paraguay, Peru, and Uruguay. The Caribbean average considers The Bahamas, Belize, the Dominican Republic, Grenada, Haiti, Jamaica, Trinidad and Tobago, and Suriname.
Source: Authors' elaboration based on LAPOP Lab (2023[3]).

StatLink https://stat.link/umn340

Lack of trust in the judiciary system is high in Caribbean countries, as 20% of people report having no trust in the courts to deliver a fair trial. Trust is particularly low in Jamaica and Trinidad and Tobago, where 34% and 27% of respondents express complete distrust in the judicial system, respectively. Finally, the Caribbean has a relatively low number of professional judges. Jamaica (3 per 100 000 inhabitants), Trinidad and Tobago (7), Barbados (8), and The Bahamas (12) all fall below the global average of 18 judges per 100 000 people. However, their numbers are close to the Latin America and the Caribbean (LAC) average of 9 judges per 100 000 (Sutton et al., 2017[4]).

Corruption perceptions in the Caribbean show important heterogeneities across countries

Citizen perceptions are a useful measure to gauge the prevalence of corruption. Of the 12 Caribbean countries with data available in the Corruption Perceptions Index, 8 are perceived as less corrupt than the world average (43) (with the understanding that higher values mean less perceived corruption). Barbados (65), The Bahamas (64), and Saint Vincent and the Grenadines (60) show levels similar to OECD countries (66.3 on average). Saint Lucia and Dominica (55 each), Grenada (52) and Jamaica (44) are also above the world's average and – except for Jamaica – above the Caribbean average. Trinidad and Tobago (42), Guyana (40) and Suriname (40) are perceived as more corrupt than the world average but still in a better position than the Latin American (36.5) average. Finally, the Dominican Republic (32) and Haiti (17) show the highest levels of perceived corruption in the Caribbean (Figure 4.2).

Figure 4.2. Corruption Perception Index, Caribbean and Latin America, 2022

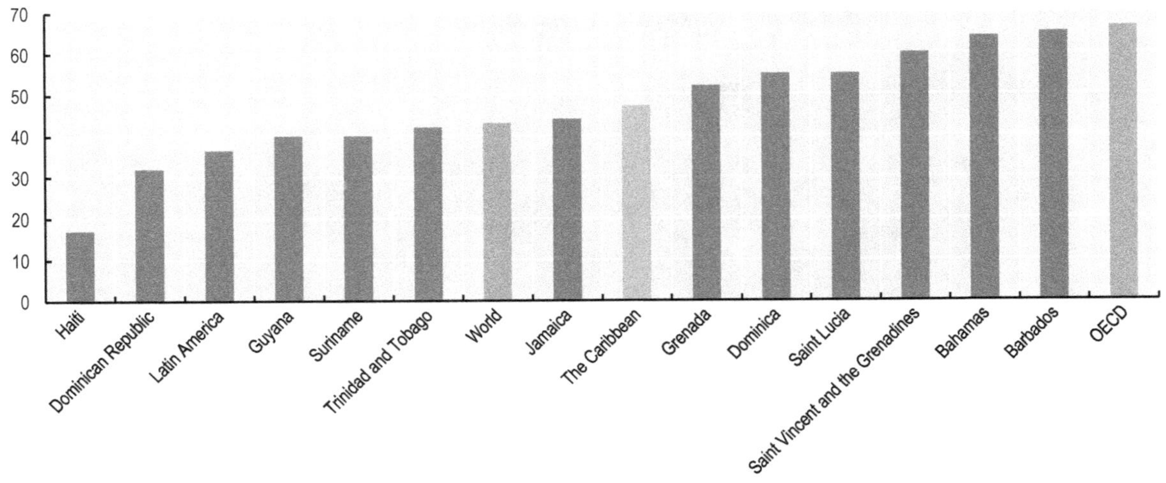

Note: The Corruption Perception Index aggregates data from various sources, reflecting perceptions of corruption in the public sector as reported by business executives and experts. It scores countries on a scale from 0 to 100, where 0 indicates total corruption, and 100 represents complete cleanliness.
Source: Authors' elaboration based on Transparency International (2022[5]).

StatLink https://stat.link/evugzn

Other data sources indicate higher levels of perceived corruption in the Caribbean. For instance, the World Justice Project conducted face-to-face interviews with representative household samples across 14 Caribbean countries to assess perceptions of public sector corruption. As much as 81% of respondents believe public officials frequently or very frequently influence the hiring of friends or relatives in the public sector. In comparison, 80% think public officials often favour friends or relatives when awarding government contracts, on average. Furthermore, 66% of respondents reported that it is frequent or very frequent for public officials to request money or gifts for public services that should be free of charge. Perceptions of corruption in politics are higher than in other parts of the public sector. On average, 66% of respondents believe that most people working in political parties are involved in corrupt practices, and 55% express the same about members of the national legislature. By contrast, public school teachers (18%), doctors and nurses in public hospitals (20%) and land registry officers (28%) are seen as less corrupt (World Justice Project, 2023[6]). Corruption also impacts business operations: 37% of Caribbean firms view corruption as a severe or very severe obstacle, particularly in Belize, Jamaica, Suriname, and Trinidad and Tobago (IDB, 2021[7]) (Chapter 1).

The satisfaction of Caribbean citizens with the quality of key public services has decreased in recent years

Citizen satisfaction with the quality of health and medical services is relatively low. In 2023, on average for the six countries with comparable available data, only 40% of Caribbean people were satisfied or very satisfied (around half of the population in the case of Latin American countries). Satisfaction with health services showed an average decline of 15.4 p.p. in the Caribbean in the last decade (from 55.4% to 40%). This decline was almost three times more than in Latin American countries, where satisfaction decreased 5.6 p.p. in the same period (from 55.6% to 50%) (LAPOP Lab, 2023[3]).

Satisfaction with the quality of education is overall higher than with health. In 2023, Caribbean citizens (65.2%, on average) were satisfied or very satisfied with the quality of public schools in their countries, 7.2 p.p. above the Latin American average (58%). Nonetheless, in the last decade, satisfaction fell by

9.5 p.p. in the Caribbean on average (from 74.7% to 65.2%) (Figure 4.3). In 2023, satisfaction with the quality of public schools varied from 75.2% in Grenada to 49.4% in Trinidad and Tobago. The overall decline could be linked to factors including the reduction of total government expenditures in the sector and the negative evolution of the student-to-teacher ratio (Chapter 2). In 2023, education spending in the region accounted for 12.7% of total government expenditures, down from 13.9% a decade earlier. These figures are below the Latin America average of 16.4% in 2023 (Arias et al., 2024[8]) (Chapter 2).

Figure 4.3. Satisfaction with the quality of public schools, selected Caribbean countries and Latin America, 2014-23

Share of citizens by level of satisfaction with the quality of public schools

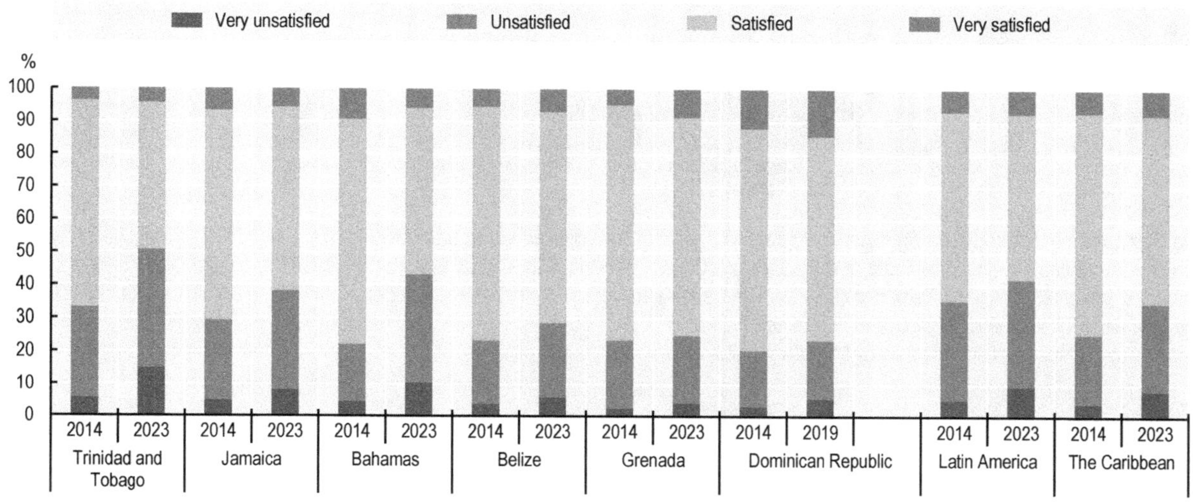

Note: The question featured in the figure is: "Are you very satisfied, satisfied, dissatisfied or very dissatisfied with the quality of public schools?". The Latin American average considers Argentina, Plurinational State of Bolivia, Brazil, Chile, Colombia, Costa Rica, Ecuador, El Salvador, Guatemala, Honduras, Mexico, Nicaragua, Panama, Paraguay, Peru, and Uruguay. The Caribbean average considers The Bahamas, Belize, the Dominican Republic, Grenada, Jamaica and Trinidad and Tobago.
Source: Authors' elaboration based on LAPOP Lab (2023[3]).

StatLink https://stat.link/w8ldbr

Regarding the condition of streets, roads and motorways, 46.7% of Caribbean people were satisfied or very satisfied in 2023, on average, 8 p.p. less than in 2014. In Latin America, half of the population was satisfied or very satisfied in 2023 with the condition of roads, a decrease of 5 p.p. from 2014.

Improving the quality of public services is paramount for sustainable development as it directly enhances well-being and productivity. Providing high-quality, efficient and effective public services can build trust, help attract investment, and encourage greater civic engagement and compliance with regulations.

Caribbean citizens are particularly concerned about security and the economy

In 2023, security issues were the most serious problem for one-third of Caribbean citizens (33.1%), on average in 8 countries with comparable available data, followed by economic issues (29.5%) and unemployment (11.3%) (Figure 4.4). Security was the top concern in Haiti (65%), Jamaica (60.1%), Trinidad and Tobago (57.6%) and Bahamas (48.4%), while economic concerns predominated in Suriname (76.3%), Belize (49.7%) and the Dominican Republic (42.2%). Unemployment was the main concern in Grenada (38.7%) and ranked second in Jamaica (12.3%).

Figure 4.4. Top concerns for citizens in Caribbean countries, 2023

Share of citizens by perceived most serious problem faced by their country

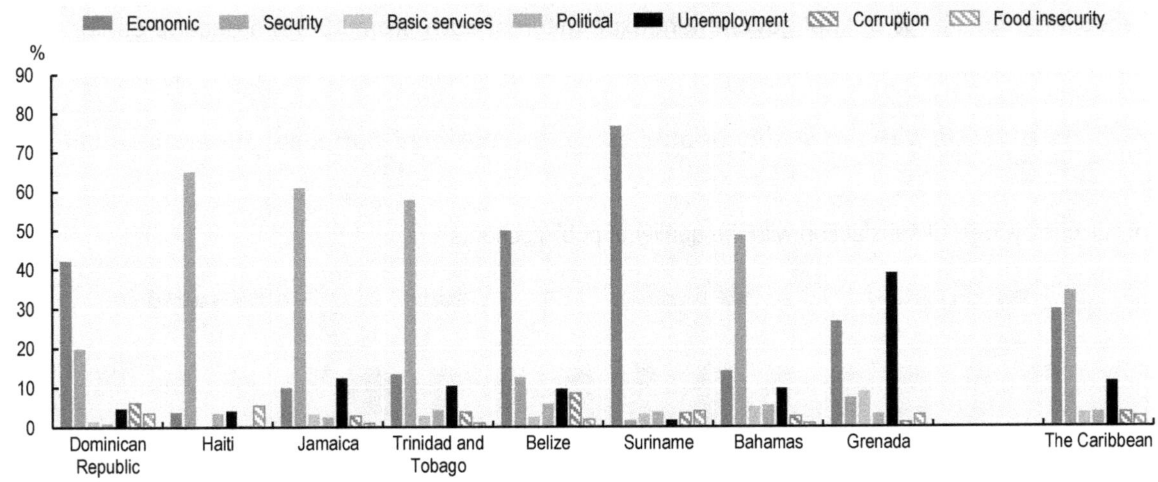

Note: The question featured in the figure is: "In your opinion, what is the most serious problem faced by the country?". The Latin America average considers Argentina, Plurinational State of Bolivia, Brazil, Chile, Colombia, Costa Rica, Ecuador, El Salvador, Guatemala, Honduras, Mexico, Nicaragua, Panama, Paraguay, Peru, and Uruguay. The Caribbean average considers The Bahamas, Belize, the Dominican Republic, Grenada, Haiti, Jamaica, Trinidad and Tobago, and Suriname.
Source: Authors' elaboration based on LAPOP Lab (2023[3]).

StatLink https://stat.link/gic5r8

Strengthening citizen security is paramount as crime and violence represent an important challenge in many Caribbean countries

Caribbean countries exhibit the highest per capita average murder rates globally, with as much as 23.7 intentional homicides per 100 000 people (well above the Latin American average, at 15.1) (Figure 4.5). The situation varies across countries but poses a shared challenge for the region (Cafferata and Scartascini, 2021[9]). The average cost of crime in the Caribbean is estimated at 3.7% of GDP (IDB, 2017[10]). To put this into context, a 3% of GDP cost is roughly equivalent to the total income of the poorest 30% of the Caribbean population, suggesting that if crime were eliminated, the income of the poorest 30% could effectively double (IDB, 2017[10]).

Significant levels of homicidal violence are associated with organised crime (UNODC, 2023[11]). The recent increase in homicidal violence is predominantly due to intense gang competition over drug markets. In Jamaica, the homicide rate reached 53.3 per 100 000 persons in 2022, with approximately 70% of these homicides linked to organised criminal groups or gangs. Saint Lucia reported a homicide rate of 36.7 per 100 000 in 2022, marking a slight decrease from the previous year. Saint Vincent and the Grenadines recorded a rate of 40.4 per 100 000 people. Trinidad and Tobago experienced a notable rise, with the homicide rate reaching 39.5 per 100 000 in 2022 (UNODC, 2022[12]). This was an increase of more than 30% from the previous year. The Bahamas reported a homicide rate of 31.2 per 100 000, and Haiti experienced a surge in its rate to 18 per 100 000 in 2022, an increase of over 35% from 2021, driven mainly by escalating gang-related tensions[1] (UNODC, 2022[12]) (Figure 4.5). Deadly violence in Haiti has continued to increase since 2022, reaching 4 448 people killed only between January and September of 2024 (BINUH, 2024[13]) (Box 4.1). Increased gang fragmentation has contributed to rising insecurity, affecting 57% of the population in Trinidad and Tobago and 35% in Jamaica between January and September 2024 (Pellegrini, 2024[14]).

The use of firearms is particularly widespread in the Eastern Caribbean (IMF, 2017[15]). Young people, particularly men aged 15-29, are disproportionately affected by violent crime, both as victims and perpetrators. Meanwhile, women are more affected by homicides linked to domestic violence and intimate partner violence. Crime prevention among young people, a better tertiary education offer, and a strengthened judicial system and police force could help reduce high crime levels (OECD, 2022[16]).

Figure 4.5. Intentional homicides rate in the Caribbean, 2022

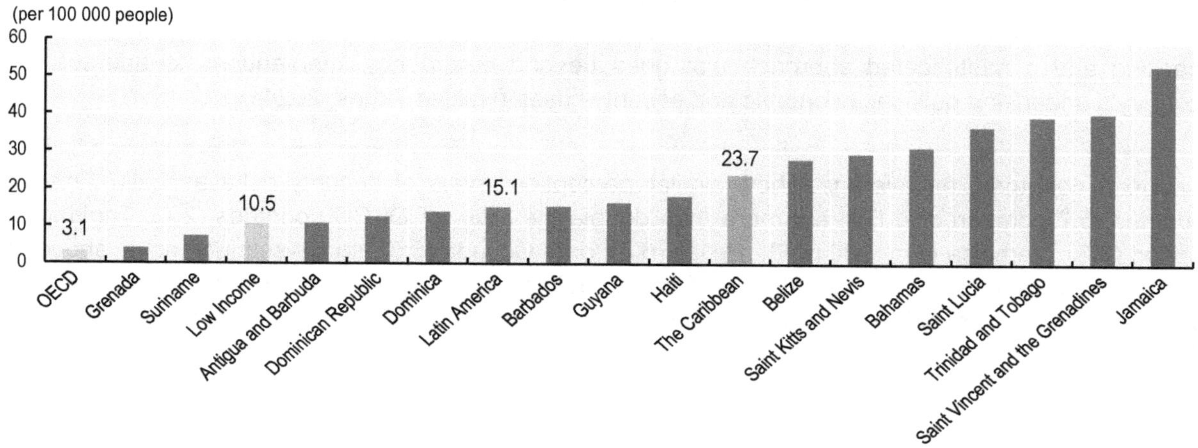

Note: The OECD average considers all OECD member states except Finland, New Zealand, and the United Kingdom. Latin American average considers Argentina, the Plurinational State of Bolivia, Brazil (2021), Chile, Colombia, Costa Rica, Ecuador, El Salvador, Guatemala (2021), Honduras, Mexico, Nicaragua, Panama, Paraguay, Peru (2020) and Uruguay. The Caribbean average considers Antigua and Barbuda, The Bahamas, Barbados, Belize, Dominica (2021), the Dominican Republic, Grenada (2021), Guyana (2021), Haiti, Jamaica, Saint Kitts, and Nevis (2021), Saint Lucia, Saint Vincent and the Grenadines, Suriname, and Trinidad and Tobago.
Source: Authors' elaboration based on UNODC (2022[12]).

StatLink https://stat.link/4uhp61

Box 4.1. Spotlight on Haiti

Haiti remains the poorest country in the LAC region and one of the poorest globally, with a GDP per capita of USD 1 694.1 in 2023 (World Bank, 2024[17]). In 2023, 90% of the population lived below the poverty line, while one third lived in extreme poverty (UNESCO, 2023[18]). Economic pressures include high unemployment, falling remittances, and limited access to essential public services, all contributing to declining income in two-thirds of households, as indicated by the 2023 High-Frequency Phone Survey (World Bank, 2024[17]). Persistent rural poverty, geographic inequalities, and one of the highest population densities in the Caribbean exacerbate infrastructure shortages and erode trust in government institutions (OECD, 2020[19]). In 2017, only 19.5% of citizens expressed satisfaction with health services (LAPOP Lab, 2023[3]). With government expenditure estimated at just 8.24% of GDP in 2022, Haiti faces substantial obstacles in addressing the needs of its citizens and building effective governance (IMF, 2022[20]).

Haiti's historical challenges in governance and socio-economic progress have been compounded by political instability, social stratification, and natural disasters since its independence, making it more difficult to consolidate democracy and political institutions (OECD, 2021[21]). The country held its first democratic election in 1990, but a military coup in 1991 disrupted this initial democratic episode, leading to a repressive regime and an international embargo. Another democratic phase began in 2000 yet was marked by allegations of fraud and low voter turnout (OECD, 2021[21]). Increasing social discontent and institutional instability followed, resulting in armed conflict. In 2004, the United Nations led international interventions aimed at supporting Haiti's democratic transition, with efforts to protect human rights and strengthen the police force and the judicial system (Heine and Thompson, 2011[22]; OECD, 2021[21]). The recent escalation in violence has intensified the calling for comprehensive international support. Currently, over 2.7 million Haitians live in areas controlled by gangs, which has severely hindered the ability of both local authorities and international organisations to provide essential services, including food, health care, and security. The recent Kenyan-led Multinational Security Support (MSS) mission aims to support the Haitian National Police. Still, Haiti continues to require sustained international backing and a multifaceted approach that goes beyond emergency interventions to address the country's underlying political, economic and security crises (Haitian Times, 2024[23]).

Caribbean countries, on average, show similar perception levels of security risks as Latin American countries (5.7 compared to 5.4) but more than double the rates of OECD countries (2.4). Trinidad and Tobago (7.3), Jamaica (7), Haiti (6.8), Belize (6.8) and Guyana (6.5) show security risks above the Caribbean average (5.7) (Figure 4.6). In Jamaica, Belize, and Trinidad and Tobago, this perception coincides with high homicide rates (Figure 4.5). Moreover, in 2022, 37% of Caribbean firms considered crime, theft, and disorder as severe or very severe obstacles to performing their operations (IDB, 2021[7]) (Chapter 1).

Figure 4.6. Security risks indicator, selected Caribbean countries, 2022

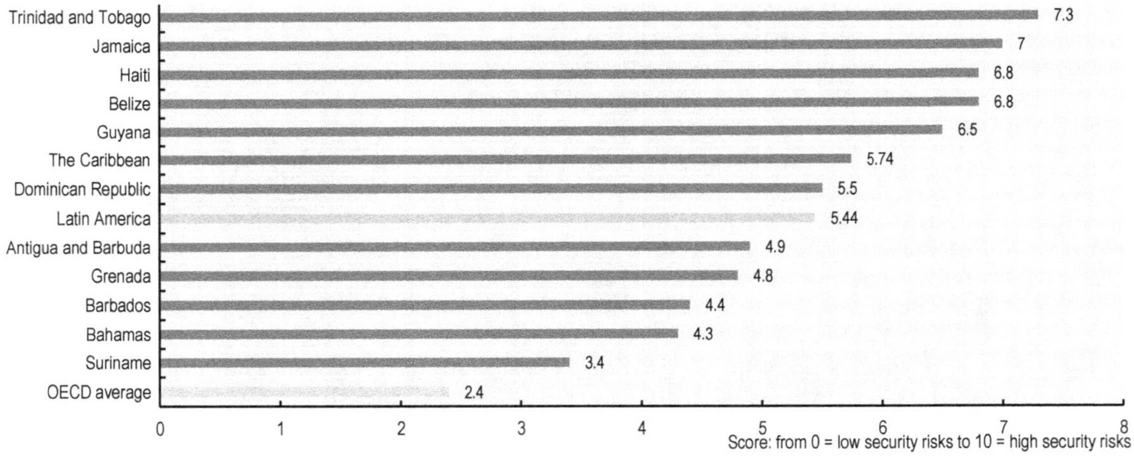

Note: The Security Risks Index measures the security threats to a state, such as bombings, attacks and battle-related deaths, rebel movements, mutinies, coups, or terrorism. The index also considers serious criminal factors, such as organised crime and homicides, and the perceived trust of citizens in domestic security.
Source: Authors' elaboration based on The Fund for Peace (2023[24]).

StatLink https://stat.link/x2egnz

Trust in the police is low in the Caribbean, although there are important variations across countries. A total of 37% of the population in Jamaica and 25% in Trinidad and Tobago reported that they do not trust the police at all (Sutton et al., 2017[4]). Substantial police investments and the region's small population have led to a high police-to-population ratio in several countries. The Bahamas has 846 police officers per 100 000 inhabitants, and Jamaica has 424, well above the world average (366). In LAC, there are 436 police officers per 100 000 inhabitants, on average. Yet, police effectiveness in the Caribbean is low.

According to the latest available data, about half or less of all homicides were resolved by the police in The Bahamas (51% detection), Jamaica (40%), and Trinidad and Tobago (14%) (Sutton et al., 2017[4]).

Caribbean citizens call for action to fight climate change

In 2023, more than 90% of citizens in the Caribbean considered climate change a serious problem if no action is taken, showing similarly high levels of concern in the seven Caribbean countries with data available. Latin Americans expressed similar levels of concern (89.4% on average) (Figure 4.7).

Figure 4.7. Caribbean citizens consider climate change a very serious problem, 2023

Share of citizens who consider that climate change will be a serious problem if no action is taken

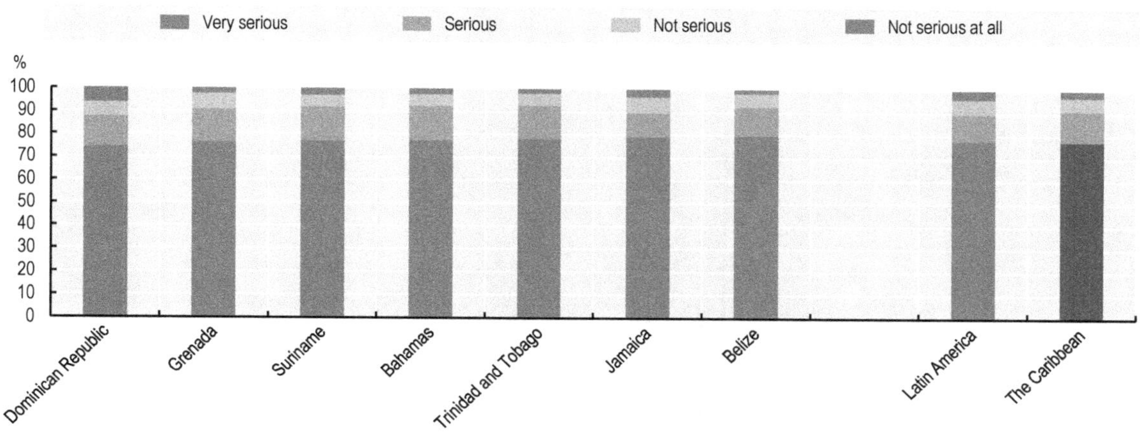

Note: The question featured in the figure is: "If nothing is done to reduce climate change in the future, how serious of a problem do you think it will be for (country)?". The Latin American average considers Argentina, Plurinational State of Bolivia, Brazil, Chile, Colombia, Costa Rica, Ecuador, El Salvador, Guatemala, Honduras, Mexico, Nicaragua, Panama, Paraguay, Peru and Uruguay. The Caribbean average considers The Bahamas, Belize, the Dominican Republic, Grenada, Haiti, Jamaica and Trinidad and Tobago.
Source: Authors' elaboration based on LAPOP Lab (2023[3]).

StatLink https://stat.link/5mdi8a

Advancing more effective and inclusive institutions in the Caribbean

To meet citizens' aspirations and rebuild trust, public institutions must become more effective and inclusive. Good government policies depend on sound data for effective, equitable and evidence-based decision making (OECD, 2020[25]). Evaluations of policies and programmes can highlight underlying problems or point to other areas of public concern, making them an essential aid to policy makers (Coglianese, 2012[26]). Similarly, digital transformation offers different opportunities to transform public institutions.

More inclusive and transparent institutions can curb the misuse of public funds, ensuring resources are effectively allocated to essential public services like education, health and strategic infrastructure. Empirical evidence shows a positive correlation between more inclusive institutions and enhanced public service delivery (e.g. health or education), improved well-being and higher levels of trust (UNDP and DIE, 2022[27]). Conversely, low political engagement and lack of transparency in LAC are associated with higher corruption, undermining economic growth and the quality of critical services like health and education (Warf and Stewart, 2016[28]). This section examines the role of improved and more accessible data, along with digital transformation, in fostering more effective institutions. It highlights the importance of promoting citizen engagement and addressing the multiple vulnerabilities faced by women in the region as key steps towards advancing more inclusive institutions.

Effective institutions: The role of better and more accessible data and digital transformation

Perceived levels of government effectiveness are diverse across Caribbean countries. Most of them score above the LAC average in the World Bank's government effectiveness indicator (Figure 4.8). Nonetheless, Belize, Guyana, Antigua and Barbuda, Suriname, and Haiti fall below this benchmark. While the effectiveness of public institutions depends on multiple, often interrelated factors, this section focuses on two key dimensions where Caribbean counties show particularly relevant challenges and opportunities: strengthening data for evidence-based policy making and the transformative potential of digital technologies.

Figure 4.8. Government effectiveness in the Caribbean, 2022

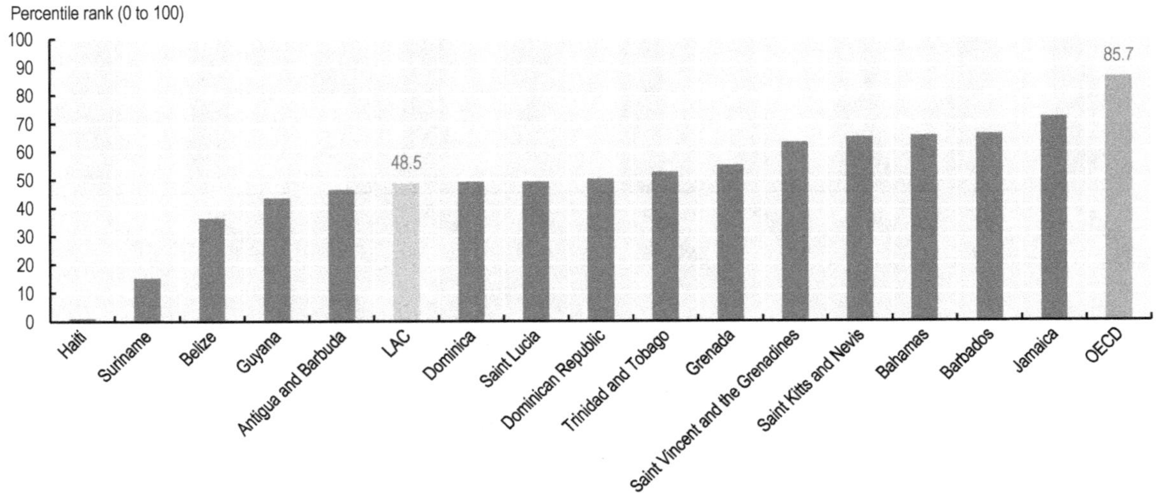

Note: The government effectiveness indicator relies exclusively on perception data from surveys of firms and households and experts' assessments. It reflects the quality of public services, the quality of the civil service and the degree of its independence from political pressures, the quality of policy formulation and implementation, and the credibility of the government's commitment to such policies. The y-axis shows the country's rank among all countries with available data for the indicator, with 0 corresponding to lowest rank and 100 to highest rank. The ranking of countries should be interpreted cautiously as the 90% confidence intervals are broad.
Source: Authors' elaboration based on World Bank (2022[29]).

StatLink https://stat.link/ivmfpj

Well-developed statistical systems are essential for fostering more effective institutions

National statistical systems (NSSs) in the region need to be improved. NSSs are essential for governments to make informed decisions and implement evidence-based policies that address citizens' needs. The Caribbean's overall Statistical Performance Indicator (SPI) score stands at 55.6, below the global average (68.8) and significantly below Latin America (74.4) and the OECD (89.7) averages (Figure 4.9). Moreover, only half of Caribbean countries with data available were implementing a statistical plan in the region in 2021 (Antigua and Barbuda, Belize, the Dominican Republic, Grenada, Jamaica, Saint Kitts and Nevis, and Suriname), which is below the percentage of countries in Latin America (60%), the world (82%), and the OECD (97%).

Caribbean countries have made efforts to enhance their statistical capacities in recent years. The overall SPI score has increased by 29%, rising from 43.1 in 2016[2] to 55.6 in 2022, compared to 18% for Latin America and the world and 10% for OECD countries over the same period. Data quality can be enhanced by generating more comprehensive and accurate survey, census, administrative, and geospatial data as well as by encouraging the private sector and citizens to contribute their own data (World Bank, 2021[30]). In addition, stronger legislation, robust institutional frameworks, consistent statistical standards and improved statistical literacy among producers and users can support the development of better data infrastructure (World Bank, 2021[30]).

Figure 4.9. Statistical Performance Indicator (SPI) overall score by region, 2022

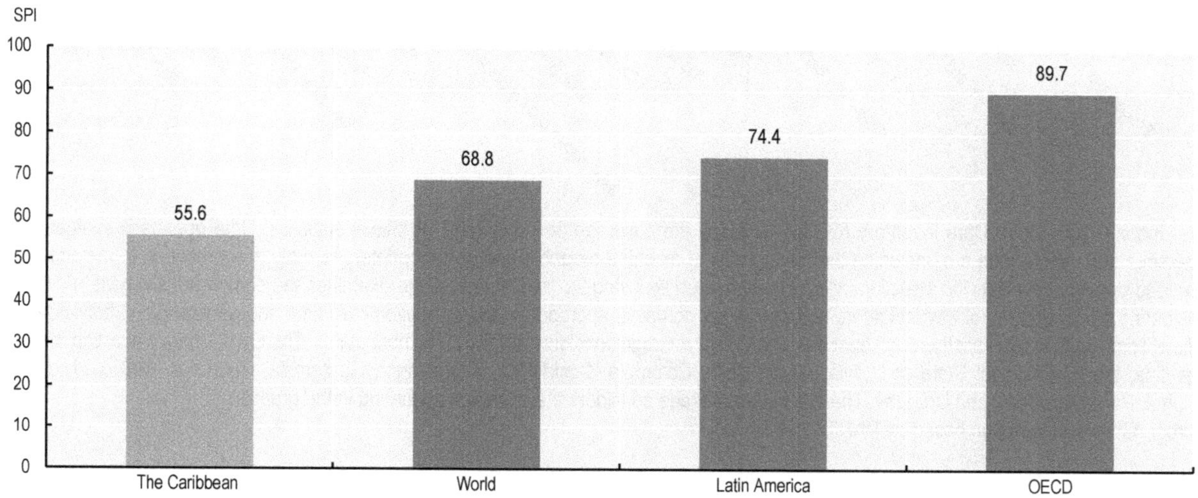

Note: The Latin American average considers 17 countries: Argentina, Bolivia, Brazil, Chile, Colombia, Costa Rica, Ecuador, El Salvador, Guatemala, Honduras, Mexico, Nicaragua, Panama, Paraguay, Peru, Uruguay, and Venezuela. The Caribbean average considers 15 countries: Antigua and Barbuda, The Bahamas, Barbados, Belize, Dominica, Dominican Republic, Grenada, Guyana, Haiti, Jamaica, Saint Kitts and Nevis, Saint Lucia, Saint Vincent and the Grenadines, Suriname and Trinidad and Tobago. The OECD average includes all OECD member states.
The SPI monitors NSSs' progress and identifies areas for further improvement among five different components: i) data use, ii) data services, iii) data products, iv) data sources, and v) data infrastructure.
Source: Authors' elaboration based on World Bank (2022[31]).

StatLink https://stat.link/5w9qsm

Data coverage and openness can be improved in the Caribbean. Open Data Inventory (ODIN) assesses the coverage and openness of official statistics to identify gaps, promote open data policies, improve access and encourage dialogue between NSOs and data users. According to this metric, data coverage and openness in the Caribbean region (40.9) in 2020 was, on average, 7.6 points lower than in Latin American countries (48.5), 9.2 points lower than the global average (50.1) and 26.9 points lower than in OECD countries (67.8) (Figure 4.10). The inventory shows high heterogeneities across Caribbean countries. Jamaica or Saint Lucia scored above 60 points, close to the OECD average, while Haiti, Trinidad and Tobago and Guyana had values below 30 points. On the positive side, the Caribbean region improved its average score by more than 15 points in four years, reaching 40.9 in 2020, compared to 25.7 in 2016 (PARIS21, 2021[32]).

Figure 4.10. Open data inventory (ODIN) overall score for data coverage and openness, selected Caribbean countries, Latin America and OECD, 2020

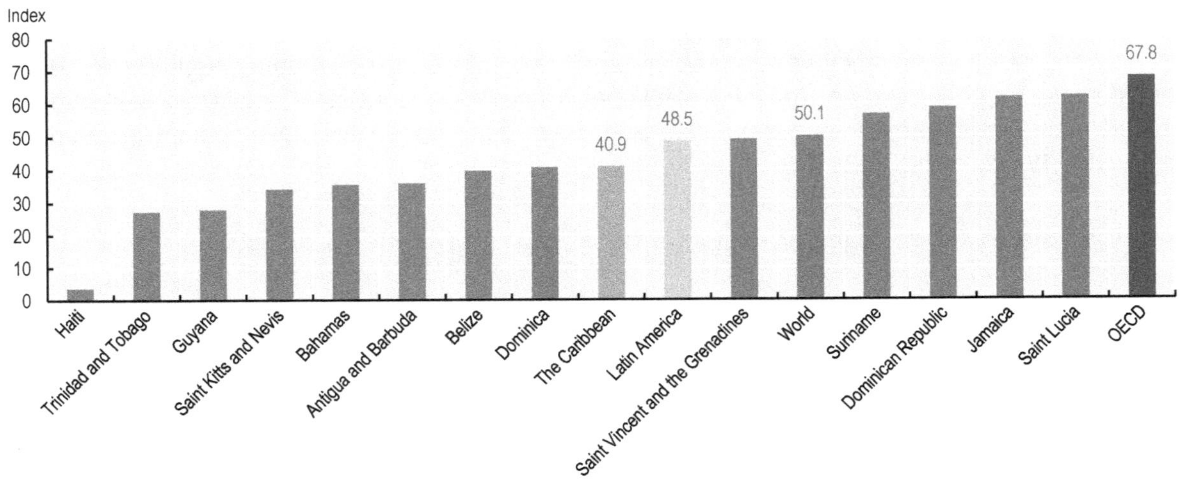

Note: Index 0-100. Open Data Inventory (ODIN) assesses the coverage and openness of official statistics. Data openness evaluates how accessible and usable data are, including their availability in machine-readable and non-proprietary formats, the presence of metadata, bulk download options, user-specific selections via APIs, and open licensing terms. Data coverage examines the comprehensiveness of the data, considering the availability of key indicators across various domains, appropriate disaggregation over time and geographic subdivisions, and sufficient time span to facilitate thorough analysis. The OECD average considers all OECD member states. The Latin America average considers Argentina, the Plurinational State of Bolivia, Brazil, Chile, Colombia, Costa Rica, El Salvador, Guatemala, Honduras, Mexico, Nicaragua, Panama, Paraguay, Peru, and Uruguay. The Caribbean average considers the countries appearing in the graph.
Source: Authors' elaboration based on PARIS21 (2021[32]).

StatLink https://stat.link/as5yfw

Data gaps are important in several Caribbean countries, particularly on social issues like poverty and inequality. In fact, among the thirteen Caribbean countries with existing poverty data, only Suriname and the Dominican Republic reported updated data on this matter after 2020, while five of these countries rely on information dating back to the early 2000s (Chapter 2). Political sensitivities often hinder the collection or publication of poverty data. Regional co-operation could help overcome these challenges by leveraging economies of scale to produce regular, high-quality statistics (OECD, 2022[16]). Without updated data, the evolution of poverty levels cannot be measured, effective policies cannot be crafted, and social welfare spending risks being misdirected (World Bank, 2023[33]).

While Caribbean countries face an increasing need to create and interpret data for informed decisions and policy development, NSOs struggle with capacity issues, including limited technical expertise, outdated legislation and lack of co-ordination. Co-ordination across data produced by NSOs and specific ministries and governmental entities that produce their own data is needed to maximise the potential impact of evidence-based policy decisions. Actions to foster the development of NSOs should prioritise several areas, including the commitment to continuous education for all staff, helping promote statistical literacy among the general population, and on a broader policy level, establishing formal co-ordination mechanisms and data-sharing agreements within the National Statistical System. For example, the Barbados Learning and Development Directorate has co-ordinated different courses to increase data literacy, which are available for workers in the public sector and the general public (OECD/CAF, 2022[34]).

Creating National and Regional Strategies for the Development of Statistics (NSDS and RSDS) can enhance data production and capacity in the Caribbean. In 2023, the OECD Partnership in Statistics for Development in the 21st Century (PARIS21) updated its NSDS Guidelines 3.0, emphasising budgeting, financing and gender mainstreaming. In the Caribbean, PARIS21 has provided technical assistance to countries like Belize to help design, review and evaluate their NSDS, aligning national statistical systems with global standards and national development plans (NDPs). These efforts focused on improving the alignment of data supply with demand and supporting resource mobilisation. PARIS21 also facilitated workshops and regional collaborations to strengthen statistical planning and address gender and climate change considerations (PARIS21, 2024[35]). Similarly, the OECS Regional Strategy for the Development of Statistics (RSDS) 2017-30 prioritises statistical literacy, user needs, and data dissemination, while CARICOM's RSDS 2019-30 focuses on producing and using quality data to inform decision making (CARICOM, 2018[36]; Floyd, Mkrtchyan and Abdulkadr, 2023[37]). From 2015 to 2023, the Project for Regional Advancement of Statistics in the Caribbean (PRASC), funded by Canada, supported CARICOM's national statistical agencies by improving national accounts systems, strengthening business and household surveys, introducing new information-sharing mechanisms, and creating an online knowledge base with training and resources for NSOs (Statistics Canada, 2023[38]).

Digital transformation can enable more efficient public services

The digital transformation can help increase the efficiency of public services. Action on five key areas is needed to advance digital transformation: governance and institutional framework, legal and regulatory framework, digital talent and change management, infrastructure and technology, and new digital processes and services (Cristia et al., 2022[39]; Cubo et al., 2022[40]).

Some key challenges Caribbean countries face relate to bridging digital gaps and developing comprehensive digital government strategies. Prioritising data-driven approaches and enhancing the interoperability of digital tools are needed to ensure inclusive digital transformations and advance government transparency and efficiency (OECD/CAF, 2023[41]).

Caribbean governments have started modernising their e-government services, but the results have been mixed. The 2022 United Nations E-Government Survey classified Caribbean countries with a very high, high, middle or low E-Government Development Index (EGDI) (Table 4.1). Implementing e-government services in the Caribbean can be challenging due to resource-intensive processes, small economies and limited economies of scale.

Table 4.1. E-Government Development Index (EGDI), selected Caribbean countries, 2022

	E-Government Development Index			
	Low	**Middle**	**High**	**Very High**
Countries	Haiti faces significant challenges in terms of information and communication technology (ICT) infrastructure and human capital, resulting in limited e-government services.	Saint Kitts and Nevis, Saint Lucia, Saint Vincent and the Grenadines, Grenada and Antigua and Barbuda are working towards enhancing their e-government services.	Trinidad and Tobago, Jamaica, and the Dominican Republic	Barbados and The Bahamas

Source: Authors' elaboration based on United Nations (2022[42]).

Moreover, seven Caribbean countries – The Bahamas, Dominican Republic, Grenada, Guyana, Jamaica, Saint Lucia and Suriname – have shown a decline in their rankings since 2018. The Online Services Index, part of the EGDI that evaluates e-government service maturity, indicates that most services in the Caribbean are in the early stages and offer limited interactive capabilities (United Nations, 2022[42]).

The development of technologies like artificial intelligence (AI) can offer significant benefits to governments and the public sector when used effectively. It is estimated that public servants spend 30% of their time on repetitive administrative tasks (Eggers, Schatsky and Viechnicki, 2017[43]). AI can serve as a tool to enhance resource and time efficiency, enabling public servants to focus on higher-value tasks while improving communication, citizen engagement, and service delivery quality (OECD/CAF, 2022[34]; Ubaldi et al., 2019[44]). The successful integration of AI in the public sector and the broader economy will also require new skills to ensure effective service delivery and mitigate the adverse effects of increased task automation (Acemoglu, 2021[45]).

In the Caribbean, only the Dominican Republic has expressed explicit interest in developing a national AI approach. Barbados and Jamaica are developing legal frameworks for data protection, an essential foundation for AI adoption in the public sector. Trinidad and Tobago is gradually exploring AI's potential benefits, but progress will likely require significant effort and international support (OECD/CAF, 2022[34]).

At the High Level Conference: "SIDS 2.0: Defining the pathway for Small Islands Digital States in the Caribbean", which took place in Trinidad and Tobago in May 2024, more than 100 Caribbean officials[3] committed to advancing their digital transformation through the "SIDS 2.0" joint initiative, defining five key core pathways: digital infrastructure; governance; regulation and cybersecurity; business and economy; and people. This people-centred regional collaboration aims to overcome resource challenges and promote sustainable development (CAF, 2024[46]; UNDP, 2024[47]).

Inclusive Institutions: Promoting citizen engagement

Involving citizens in public decision-making enhances trust in government and democratic institutions (OECD, 2022[48]). More inclusive institutions can promote social cohesion and reduce marginalisation by amplifying the voices of underrepresented groups, including women, indigenous peoples, LGBTI communities, migrants, and informal workers (OECD, 2022[48]). Leveraging citizens' views to identify and address pressing needs also contributes to more legitimate and effective policies (OECD, 2022[48]). Extensive evidence highlights the positive impacts of civic engagement in improving access to essential services, such as healthcare (Wickremasinghe et al., 2018[49]; Nwobashi and Itumo, 2017[50]) and water and sanitation (Guimarães, Malheiros and Marques, 2016[51]), while also reducing poverty and inequality (Nieto-Aleman et al., 2019[52]; Akobeng, 2016[53]; Das and Das, 2017[54]). This section presents citizen participation experiences across the Caribbean and highlights the need to address the multiple vulnerabilities experienced by women in the region.

Citizen participation experiences in Caribbean countries

Efforts to foster citizen engagement and strengthen social cohesion in the Caribbean encompass a range of initiatives. These include institutional transitions linked to constitutional reforms, independence, and the establishment of republics; social programmes aimed at vulnerable populations such as indigenous communities and high-violence areas; the adoption of digital tools; and the implementation of open government initiatives. While differing in scope and varying degrees of success in participation and impact, these experiences can offer lessons on engaging civil society.

The Constitutional reform process in Trinidad and Tobago, launched in January 2024, aims to gather citizens' views in drafting a more inclusive constitution. A National Advisory Committee has organised 16 town hall meetings across all municipalities, three youth forums and launched a dedicated website[4] to gather public input and raise awareness of the reform. Public consultations revealed concerns about strengthening democracy, combating corruption, and protecting environmental, social, and cultural rights. Expert meetings supported the committee in evaluating the reform's practicality and feasibility (National Advisory Committee on Constitutional Reform, 2024[55]). Critics of the reform process emerged, alleging low participation and a lack of clarity on participation procedures and input evaluation.

Citizen engagement has also played a role in political transitions across the Caribbean. In 2021, 55 years after gaining independence, the government of Barbados expressed its will to start the process of becoming a republic. An independent study conducted by researchers from the University of the West Indies, in collaboration with the University of London, found that half of the respondents agreed the country should have its own elected head of state (Barrow-Giles and Devonish, 2021[56]), while 30% were indifferent between a republic or a monarchy (Barrow-Giles, 2021[57]). Since then, the country has been advancing towards a new Constitution. The Constitutional Reform Commission released a dedicated report in November 2024 outlining key recommendations to guide the reform process. These include empowering citizens through strengthening protections for basic rights, promoting gender parity in the Upper House of Parliament and increasing the number of seats to opposition parties in the Senate to enhance representation (ConstitutionNet, 2024[58]). In some Caribbean countries, referendums are necessary for transitioning to a republic. In Jamaica, Saint Kitts and Nevis, Saint Lucia, and The Bahamas, a simple majority is sufficient to consider the referendum valid, while in Antigua and Barbuda, Grenada and Saint Vincent and the Grenadines, a two-thirds majority is needed. In 2009, Saint Vincent and the Grenadines held a referendum to become a republic, which failed as only 45% of the voters supported the change. (Carrington, 2022[59]). Similarly, in 2011, the Constitutional Reform Commission (CRC) in Saint Lucia recommended several political reforms, including a move towards a republic (Barrow-Giles, 2024[60]). Over five years, the CRC held over 200 engagements with community groups, schools, and constitutional officeholders, in addition to organising public lectures and panel discussions (Barrow-Giles, 2024[60]; CRC, 2011[61]).

In terms of citizen engagement to improve the impact of specific social programmes, an interesting example is the Amerindian Development Fund, created in 2012 in Guyana by the Ministry of Amerindian Affairs in collaboration with the UNDP. Its main objective is to promote the socio-economic development of Amerindian communities, which generally face marginalisation and high poverty rates (MoAA, 2016[62]). By 2019, 154 communities had participated, resulting in nearly 1 000 new jobs and locally driven development projects. The programme aimed to create Community Development Plans and fund community development projects identified by the communities themselves through an open and democratic dialogue process (GRIF, 2023[63]).

Caribbean countries are exploring the use of technology to enhance democratic engagement through e-participation tools that expand citizen involvement in decision making. For example, Jamaica's Digital Citizen Participation pilot initiative, "Tell your MP", was designed to familiarise civil society with the Constituency Development Fund (CDF) process and to increase constituent participation through a combination of digital and in-person methods (The Caribbean Open Institute, 2024[64]).

Public institutions in Caribbean countries are gradually becoming more open. Open government practices can help build public trust by fostering inclusiveness in public policy decisions (OECD, 2015[65]; Matasick, 2017[66]). The Dominican Republic and Jamaica have joined the Open Government Partnership (OGP).[5] Guyana and Trinidad and Tobago meet the necessary criteria regarding fiscal transparency, access to information, disclosure of public officials' assets, and citizen engagement, and are thus considered eligible for membership (OGP, 2024[67]). Jamaica joined OGP in 2021 and has prioritised modernising its legal framework for information access, youth involvement in environmental issues, and establishing an open justice data portal. The Dominican Republic, an OGP member since 2016, has focused on enhancing government transparency and citizen engagement through accessible data and participatory mechanisms. Its commitments have fostered reforms in areas like public procurement and environmental sustainability while creating a strong multistakeholder forum to amplify civil society voices (OGP, 2024[68]).

As a concrete example of open government actions, Jamaica, Trinidad and Tobago and the Dominican Republic are implementing participatory budgeting initiatives to strengthen civic participation. Evidence shows that countries with a higher level of openness in the budget process tend to exhibit, on average, lower levels of inequality and higher levels of democracy (IBP, 2023[69]).

The Dominican Republic has implemented public consultations, with the General Directorate of Budget (Digepres) launching an online citizen budget consultation in 2023 to gather feedback and enhance transparency (Ministerio de Hacienda, 2022[70]). In Jamaica, the Jamaica Accountability Meter Portal (JAMP) aims to strengthen democratic governance beyond elections, promoting public oversight by using data to track public resources use and providing tools to help ensure parliamentary accountability (JAMP, 2018[71]). Outside the Caribbean, the Brazilian Transparency Portal exemplifies how open access to public information enables citizens to monitor public expenditures and hold officials accountable, leading to a 25% reduction in government credit card spending and the revision of social welfare programme rules following reports of fund mismanagement and nepotism, prompted by the publication of public officials' salaries (OECD-OPSI, 2018[72]).

Policy reforms often directly impact specific communities and territories, hence the importance of involving them from the beginning of projects. Participatory tools should ensure the widest access for all citizens, especially the most vulnerable groups. Early citizen participation is crucial in decisions such as the location of facilities associated with an investment or the terms of an environmental impact assessment. Among other useful practices, neighbourhood assemblies and facility visits can allow broad consultations with enterprises and government representatives. Temporary co-ordination committees can be instrumental in forming smaller groups that bring together representatives from companies, civil associations, neighbourhood groups, and local governments to supervise the progress of projects. In turn, collaboration with local universities or non-governmental organisations can be useful for providing technical assistance, especially at key moments such as pre-feasibility studies or environmental or social impact assessments (OECD et al., 2023[73]).

Local-level open government participation initiatives are emerging across the Caribbean. These include interactive community mapping projects in Jamaica aimed at boosting community-based tourism (Young and Verhulst, 2017[74]) and urban development initiatives led by UN-Habitat with local communities in several Haitian cities (Dame Marie, Jérémie, Beaumont, Les Cayes and Port-au-Prince) to design potential interventions and tailor urban planning to local needs and public space usage (UN-Habitat, 2024[75]).

Women are largely under-represented in the political and business life

Women in the Caribbean region face different obstacles – from gender-based violence to unequal pay and limited access to education and health care (Chapter 2). Women's representation in politics in the Caribbean is also low. In 2022, women held only 23.7% of parliamentary seats compared to 33.8% in LAC on average (Figure 4.11). Guyana (35.4%) and Dominica (34.4%) show the highest female parliamentary representation, surpassing Latin America's average. At the firm level, respondents in 6 Caribbean countries[6] show that, on average, 70.3% of the owners and shareholders of the firms where they work are all male or predominantly male. This ranges from 60% in Jamaica to almost 80% in Barbados (78%) and Trinidad and Tobago (76%) (IDB, 2021[7]). Moreover, only 18.5% of Caribbean firms actively seek to employ, retain, develop and promote women, ranging from 8% in Barbados to 28% in Guyana (IDB, 2021[7]). Based on these figures, inclusive institutions need to promote women's empowerment and gender equality in the region, both in the public and private sectors and at the household level.

Figure 4.11. Women's political representation in Caribbean countries, 2022

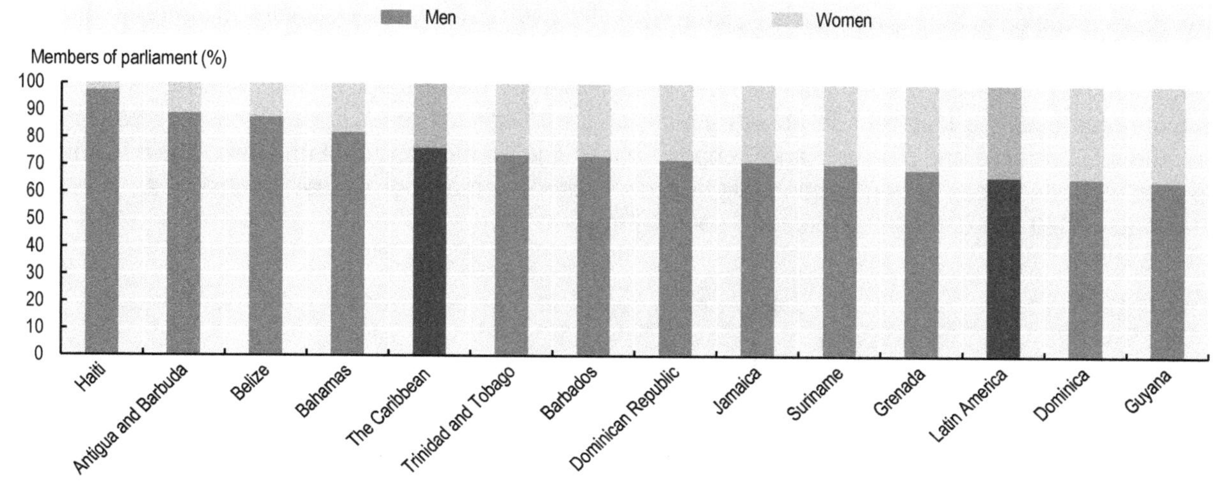

The Latin American average considers Argentina, Bolivia, Brazil, Chile, Colombia, Costa Rica, Ecuador, El Salvador, Guatemala, Honduras, Mexico, Nicaragua, Panama, Paraguay, Peru, Uruguay and Venezuela. The Caribbean average considers Antigua and Barbuda, The Bahamas, Barbados, Belize, Dominica, the Dominican Republic, Grenada, Guyana, Haiti, Jamaica, Suriname and Trinidad and Tobago.
Source: Authors' elaboration based on OECD (2023[76]).

StatLink https://stat.link/j6i2gx

Towards a renewed social contract

Caribbean citizens report declining satisfaction with democratic institutions and the quality of key public services, while their concerns about critical policy dimensions, including security, the economy and climate change, remain high. In this context, addressing society's aspirations and rebuilding trust will require public institutions that are more efficient and inclusive. This section argues that these priorities should converge around a strengthened social contract, fostering a shared vision for Caribbean development built through consensus with citizens.

The section presents, first, the importance of rethinking the social contract in the region and analyses key pillars to make it strong, including how citizens trust and interrelate with each other and their support for policies that redistribute wealth and opportunities. Second, this section analyses how to make this renewed social contract possible, focusing on the importance of having a shared and co-ordinated vision of long-term development in Caribbean countries, built around a CoG approach and sound and inclusive National Development Plans (NDPs).

Caribbean citizens think their basic rights should be better protected, yet they have high trust in local communities and broad support for inequality reduction policies

The social contract is an implicit agreement encompassing a broad set of social norms, conventions, and shared expectations among various actors within a society. It represents a shared understanding of how power and resources should be allocated among various groups – notably citizens, the state, workers, and businesses – to achieve collective goals and what each social group gives to and receives from the state (OECD et al., 2023[73]; OECD et al., 2022[77]).

Strengthening the social contract in the Caribbean involves addressing society's main concerns. It means, for instance, addressing the protection of basic rights, as more than half of Caribbean citizens (54.6%)

believe these are not well protected (Figure 4.12). This represents an increase of more than 10 percentage points compared to a decade ago (43.6%) when levels were similar to the Latin American average (42.1%). While dissatisfaction in Latin America has also grown (+ 6.8%), it has done so slowly, rising from 42.1% to 48.9%. Dissatisfaction levels regarding basic rights protection in the Caribbean vary widely, ranging from one-third of the population in Grenada to 75% in Haiti. However, dissatisfaction with basic rights protection has increased over the last decade across almost all Caribbean countries. The highest increases were observed in Suriname and Trinidad and Tobago, where figures almost doubled, while in the Dominican Republic and Jamaica, dissatisfaction slightly decreased, remaining almost unchanged. In Belize, dissatisfaction fell by nearly six percentage points (Figure 4.12).

Figure 4.12. Perception of citizens' basic rights protection, selected Caribbean countries, 2014 and 2023

Share of citizens who consider that citizens' basic rights are well protected by the political system

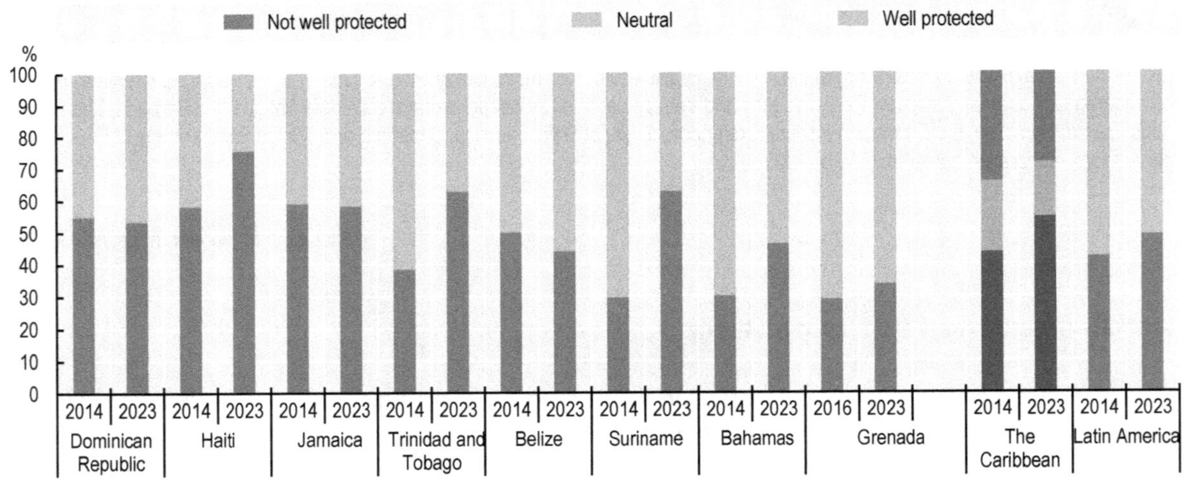

Note: The question featured in the figure is: "To what extent do you think that citizens' basic rights are well protected by the political system of (demonym)?". The Caribbean Average comprises eight countries: The Bahamas, Belize, Dominican Republic, Grenada, Haiti, Jamaica, Suriname, and Trinidad and Tobago. The Latin American average consists of 16 countries: Argentina, Bolivia, Brazil, Chile, Colombia, Costa Rica, Ecuador, El Salvador, Guatemala, Honduras, Mexico, Nicaragua, Panama, Paraguay, Peru and Uruguay.
Source: Authors' elaboration based on LAPOP Lab (2023[3]).

StatLink https://stat.link/xavy5l

Despite growing dissatisfaction among citizens, relatively high levels of interpersonal and strong support for policies aimed at reducing inequality are key aspects that can help Caribbean societies progress towards a new social contract. Interpersonal trust serves as a foundation for collective action, particularly through civil society organisations, which can be powerful channels to foster a collective dialogue and advocate for better public policies at the local level (Keefer, Scartascini and Vlaicu, 2018[78]). Trust among citizens and the norms governing their interactions contribute significantly to economic growth. They encourage the accumulation of both physical and human capital, improve the provision of public goods, and cultivate an environment conducive to market development and knowledge exchange (Beuermann et al., 2018[2]).

Caribbean society is characterised by relatively high levels of trust within communities. An average of 70% of citizens believe their neighbours and those living in their community are very or somewhat trustworthy (Figure 4.13). These levels have remained stable over the past decade, in contrast to a notable decline in Latin America, where community trust dropped by 10 percentage points, from 67.7% in 2014 to 57.2% in

2023. In all Caribbean countries, more than half of the population expressed some level of trust in their local community, with rates ranging from a minimum of 52.2% in Haiti to 87% in The Bahamas and 79.6% in Suriname (Figure 4.13).

Figure 4.13. High levels of trust in the local community, selected Caribbean countries, 2014 and 2023

Share of citizens by level of trust in the people living in their community/neighbourhood

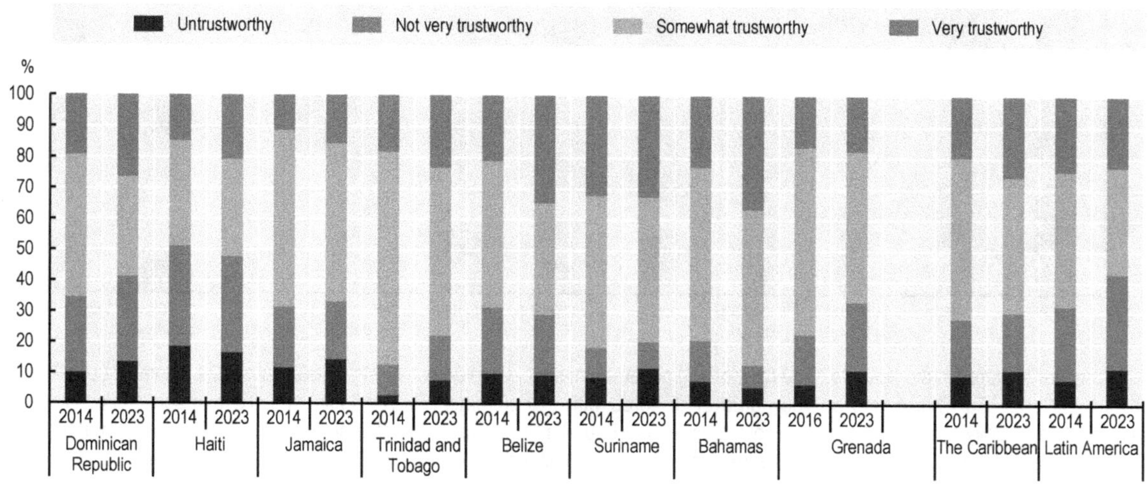

Note: The question featured in the figure is: "Speaking of the people from around here, would you say that people in this community/neighbourhood are very trustworthy, somewhat trustworthy, not very trustworthy or untrustworthy...?". The Caribbean Average comprises eight countries: The Bahamas, Belize, Dominican Republic, Grenada, Haiti, Jamaica, Suriname, and Trinidad and Tobago. The Latin American average comprises 16 countries: Argentina, Bolivia, Brazil, Chile, Colombia, Costa Rica, Ecuador, El Salvador, Guatemala, Honduras, Mexico, Nicaragua, Panama, Paraguay, Peru and Uruguay.
Source: Authors' elaboration based on LAPOP Lab (2023[3]).

StatLink https://stat.link/kyjlu9

Policies aimed at reducing inequality have broad support in the Caribbean (Figure 4.14). Almost 70% of Caribbean citizens (68.4%) support the implementation of policies to reduce income inequalities, similar to the Latin American average (68.9%). Support for policies to reduce income inequalities remains consistently high across all Caribbean countries, with the strongest support observed in Suriname (71.9%) and the Dominican Republic (75.1%).

Figure 4.14. Citizens' support for policies to reduce income inequality, selected Caribbean countries, 2023

Share of people who consider that strong policies should be implemented to reduce income inequalities

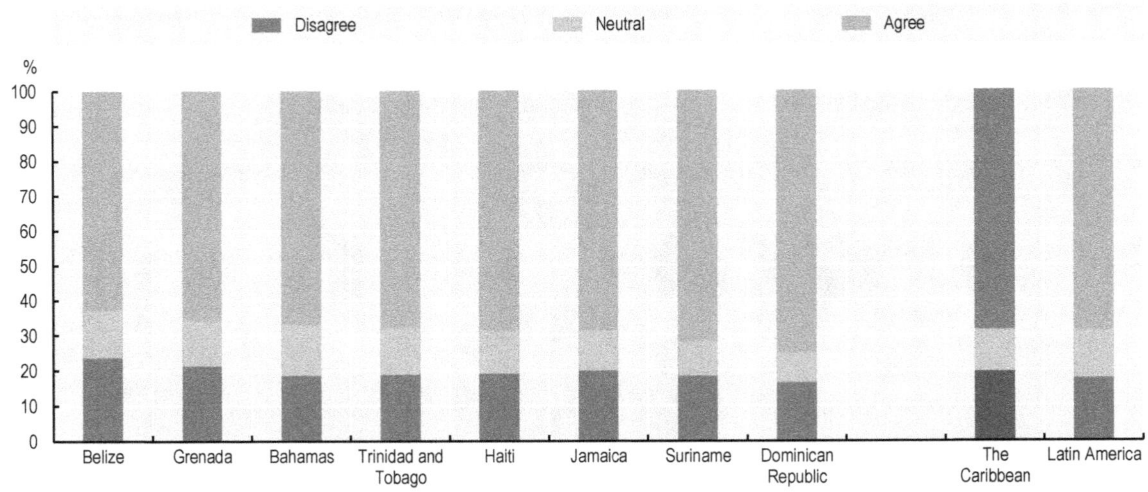

Note: The question featured in the figure is: "The (demonym) government should implement strong policies to reduce income inequality between the rich and the poor. To what extent do you agree or disagree with this statement?". The Latin America average considers Argentina, Plurinational State of Bolivia, Brazil, Chile, Colombia, Costa Rica, Ecuador, El Salvador, Guatemala, Honduras, Mexico, Nicaragua, Panama, Paraguay, Peru and Uruguay. The Caribbean average considers The Bahamas, Belize, the Dominican Republic, Grenada, Haiti, Jamaica, Trinidad and Tobago, and Suriname.
Source: Authors' elaboration based on LAPOP Lab (2023[3]).

StatLink https://stat.link/7vz5rc

Making a renewed social contract possible through institutional mechanisms to foster consensus and build a long-term vision of development

A renewed social contract requires far-reaching political agreement and consensus, re-balancing the roles of the state, market, society and the environment (OECD et al., 2021[79]; ECLAC, 2022[80]; Beuermann et al., 2021[81]), and taking into account citizens' needs. This social contract should serve to rethink the current development model from a multi-dimensional perspective, putting sustainable development and citizen well-being at the centre. This involves advancing sustainable production and consumption strategies, strengthening welfare systems, and ensuring sustainable financing for development models (Table 4.2). As sustainable policies disproportionally affect different socio-economic groups, territories and generations, an intersectional approach is crucial to balancing costs and benefits and garnering support while avoiding backlash against the sustainable agenda.

Such a renewed social contract will only endure and bear long-term effects if it secures buy-in and support from a wide stakeholder base. Engaging opponents of reform through an inclusive and consultative policy process usually pays dividends by fostering greater trust among involved parties. Consequently, stakeholders become more willing to commit to measures that mitigate personal costs resulting from changes (OECD, 2022[16]).

In practice, the sustainable development agenda involves policy trade-offs and the reallocation of resources among economic sectors and political constituencies that could trigger the opposition of some interest groups. Building consensus necessitates establishing inclusive and shared platforms for negotiated stances. Encouraging citizen participation, including vulnerable or marginalised groups, throughout the policy-making process can enhance local ownership and generate more inclusive policies that address local needs.

Policy makers should also engage the private sector by promoting awareness of responsible business conduct practices and establishing stronger integrity policies to prevent policy capture by powerful groups. Adapting strategies to socio-political contexts and devising empowering and empathic communication strategies for proposed sustainable reforms are vital. Strategies must also include ways to compensate vulnerable groups adversely affected in the short term.

A renewed social contract involves virtually every domain of public policy. Policy makers must work strategically and co-ordinate across sectors and levels of government to ensure a coherent policy agenda. An integrated approach is necessary to balance economic, social, and environmental trade-offs while leveraging policy spillovers among these fields.

The Centre of Government (CoG) can play a significant role in setting priority objectives and delivering results to citizens as it operates beyond the sector-specific limitations of ministries, departments, and agencies (Shostak et al., 2023[82]). While there is not a single institutional framework across countries, the CoG consists of the countries' chief executive (President or Prime Minister), institutions, units and individuals that participate in the policy cycle, and of the functions shaping this process (Santiso, Lafuente and Martín, 2013[83]). These functions encompass identifying needs and setting priorities, allocating the necessary resources, co-ordinating efforts among the government actors and external stakeholders to deliver on these priorities, and evaluating, monitoring, and communicating the outcomes. (Shostak et al., 2023[82]).

Moreover, the CoG can act as: a bridge between the political and administrative layers; a steward of strategic vision driving cohesive actions; a guide of good governance to enhance public sector efficiency; a stabiliser during crises, building resilience; a communicator fostering trust while combatting misinformation; and a system to maximise its potential (OECD, 2024[84]). Ultimately, a well-co-ordinated and efficient CoG strengthens long-term government capabilities, enhances the pursuit and delivery of policy priorities to tackle multi-dimensional challenges, fosters co-ordination across ministries and agencies, and encourages the development of actionable delivery plans to meet promises and objectives. It also rigorously evaluates policies, tailoring them to specific needs and preventing costly errors while managing the political economy of reform (Shostak et al., 2023[82]).

A snapshot of national development plans in the Caribbean: A critical tool to foster a new social contract

National development plans (NDPs) represent an instrumental tool to support a shared long-term vision for national development pathways in the Caribbean, outlining strategic goals and objectives and linking policy objectives with long-term plans and citizens' priorities. NDPs can help achieve consistent policy implementation over time, beyond short-term political cycles. This section presents existing NDPs in Caribbean countries and relevant aspects needed to advance towards a new social contract in the region.

A total of 12 Caribbean countries have NDPs or long-term visions in place: The Bahamas, Belize, Dominica, the Dominican Republic, Grenada, Guyana, Haiti, Jamaica, Saint Kitts and Nevis, Saint Vincent and the Grenadines, Suriname, and Trinidad and Tobago (Table 4.2). NDPs integrate various development areas, such as economic growth, social welfare, environmental sustainability and governance, to promote a co-ordinated approach to policy making.

NDPs in the Caribbean do not have a common structure, but there are similarities in their main strategic areas. Environmental sustainability is a common priority. The Bahamas, Dominica, Grenada, Guyana, and Trinidad and Tobago all emphasise the need for sustainable management of natural resources, while the Dominican Republic and Grenada emphasise the need to address climate change and build disaster-resilient infrastructure.

Belize explicitly mentions health and well-being objectives, while most Caribbean countries include them more indirectly in broader human development goals. Saint Vincent and the Grenadines and Trinidad and Tobago highlight improving infrastructure and adopting modern technology, linking economic growth with technological development. Cultural identity and national pride are integrated into the plans of Saint Vincent and the Grenadines and Jamaica, underscoring the importance of social cohesion and cultural preservation in national development.

Governance and efficient public administration are emphasised across the region, with countries like The Bahamas, Belize, the Dominican Republic, and Suriname prioritising institutional transparency goals. Human capital and social development are also central, with The Bahamas, Belize, Grenada, and Saint Vincent and the Grenadines focusing on education and social well-being. Economic growth and resilience feature prominently, with Belize, Dominica, Grenada and Jamaica targeting economic development and transformation.

Interconnected themes demonstrate comprehensive notions of development in the Caribbean. The themes include governance, human capital, economic resilience, environmental sustainability, social equity, and cultural identity. Countries need to enhance implementation, monitoring, and evaluation capacities to help make these goals a reality.

OECS countries have adopted the OECS Development Strategy 2019-28. This strategy is organised around three main pillars: generating economic growth; promoting human and social well-being; and the sustainable use of natural endowments (OECD, 2022[16]).

Table 4.2. National Development Plans, selected Caribbean countries

Country	Year	Strategic pillars
The Bahamas	2040	(1) Governance; (2) Human capital; (3) Environment; (4) Economy
Belize	2030	(1) Democratic governance for effective public administration and sustainable development; (2) Education for development; (3) Economic resilience; (4) Healthy citizens and a healthy environment
Dominica	2030	(1)E conomic development and transformation; (2) Environmental management; (3) Social development, social protection and poverty reduction
Dominican Republic	2030	(1) A state with efficient and transparent institutions; (2) Cohesive society; (3) An articulated, innovative and sustainable economy; (4) Sustainable environmental management and adequate adaptation to climate change
Grenada	2035	(1) High human and social development; (2) Vibrant economy with supporting climate-and-disaster resilient infrastructure; (3) Environmental sustainability and security
Guyana	2030	(1) Sustainable forestry and low-impact mining; (2) Implement mineral mapping; (3) Integrated planning and management of the mining and forest sectors; (4) Sustainable forest management; (5) Low-impact mining; (6) Forest climate services; (7) Ecosystem services; (8) Forest ecosystems; (9) Biodiversity conservation and protection
Haiti	2030	(1) Territorial reform; (2) Economic reform; (3) Social reform; (4) Institutional reform
Jamaica	2030	(1) Jamaicans are empowered to achieve their fullest potential; (2) The Jamaican society is secure, cohesive and just; (3) Jamaica's economy is prosperous; (4) Jamaica has a healthy natural environment
Saint Kitts and Nevis	2030	(1) Human capital and well-being; (2) Poverty and inequality reduction; (3) Sustainable economic growth and innovation; (4) Environmental sustainability; (5) Peace, justice and institutions; (6) International partnerships; (7) Sustainable urban planning
Saint Vincent and the Grenadines	2025	(1) Re-engineering economic growth; (2) Enabling increased human and social development; (3) Promoting good governance and increasing the effectiveness of public administration; (4) Improving physical infrastructure, preserving the environment and building resilience to climate change; (5) Building national pride, identity and culture
Suriname	2026	(1) Good governance; (2) Security; (3) Employment; (4) Value addition; (5) Profitable industries; (6) Green growth; (7) International and local access; (8) Land rights
Trinidad and Tobago	2030	(1) Putting people first: Nurturing our greatest asset; (2) Delivering good governance and service excellence; (3) Improving productivity through quality infrastructure and transportation; (4) Building globally competitive businesses; (5) Placing the environment at the centre of social and economic development.

Source: Authors' elaboration based on ECLAC (2024[85]).

A sectoral analysis of NDPs in 12 Caribbean countries sheds light on the current long-term national priorities across the seven key areas of opportunity for development in the Caribbean identified in Chapter 3 (Figure 4.15). The results derive from a text-mining analysis reflecting the relative frequency within each NDP of certain topics linked to the seven priority areas. These areas are energy transition, the blue economy, digital transformation, nature-based solutions, the circular economy, sustainable tourism and sustainable transport.

Figure 4.15. Key areas of opportunity in Caribbean NDPs

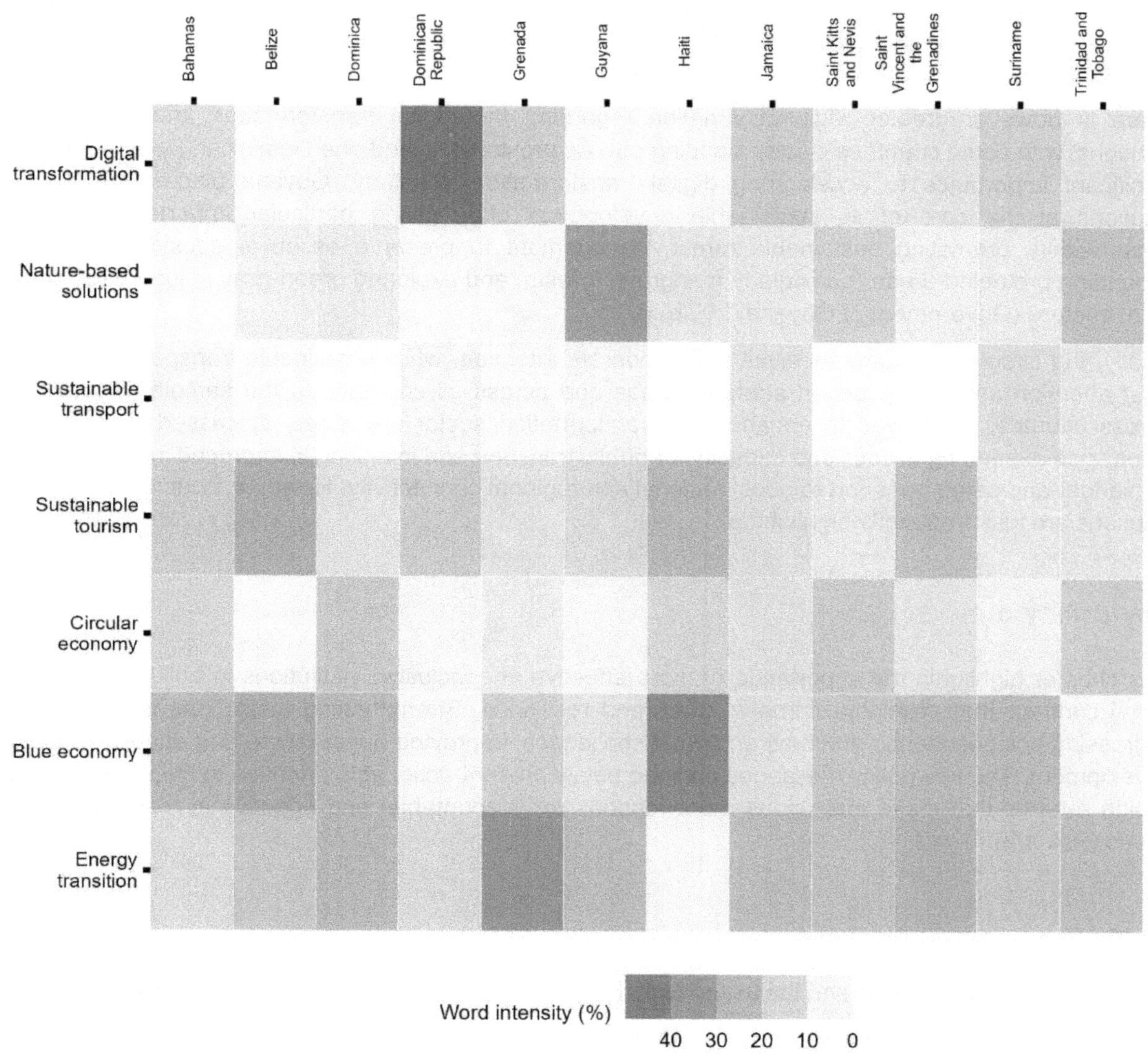

Note: Colour intensity indicates the frequency of mentions in the NDPs of 12 Caribbean countries. The darker the colour, the higher the frequency of mentions. The sum of the relative frequencies across all sectors in a country's NDP is 100. Each country's text data comes from their latest NDP.
Source: Authors' elaboration.

StatLink https://stat.link/amto8v

Energy transition is frequently mentioned across most countries, particularly in Grenada. Due to its high reliance on non-renewable energy imports, which represent 91% of the country's energy consumption, Grenada faces challenges with volatile energy markets and important CO_2 emissions (MoF, 2019[86]). To address these issues, the country aims to ensure energy security and efficiency by implementing strategies such as feed-in tariffs to encourage investment and uptake of renewable energies, alongside implementing Minimum Energy Performance Standards (MEPS) to promote more efficient energy consumption (MoF, 2019[86]). Guyana, a commodity exporter, also places considerable relative importance in the energy transition and is committed to channelling revenues from carbon and ecosystem services into building a more sustainable energy system centred on hydropower, solar and wind power and fostering low-carbon growth by 2030 (Government of Guyana, 2022[87]).

The blue economy also appears to be a crucial area for most Caribbean countries. For instance, Belize is making considerable efforts to develop the blue economy, followed by Dominica and The Bahamas. Sustainable tourism is another primary priority in Caribbean NDPs, with particular relevance in countries like Belize, Haiti, and Saint Vincent and the Grenadines.

There is however greater regional variation regarding the digital transformation and nature-based solutions, with some countries clearly standing out. As previously noted, the Dominican Republic is giving significant importance to accelerating digital transformation. Similarly, Guyana places nature-based solutions at the core of its sustainable development plan, giving particular importance to forest conservation, promoting sustainable forest management to preserve essential ecosystem services, expanding protected areas (particularly mangrove forests) and exploring green-grey solutions for coastal infrastructure (Government of Guyana, 2022[87]).

Finally, the circular economy receives only moderate attention, while sustainable transport receives the least attention among the seven strategic areas and across all countries in the sample (Figure 4.15). Across countries, initiatives to enhance the transportation sector are widely discussed. These efforts emphasise expanding access and capacity for public transport and investing in improved infrastructure for passenger and cargo transport to boost national and regional connectivity. However, concrete sustainable solutions are less frequently highlighted.

Key policy messages

This chapter highlights the importance of more effective and inclusive institutions in building a renewed social contract that promotes fairness, trust, and resilience. Strengthening institutions is essential for addressing socioeconomic and environmental challenges, improving governance, and enabling inclusive development. The key policy messages outlined below present actionable priorities to help policy makers design reforms that make institutions more responsive, accountable, and effective in meeting people's needs (Box 4.2).

Box 4.2. Key policy messages

Improve statistical systems and the use of digital technologies for more effective institutions

- Strengthen national statistical systems to close data gaps by improving data infrastructure, promoting statistical literacy, fostering stronger legislation and standards, and establishing co-ordination mechanisms and data-sharing agreements.
- Enhance data quality by generating more comprehensive and accurate survey, census, administrative, and geospatial data by encouraging the private sector and citizens involvement as well as regional co-operation.
- Advance digital transformation by investing in digital tools, e-government and AI in at least five key areas: governance and institutions, legal and regulatory framework, digital talent and change management, infrastructure and technology, and new digital processes and services.

Advance more inclusive institutions

- Promote citizen participation in public decision making to enhance trust in government and democratic institutions while addressing citizens' growing expectations including security, the economy, the environment, and the quality of public services.
- Amplify the voices of underrepresented groups, including women, indigenous peoples, LGBTI communities, migrants, and informal workers to promote social cohesion and reduce marginalisation. Inclusive institutions should particularly promote women's empowerment and gender equality across the public and private sectors, and within households.

Renew and strengthen the social contract

- Develop a shared and co-ordinated vision for long-term development, built around a Centre of Government approach and sound and inclusive National Development Plans.
- Develop inclusive and shared platforms for dialogue and negotiation, encouraging private sector and citizen participation, including vulnerable or marginalised groups, throughout the policy making process to enhance ownership and foster alignment with citizen needs.
- Tailor strategies to socio-political contexts, incorporating measures to compensate short-term impacts on vulnerable groups and prioritising clear communication strategies to build support for necessary policy reforms.

Notes

[1] At least 4 324 homicides were reported in 2023 in Haiti (BINUH, 2024[13]); 2 088 were reported in 2022, up from 1 489 in 2021 (UNODC, 2023[11]).

[2] Data analysed starts from 2016 as the World Bank's Statistical Capacity Indicator (SCI) was replaced by the Statistical Performance Indicator (SPI) that year. The SPI covers more economies, uses a broader range of data sources and incorporates additional components in assessing statistical systems compared to the SCI.

[3] Participating countries: Aruba, Barbados, British Virgin Islands, Cuba, Curaçao, Dominica, Dominican Republic, Grenada, Guyana, Montserrat, Saint Lucia, Saint Kitts and Nevis, Suriname and Trinidad and Tobago. Representatives from Belize and Jamaica also participated.

[4] www.constitutionalreform2024.gov.tt.

[5] A global initiative aimed at promoting transparency, empowering citizens and fighting corruption. Member countries craft open plans with commitments elaborated by government authorities in consultation with civil society and multiple stakeholders.

[6] The Bahamas, Barbados, Guyana, Jamaica, Suriname, and Trinidad and Tobago.

References

Acemoglu, D. (2021), *Redesigning Ai*, MIT Press. [45]

Akobeng, E. (2016), "Growth and Institutions: A Potential Medicine for the Poor in Sub-Saharan Africa", *African Development Review*, https://doi.org/10.1111/1467-8268.12163. [53]

Arias, E. et al. (2024), "The state of education in Latin America and the Caribbean 2023", *Technical Note*, No. IDB-TN-02708, Inter-American Development Bank, Washington, DC, https://doi.org/10.18235/0005515. [8]

Barrow-Giles, C. (2024), "Reviving Constitutional Reform in Saint Lucia: The Role of the Parliamentary Constitutional Review Committee", *Voices from the Field*, https://constitutionnet.org/news/voices/reviving-constitutional-reform-st-lucia-role-parliamentary-constitutional-review-committee. [60]

Barrow-Giles, C. (2021), "Barbados' Long-drawn-out Promise of a Republic", *Voices from the Field*, https://constitutionnet.org/news/barbadoss-long-drawn-out-promise-republic. [57]

Barrow-Giles, C. and D. Devonish (2021), "Visible Crown Project", *Monarchy vs Republicanism: Barbadians Have their Say*, https://irp.cdn-website.com/8ca726a8/files/uploaded/Barbadian%20Public%20Opinion%20Survey%20Analysis%20Presentation%20191221%20.pdf. [56]

Beuermann, D. et al. (2021), *Economic Institutions for a Resilient Caribbean*, Inter-American Development Bank, Washington, DC, https://doi.org/10.18235/0003053. [81]

Beuermann, D. et al. (2018), *Nurturing Institutions for a Resilient Caribbean*, Inter-American Development Bank, Washington, DC, https://doi.org/10.18235/0001333. [2]

BINUH (2024), *Haiti Security and Crime Statistics Dataset (2018–2024)*. [13]

CAF (2024), "Leaders From Caribbean small Islands set priorities to ensure a digital transformation that leaves no one behind", 1 May, Press Release, Development Bank of Latin America and the Caribbean, Port-of-Spain, https://www.caf.com/en/currently/news/2024/05/leaders-from-caribbean-small-islands-set-priorities-to-ensure-a-digital-transformation-that-leaves-no-one-behind/. [46]

Cafferata, F. and C. Scartascini (2021), *Combating Crime in Latin America and the Caribbean: What Public Policies Do Citizens Want?*, https://doi.org/10.18235/0003306. [9]

CARICOM (2018), *The CARICOM Regional Strategy for the Developmet of Statistics (RSDS)*, https://caricom.org/wp-content/uploads/RSDS2020.pdf. [36]

Carrington, G. (2022), "The Visible Crown, Queen Elizabeth II and the Caribbean, 1952 to the present", *Routes to Republicanism in the Caribbean*, https://www.visiblecrown.com/routes-to-republicanism-in-the-caribbean. [59]

Coglianese, C. (2012), *Measuring Regulatory Performance: Evaluating the Impact of Regulation and Regulatory Policy*, https://citeseerx.ist.psu.edu/document?repid=rep1&type=pdf&doi=47319685d34eb420539054e461496732715207a2. [26]

ConstitutionNet (2024), *Barbados' constitutional reform commission releases report of recommendations*. [58]

CRC (2011), *Report of the Saint Lucia Constitutional Reform Commission*, https://www.govt.lc/media.govt.lc/www/resources/publications/FINAL%20REPORT%2030-03-2011.pdf. [61]

Cristia, J. et al. (2022), *A Cost-Benefit Analysis of Selected Digital Projects in Latin America and the Caribbean*, Inter-American Development Bank, Washington, DC, https://doi.org/10.18235/0004525. [39]

Cubo, A. et al. (2022), *Government Digital Transformation Guide: Executive Summary*, Inter-American Development Bank, Washington, DC, https://doi.org/10.18235/0004556. [40]

Das, S. and G. Das (2017), "Public Resource Allocation through Grassroots Democratic Institutions: Evidence from Assam, India", *International Journal of Public Administration*, https://doi.org/10.1080/01900692.2017.1387918. [54]

ECLAC (2024), *Regional Observatory on Planning for Development in Latin America and the Caribbean (website)*, United Nations Economic Commission for Latin America and the Caribbean, Santiago, https://observatorioplanificacion.cepal.org/en. [85]

ECLAC (2022), *Building a New Future: Transformative Recovery with Equality and Sustainability*, United Nations Economic Commission for Latin America and the Caribbean, Santiago, http://www. cepal.org/en/publications/46226-building-new-future-transformative-recovery-equality-and sustainability-summary. [80]

Eggers, W., D. Schatsky and P. Viechnicki (2017), *AI-Augmented Government: Using cognitive technologies to redesign public sector work*, Deloitte University Press, https://www2.deloitte.com/content/dam/insights/us/articles/3832_AI-augmented-government/DUP_AI-augmented-government.pdf. [43]

Floyd, S., I. Mkrtchyan and A. Abdulkadr (2023), "Statistical literacy: An enabler of statistical capacity in the Caribbean", *Studies and Perspectives*, No. 113, United Nations Economic Commission for Latin America and the Caribbean, Santiago, https://repositorio.cepal.org/server/api/core/bitstreams/2658a704-4899-4ae6-9620-2afca2bda6cd/content. [37]

Government of Guyana (2022), *Guyana's Low Carbon Development Strategy 2030*, https://lcds.gov.gy/. [87]

GRIF (2023), *Amerindian Development Fund - Village Economy Development*, https://www.guyanareddfund.org/project/amerindian-development-fund-phases-1-2/. [63]

Guimarães, E., T. Malheiros and R. Marques (2016), "Inclusive governance: New concept of water supply and sanitation services in social vulnerability areas", *Utilities Policy*, Vol. 43, pp. 124-129, https://doi.org/10.1016/j.jup.2016.06.003. [51]

Haitian Times (2024), *UN Security Council briefing highlights escalating crisis in Haiti amid calls for greater international support*. [23]

Heine, J. and A. Thompson (2011), *Introduction: Haiti's governance challenges and the international community*, United Nations University Press, https://doi.org/10.18356/32a14fca-en. [22]

IBP (2023), *Open Budget Survey 2023, 9th edition*, https://internationalbudget.org/wp-content/uploads/IBP-OBS-Global-Report-2023-v4-Final-Artwork.pdf. [69]

IDB (2021), *Compete Caribbean. Innovation, Firm Performance and Gender Survey*, (database), https://www.competecaribbean.org/docs/ifpg-survey/index.html (accessed on 2024 July 2024). [7]

IDB (2017), *Restoring Paradise in the Caribbean: Combatting Violence with Numbers*, Inter-American Development Bank, Washington, DC, https://publications.iadb.org/en/restoring-paradise-caribbean-combatting-violence-numbers-executive-summary. [10]

IMF (2022), *Publc Finances in Modern History [dataset]*, https://www.imf.org/external/datamapper/exp@FPP/HTI. [20]

IMF (2017), *Unleashing Growth and Strengthening Resilience in the Caribbean*, International Monetary Fund, Washington, DC, https://www.imf.org/en/Publications/Books/Issues/2018/02/26/Unleashing-Growth-and-Strengthening-Resilience-in-the-Caribbean-44910. [15]

JAMP (2018), *Jamaica Accountability Meter Portal*, https://www.jampja.org/who-we-are/about-us/. [71]

Keefer, P. and C. Scartascini (eds.) (2022), *Trust: The Key to Social Cohesion and Growth in Latin America and the Caribbean (Executive Summary)*, Inter-American Development Bank, https://doi.org/10.18235/0003911. [1]

Keefer, P., C. Scartascini and R. Vlaicu (2018), *Shortchanging the Future: The Short-Term Bias of Politics*, https://publications.iadb.org/en/shortchanging-future-short-term-bias-politics. [78]

LAPOP Lab (2023), *The AmericasBarometer*, LAPOP Lab, http://www.vanderbilt.edu/lapop. [3]

Matasick, C. (2017), “Open government: How transparency and inclusiveness can reshape public trust”, in *Trust and Public Policy: How Better Governance Can Help Rebuild Public Trust*, OECD Publishing, Paris, https://doi.org/10.1787/9789264268920-8-en. [66]

Ministerio de Hacienda (2022), *Digepres presenta Consulta Abierta sobre Presupuesto Ciudadano 2023*, https://www.hacienda.gob.do/digepres-presenta-consulta-abierta-sobre-presupuesto-ciudadano-2023/. [70]

MoAA (2016), *GRIF Amerindian Development Fund (ADF) Project*, https://moaa.gov.gy/amerindian-development-fund/. [62]

MoF (2019), *National Sustainable Development Plan 2020-2035 (Grenada)*, National Plan Secretariat, https://observatorioplanificacion.cepal.org/sites/default/files/plan/files/GRANADA-NSDP20202035.pdf. [86]

National Advisory Committee on Constitutional Reform (2024), *e the People: Report of the National Advisory Committee on Constitutional Reform*, https://constitutionalreform2024.gov.tt/wp-content/uploads/2024/08/Report-of-the-National-Advisory-Committee-on-Constitutional-Reform.pdf. [55]

Nieto-Aleman, P. et al. (2019), “Factors of regional poverty reduction in Colombia: Do institutional conditions matter?”, *Social Policy and Administration*, https://doi.org/10.1111/spol.12474. [52]

Nwobashi, H. and A. Itumo (2017), "Democracy, Town Unions and Provision of Health Facilities in Rural Communities of Ebonyi State: Evaluation of some Selected Communities", *European Journal of Social Sciences*, https://www.europeanjournalofsocialsciences.com/issues/PDF/EJSS_55_4_06.pdf. [50]

OECD (2024), *Steering from the Centre of Government in Times of Complexity: Compendium of Practices*, OECD Publishing, Paris, https://doi.org/10.1787/69b1f129-en. [84]

OECD (2023), *Social Institutions & Gender Index*, (database), https://www.oecd.org/en/data/dashboards/social-institutions-gender-index.html. [76]

OECD (2022), *Development Strategy Assessment of the Eastern Caribbean*, OECD Development Pathways, OECD Publishing, Paris, https://doi.org/10.1787/f1566c7a-en. [16]

OECD (2022), *OECD Guidelines for Citizen Participation Processes*, OECD Publishing, Paris, https://doi.org/10.1787/f765caf6-en. [48]

OECD (2021), *OECD Public Governance Reviews: Haiti, Strengthening Public Administration For Resilient and Sustainable Governance*, OECD Publishing, Paris, https://doi.org/10.1787/dfd5f806-en. [21]

OECD (2020), *Government at a Glance: Latin America and the Caribbean 2020*, OECD Publishing, Paris, https://doi.org/10.1787/13130fbb-en. [19]

OECD (2020), *Policy Framework on Sound Public Governance: Baseline Features of Governments that Work Well*, OECD Publishing, Paris, https://doi.org/10.1787/c03e01b3-en. [25]

OECD (2015), *Government at a Glance 2015*, OECD Publishing, Paris, https://doi.org/10.1787/gov_glance-2015-50-en. [65]

OECD et al. (2023), *Latin American Economic Outlook 2023: Investing in Sustainable Development*, OECD Publishing, Paris, https://doi.org/10.1787/8c93ff6e-en. [73]

OECD et al. (2022), *Latin American Economic Outlook 2022: Towards a Green and Just Transition*, OECD Publishing, Paris, https://doi.org/10.1787/3d5554fc-en. [77]

OECD et al. (2021), *Latin American Economic Outlook 2021: Working Together for a Better Recovery*, OECD Publishing, Paris, https://doi.org/10.1787/5fedabe5-en. [79]

OECD/CAF (2023), *Digital Government Review of Latin America and the Caribbean: Building Inclusive and Responsive Public Services*, OECD Digital Government Studies, OECD Publishing, Paris, https://doi.org/10.1787/29f32e64-en. [41]

OECD/CAF (2022), *The Strategic and Responsible Use of Artificial Intelligence in the Public Sector of Latin America and the Caribbean*, OECD Publishing, Paris, https://doi.org/10.1787/1f334543-en. [34]

OECD-OPSI (2018), *Brazilian Transparency Policy and the Transparency Portal*, https://oecd-opsi.org/innovations/brazilian-transparency-policy-and-the-transparency-portal/. [72]

OGP (2024), *Dominican Republic*, https://www.opengovpartnership.org/members/dominican-republic/. [68]

OGP (2024), *Eligibility Criteria & OGP Values Check Assessment*, https://www.opengovpartnership.org/process/joining-ogp/eligibility-criteria/. [67]

PARIS21 (2024), *Guidelines for National Strategy for the Development of Statistics (NSDS)*. [35]

PARIS21 (2021), "ODIN Overall Score in 2020", *Statistical Capacity Monitor*, Paris 21, https://statisticalcapacitymonitor.org/indicator/136. [32]

Pellegrini, S. (2024), *ACLED*, https://acleddata.com/2024/10/23/gang-violence-in-the-caribbean-reaches-farther-than-haiti/. [14]

Santiso, C., M. Lafuente and A. Martín (2013), *The Role of the Center of Government: A Literature Review*, https://doi.org/10.18235/0009130. [83]

Shostak, R. et al. (2023), *The Center of Government, Revisited: A Decade of Global Reforms*, Inter-American Development Bank, https://doi.org/10.18235/0004994. [82]

Statistics Canada (2023), *Project for the Regional Advancement of Statistics in the Caribbean (PRASC)*, https://www.statcan.gc.ca/en/about/cooperation/prasc. [38]

Sutton, H. et al. (2017), *Restoring Paradise in the Caribbean: Combatting Violence with Numbers*, https://doi.org/10.18235/0012654. [4]

The Caribbean Open Institute (2024), *Digital Citizen Participation in Jamaica with Tell Your MP*, https://caribbeanopeninstitute.org/TellYourMP. [64]

The Fund for Peace (2023), "Global data", *Fragile States Index*, (database), https://fragilestatesindex.org/global-data/. [24]

Transparency International (2022), *Transparency International Corruption Perception Index*, (database), https://www.transparency.org/en/cpi/2023. [5]

Ubaldi, B. et al. (2019), "State of the art in the use of emerging technologies in the public sector", *OECD Working Papers on Public Governance*, No. 31, OECD Publishing, Paris, https://doi.org/10.1787/932780bc-en. [44]

UNDP (2024), *High Level Conference: SIDS 2.0: Defining the pathway for Small Islands DIGITAL States in the Caribbean*. [47]

UNDP and DIE (2022), *Connections that Matter: How the Quality of Governance Institutions may be the Booster Shot we need to reduce Poverty and Inequality*, https://www.undp.org/policy-centre/governance/publications/connections-matter-how-quality-governance-institutions-may-be-booster-shot-we-need-reduce-poverty-and. [27]

UNESCO (2023), *Country Office Annual Report 2023: Haiti*. [18]

UN-Habitat (2024), *Our City Plans*, https://ourcityplans.org/. [75]

United Nations (2022), *UN E-Government Survey 2022*, United Nations, https://publicadministration.un.org/egovkb/en-us/Reports/UN-E-Government-Survey-2022. [42]

UNODC (2023), *UNODC Global Study on Homicide 2023. Homicide and organized crime in latin america and the Caribbean*. [11]

UNODC (2022), "International homicide statistics", *dataUNODC*, (database), https://dataunodc.un.org/dp-intentional-homicide-victims. [12]

Warf, B. and S. Stewart (2016), "Latin American Corruption in Geograpgic Perspective", *Journal of Latin American Geography*, https://www.jstor.org/stable/43964653. [28]

Wickremasinghe, D. et al. (2018), "It's About the Idea Hitting the Bull's Eye": How Aid Effectiveness Can Catalyse the Scale-up of Health Innovations", https://pubmed.ncbi.nlm.nih.gov/30078292/. [49]

World Bank (2024), *The World Bank in Haiti*, https://www.worldbank.org/en/country/haiti/overview. [17]

World Bank (2023), *Data absence hampers poverty reduction efforts in the Caribbean*. [33]

World Bank (2022), *Statistical Performance Indicators (SPI) [dataset]*, https://datanalytics.worldbank.org/SPI/. [31]

World Bank (2022), *Worldwide Governance Indicators [dataset]*, https://www.worldbank.org/en/publication/worldwide-governance-indicators/interactive-data-access. [29]

World Bank (2021), *Measuring the Statistical Performance of Countries: An Overview of Updates to the World Bank Statistical Capacity Index*. [30]

World Justice Project (2023), *Corruption in the Caribbean: Insights from the General Public 2022*, World Justice Project, Washiington, DC, https://worldjusticeproject.org/sites/default/files/documents/Corruption-in-the-Caribbean-report-v4.pdf. [6]

Young, A. and S. Verhulst (2017), *Jamaica, Community, Tourism, and Open Data*, https://odimpact.org/files/case-jamaica-community-tourism-and-open-data.pdf. [74]

5 Financing the development agenda

Addressing the main development challenges and opportunities of the Caribbean will require the mobilisation of substantial amounts of financial resources, both public and private, domestic and international. This chapter explores the need to strengthen tax collection, make the taxation system more progressive and rationalise tax exemptions while fighting tax evasion. It argues these steps are essential to spur public investment, finance key policy reforms and improve the quality of public services. It also analyses how managing debt sustainably and strengthening fiscal frameworks will be critical in countries with high levels of debt. To that end, it points to emerging opportunities on the back of new debt instruments that can be linked to green, social and blue development objectives. The chapter also examines the need to develop financial markets to facilitate access to finance.

Introduction

Caribbean countries need to mobilise substantial financial resources to face their development challenges and seize emerging opportunities. The region's climate vulnerability imposes significant economic and social costs, necessitating considerable investment in adaptation strategies and resilient infrastructure. Furthermore, climate-related risks contribute to higher financing costs for Caribbean nations, which already face difficulties in mobilising sufficient domestic financial resources, partly due to their small economic size. Beyond climate considerations, Caribbean countries confront pressing economic, social, and institutional challenges that require substantial funding. At the same time, the region has significant potential to unlock development opportunities, such as those linked to its rich biodiversity and natural resources. However, realizing this potential will also depend on the successful mobilization of financing.

This chapter examines ways to mobilise both domestic and international resources, from public and private sources. It underscores the need for tax reform, advocating for enhanced tax collection, a more progressive taxation system, the rationalisation of tax exemptions while fighting tax evasion. The chapter also emphasizes the importance of sustainable debt management and robust fiscal frameworks, particularly for countries facing high debt levels. In the context, this chapter explores the emerging potential of innovative debt instruments linked to green, social, and blue development objectives, where Caribbean countries have been pioneers. Finally, the chapter analyses the need to develop financial markets to improve access to finance across the region.

Tax revenues in the Caribbean can be strengthened to finance the development agenda

Tax-to-GDP ratios are, on average, below OECD and Latin American levels, though with high heterogeneity across Caribbean countries

In 2022, average tax revenues in the Caribbean region were 21% of gross domestic product (GDP), slightly below the 22.4% of GDP in Latin America and significantly lower than the OECD average of 34% (Figure 5.1, Panel A). The Caribbean average includes The Bahamas, Barbados, Belize, Dominican Republic, Guyana, Jamaica, Saint Lucia, and Trinidad and Tobago, the eight Caribbean countries for which comparable data are available (OECD et al., 2024[1]).

Heterogeneity is large across Caribbean economies. Tax revenues as a share of GDP varied greatly from Barbados (31.9%) to the Dominican Republic (14.5%) and Guyana (10.6%) (Figure 5.1, Panel B) (OECD et al., 2024[1]). Average tax-to-GDP ratios in the Caribbean fell below the Latin American average in 2022, in large part due to the evolution of specific countries. Guyana experienced the most pronounced decline in the region in the tax-to-GDP ratio, with a loss of 10.7 percentage points since 2020. It was followed by Barbados and Saint Lucia, each with a loss of 2.9 percentage points. Guyana's substantial GDP growth in recent years (an increase of 83% in nominal GDP and 63% in real terms) resulted from strong growth in oil production and high oil prices. This growth, combined with a slower increase in nominal tax revenue (only 15%), contributed to the large decreases (OECD et al., 2024[1]).

Figure 5.1. Evolution of tax-to-GDP ratios, regional averages and Caribbean countries, 2010-22

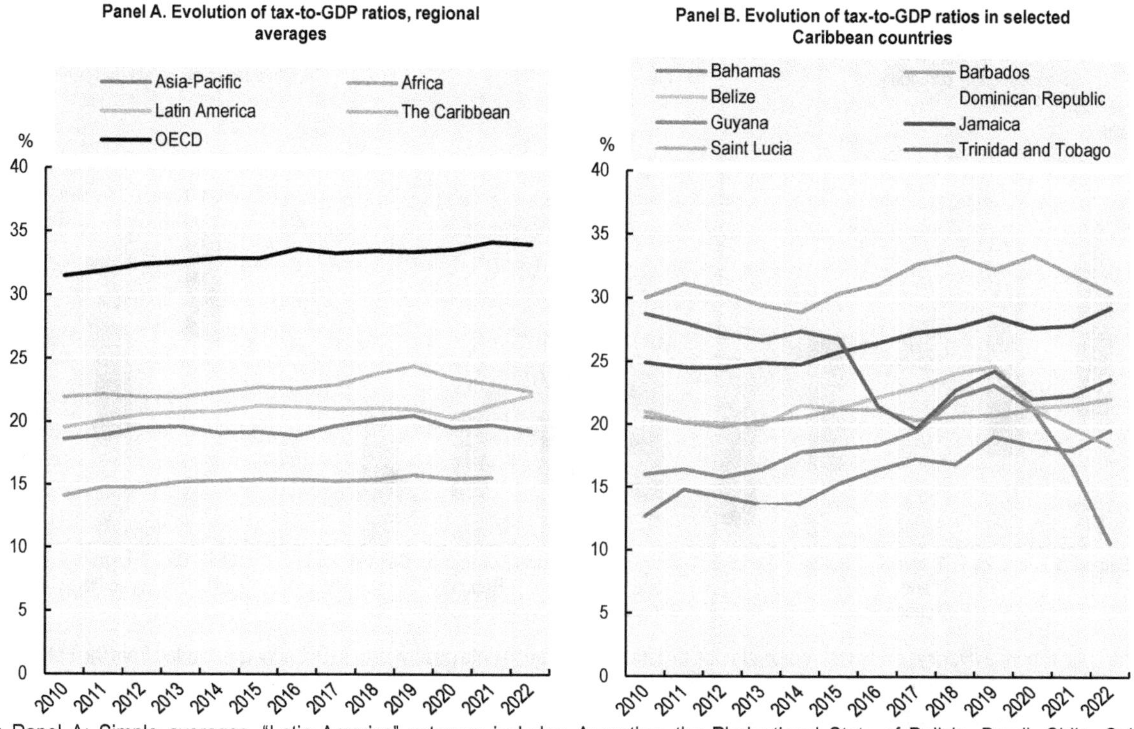

Note: Panel A: Simple averages. "Latin America" category includes Argentina, the Plurinational State of Bolivia, Brazil, Chile, Colombia, Costa Rica, Ecuador, El Salvador, Guatemala, Honduras, Mexico, Nicaragua, Panama, Paraguay, Peru and Uruguay. The Caribbean includes The Bahamas, Barbados, Belize, the Dominican Republic, Guyana, Jamaica, Saint Lucia, and Trinidad and Tobago. Data for Africa in 2022 are not available.

Source: (OECD et al., 2024[1]; OECD, 2023[2]).

StatLink https://stat.link/ow9fj2

In Barbados, tax-to-GDP ratios are still the highest in the Caribbean, but there has been a decline in tax revenues primarily due to a slower recovery in the tourism sector. This slower recovery has led to reduced revenues from value-added tax (VAT) and lower excise tax revenues. Additionally, the decrease in tax revenues is also attributed to reduced imports, including fuel, lower domestic sales and increased tax refunds (The Barbados Advocate, 2021[3]; Ministry of Finance of Barbados, 2024[4]).

There is space to improve the structure of taxation systems to make them more efficient and equitable

The tax structure in the region is characterised by a low contribution of direct taxes, notably personal income taxes (PIT) and social security contributions (SSCs), alongside a high reliance on indirect taxes. This structure is similar to the average of Latin American countries and contrasts with OECD countries (Figure 5.2).

As a percentage of total tax revenues, indirect taxes (VAT plus other taxes on goods and services) accounted for an average of 55% in the Caribbean. This was higher than the Latin American average of 48%. It was also significantly above the OECD average of 32%.

Corporate income tax (CIT) represented a larger share for the Caribbean than for the OECD, although with heterogeneity across countries. On average, CIT revenues represented 17.5% of total tax revenues in the Caribbean, compared to 12% in the OECD average. As a share of GDP, CIT revenues represented 3.6% in the Caribbean and 3.9% in the OECD averages (OECD et al., 2024[1]). In Trinidad and Tobago, CIT revenues accounted for 12.2% of GDP, while in the Dominican Republic, these represented 2.2%, and in The Bahamas, 0%.

Figure 5.2. Tax structure in selected Caribbean economies and Latin America and OECD averages, 2022

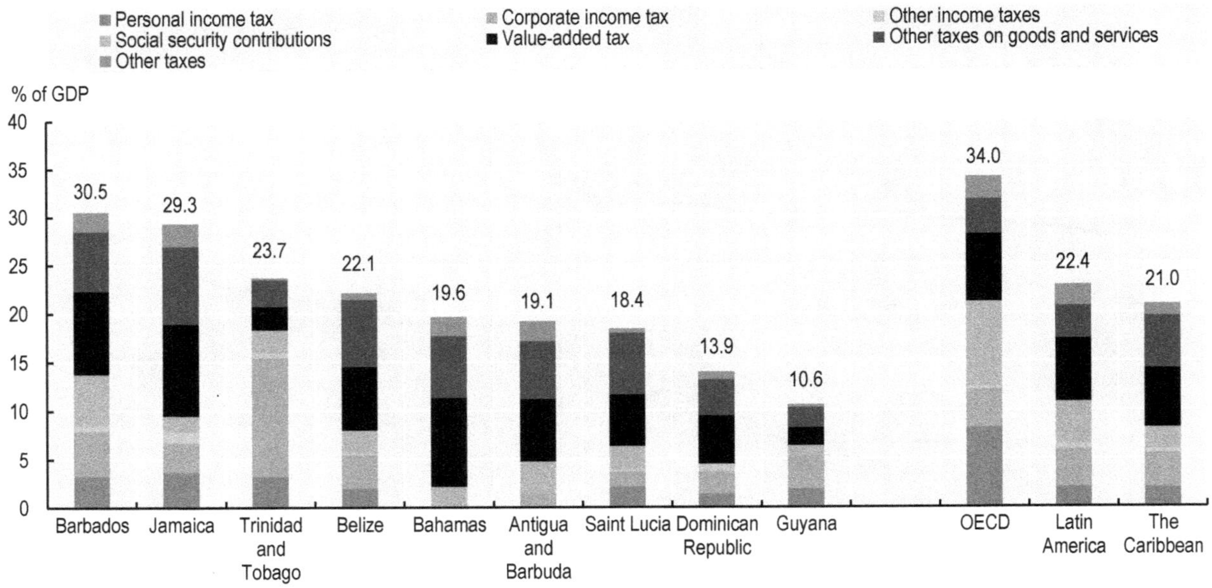

Note: The Latin America average excludes Venezuela due to data issues. Due to data quality issues, Ecuador is excluded from the Latin America average for PIT and CIT revenues. The OECD average represents the unweighted average of the 38 OECD member countries. Chile, Colombia, Costa Rica and Mexico are also part of the OECD (38).
Source: (OECD et al., 2024[1]).

StatLink https://stat.link/3l48or

Improving the collection levels of direct taxes, particularly PIT, can increase revenues while enhancing the redistributive impact of the tax system in some Caribbean countries. Recognising the heterogeneity in PIT collection is key in this region. Countries like Jamaica, Barbados, and Trinidad and Tobago have collection levels exceeding 3% of GDP. Conversely, the Dominican Republic has a level as low as 1.4%, while some countries, like Antigua and Barbuda and The Bahamas, do not have PIT at all.

Enhancing and re-assessing PIT design for some countries with low levels of PIT collection but high collection of indirect taxes holds promise for increasing progressivity and revenue generation. Factors contributing to low PIT collection in the region include: i) high levels of tax relief; ii) a narrow tax base of mostly formal-sector wages; and iii) high rates of tax evasion (Núñez and Lasso, 2023[5]). For instance, re-assessing PIT in the region could favour targeted tax relief measures over more general tax benefits.

Re-assessing the design of PIT must also be accompanied by a re-evaluation of indirect taxes. In many countries, indirect taxes are regressive, placing a disproportionate burden on low-income populations. Eliminating or phasing out inefficient VAT exemptions can improve the progressivity of the tax system in the region. VAT-targeted tax benefits should be more precise, and VAT exemptions should benefit poor households and vulnerable populations through effective and well-targeted compensation mechanisms.

To further increase revenues, Caribbean countries can also consider other untapped revenue sources, including non-tax revenues

Non-tax sources of revenue play an important role in several Caribbean countries. Non-tax revenues include non-tax income, capital income and grants. Similar to tax revenue trends in the region, revenues from these sources vary significantly across Caribbean countries, highlighting substantial differences between service exporters and natural resource exporters. In 2023, non-tax revenues accounted, on average, for 6.7% of GDP in 12 Caribbean countries (ECLAC, 2024[6]).[1]

Citizenship-by-investment programmes are a major source of non-tax revenues in some Caribbean countries. These government-run programmes grant foreign investors citizenship and a passport in exchange for contributing to the economy through approved investment channels. Receipts from citizenship-by-investment programmes represent an important share of non-tax revenues in some Caribbean countries. In Saint Kitts and Nevis, for example, receipts from such programmes amounted to 20.9% of GDP in 2023, although this was a drop from 25.5% of GDP in 2022. For its part, Grenada saw the revenue generated from these programmes grow from 2.2% of GDP in 2022 to 9.9% of GDP in 2023 (ECLAC, 2024[6]). However, there are several risks associated with these programmes. First, potential policy changes in source countries, such as increased exit taxes for those renouncing citizenship or new visa restrictions, can raise costs and reduce the attractiveness of citizenship-by-investment programmes. Second, there are financial crime risks due to the misuse of these programmes, often exacerbated by inconsistent risk mitigation measures (FATF/OECD, 2023[7]). Effective oversight and adherence to best practices, such as those outlined by the Financial Action Task Force (FATF), can be crucial to preventing illicit activities, including money laundering (FATF/OECD, 2023[7]).

Among natural resource-exporting countries, non-tax revenues increased from 6.4% of GDP in 2022 to 7.3% in 2023. This was mainly due to withdrawals from the National Resource Fund by the government of Guyana. In Trinidad and Tobago, higher oil royalty payments boosted non-tax revenue sources (ECLAC, 2024[6]).

Some Caribbean countries could benefit from environmentally related taxes, but these should be approached with caution. Many countries in the region are fuel importers. Consequently, such taxes can increase price pressures on vulnerable populations. When relevant, these taxes should be accompanied by protections like cash transfers, in-kind support, active labour market policies, and entrepreneurship programmes to cushion social costs and strengthen social protection systems.

Environmentally related tax revenues (ERTR) vary significantly across the Caribbean. ERTR in the Caribbean average 0.8% of GDP, which matches the Latin American average but is below the OECD average of 1.8% (Figure 5.3). ERTR range from 1.7% of GDP in the Dominican Republic to 0.1% in Belize.

Most Caribbean countries rely on transport taxes for ERTR, in contrast with the energy taxes prevalent in the OECD and Latin America. The Dominican Republic and Barbados are exceptions, primarily relying on energy tax revenues at 1.3% and 0.7% of GDP, respectively (Figure 5.3).

Most environment-related tax policy instruments include motor vehicle and travel-related taxes. These are followed in popularity by fuel/hydrocarbon taxes. Only the Dominican Republic and Guyana directly impose environmental or carbon taxes.

Figure 5.3. Environmentally related tax revenues by main tax base in Caribbean countries, 2022

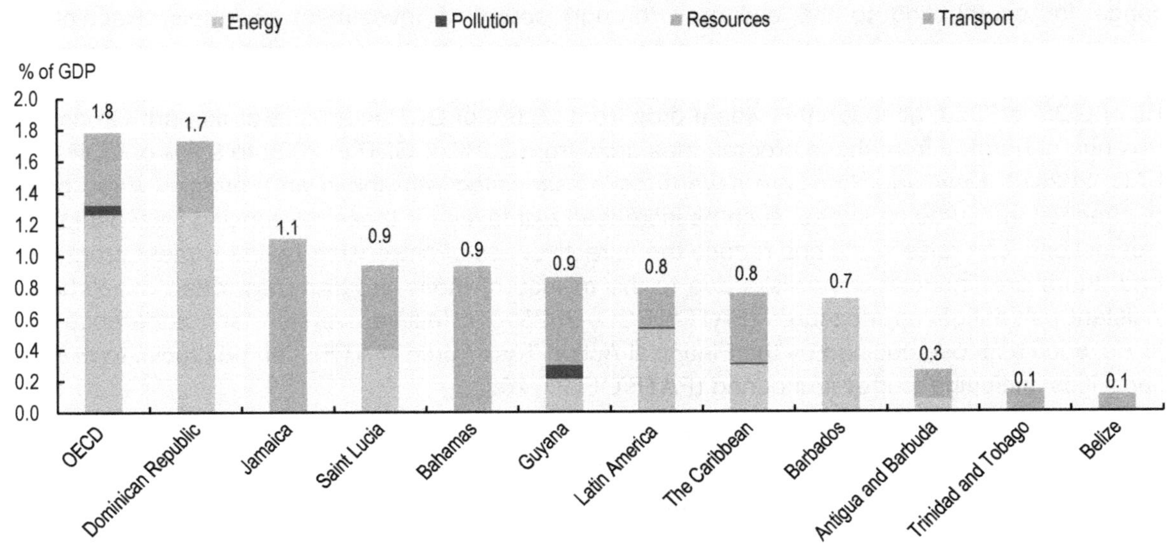

Note: The Caribbean average represents the unweighted average of nine Caribbean countries. The figure does not include Jamaica's revenues from the special consumption tax on petroleum products (estimated to be more than 2.0% of GDP in 2018), as the data are unavailable. The OECD average represents the unweighted average of 37 OECD member countries, excluding Costa Rica.
Source: Panel A: (OECD et al., 2024[1]).

StatLink https://stat.link/wpd2a5

Caribbean countries can further explore and develop explicit carbon pricing mechanisms such as carbon credits, which can help increase revenues in the Latin American and Caribbean (LAC) region. On average, such instruments could raise revenues to 2% of GDP in the region (OECD et al., 2022[8]). A carbon credit allows the permit holder to emit one metric tonne of carbon dioxide or its equivalent. Earned through activities that reduce emissions, these credits can be traded or used to offset emissions, helping meet reduction targets. Establishing a carbon credit market can also open new avenues for taxation, such as taxes on transactions or administrative fees for registering and transferring credits.

The Dominican Republic, through the World Bank's Forest Carbon Partnership Facility, is set to receive payments of up to USD 25 million for verified reductions in carbon emissions from forest carbon until 2025 as part of its emissions reduction programme. In 2022, The Bahamas took a significant step towards credit market development by publishing a Carbon Credit Trading Bill, which establishes a regulatory framework for trading carbon credits within the country (KPMG, 2023[9]). In the same year, Guyana entered the carbon market through a USD 750 million deal with Hess Corporation, which will be disbursed between 2022 and 2032 (Government of Guyana, 2022[10]). The funds will be allocated to community- and village-led sustainability programmes for Indigenous peoples and local communities and initiatives for renewable energy, land titling, canal repairs, and climate change protection (Government of Guyana, 2022[10]). These initiatives align with global efforts to establish a market for carbon credits, highlighting the importance of achieving balanced emissions reductions (DGB Group, 2023[11]).

Rationalising tax expenditures can contribute to stronger and fairer tax systems in the Caribbean

Revenues forgone due to tax expenditures are significant for some Caribbean countries, although there is great heterogeneity. In 2022, despite a decline since 2016, tax expenditures in the Dominican Republic averaged 4.6% of GDP, equivalent to 32.5% of general government tax revenues (Redonda, von

Haldenwang and Aliu, 2024[12]). In the same year, tax expenditures in Jamaica averaged 3.3% of GDP, equivalent to 11.8% of general government tax revenues (Redonda, von Haldenwang and Aliu, 2024[12]). In Barbados, the government, with technical assistance from the International Monetary Fund (IMF), has modernised procedures for granting and managing duty and tax exemptions (IMF, 2023[13]). Key provisions include: i) exemptions must be "in the public interest"; ii) the Minister of Finance or Cabinet must approve exemptions above a certain threshold; and iii) recipients must repay if they breach the laws of Barbados (IMF, 2023[13]). IMF authorities also expect that rationalising the exemption framework will gradually increase public revenue over the medium term.

Some countries in the region have made progress in estimating the revenues forgone due to tax expenditures. Other countries are not so advanced and should make efforts to adopt this practice.

The estimate of revenues forgone to tax expenditures requires a thorough assessment of overall benefits and costs. Such assessments should consider the real impact of tax incentives, including increased revenues from new investments and their associated social benefits. They should also consider the costs associated with revenues that would have been received even without the tax incentives. Additionally, they should account for the increased costs of tax administration, potential abuse of incentives leading to tax evasion, economic distortions, distributional effects and the impact of such abuse on macroeconomic variables (ECLAC, 2023[14]).

International tax co-operation in the Caribbean will be essential for addressing high levels of tax evasion, increasing transparency and enhancing domestic resource mobilisation

To increase revenues while developing a fairer tax system, it is also crucial to address high levels of tax evasion and tax avoidance in some Caribbean countries by adopting and implementing key international tax standards and supporting multilateral efforts for combating tax evasion and avoidance in the region. Multinational enterprises sometimes use tax planning strategies to avoid paying taxes, eroding the tax base by artificially shifting profits to low or no-tax jurisdictions. This has an important impact internationally in terms of lost revenue, estimated by the OECD to be USD 100-240 billion per annum. Financial secrecy allows taxpayers to conceal wealth and income from tax auditors. Over the past 15 years, significant improvements to the international tax framework have helped tax administrations enforce tax compliance more effectively, improving their ability to make sure corporations pay taxes where their profits are earned and re-imagined key rules to ensure they pay a minimum level of taxes, bringing an end to the race to the bottom on competition for foreign direct investment.

Tax transparency

To address tax transparency, the Global Forum on Transparency and Exchange of Information for Tax Purposes (Global Forum) has been providing capacity-building on the implementation and effective use of the internationally recognised transparency and exchange of information standards to fight tax evasion and other illicit financial flows and mobilise sustainable domestic resources. Today, 23 Caribbean jurisdictions participate in the work of the Global Forum, including all CARICOM members but Suriname. They benefit from an extensive capacity-building programme supported by the Standard on Transparency and Exchange of Information on Request, the Standard on Automatic Exchange of Financial Account Information, and the newly established Crypto-Asset Reporting Framework. This is done by providing knowledge tools (e.g. toolkits, guidance, e-learning), delivering virtual and in-person training and workshop events, and implementing bilateral jurisdiction-specific technical assistance programmes. For instance, in 2023, 15 Caribbean jurisdictions benefitted from technical assistance supporting legal and regulatory changes, including beneficial ownership and supervisory efforts; 347 officials participated in Global Forum's training events.

In addition, Caribbean jurisdictions have also benefitted from other Global Forum's capacity-building initiatives, such as the Women Leader in Tax Transparency Programme, which aims at supporting female development and gender equality in tax authorities. A dedicated Train the Trainer programme, which aims at building a sustainable knowledge-development capacity in tax authorities to ensure effective use of the tax transparency tools to tackle tax evasion, was also launched in 2024 with the participation of 14 officials from 6 Caribbean jurisdictions. The Global Forum is also working with the CARICOM Secretariat, an observer of the Forum's work, to assist its members in implementing and benefiting from the tax transparency standards (Box 5.1).

Box 5.1. Tax transparency in the Caribbean region: Progress and remaining challenges

Since 2009, through the Global Forum on Transparency and Exchange of Information for Tax Purposes (Global Forum), global work has been carried out to ensure that the international tax transparency standards, being exchange of information on request (EOIR) and automatic exchange of information (AEOI), are consistently implemented to promote a level playing field, combat tax evasion and other illicit financial flows, and assist in domestic revenue mobilisation. Caribbean jurisdictions have a long history of working on the issues of tax transparency through their membership in the Global Forum. The active participation and progress of 23 Caribbean jurisdictions have been key to the global success of the tax transparency initiatives, especially the end of bank secrecy.

Advancements have been identified in the Caribbean region in the implementation of tax transparency standards; however, there is still room for improvement, particularly in terms of effectiveness in practice.

- For the implementation of the EOIR standard, which includes strengthened requirements on availability of beneficial ownership, the peer review results have been quite satisfactory with 71% of reviewed Caribbean jurisdictions having received a satisfactory rating (i.e. largely compliant). However, there is still room for improvement in the remaining 29% of the jurisdictions.
- The Caribbean region is also making progress in implementing the AEOI standard, as highlighted in the effectiveness review published at the end of 2022. Caribbean jurisdictions are highly committed, with room for further improvement.

Looking ahead, Caribbean jurisdictions need to swiftly improve their legal framework and/or its effectiveness in practice to ensure their compliance with the tax transparency standards.

In the current demanding and evolving environment, the Caribbean region would benefit from further identifying tax transparency opportunities and challenges for the region and seeking opportunities and solutions to collectively address any deficiencies in the implementation of the tax transparency standards. Capacity building from the Global Forum has been available to help Caribbean jurisdictions implement the tax transparency standards and benefit from them for domestic revenue mobilisation. Bilateral technical assistance has been provided to put in place or amend the legal framework and ensure an effective supervision of the legal obligations in practice. Toolkits and other tools are made available to Caribbean jurisdictions, and they participate in the various training and workshop events organised in person or virtually. The Global Forum can further assist these jurisdictions in their commitment to implement and benefit from the tax transparency standards.

Source: (OECD, 2023[15]) (OECD, 2023[16]).

Protecting the corporate tax base from base erosion and profit shifting

The OECD and the G20 have been working with more than 140 jurisdictions globally under the Inclusive Framework on BEPS (Base Erosion and Profit Shifting) to implement measures to tackle international tax avoidance, improve the coherence of international tax rules, and ensure a more transparent tax environment. Members of the Inclusive Framework have committed to implementing the BEPS measures, including minimum standards on Harmful Tax Practices, countering tax treaty abuse, exchanging country-by-country reports for risk assessment and mutual agreement procedures. The Inclusive Framework includes 19 members from the Caribbean.[2]

In addition to the BEPS measures, the Inclusive Framework is in the final stages of completing its Two-Pillar Solution to address the tax challenges arising from the digitalisation of the economy. The Two-Pillar Solution is a modernisation of the international tax rules that:

- re-allocates taxing rights over a portion of the residual profits of the largest and most profitable multinational enterprises (MNEs)
- provides a simpler approach by applying transfer pricing rules in certain types of cases, taking into account the needs of low-capacity countries
- establishes a global minimum corporate tax (GMT) of 15%; and
- provides for a Subject to Tax Rule (STTR), which allows source jurisdictions to "tax back" where defined categories of intra-group covered income are subject to nominal corporate income tax rates below the STTR minimum rate of 9% and domestic taxing rights over that income have been ceded under a treaty.

These transformations in international taxation have – and will continue to have – implications for Caribbean economies. The GMT will be of particular significance, as it is expected to generate increased CIT revenues of USD 155-192 billion annually (6.5-8.1% of global CIT revenues). The GMT is already in effect in around 40 jurisdictions, with many more set to implement in 2025. It will have a profound impact by neutralising tax planning through investment hubs, which is highly relevant for the Caribbean region. It will also create opportunities for governments in the region to re-evaluate tax incentives that are impacted by the GMT, since MNEs that benefit from these regimes will now be required to pay the minimum tax either in the source country or another jurisdiction where the MNE has activities. Given this, jurisdictions in the region need to assess the possibility of imposing that tax themselves rather than allowing it to be collected elsewhere. The OECD launched a series of pilot programmes to help developing countries assess the impact of the GMT and evaluate policy options, including a pilot programme in Jamaica.

Other tax policy options for domestic resource mobilisation

Beyond the work on tax transparency and BEPS, a range of other international tax issues are relevant for governments in the region and can support domestic resource mobilisation. This includes the work on VAT, given the strong reliance on VAT among Caribbean jurisdictions, and digitalisation of tax administrations as many jurisdictions are modernising their systems to improve compliance and efficiency and transfer pricing, where several jurisdictions are contemplating bringing transfer pricing rules into place.

Tax morale – the intrinsic willingness to pay tax – can greatly assist governments in designing and administering tax policies, particularly in developing countries with low compliance rates (OECD, 2019[17]). Improving tax morale could significantly reduce tax evasion levels across many Caribbean countries. Over the past decade, tax morale has fluctuated in Latin America and the Caribbean, but recent trends indicate a deterioration (Latinobarometro, 2023[18])). For instance, in 2023, approximately 18.1% of respondents in the Dominican Republic viewed tax evasion as justifiable. This represents the highest rate among 18 Latin American countries.[3]

Support implementation through capacity building

Many Caribbean jurisdictions receive technical assistance from the OECD Secretariat to help implement the BEPS standards and issues such as transfer pricing and value added tax. Other Caribbean jurisdictions participate in OECD tax projects and publications. For instance, nine jurisdictions in the region are included in the Revenue Statistics in Latin America and the Caribbean and in the Global Revenue Statistics Database, and Jamaica contributed to the *VAT Digital Toolkit for Latin America and the Caribbean* and to a publication on Taxpayer Education (OECD et al., 2021[19]; OECD, 2021[20]) As noted above, Jamaica participates in a pilot programme on Tax Incentives and the GMT. Going forward, it would be important to have more Caribbean jurisdictions participating in the Revenue Statistics Database and other tax projects and publications. This participation can enhance regional data collection, improve policy making, and promote a deeper understanding of Caribbean tax systems and revenue trends.

The OECD has organised several regional Caribbean conferences with a focus on BEPS and other strategic issues, as well as different rounds of regional consultations on international tax developments, with an emphasis on the Two-Pillar Solution. These meetings have ensured that Caribbean developing states, whether members or not of the Inclusive Framework, keep up to date with international tax developments and actively contribute to the agenda of the Inclusive Framework. In addition to existing bilateral programmes, ad-hoc assistance on specific issues has been provided to several islands.

At a political level, the OECD has been active at the Ministerial meetings of the CARICOM Council for Finance and Planning (COFAP), where CARICOM member states have noted the advice from the OECD on international and regional tax matters and have agreed on updating regional instruments to ensure they comply with the international tax standards.

Rethinking debt management and strengthening fiscal frameworks will help Caribbean countries cope with high debt levels

Public debt levels have grown significantly in most Caribbean economies in the last decade (Chapter 1). In 2022, central government total public debt averaged 78.8% of GDP (well above the average for Latin America, at 52.9%), more than 10 percentage points higher than in 2012, when it stood at 69.2% of GDP.

High debt levels reduce fiscal space and limit social expenditure

High debt principal and interest payments are depleting domestic resources for public investment and social spending. Besides, it limits fiscal flexibility to face economic shocks and affects the sustainability of public finance. Debt service is indeed high in many Caribbean countries. The Caribbean average debt service to tax revenue ratio reached 12.9% in 2022, above the average levels in Latin America (11.5%) and much higher than those of the OECD (4.8%). Although significant, the level in the Caribbean is lower than a decade earlier, when it reached 14.1%. (Figure 5.4).

Some Caribbean countries have been more successful in reducing tax-debt ratios than others. Countries such as Jamaica, Saint Kitts and Nevis, Grenada, Barbados, and Guyana have significantly reduced their tax-debt ratio. Jamaica is a notable case due to its adoption of a well-designed fiscal rule and a partnership agreement that ensured the equitable distribution of adjustment burdens among creditors (Arslanalp, Eichengreen and Blair, 2024[21]). In other countries, notably the Dominican Republic, The Bahamas and Suriname, the share of debt service as a percentage of tax revenues has increased.

Figure 5.4. Debt service to tax revenues ratio, 2012 and 2022

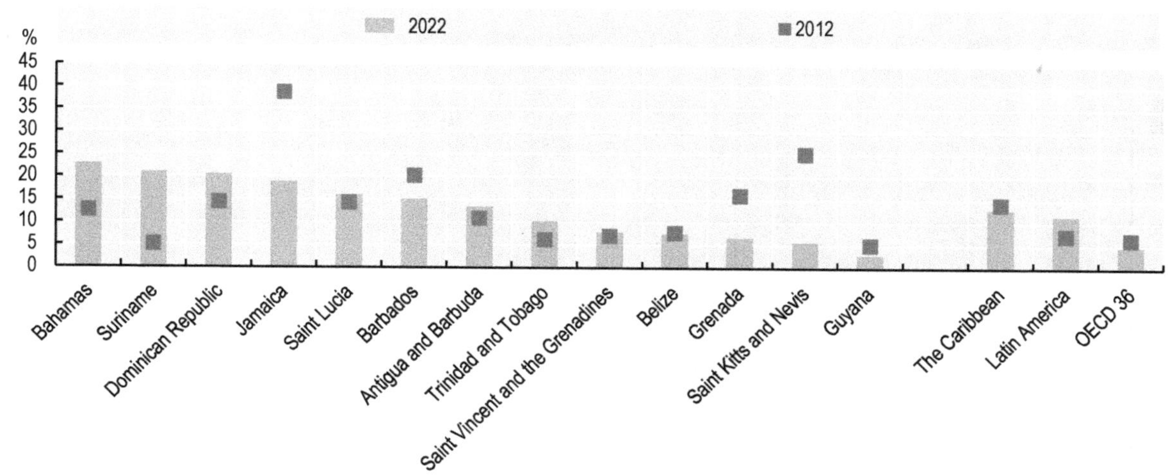

Source: Authors' elaboration based on (IMF, 2023[22]) and (OECD et al., 2024[1]).

StatLink https://stat.link/4itq6x

Debt management must be strengthened to reduce financial vulnerabilities of Caribbean economies

The composition of public debt differs across countries in terms of the currency of denomination and the external-domestic legislation under which it is issued. For instance, Suriname, Jamaica and the Dominican Republic have mainly external debt, comprising 63-71% of their total debt. In contrast, countries such as Trinidad and Tobago, Barbados, The Bahamas, and Haiti exhibit figures ranging between 34% and 46% (IDB, 2021[23]).

Foreign and domestic currency denominated debt have advantages and drawbacks, underscoring the importance of a balanced approach to debt composition in Caribbean countries. Foreign currency issuances are significant for some Caribbean economies, which therefore face greater exposure to exchange rate fluctuations. Suriname, the Dominican Republic and Jamaica hold sizeable shares of their debt in foreign currency (63-80%). In contrast, Haiti, Guyana, The Bahamas, and Trinidad and Tobago mostly have domestic currency debt, representing 55-64% of their total debt (IDB, 2021[23]).

Maturity of public debt in many Caribbean economies is oriented to the long term, thus reducing the vulnerability associated with potential domestic fiscal pressures or volatility in financial markets. Longer amortisation profiles are associated with less exposure to financial market fluctuations, especially in interest rates. However, some countries have short- and medium-term obligations requiring attention and rigorous debt management (Figure 5.5). Countries such as Suriname and The Bahamas have sizeable shares of debt obligations maturing over the next five years, representing about 40% of their GDP.

Figure 5.5. Public debt by remaining maturity as percentage of GDP, selected Caribbean countries, 2021

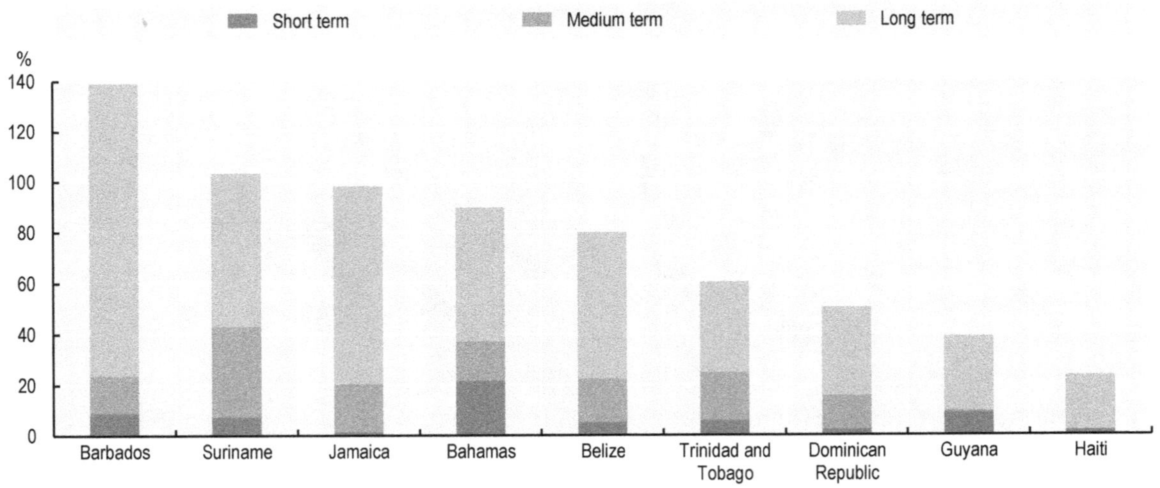

Note: Short term refers to a remaining maturity of less than one year, medium term comprises one to five years, and long term exceeds five years.
Source: Authors' elaboration based on the Standardized Public Debt Database (IDB, 2021[23]).

StatLink https://stat.link/u2ohvd

External debt in the Caribbean is mainly held with bilateral and multilateral creditors, reflecting constrained access to financial markets. On average, the creditor structure is composed of multilateral banks (59%), bonds held by private investors (22%) and bilateral creditors (19%) (Figure 5.6). Countries such as Jamaica and the Dominican Republic, which have had better access to international capital markets, have mainly raised funds by issuing bonds. Conversely, economies like Haiti, Saint Vincent and the Grenadines and Dominica mainly rely on debt financed by multilateral and bilateral creditors.

Figure 5.6. External public debt stock by creditor (public and private) in Caribbean countries, 2022

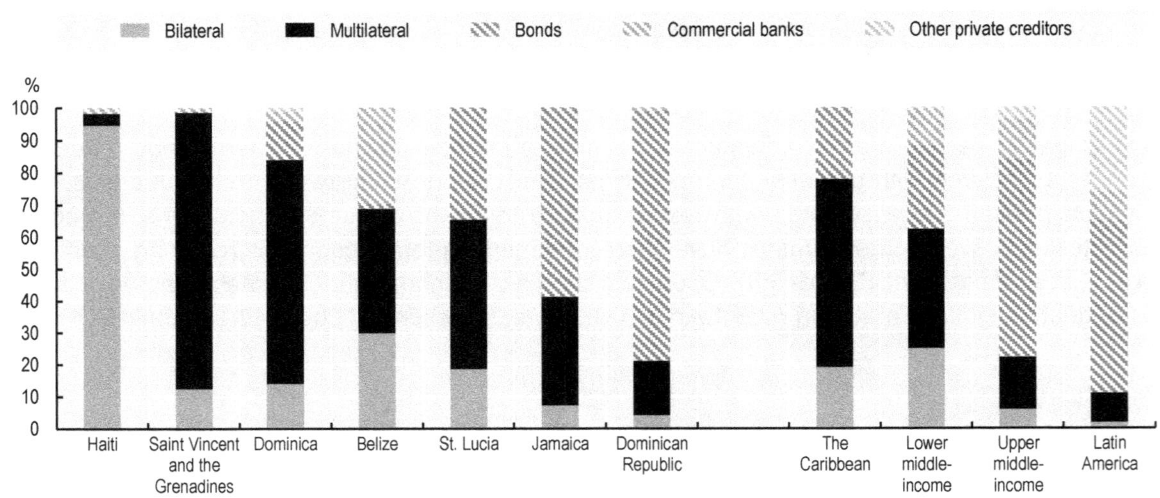

Note: Caribbean, low middle-income (LMI), upper middle-income (LMI) and Latin America are weighted average figures.
Source: Authors' calculations based on World Bank International Debt Statistics (World Bank, 2022[24]).

StatLink https://stat.link/bdox57

Fiscal frameworks are essential to support fiscal and debt sustainability while protecting investment

Fiscal frameworks are an essential tool to preserve medium- and long-term stability. They establish rules that can help fiscal policy to be countercyclical, reduce discretionary public spending and guarantee debt sustainability. They can also help protect public investment that is essential to transform production. In episodes of fiscal consolidation, for example, governments tend to reduce capital expenditures because this may have lower political costs than reducing current spending (Ardanaz and Izquierdo, 2022[25]). However, reducing capital spending affects both long-term growth and economic recovery. Protecting investment during the fiscal consolidation period can mitigate economic contraction and, in some cases, lead to an expansion (Ardanaz and Izquierdo, 2022[25]; OECD et al., 2023[26]).

Fiscal rules are a central component of the fiscal framework. They are designed to solve the temporal inconsistency of public finances and mitigate debt accumulation by establishing debt limits (Andrian et al., 2022[27]). By decoupling spending from the business cycle, fiscal rules prevent spending from rising during economic upturns and protect public investment during downturns. Moreover, fiscal rules help stabilise debt-to-GDP ratios, ensuring long-term fiscal stability. Additionally, they have the potential to alleviate the perception of sovereign risk (Gomez-Gonzalez, Valencia and Sánchez, 2024[28]).

The mere existence of fiscal rules is not sufficient to ensure sustainability. Quality and compliance are key. Quality rules are supported by institutions and comprise robust legal frameworks, flexibility against economic shocks, and monitoring and enforcement mechanisms. High-quality fiscal rules stabilise debt growth and reduce its volatility (Galindo and Izquierdo, 2024[29]). Compliance is crucial since periods of adherence correlate with fewer events of debt acceleration, lower bond spreads and higher credit ratings (Ardanaz, Ulloa-Suarez and Valencia, 2023[30]).

Caribbean economies have implemented various fiscal rules to enhance economic stability and reduce public debt. Jamaica introduced a Fiscal Responsibility Framework (FRF) in 2014. It includes a balanced budget rule and a debt rule, accompanied by a well-designed escape clause for emergencies such as natural disasters or severe economic downturns. The FRF also imposes a ceiling on the public wage bill to control current expenditures (Rosenblatt et al., 2023[31]; Arslanalp, Eichengreen and Blair, 2024[21]). In Grenada, the Fiscal Responsibility Act (FRA) of 2016 mandates a primary surplus of 3.5% of GDP and targets a debt-to-GDP ratio of 60%. It also restricts the growth of primary expenditures and the public wage bill to maintain fiscal sustainability. The legislation permits suspension of fiscal rules in the event of natural disasters, severe economic contractions or financial crises, allowing three years for corrective actions (Wright, Grenade and Scott-Joseph, 2017[32]). Similarly, The Bahamas enacted its own FRA in 2018, establishing fiscal rules such as a budget deficit ceiling of 0.5% of GDP, a cap on the annual growth rate of current expenditures, and a government debt ceiling of 50% of GDP expected to be met by 2025. In addition, it includes an escape clause for unexpected external shocks (Rosenblatt et al., 2023[31]).

Fiscal rules must be flexible enough to accommodate exogenous shocks. In economies with no fiscal rules or rigid ones, a fiscal consolidation of 2% of GDP is associated with a reduction of 10% in public investment. By contrast, in countries with flexible fiscal rules, investment is not affected during fiscal consolidation periods (Ardanaz et al., 2021[33]). This flexibility can take the form of cyclically adjusted fiscal targets, well-defined escape clauses or differential treatment of investment expenditures.

Innovative debt financing mechanisms can mobilise resources to support environmental, social and ocean-related objectives

Innovative debt financing mechanisms can help mobilise financial resources and connect them to areas where Caribbean countries have important financing gaps. Among these instruments, green, social, sustainability, sustainability-linked and blue (GSSSB) bonds have been gaining prominence worldwide.

These instruments can bring financing to key development objectives, including promoting renewable energy and marine conservation projects, enhancing adaptation and resilience to climate change, and contributing to debt sustainability or significant debt reduction across the region. Similarly, other financing mechanisms like catastrophe bonds, natural disaster clauses and debt-for-nature swaps are particularly relevant for Caribbean economies, given their combination of high levels of debt, high exposure to climate risks, and rich natural capital.

GSSSB bonds are emerging as a powerful tool for financing sustainable initiatives in the Caribbean region

The international GSSSB bonds market in the Caribbean has expanded in recent years. Between 2019 and November 2024, the GSSSB international bond market in the Caribbean reached a cumulative value of USD 1.5 billion (Figure 5.7, Panel A). Green bonds lead the way with USD 804 million, followed by blue bonds at USD 385 million and sustainability-linked bonds (SLBs) at USD 300 million. Corporate issuers account for 45% of total issuances, sovereigns make up 33%, and quasi-sovereign issuers comprise the remaining 22% (Figure 5.7, Panel B). The gradual shift towards sustainable debt securities over conventional bonds indicates a growing investor appetite for sustainable projects. This trend can help both private and public issuers meet their sustainability goals. These bonds, driven by increasing investor interest in thematic and sustainable investments, offer Caribbean countries a significant avenue for funding sustainable development and promoting economic progress (OECD, 2024[34]).

Figure 5.7. International GSSSB bond issuance in the Caribbean by type and issuer, 2019 - November 2024

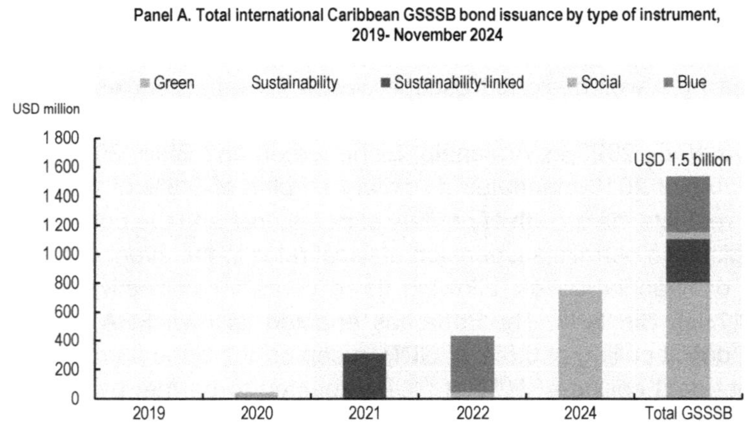

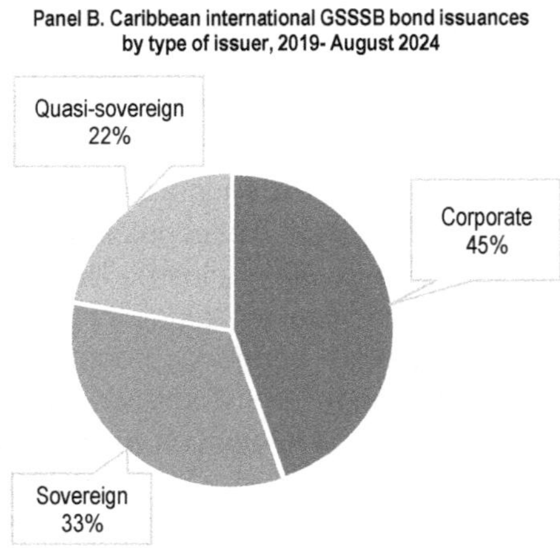

Note: GSSSB = Green, social, sustainability, sustainability-linked, and blue bonds. Quasi-sovereign issuers are defined as companies with full or partial government ownership.
Source: Authors' elaboration based on official figures (Núñez, G., H. Velloso and F. Da Silva, 2022[35]; ECLAC, 2023[36]; OECD et al., 2023[26]).

StatLink https://stat.link/m7vsdy

Blue bonds can help safeguard oceans and nurture sustainable "blue economies"

Blue bonds are emerging as a powerful tool in the region for financing initiatives aimed at safeguarding oceans and nurturing sustainable "blue economies" – economic activities that depend on or affect the use of coastal and marine resources (Chapter 3). In 2021, BB Blue, a Special Purpose Vehicle created to manage Barbados' debt-for-nature swap, issued two blue bonds totalling USD 71.6 million, allowing Barbados to buy back USD 77.6 million worth of Eurobonds due in 2029 at a discounted price. BB Blue was backed by Credit Suisse and received guarantees from the Inter-American Development Bank (IDB) and The Nature Conservancy (TNC), enabling BB Blue to issue these two bonds with strong credit ratings. This setup demonstrated a unique blended finance approach, facilitated by financial institutions such as CIBC FirstCaribbean and Credit Suisse (The Nature Conservancy, 2023[37]). In the same year, a TNC subsidiary, Belize Blue Investment Company, LLC (BZBIC), backed by Credit Suisse, arranged blue bonds that funded a USD 364 million loan to Belize to repurchase a USD 553 million "superbond". This superbond represented the government's entire external commercial debt, equivalent to 30% of GDP (Owen, 2022[38]). In 2022, The Bahamas issued two blue bonds totalling USD 385 million, which attracted high demand in the international debt market (ECLAC, 2023[39]).

Blue bonds offer a promising avenue to unlock the untapped financial potential of blue economies in the Caribbean, presenting opportunities for larger and longer-term financing. They can also enhance investor diversification, broadening funding sources and potentially mitigating risks associated with bond demand fluctuations (ADB/IFC, 2023[40]).

Sustainability-linked bonds and social bonds are also gaining traction in the region

SLBs raise capital for climate-related or environmental projects, reflecting a growing trend towards sustainable investing. In 2019, Williams Caribbean Capital, based in Barbados, issued the region's first green bond valued at USD 2 million. This was followed by another issuance in 2021, amounting to USD 7 million. Both bonds were earmarked for solar energy projects and certified under the Climate Bonds Standard Solar Energy Criteria (Climate Bonds Initiative, 2022[41]). In 2020, the Dominican Republic's Banco Popular Dominicano issued a USD 45 million green bond aimed at financing renewable energy, electro-mobility and eco-efficiency projects (Garcia, 2022[42]). In 2021, the Dominican Republic's quasi-sovereign issuer, *Empresa Generadora de Energía Haina*, issued an SLB of USD 100 million. Regarding social bonds, Trinidad and Tobago issued a USD 44.2 million social bond in 2020 by the local financial institution Home Mortgage Bank. This bond supports the country's subsidised housing programmes. It aims to tackle inequalities and poverty, promote sustainable cities, create decent work opportunities, and advance climate action goals (HMB, 2020[43]).

Technical assistance and capacity building to develop sustainable, bankable project pipelines are essential for helping Caribbean countries gain access to and effectively utilise green/sustainable funds (OECD et al., 2022[8]; Piemonté, Kim and Cattaneo, 2024[44]). This assistance is particularly relevant for GSSS and other sustainable finance instruments, which can only work effectively if a pipeline of bankable sustainable projects is developed. Even if regulatory frameworks are established and investment appetite is high, effective project feasibility planning is essential for efficient resource allocation (OECD, 2024[34]). Helping countries create a pipeline of projects, including those focused on the green transition, to present to potential international investors seeking business opportunities could help bridge the information gap that hinders matching supply with demand. Such an initiative could attract new capital to Caribbean economies (Piemonté, Kim and Cattaneo, 2024[44]). Enhancing project governance and implementation, technical assistance, and capacity building can reduce disbursement delays and ensure the effective allocation of resources (Piemonté, Kim and Cattaneo, 2024[44]).

Catastrophe bonds present a unique opportunity for Caribbean countries to expand their external borrowing capacity to fund natural disaster responses

Catastrophe (CAT) bonds can be useful for countries with a higher risk of being struck by natural disasters. A higher level of risk leaves such countries more vulnerable to defaulting on their debt obligations and, in turn, higher capital costs or lack of access to financial markets. This is the case for the Caribbean, a region with tight fiscal constraints and high vulnerability to natural catastrophes. CAT bonds can offer an innovative insurance-linked risk transfer mechanism to fund natural disaster responses in the Caribbean. CAT bonds can also provide countries in the region with flexibility and price stability.

Globally, the CAT bond market has grown steadily. In 2021, CAT bond issuances peaked at USD 12.7 billion, slightly decreasing to USD 10 billion in 2022 (Figure 5.8, Panel A). Advanced economies dominate these issuances. Among countries and regions with emerging economies, the Caribbean (2.1%) is covered more frequently than many others (OECD, 2024[45]) (Figure 5.8, Panel B).

Figure 5.8. Cumulative CAT bond issuance and geographical coverage of CAT bonds issued, 1996-2022

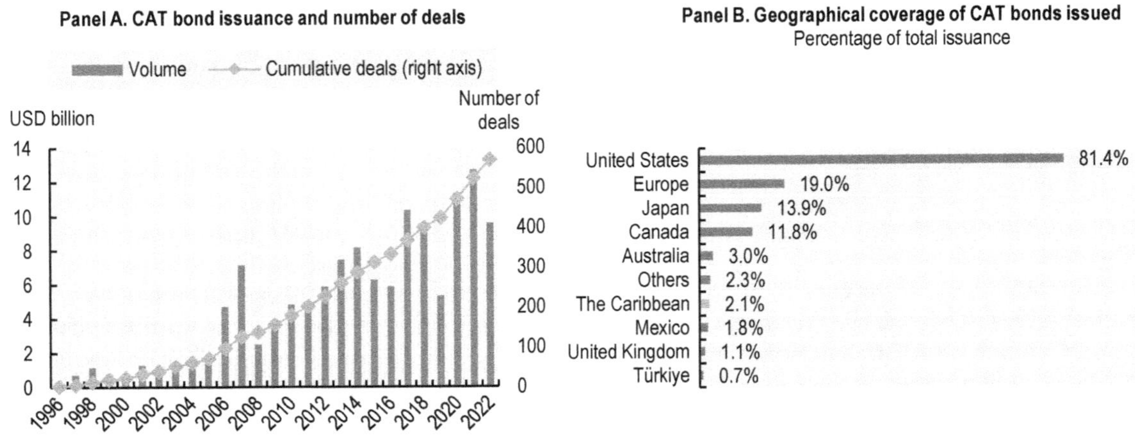

Note: Panel A: Only 144A CAT bonds or similar are included; 144A CAT bonds are privately placed CAT bonds under Rule 144A of the US Securities Act. Panel B: Only 144A CAT bonds or similar issued in 1996-2022 are included. "Others" include Chile, the People's Republic of China, Cyprus, Colombia, El Salvador, Guatemala, Israel, New Zealand, Peru, the Philippines and Chinese Taipei. Some percentages involve multiple counting; this applies to a CAT bond transaction that covers multiple countries or regions.
Source: (Artemis, 2024[46]), www.artemis.bm/deal-directory/.

StatLink https://stat.link/5iywbz

CAT bonds present Caribbean countries with a unique opportunity to expand their external borrowing capacity (OECD et al., 2022[8]). They are financial instruments that use securitisation processes to transform natural disaster risks into tradeable assets (OECD, 2024[45]). These bonds typically last three years and are fully collateralised with high-quality securities to mitigate counterparty default risk (OECD, 2024[45]).

In 2014, the World Bank issued its first CAT bond in a USD 30 million deal to provide hurricane and earthquake reinsurance protection to the Caribbean Catastrophe Risk Insurance Facility (CCRIF), which comprises 16 member island nations.[4] The main investors in this issuance were specialists in insurance-linked securities funds, CAT funds, hedge funds and other investment companies (Artemis, 2014[47]).

In 2021, the World Bank issued a USD 185 million CAT bond for Jamaica, providing coverage for 3 hurricane seasons. This bond addressed Jamaica's financing gap and made it the first small island state to independently sponsor a CAT bond (World Bank, 2024[48]). In 2024, the World Bank announced the renewal of this CAT bond for USD 150 million. Through this mechanism, Jamaica stands to receive vital funds should future storms surpass predefined intensity thresholds. Jamaica's experience underscores the significance of collaboration with international financial institutions throughout the pre-issuance and issuance stages of CAT bond transactions.

Multi-country CAT bonds can provide a strategic solution for Caribbean nations that cannot issue such bonds independently. By enabling multiple countries to pool their resources, these bonds can offer regional benefits and collective risk mitigation against natural disasters (World Bank, 2013[49]). Efforts are underway, supported by the World Bank, to develop a regional CAT bond for the Caribbean, mirroring successful initiatives like the Pacific Alliance CAT bonds. These bonds streamline transaction costs and attract a broader investor base. This, in turn, leads to lower premium rates and bolsters resilience against catastrophic events across borders (OECD, 2024[45]). They enable multiple sovereign nations to enter the CAT bond markets independently, without the need for a risk pooling (OECD, 2024[45]).

Natural disaster clauses can significantly enhance fiscal resilience in the region

Natural disaster clauses in debt contracts allow for the temporary suspension of payments when a country is affected by a disaster. Natural disaster clauses have emerged as crucial components in debt contracts in the Caribbean. At present, they cover losses of up to USD 30 million.

In 2024, in a world first, Grenada was able to pause debt repayment due to a hurricane debt suspension clause after Hurricane Beryl, saving the country USD 28 million. In 2015, Grenada pioneered the inclusion of a natural disaster clause in its debt restructuring (Ho and Fontana, 2021[50]). Grenada's bonds, due in 2030, allow deferring principal and interest payments for the next semi-annual payment date if a tropical cyclone results in USD 15-30 million in losses (Ho and Fontana, 2021[50]). If losses exceed USD 30 million, payments can be deferred for the next two semi-annual dates.

In 2018 and 2019, Barbados introduced innovations to debt restructuring contracts by expanding the range of trigger events – specific natural disasters that activate clauses for the suspension of debt payments – to include earthquakes and excess rainfall while lowering the loss threshold required to activate these measures to USD 5 million (Ho and Fontana, 2021[50]). In 2019, a transparency mechanism was added, allowing bondholders holding half of the principal to block deferrals within 15 days of notice. This veto right addressed bondholders' concerns about potential opportunistic or abusive triggering of the clause by the issuer.

For both Grenada and Barbados, conditions of their natural disaster clauses are linked to their insurance policies from the CCRIF. The Facility offers coverage for hurricanes, earthquakes and excess rainfall in Caribbean and Central American countries (Ho and Fontana, 2021[50]).

Multilateral Development Banks can also play a key role in helping Caribbean countries access innovative financial solutions to provide coverage for natural disaster events. For instance, financial mechanisms such as Principal Payment Options (PPO) allow Caribbean countries to defer principal repayments for two years following an eligible natural disaster and repay those amounts in future amortisation instalments (IDB, 2024[51]). The IDB was the first to offer a PPO to three Caribbean countries – Belize, The Bahamas and Barbados. These countries have activated the option for loans totalling over USD 1.1 billion (IDB, 2024[51]).

However, disaster clauses may carry a cost as they incentivise governments to borrow more and pay higher yields. Introducing disaster clauses exposes investors to the risk of delayed repayments and the need to be compensated accordingly through higher spreads. However, recent analyses suggest that borrowing terms generally improve with the introduction of these clauses. Evidence shows that governments take advantage of the better borrowing terms. Specifically, they expand their borrowing up to the point that default risk reaches levels such as those observed in the economy without disaster clauses. Since governments expect to postpone repayments, the expected cost of servicing debt declines even when spreads increase due to the risk of delay (OECD et al., 2022[8]).

For richly biodiverse and highly indebted countries, debt-for-nature swaps can serve as important sustainable financing instruments

A debt-for-nature swap is a liability management exercise where the country issues a guaranteed instrument (loan or bond) at more favourable terms and then uses the proceeds to buy back outstanding, more expensive sovereign debt, generating savings on the interest rate coupon and/or the principal. These savings will be used to finance nature conservation and/or climate change mitigation/adaptation activities. Debt-for-nature swaps offer a dual advantage for Caribbean countries: refinancing part of their external debt under more favourable terms while advancing their commitments to the Global Biodiversity

Framework and the Nationally Determined Contributions under the Paris Agreement. Such swaps are particularly relevant for enhancing debt sustainability in highly biodiverse countries.

To date, the Caribbean region has executed four debt-for-nature swaps amounting to more than USD 400 million destined for marine conservation. In 2022, Barbados conducted a USD 150 million debt-for-nature conversion, resulting in USD 50 million allocated to marine conservation initiatives (Box 5.2) (Savage, 2023[52]). In July 2024, the EIB and IDB approved USD 300 million in guarantees for an innovative debt-for-climate-resilience swap, structured as a sovereign sustainability-linked loan. This initiative will save USD 125 million for new resilience investments and marks the first such loan tied to a sovereign water security project (European Investment Bank, 2024[53]; IDB, 2024[54]). In November 2024, the Bahamas launched a new debt conversion project that is expected to save an estimated USD 124 million over the next 15 years and enable improvements in ocean conservation and the management of the Bahamas Protected Areas System (IDB, 2024[56]). The project, supported by the IDB, The Nature Conservancy's Nature Bonds Program, and others, enabled the Bahamas to buy back USD 300 million in debt using proceeds from a new USD 300 million loan arranged by Standard Chartered Bank (IDB, 2024[55]). In 2021, The Nature Conservancy and the government of Belize finalised a USD 364 million debt conversion aimed at protecting 30% of Belize's ocean. This initiative reduced Belize's debt by 8.7% of GDP and generated an estimated USD 178 million for marine conservation (Green Finance Institute, 2021[56]).

Box 5.2. Barbados debt-for-nature conversion

In late 2022, Barbados completed a debt-for-nature conversion backed by a USD 100 million guarantee from the Inter-American Development Bank (IDB) and USD 50 million guarantee from The Nature Conservancy (TNC) that enhanced a loan provided to Barbados (blue loan), allowing the country to reduce borrowing costs and use the proceeds to buy back existing debt. The transaction enabled Barbados to replace relatively expensive pre-existing debt (7.2% average cost) with significantly lower all-in cost of financing (4.9%), generating USD 50 million in savings that will be used to fund a Conservation Trust Fund (CTF) and finance marine conservation activities over a 15-year period.

As part of the transaction, Barbados committed to the following specific marine conservation milestones: i) completing an ocean-wide Marine Spatial Plan (MSP) using global best practices to protect up to 30% of Barbados' Exclusive Economic Zone and promote ocean sustainability, ii) designing and implementing legal, regulatory, and institutional frameworks to effectively implement the MSP and manage Barbados' ocean, and iii) complete and adopt comprehensive management plans for all protected areas.

To continue advancing the sustainability agenda, in July 2024, the IDB and the European Investment Bank approved guarantees totalling USD 300 million to support a debt-for-climate-resilience operation in Barbados. The debt conversion will create the fiscal space that allows the government to make water resilience investments that would not be otherwise possible given the current fiscal limitations. The operation will provide Barbados with the resources for infrastructure investments, including the South Coast sewage treatment plant, which will increase the island's water security in the context of climate change impacts and improve sanitation services. A monitoring mechanism will ensure that sustainability targets, focused on the volume and quality of reclaimed water from the upgraded plant, are met. If the targets are not achieved, the government will incur a financial penalty, which will be directed to the Barbados Environmental Sustainability Fund, a specialised trust for environmental investments.

Source: (IDB, 2022[57]; IDB, 2024[58]; IDB, 2024[54]).

Scaling up debt-for-nature swaps through concerted multilateral efforts in the region offers new opportunities for enhancing sustainable financing. In 2018, Antigua and Barbuda, Saint Lucia, and Saint

Vincent and the Grenadines began negotiating with creditors for debt swaps to reduce their debt-to-GDP ratio. Reducing the debt-to-GDP ratio by at least 12.2 percentage points for each country could lead to a minimum of a 1% increase in economic growth. This boost would raise the average growth rate of these three countries back to levels seen before the global financial crisis (ECLAC, 2018[59]).

Countries in the region must assess the requirements of debt-for-nature swaps before engaging in them. These swaps alone cannot structurally reduce debt or improve sovereign creditworthiness (Caballero, Gonzalez and Nieto, 2024[60]). It is important to establish robust verification systems and legal frameworks to ensure the fulfilment of long-term conservation commitments and to mitigate the risk of green/blue washing. The extended duration of environmental commitments and their potential vulnerability to political changes make it essential to develop Conservation Commitment Agreements that address these risks. Such agreements should include legal and financial incentives, as well as penalties for non-compliance, to ensure the fulfilment of commitments. For this reason, effective enforcement of climate contracts is crucial for debt-for-nature swaps (Caballero, Gonzalez and Nieto, 2024[60]). Moving forward, robust governance structures, effective monitoring and oversight mechanisms, and a long-term, integrated approach aligned with national development plans will be essential (Fuller et al., 2018[61]).

Enhanced regulation and oversight play pivotal roles in ensuring the efficacy of sustainable finance instruments while mitigating associated risks

Establishing robust, sustainable finance frameworks is essential for enhancing transparency and attractiveness in regional markets while mitigating risks. Given the vulnerability of many Caribbean countries to climate change, transparent, sustainable frameworks are crucial to ensure investment and promote innovation across various fronts (UNDP, 2023[62]). This requires developing and refining various mechanisms, including taxonomies, standards, guidelines, policies, international co-operation initiatives and regulations. These mechanisms may be created by the public sector, the private sector or through collaboration between both.

Frameworks often follow three key objectives: integrating economic, social and governance principles into financial sector operations; climate risk management; and sustainability financing. The diverse components of these frameworks make a unified definition challenging, requiring enhanced co-ordination. Greater efforts in the Caribbean region are needed to foster more consolidated sustainable finance frameworks, ensuring comparability, certainty, credibility, integrity and transparency in the market.

While the Dominican Republic remains the only Caribbean country to have put in place a green taxonomy, other nations in the region are advancing in the design of sustainable finance frameworks (Figure 5.9). Efforts focus on green protocols, surveys and climate risk guidelines involving diverse stakeholders. In 2018, the Stock Exchange of the Dominican Republic took a pioneering step by establishing the Green Finance Segment, followed by the issuance of the Green Bond Guide in 2019. In June 2024, it published the first green taxonomy in the Caribbean and the Framework for Green, Social, and Sustainable Bonds through the Ministry of Finance. This aimed to help investors, companies and other market participants more easily identify strategic investment opportunities that align with the country's environmental objectives, such as those outlined in the Paris Agreement.

In 2022, Jamaica published a report on climate-related financial risks and conducted surveys to enhance its sustainable finance framework. By 2024, the country developed a framework for green bond issuance with support from the IMF Resilience and Sustainability Facility programme and technical assistance from the IDB (IMF, 2024[63]). That same year, Eastern Caribbean states launched a three-year pilot programme to green the Eastern Caribbean Currency Union (ECCU) financial system. The participating states comprised Anguilla, Antigua and Barbuda, Dominica, Grenada, Montserrat, Saint Lucia, Saint Vincent and the Grenadines, and Saint Kitts and Nevis. In 2024, the Eastern Caribbean Central Bank also developed regional frameworks for climate stress testing and green finance, including a Regional Renewable Energy Infrastructure Investment Facility.

Figure 5.9. Sustainable finance framework development in the Caribbean, 2018-24

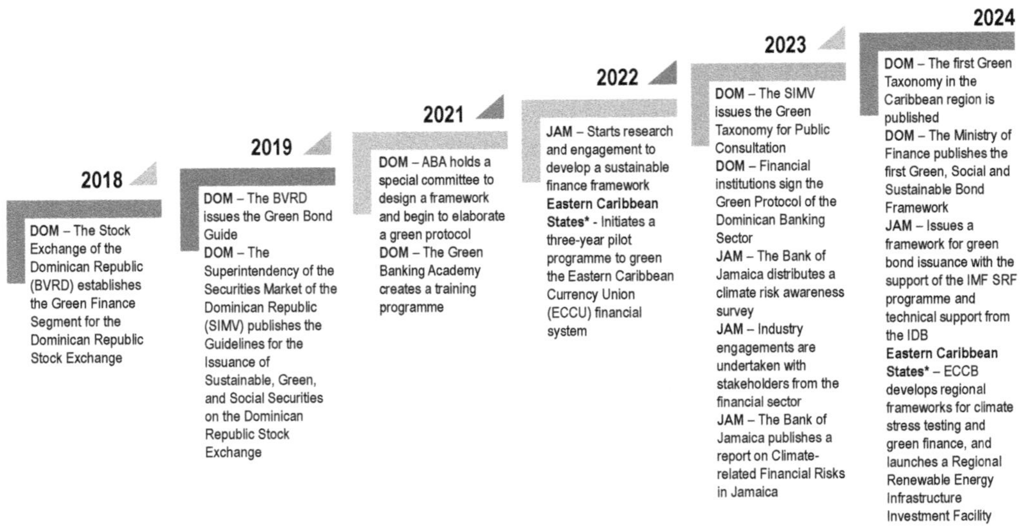

Note: *Eastern Caribbean States include Anguilla, Antigua and Barbuda, Dominica, Grenada, Montserrat, Saint Lucia, Saint Vincent and the Grenadines, and Saint Kitts and Nevis. DOM=Dominican Republic; JAM=Jamaica. IMF SRF=International Monetary Fund's Resilience and Sustainability Facility.
Source: Authors' elaboration based on (SBFN, 2024[64]).

It is crucial for public and private issuers in the region to establish clearer and more binding standards and taxonomies. In June 2023, in a significant step towards this direction, the UN system in LAC launched the first Common Framework of Sustainable Finance Taxonomies in the region through the Working Group on Taxonomies of Sustainable Finance. This regional framework is intended as a voluntary guide for actors in the region developing or intending to develop taxonomies. The framework also provides guidance for the interoperability of taxonomies within LAC and globally. Harmonising the methodologies behind the different taxonomies will increase trust among investors and reduce transaction costs (OECD et al., 2023[26]).

Financial markets need development to improve access to financing

The development of financial markets differs significantly across Caribbean economies, and more efforts are needed to improve their role in effectively channelling financial resources towards sustainable and inclusive development. Specifically, it is useful to look at four aspects: "depth", which measures the size of financial markets; "access", which examines the extent to which individuals can use these markets; "efficiency", which evaluates the system's effectiveness in delivering services, and "stability", which refers to the ability of the system to manage risks and absorb shocks.

Financial depth in the Caribbean has been historically low, constraining households and business participation in the financial system

Domestic credit to the private sector as a percentage of GDP – the standard measure of financial depth – stood at an average of 42% for the Caribbean in 2022, lagging behind the averages in Latin America (55%) and OECD countries (149%) (Figure 5.10, Panel A). Although most countries in the Caribbean are classified as high or upper middle-income, the financial depth of the region remains comparatively low within these groups of countries.

The level of financial depth differs across countries in the region. Measured by domestic bank credit to GDP, two high-income countries – Barbados and Saint Kitts and Nevis – demonstrate the highest levels of financial depth, at 73% and 64%, respectively. Bank deposits relative to GDP in these two countries remain at 111% and 105%, respectively. Conversely, Guyana and Haiti exhibit the lowest levels, with 12% and 8% for domestic bank credit and 36% and 24% for bank deposits (Figure 5.10, Panel B). Financial depth in the Caribbean reflects both common challenges and country-specific characteristics. For instance, high levels of government debt have limited private credit and financial development in some countries, resulting in significant crowding out of private financing (Beck and Mooney, 2021[65]).

Figure 5.10. Domestic credit to private sector as percentage of GDP by region 2000-22 and domestic bank credit and deposits as percentage of GDP in the Caribbean, 2022

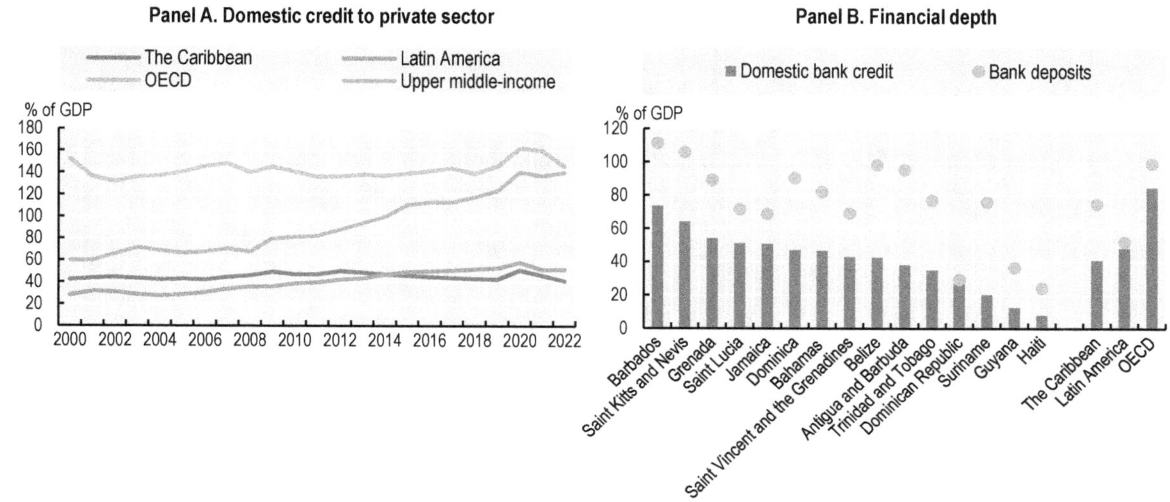

Note: Panel A – OECD and upper middle-income belong to World Bank data classification. Panel B – Figures for bank deposits as percentage of GDP correspond to 2021 due to data availability.
Source: Authors' elaboration based on World Development Indicators (World Bank, 2022[66]).

StatLink https://stat.link/5zhbdl

Financial access in many Caribbean countries is low, highlighting the importance of enhancing financial inclusion

In 2022, the number of deposit accounts with commercial banks per 1 000 adults stood at 1 162 for the Caribbean average, showing lower levels than Latin America (1 750) and the OECD (3 000) (Figure 5.11). Access to formal financial services enables households to manage their finances, smoothing consumption more effectively over time and facilitating wealth accumulation. This, in turn, reduces economic vulnerability. With enhanced access to high-quality financial products and services, households can increase their savings, manage consumption more effectively, and invest in housing, education, and health. These measures can lead to improved living standards and reduced poverty.

Caribbean countries encounter geographical challenges that hinder access to financial services. Countries in the region face common obstacles among Small Island Developing States, such as inadequate physical and digital infrastructure. Deficient roads and transportation networks hinder the expansion of financial services to remote communities. Additionally, unreliable electricity and costly digital connectivity impede efforts to promote digital financial inclusion (UNSGSA, 2024[67]).

Financial literacy remains a significant barrier to achieving financial inclusion. In the five member countries of the Eastern Caribbean Currency Union (ECCU, comprising Antigua and Barbuda, Dominica, Grenada, Saint Kitts and Nevis, Saint Lucia, and Saint Vincent and the Grenadines), only one in two adults meet the minimum target score of five out of seven for financial knowledge. Financial literacy scores ranged from 12.7 in Antigua and Barbuda to 11.7 in Saint Vincent and the Grenadines (ECCB, 2023[68]).

Figure 5.11. Number of deposit accounts with commercial banks per 1 000 adults, 2022

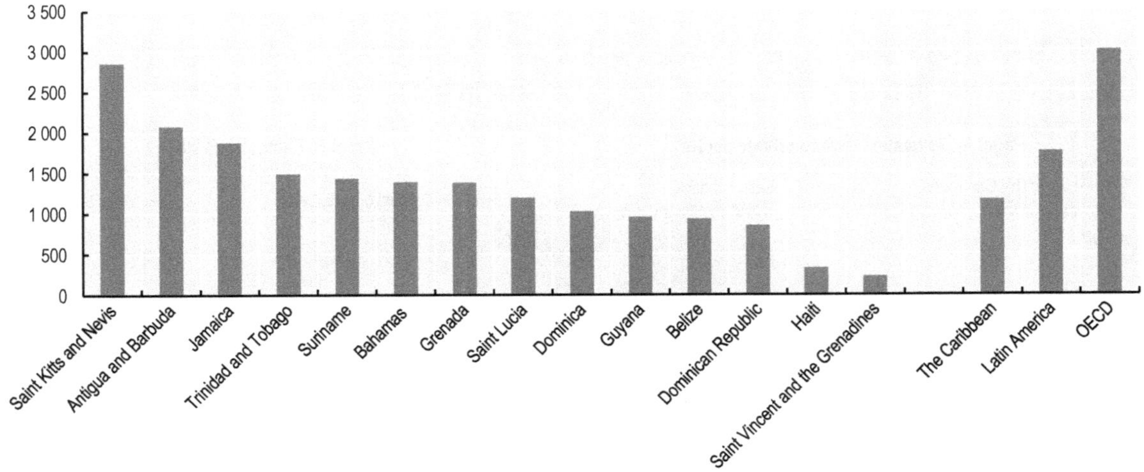

Note: Deposit accounts with commercial banks per 1 000 adults denote the total number of deposit accounts held by resident non-financial corporations and individuals from the household sector at commercial banks for every 1 000 adults in the country.
Source: Authors' elaboration based on the Financial Access Survey (IMF, 2022[69]).

StatLink https://stat.link/bnld37

The banking system remains concentrated and shows high profitability, wide interest rate margins and high operational costs, thus limiting access to credit

The banking system in the Caribbean exhibits high profitability and net interest margins. In 2021, the average Return on Assets – measuring a bank's net income relative to its total assets – stood at 1.7% in the Caribbean. This was similar to Latin America (1.6%) and higher than the OECD average of 0.9% (Figure 5.12). High profitability is often associated with low revenue diversification, high concentration and market power. For similar reasons, the Net Interest Margin – showing the difference between interest income from assets and interest paid to depositors for savings – stood at 4.8% in 2021, well above the OECD average of 1.7%. A high credit spread limits access to credit, making it costly for individuals and businesses and discouraging savings.

High banking costs are prevalent in the region. In 2021, banks in the region faced an overhead cost to total assets ratio of 3.3%, higher than the OECD average (1.4%) and lower than in Latin America (3.8%). This indicator evaluates the operational efficiency of a bank by quantifying operating expenses relative to total assets. High costs may be attributed to premiums associated with greater underlying macroeconomic risks, tighter regulatory requirements and the absence of strong competitive pressures within the banking sector. High overhead costs in banks can lead them to charge higher fees or offer less favourable terms to businesses and households. Additionally, they may limit the ability of banks to invest in new technologies and services that could benefit users.

Figure 5.12. Banking system efficiency, 2021

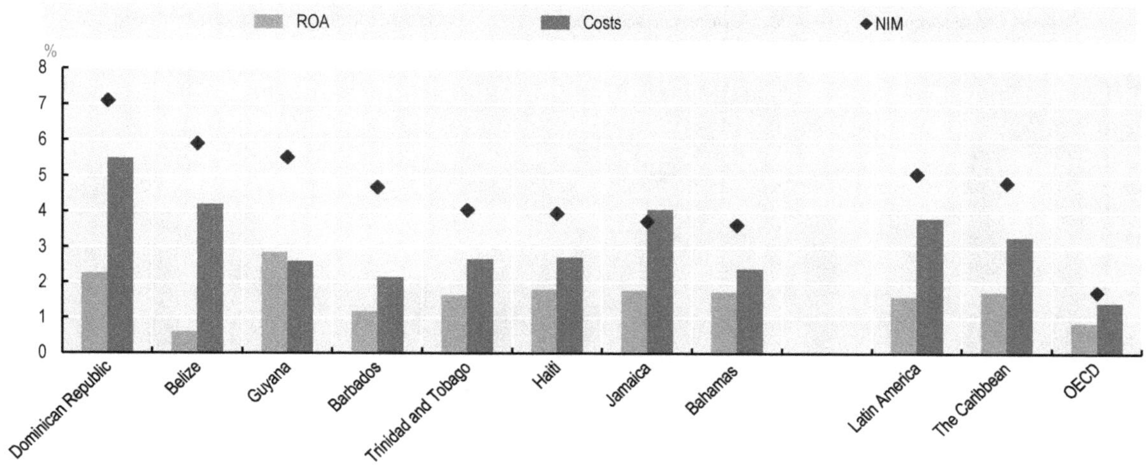

Note: ROA=Return on Assets (ROA); Costs=Overhead Costs to Assets; NIM=Net Interest Margin.
Source: Authors' elaboration based on Global Financial Development Database (World Bank, 2022[66]).

StatLink https://stat.link/ju42rp

The banking system maintains solid capitalisation and liquidity levels, enhancing stability and resilience, but asset quality remains a potential risk for some countries

Recurring natural disasters and volatile commodity prices are challenges to achieving economic growth and resilience in the Caribbean. Sound financial systems contribute to mitigate these risks, ensuring stability amid economic shocks (Rojas-Suarez and Zegarra, 2021[70]). Banks with robust capital and liquidity buffers play a vital role in maintaining credit flows during crises, supporting effective capital allocation, risk management, and sustained growth (World Bank, 2016[71]).

In 2022, the capital adequacy ratio of banks in the region stood at 17%, slightly below the 19% observed in OECD countries and above the regulatory minimum of 8% stipulated by Basel (BIS, 2020[72]). This indicates a robust capital position that provides a buffer against financial shocks and supports lending activities through the business cycle. The liquid assets to deposits and short-term funding ratio remained robust at 48%, in line with the OECD average of 50% (Figure 5.13). High liquidity levels reflect the ability to meet short-term obligations and cover unexpected liquidity shocks.

Figure 5.13. Banking system soundness indicators, 2022

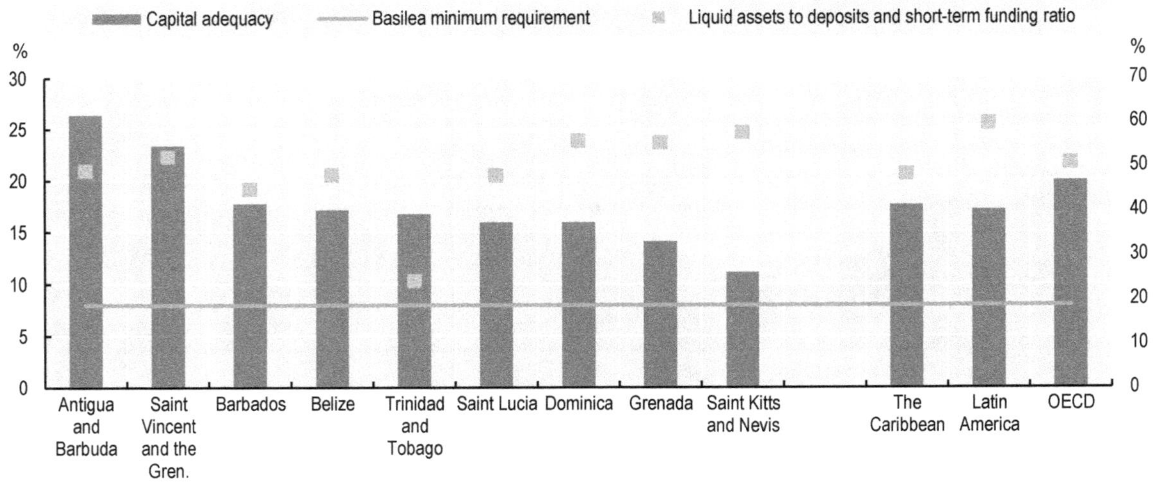

Note: Capital adequacy data are shown on the primary axis, while liquid assets to deposits and short-term funding ratio are on the secondary one.
Source: Authors' elaboration based on Financial Soundness Indicators (IMF, 2022[73]).

StatLink https://stat.link/3ui7nj

Banks with high ratios of non-performing loans (NPLs) to gross loans represent a potential risk to financial stability in the region. In 2022, the NPL ratio in the region stood at 9.3%, above Latin America and OECD figures of 2.3% and 2.2%, respectively. This indicator assesses the percentage of unpaid, delayed and unlikely-to-be-repaid loans within a bank's total portfolio. As such, the level of NPLs provides insight into credit quality and potential credit risks that could threaten the institution's stability. Additionally, low levels of NPLs indicate increased lending capacity, as more funds are available for loans rather than to cover potential losses.

Key policy messages

This chapter has examined challenges, opportunities and strategies for mobilising domestic and international resources, from both public and private sources, to finance the reforms needed to boost development in the Caribbean. Box 5.3 provides actionable recommendations based on the analysis presented, offering guidance to Caribbean countries in shaping their policy initiatives. Given the region's diverse socioeconomic characteristics, challenges, and opportunities, tailored approaches are essential for each country. However, certain overarching considerations can orient countries in designing effective "policy menus" and achieving an optimal policy mix.

Box 5.3. Key policy messages

Enhance collection and progressivity of tax systems

- Rethink the structure of tax systems to move towards a larger relative contribution of direct taxes in the region.
- Work further in assessing the overall benefits and costs of revenues forgone due to tax expenditures to determine the effectiveness of certain incentives and exemptions.

- Continue the implementation of key international tax guidelines, including the OECD/G20 Inclusive Framework on BEPS, to combat tax evasion more effectively.
- Enhance analysis and data on tax morale to foster a stronger taxpaying culture.

Promote and scale-up debt tools to channel resources to specific goals while managing debt pressures

- Scale up GSSSB bonds, in particular blue bonds, by enhancing the domestic debt market, issuing bonds in local currency and fostering digital and technological advances.
- Support expansion and improvement of innovative structures for SLBs, as they offer an opportunity to redirect capital flows towards high-impact socio-environmental projects.
- Participate in debt-for-nature swaps to finance the green transition, scaling up through improved governance, oversight, and a whole-of-government participatory approach, and promote natural disaster clauses in debt contracts to link repayment to risk exposure.

Foster resilient debt management and support implementation of sustainable finance frameworks

- Enhance debt management strategies to reduce the vulnerability associated with external and foreign currency-denominated debt.
- Consider the establishment of fiscal rules to support debt sustainability, including rules for spending and balanced budgets and debt, coupled with improved monitoring, evaluation and compliance mechanisms for fiscal rules.
- Expand and enhance regulatory tools (e.g. sustainability, green or transition bonds standards and taxonomies) to boost sustainable investments and avoid greenwashing.

Promote financial inclusion and financial markets development

- Develop National Financial Inclusion Strategies and financial education initiatives to enhance financial literacy among individuals and businesses.
- Support digital infrastructure development to facilitate mobile banking and digital financial services, particularly in remote areas.

Notes

[1] The 12 Caribbean countries covered in the analysis are Saint Kitts and Nevis, Suriname, Barbados, Trinidad and Tobago, Antigua and Barbuda, The Bahamas, Belize, Saint Lucia, Jamaica, Guyana, and Grenada (ECLAC, 2024[6]).

[2] Anguilla, Antigua and Barbuda, The Bahamas, Barbados, Belize, British Virgin Islands, Cayman Islands, Curacao, Dominica, Dominican Republic, Grenada, Haiti, Jamaica, Montserrat, Saint Kitts and Nevis, Saint Lucia, Saint Vincent and the Grenadines, Trinidad and Tobago, and Turks and Caicos Islands.

[3] The Latinobarómetro survey comprises 18 Latin American countries: Argentina, Bolivia, Brazil, Chile, Colombia, Costa Rica, Dominican Republic, Ecuador, El Salvador, Guatemala, Honduras, Mexico, Nicaragua, Panama, Paraguay, Peru, Uruguay and Venezuela (Latinobarometro, 2023[18]).

[4] The 16 current members of the CCRIF are: Anguilla, Antigua and Barbuda, The Bahamas, Barbados, Belize, Bermuda, Cayman Islands, Dominica, Grenada, Haiti, Jamaica, Saint Kitts and Nevis, Saint Lucia, Saint Vincent and the Grenadines, Trinidad and Tobago, and Turks and Caicos Islands.

References

ADB/IFC (2023), *Bonds to Finance the Sustainable Blue Economy: A Practitioner's Guide*, Asian Development Bank/International Finance Corporation, Manila, https://www.greenfinanceplatform.org/sites/default/files/downloads/tools/Bonds-to-Finance-the-Sustainable-Blue-Economy-a-Practitioners-Guide-September-2023.pdf. [40]

Andrian, L. et al. (2022), *Fiscal Rules and Economic Cycles: Quality (Always) Matters*, Inter-American Development Bank, Washington, DC, https://doi.org/10.18235/0004570. [27]

Ardanaz, M. et al. (2021), "Growth-friendly fiscal rules? Safeguarding public investment from budget cuts through fiscal rule design", *Journal of International Money and Finance*, Vol. 111, https://doi.org/10.1016/j.jimonfin.2020.102319. [33]

Ardanaz, M. and A. Izquierdo (2022), "Current expenditure upswings in good times and public investment downswings in bad times? New evidence from developing countries", *Journal of Comparative Economics*, Vol. 50/1, pp. 118-134, https://doi.org/10.1016/j.jce.2021.06.002. [25]

Ardanaz, M., C. Ulloa-Suarez and O. Valencia (2023), "Why don't we follow the rules? Drivers of compliance with fiscal policy rules in emerging markets", *IBD Working Paper*, No. IDB-WP-1497, Inter-American Development Bank, Washington, DC, https://doi.org/10.18235/0005165. [30]

Arslanalp, S., B. Eichengreen and P. Blair (2024), "Sustained debt reduction: The Jamaica exception", *Brooking Papers on Economic Activity*, Brookings Institution, Washington, DC, https://www.brookings.edu/articles/sustained-debt-reduction-the-jamaica-exception/. [21]

Artemis (2024), *Catastrophe Bonds and Insurance-linked Securities Deal Directory*, (database), https://www.artemis.bm/dashboard/cat-bonds-ils-cumulative-issuance/. [46]

Artemis (2014), *World Bank - CCRIF 2014-1*, Artemis, https://www.artemis.bm/deal-directory/world-bank-ccrif-2014-1/. [47]

Beck, B. and H. Mooney (2021), "Financial development", in *Economic Institutions for a Resilient Caribbean*, Inter-American Development Bank, Washington, DC, https://doi.org/10.18235/0003053. [65]

BIS (2020), "Risk-based Capital Requirements", webpage, https://www.bis.org/basel_framework/standard/RBC.htm. [72]

Caballero, C., K. Gonzalez and F. Nieto (2024), *Debt-For-Nature Swaps are Gaining Traction among Lower-Rated Sovereigns*, S&P Global, https://www.spglobal.com/ratings/en/research/articles/240227-debt-for-nature-swaps-are-gaining-traction-among-lower-rated-sovereigns-13010020. [60]

Climate Bonds Initiative (2022), *Latin America and the Caribbean Sustainable Debt: State of the Market 2022*, Climate Bonds Initiative, London, https://www.climatebonds.net/files/reports/cbi_lac_sotm_2022_en__0.pdf. [41]

DGB Group (2023), "Dominican Republic received $6 million boost in carbon credits from the World Bank", 30 October, DGB Group, https://www.green.earth/news/dominican-republic-receives-6-million-boost-in-carbon-credits-from-the-world-bank. [11]

ECCB (2023), *The ECCU's Financial Literacy and Financial Inclusion Report on Survey Results 2022/2023*, Eastern Caribbean Central Bank, https://www.eccb-centralbank.org/viewPDF/documents/2023-09-15-09-55-07-ECCU-Financial-Literacy-and-Financial-Inclusion-Survey-Report.pdf. [68]

ECLAC (2024), *Fiscal Panorama of Latin America and the Caribbean, 2024*, United Nations Economic Commission for Latin America and the Caribbean, Santiago, https://repositorio.cepal.org/server/api/core/bitstreams/7b6e3da2-68e3-431e-a9ed-29a931883693/content. [6]

ECLAC (2023), *Capital Flows to Latin America and the Caribbean: 2022 Year-in-review and Early 2023 Developments*, United Nations Economic Commission for Latin America and the Caribbean, Washington, DC, https://repositorio.cepal.org/server/api/core/bitstreams/7e7681e0-0855-45f3-9bbe-38ad9feedd63/content. [39]

ECLAC (2023), *Capital Flows to Latin America and the Caribbean: First 10 months of 2023*, United Nations Economic Commission for Africa and the Caribbean, Washington, DC, https://www.cepal.org/en/publications/68745-capital-flows-latin-america-and-caribbean-first-10-months-2023#:~:text=Latin%20American%20and%20Caribbean%20bond,higher%20than%20the%20annual%20volume. [36]

ECLAC (2023), *Fiscal Panorama of Latin America and the Caribbean*, United Nations Economic Commission for Latin America and the Caribbean, Santiago, https://www.cepal.org/en/publications/48900-fiscal-panorama-latin-america-and-caribbean-2023-fiscal-policy-growth. [14]

ECLAC (2018), *Debt for Climate Adaptation: Swap Initiative for Caribbean SIDS*, United Nations Economic Commission for Latin America and the Caribbean, Santiago. [59]

European Investment Bank (2024), *Barbados: EIB and Inter-American Development Bank approve guarantees to support climate and fiscal resilience*, European Investment Bank, https://www.eib.org/en/press/all/2024-300-inter-american-development-bank-and-european-investment-bank-approve-guarantees-to-support-climate-and-fiscal-resilience-in-barbados. [53]

FATF/OECD (2023), *Misuse of Citizenship and Residency by Investment Programmes*, The Financial Action Task Force, Paris, https://www.fatf-gafi.org/content/dam/fatf-gafi/reports/Misuse-CBI-RBI-Programmes.pdf.coredownload.pdf. [7]

Fuller, F. et al. (2018), *Debt for Climate Swaps: Caribbean Outlook*, Climate Analytics, https://climateanalytics.org/publications/debt-for-climate-swaps-caribbean-outlook. [61]

Galindo, A. and A. Izquierdo (2024), *2024 Latin American and Caribbean Macroeconomic Report: Ready for Take-Off? Building on Macroeconomic Stability for Growth*, Inter-American Development Bank, Washington, DC, https://doi.org/10.18235/0005667. [29]

Garcia, D. (2022), "Banco Popular Dominicano approves green bond and increase in share capital", 21 March, Bloomberg, https://www.bloomberglinea.com/2022/03/21/banco-popular-dominicano-aprueba-bono-verde-y-aumento-del-capital-social/?outputType=amp. [42]

Gomez-Gonzalez, J., O. Valencia and G. Sánchez (2024), "Debt affordability in developed and emerging market economies: The role of fiscal rules", *Journal of Economic Finance*, https://doi.org/10.1007/s12197-024-09660-3. [28]

Government of Guyana (2022), *Guyana Receives First Payments Under World Leading Carbon Credit Sales Agreement*, Low Carbon Development Strategy, Government of Guyana, https://lcds.gov.gy/guyana-receives-first-payments-under-world-leading-carbon-credit-sales-agreement/. [10]

Green Finance Institute (2021), "Government of Belize Debt Conversion for Marine Conservation", webpage, https://www.greenfinanceinstitute.com/gfihive/case-studies/government-of-belize-debt-conversion-for-marine-conservation/. [56]

HMB (2020), "HMB partners with IDB Invest to issue the first social bond in Trinidad and Tobago and the Caribbean region", 6 February, Home Mortgage Bank, Port of Spain, https://hmbinvest.com/news/hmb-invest-partners-to-issue-social-bond/#:~:text=About%20the%20Social%20Bond&text=The%20bond%20issuance%20will%20contribute,inclusive%2C%20safe%2C%20resilient%20and%20sustainable. [43]

Ho, S. and S. Fontana (2021), "Sovereign debt evolution: The natural disaster clause", *Emerging Markets Restructuring Journal* 11, https://www.clearygottlieb.com/-/media/files/emrj-materials/issue-11-spring-2021/article_natural_disaster_clause_v3-pdf.pdf. [50]

IDB (2024), *Barbados Launched the World's First Debt-for-Climate-Resilience Operation*, Inter-American Development Bank, Washington D.C., https://www.iadb.org/en/news/barbados-launched-worlds-first-debt-climate-resilience-operation. [54]

IDB (2024), *Flexible Financing Facility (FFF)*, https://www.iadb.org/en/how-we-can-work-together/public-sector/financing-solutions/flexible-financing-facility-fff#:~:text=Through%20the%20Principal%20Payment%20Option,amounts%20in%20future%20amortization%20installments. [51]

IDB (2024), *IDB, EIB Approve Guarantees to Support Climate and Fiscal Resilience in Barbados*, Inter-American Development Bank, https://www.iadb.org/en/news/idb-eib-approve-guarantees-support-climate-and-fiscal-resilience-barbados#:~:text=The%20Inter%2DAmerican%20Development%20Bank,adaptation%20projects%2C%20while%20safeguarding%20other. [58]

IDB (2024), *The Bahamas Launches Debt for Ocean Conservation Swap with the support of IDB*, Inter-American Development Bank, Washington D.C., https://www.iadb.org/en/news/bahamas-launches-debt-ocean-conservation-swap-support-idb. [55]

IDB (2022), *Barbados Places Climate Financing Firmly on Agenda with IDB, Nature Conservancy Support*, Inter-American Development Bank, Washington, DC, https://www.iadb.org/en/news/barbados-places-climate-financing-firmly-agenda-idb-nature-conservancy-support. [57]

IDB (2021), *IDB Standardized Public Debt*, (database), https://mydata.iadb.org/Finance/Standardized-Public-Debt-Database/3bvi-edbq/about_data. [23]

IMF (2024), *IMF Reaches Staff-Level Agreement with Jamaica on the Third Reviews of the Precautionary and Liquidity Line (PLL) and the Resilience and Sustainability Facility (RSF) Arrangement*, International Monetary Fund, Washington, DC, https://www.imf.org/en/News/Articles/2024/06/28/pr24256-jamaica-imf-reaches-sla-3rd-rev-pll-rsf-arr. [63]

IMF (2023), "Barbados: First Reviews Under the Extended Fund Facility and Under the Resilience and Sustainability Facility, Requests for Modification of Performance Criteria and Reform Measures, and Rephasing of Access Under the Resilience and Sustainability Facility"*, IMF Staff Country Reports*, No. 241, International Monetary Fund, Washington, DC, https://www.imf.org/en/Publications/CR/Issues/2023/06/30/Barbados-First-Reviews-Under-the-Extended-Fund-Facility-and-Under-the-Resilience-and-535462. [13]

IMF (2023), *World Economic Outlook*, (database), https://www.imf.org/en/Publications/WEO/weo-database/2023/October. [22]

IMF (2022), "Financial Access Survey"*, IMF Data*, (database), https://data.imf.org/?sk=e5dcab7e-a5ca-4892-a6ea-598b5463a34c. [69]

IMF (2022), *Financial Soundness Indicators*, (database), http://Add URL. [73]

KPMG (2023), "Blue bonds and climate finance in island economies", September, KPMG, https://assets.kpmg.com/content/dam/kpmg/bb/pdf/2023/Blue%20Bonds%20and%20Climate%20Finance%20in%20Island%20Economies.pdf. [9]

Latinobarometro (2023), *Latinobarometro (database)*, https://www.latinobarometro.org/latContents.jsp. [18]

Ministry of Finance of Barbados (2024), *Barbados Fiscal Framework 2023/24 - 2025/26*, Parliament of Barbados, https://www.barbadosparliament.com/uploads/sittings/attachments/31e29c0865c2de076a924af88b7e2416.pdf. [4]

Núñez, G., H. Velloso and F. Da Silva (2022), *Corporate Governance in Latin America and the Caribbean: Using ESG Debt Instruments to Fiinance Sustainable Investment Projects*, United Nations Economic Commission for Latin America and the Caribbean, Santiago, https://repositorio.cepal.org/handle/11362/47778. [35]

Núñez, J. and D. Lasso (2023), *Fiscal Incidence and Public Spending: Public Policy Scenarios for Colombia*, Agence Française de Développement, Paris, https://www.afd.fr/en/ressources/fiscal-incidence-and-public-spending-public-policy-scenarios-colombia. [5]

OECD (2024), *Fostering Catastrophe Bond Markets in Asia and the Pacific*, The Development Dimension, OECD Publishing, Paris, https://doi.org/10.1787/ab1e49ef-en. [45]

OECD (2024), *The surge of green, social, sustainability and sustainability-linked (GSSS) bonds in Latin America and the Caribbean: Facts and policy implications*, OECD Development Policy Papers, No. 56, OECD Publishing, Paris, https://doi.org/10.1787/f1c893a3-en. [34]

OECD (2023), *Global Forum Capacity Building Report*, OECD Publishing, Paris, https://web-archive.oecd.org/tax/transparency/documents/2023-global-forum-capacity-building-report.pdf. [16]

OECD (2023), *Global Revenue Statistics*, (database), https://stats.oecd.org/Index.aspx?DataSetCode=RS_GBL# (accessed on 13 June 2024). [2]

OECD (2023), *Pioneering Global Progress in Tax Transparency: A Journey of Transformation and Development – 2023 Global Forum Annual Report*, Global Forum on Transparency and Exchange of Information for Tax Purposes, OECD Publishing, Paris, https://www.oecd.org/tax/ transparency/documents/global-forum-annual-report-2023.pdf. [15]

OECD (2021), *Building Tax Culture, Compliance and Citizenship: A Global Source Book on Taxpayer Education, Second Edition*, OECD Publishing, Paris, https://doi.org/10.1787/18585eb1-en. [20]

OECD (2019), *Tax Morale: What Drives People and Businesses to Pay Tax?*, OECD Publishing, Paris, https://doi.org/10.1787/f3d8ea10-en. [17]

OECD et al. (2023), *Latin American Economic Outlook 2023: Investing in Sustainable Development*, OECD Publishing, Paris, https://doi.org/10.1787/8c93ff6e-en. [26]

OECD et al. (2024), *Revenue Statistics in Latin America and the Caribbean 2024*, OECD Publishing, Paris, https://doi.org/10.1787/33e226ae-en. [1]

OECD et al. (2022), *Latin American Economic Outlook 2022: Towards a Green and Just Transition*, OECD Publishing, Paris, https://doi.org/10.1787/3d5554fc-en. [8]

OECD et al. (2021), *VAT Digital Toolkit for Latin America and the Caribbean*, OECD Publishing, Paris, https://www.oecd.org/tax/consumption/vat-digital-toolkit-for-latin-america-and-the-caribbean.htm. [19]

Owen, N. (2022), "Belize: Swapping debt for nature", *IMF Country Focus*, 4 May, International Monetary Fund, Washington, DC, https://www.imf.org/en/News/Articles/2022/05/03/CF-Belize-swapping-debt-for-nature. [38]

Piemonté, C., J. Kim and O. Cattaneo (2024), "Financing sustainable development in the Organisation of Eastern Caribbean States: A transition finance diagnostic", *OECD Development Co-operation Working Papers*, No. 115, OECD Publishing, Paris, https://doi.org/10.1787/62a4deae-en. [44]

Redonda, A., C. von Haldenwang and F. Aliu (2024), "Global tax expenditures dataset, version 1.2.2", 25 January, German Institute of Development and Sustainability, Bonn, https://doi.org/10.5281/zenodo.10796848. [12]

Rojas-Suarez, L. and M. Zegarra (2021), "Financial regulation and supervision in Caribbean countries", *Economic Institutions for a Resilient Caribbean*, Inter-American Development Bank, Washington, DC, https://doi.org/10.18235/0003053. [70]

Rosenblatt, D. et al. (2023), "Dealing with debt in the Caribbean", *Caribbean Economics Quarterly*, Vol. 12/3, https://doi.org/10.18235/0005372. [31]

Savage, R. (2023), "Barbados 'debt-for-climate' swap backed by $300 mln EIB, IADB guarantee – statement", 10 November, Reuters, https://www.reuters.com/sustainability/sustainable-finance-reporting/barbados-debt-for-climate-swap-backed-by-300-mln-eib-iadb-guarantee-statement-2023-11-10/#:~:text=In%20September%202022%2C%20Barbados%20carried,vital%20for%20the%20tourism%20sector. [52]

SBFN (2024), "Country Profiles", *SFB Network*, (database), https://data.sbfnetwork.org/country-profiles. [64]

The Barbados Advocate (2021), "Business Monday: VAT revenue falling short, says business analyst", 10 May, The Barbados Advocate, https://www.barbadosadvocate.com/business/business-monday-vat-revenue-falling-short-says-business-analyst. [3]

The Nature Conservancy (2023), *Case Study: Barbados Blue Bond for Ocean Conservation*, The Nature Conservancy, Arlington, Virginia, https://www.nature.org/content/dam/tnc/nature/en/documents/TNC-Barbados-Blue-Bonds_Case-Study.pdf. [37]

UNDP (2023), *Common Framework of Sustainable Finance Taxonomies for Latin America and the Caribbean*, United Nations Development Programme, New York, https://climatepromise.undp.org/sites/default/files/research_report_document/common-framework-of-sustainable-finance-taxonomies-lac.pdf. [62]

UNSGSA (2024), *Financial Inclusion and Small Island Developing States*, United Nations Secretary-General's Special Advocate for Inclusive Finance and Development, https://sdgs.un.org/sites/default/files/2024-05/OUNSGSA_SIDS4%20Brief_final.pdf. [67]

World Bank (2024), "World Bank returns to the Cat bond market providing financial protection to Jamaica", 25 April, Press Release, World Bank, Washington, DC, https://www.worldbank.org/en/news/press-release/2024/04/25/world-bank-returns-to-the-cat-bond-market-providing-financial-protection-to-jamaica. [48]

World Bank (2022), *Global Financial Development*, (database). [66]

World Bank (2022), *International Debt Statistics*, (database), https://www.worldbank.org/en/programs/debt-statistics/ids. [24]

World Bank (2016), "Financial Stability", webpage, https://www.worldbank.org/en/publication/gfdr/gfdr-2016/background/financial-stability. [71]

World Bank (2013), "Mexico multiCat bond: Transferring catastrophe risk to the capital markets", (brochure), World Bank Group, Washington, DC, https://openknowledge.worldbank.org/server/api/core/bitstreams/42f4a9ed-6f3d-5bbb-bb5b-e5c2cc6703ae/content. [49]

Wright, A., K. Grenade and A. Scott-Joseph (2017), "Fiscal rules: Towards a new paradigm for fiscal sustainability in small states", *IDB Working Paper Series*, No. IDB-WP-780, Inter-American Development Bank, Washington, DC, https://asip.org.ar/wp-content/uploads/2017/09/Fiscal-Rules-Towards-a-New-Paradigm-for-Fiscal-Sustainability-in-Small-States-BID.pdf. [32]

6 Regional integration and international partnerships

Regional integration and international partnerships are vital for Caribbean countries to foster economic resilience and productivity, improve global market positioning, and enhance responses to climate change and other development challenges. The Caribbean has room to improve intra- and extra-regional trade by diversifying partners and improving transport connectivity. Harnessing regional co-operation, the Caribbean can extend successful disaster risk strategies to promote a resilient green transition, leverage digital advancements to tackle common challenges, unlock renewable energy potential and enhance intra-regional mobility of persons. Further, the chapter highlights the relevance of advancing a Development in Transition approach to international partnerships to leverage different sources of international funding, while improving their development impact in line with nationally determined priorities. New partnerships can be particularly helpful in aiding the Caribbean's climate adaptation needs by providing the Caribbean with equal-footing platforms in the multilateral sphere, introducing innovative financial instruments and enhancing support from global climate funds.

Introduction

Caribbean countries face several common challenges and opportunities that underscore the strategic relevance of collective action. These challenges include small territorial and population sizes, which limit economic scale and diversification, making the region vulnerable to shocks and crises. This vulnerability has contributed to high levels of international debt and significant impacts of climate disasters. At the same time, the Caribbean possesses abundant assets, including its rich biodiversity and large ocean resources. These assets offer significant development opportunities, particularly in the context of the green transition.

Deepening regional integration and co-operation among Caribbean nations – and with the rest of the world - is instrumental to address vulnerabilities and potentially generate new development opportunities. First, greater integration can enable economies of scale for production transformation, increased productivity, and job creation. This, in turn, improves intra-regional trade and the position of the region in global markets and global value chains (GVCs). Second, co-operation can allow for more efficient responses to development challenges like climate change, digitalisation, indebtedness and the energy transition. Third, international partnerships can help in amplifying the Caribbean's voice in multilateral fora and advancing the region's interest in relation to global public goods.

Targeted regional strategies can improve trade outcomes for the Caribbean

Regional integration has been a long-standing strategy in the Caribbean, yet there is room to harness the potential of existing integration and co-operation mechanisms

For decades, Caribbean countries have pushed for regional solutions to overcome development challenges through collective action. Since the 1960s, they have fostered regional integration and co-operation, conforming today to a rich weave of organisations working towards shared goals (Figure 6.1). This includes well-grounded integration and co-operation schemes, including the Caribbean Community (CARICOM), the Association of Caribbean States (ACS) and the Organisation of Eastern Caribbean States (OECS), among others. Other sub-regional organisations focus on co-operation and/or development financing, like the Caribbean Development Bank (CDB) or the Caribbean Export Development Agency. Simultaneously, all Caribbean states form part of the Community of Latin American and Caribbean States, the largest Latin American and Caribbean organisation for regional political and policy co-ordination. Some are also part of other integration mechanisms, like the Centro American System of Integration (SICA), of which the Dominican Republic and Belize are members.

Figure 6.1. Main regional and sub-regional organisations with Caribbean membership

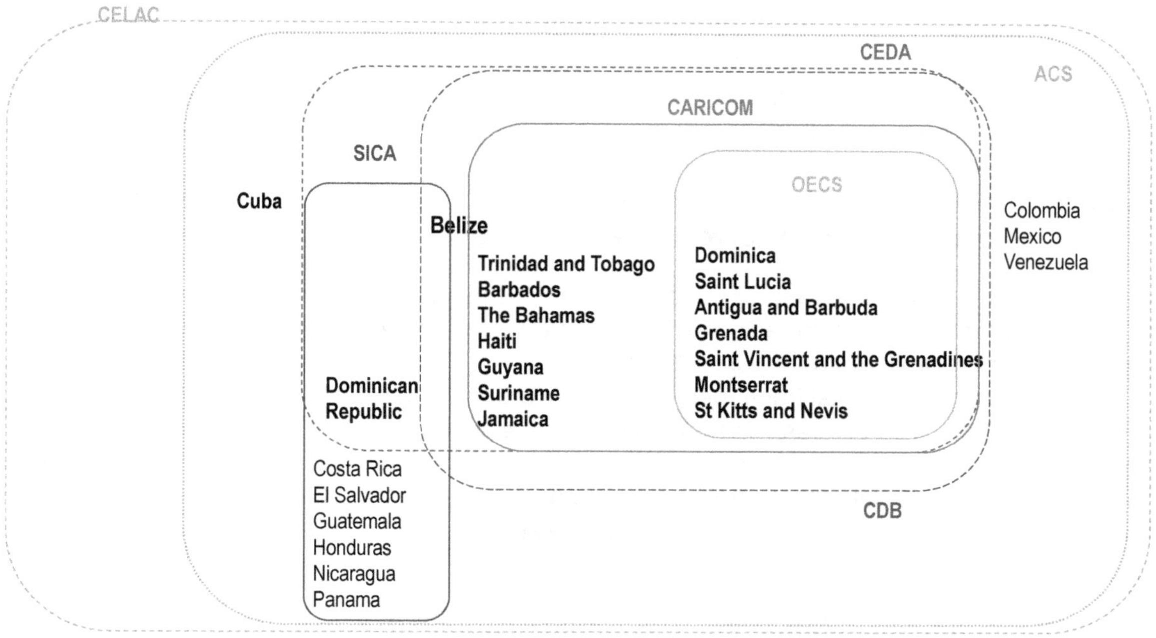

Note: Dashed borders indicate co-operation and/or financing organisations, while continued borders indicate integration blocs.
Source: Authors' elaboration.

CARICOM, OECS and SICA are regional intergovernmental organisations that have advanced the integration process, achieving significant milestones since the early 2000s. In 2001, the 15 member states of CARICOM set the goal of establishing its Single Market and Economy (CSME). This would include a customs union, a common market with free movement of capital, labour, goods, and services, and an economic union with co-ordinated sectoral and macroeconomic policies (Allub and Schliesser, 2023[1]). In 2010, the OECS approved the revision of the original Treaty of Basseterre. This created an economic union and a single market with a customs union where the seven OECS countries agreed to trade without tariffs or other barriers.

While progress has been made in liberalising the movement of goods, services and skilled labour within the region, the pace of integration has been slow and remains incomplete (IDB, 2020[2]). The region has concluded only 57% of the required actions to complete the CSME since its agreement more than 20 years ago (IMF, 2020[3]). Persistent non-tariff barriers (NTBs) to trade, such as distance and culture, bilateral exchange rates, transfer fees, and required documentation, have negative effects on trade and could erase trade gains achieved through the removal or reductions of tariffs. Addressing this issue in the Caribbean is particularly relevant as intra-CARICOM NTBs, measured by the variations in non-tariff costs (the percentage increase in trade cost compared to the average domestic cost of goods), increased 35% between 2000 and 2015 (Allende López et al., 2020[4]).

Regional integration is particularly relevant for Caribbean countries for several reasons. These countries have small territories and populations with associated limited economic scale. They are also remote from international markets, with high levels of external openness and high exposure to external shocks and climate change. Additionally, most countries have elevated public debt and are highly dependent on external capital.

Regional integration can enhance welfare, productivity, and resilience through the expansion of market opportunities, specialisation gains, economies of scale, and pooled power to negotiate and trade with international partners. Advancing regional integration appears even more relevant, primarily in the context of free-trade areas and customs unions among Caribbean nations (Giordano, 2012[5]). In recent years, value chains have been turning more regional and less global. Furthermore, the COVID-19 pandemic prompted companies worldwide to implement a variety of localisation strategies, including relocation, nearshoring and reshoring (Lund et al., 2019[6]; OECD/UNCTAD/ECLAC, 2020[7]). Considering the institutional network in place in the region, the Caribbean could make efforts within and between regional organisations, optimising results through increased inter-institutional synergies.

Expanding intra-regional trade can bring resilience and productivity gains, although it will have to be accompanied by diversification and upgrading of production

The progress in liberalising the trade of goods and services has not been enough to foster intra-regional trade. While progress has been made in the CSME, intra-regional trade in CARICOM is relatively low and has decreased in recent years (Figure 6.2) (IMF, 2020[3]). Total intra-regional trade in CARICOM, measured as a proportion of total trade, decreased from around 8% in 1995-99 to 6.7% in 2015-18 (Allub and Schliesser, 2023[1]). In contrast, the regional bloc comprised of SICA and the Dominican Republic showed a higher level of intra-regional trade, increasing from 12.4% in 1995-99 to 14.1% in 2015-18. Both sub-regions show lower levels of intra-regional trade than other regional blocs like the European Union (EU) and the Association of Southeast Asian Nations (ASEAN).

Figure 6.2. Intra-regional trade as a proportion of total trade, selected regional blocs, 1995-99 and 2015-18

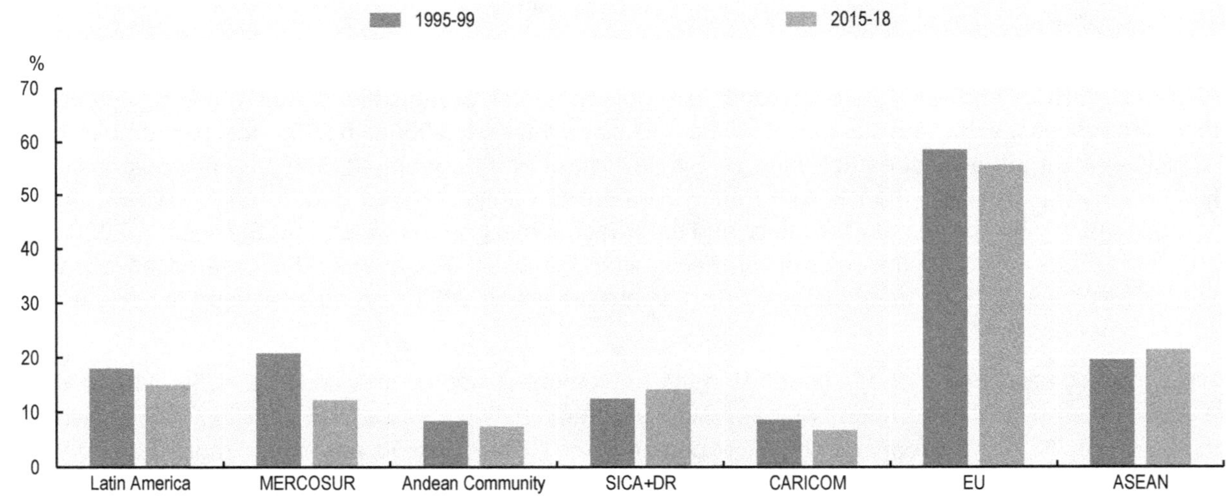

Notes: ASEAN = Association of Southeast Asian Nations; CARICOM = Caribbean Community; EU = European Union; MERCOSUR = Southern Common Market; SICA+DR = Central American Integration System + Dominican Republic.
Source: Authors' elaboration based on (Allub and Schliesser, 2023[1]).

StatLink https://stat.link/sl45ip

Intra-regional trade is further limited by the low diversification and complementarity of economies in the Caribbean. The region continues to specialise in relatively low value-added segments of GVCs, both in the service sector (tourism) and natural resources (agricultural products, minerals, and fossil fuels). Indeed, 52.5% of exported goods are primary products and resource-based manufactures, while only 4.1% are high-technology manufactures. Most intra-regional trade is between commodity and non-commodity exporting economies, while trade within each group is less than 1% of gross domestic product (GDP) (IMF, 2020[3]). In addition, the CSME has not been able to reverse regional asymmetries. Countries with stronger manufacturing economies have benefited most from the CSME. Trinidad and Tobago, for example, accounted for 62% of intra-regional trade in 2019 (ECLAC, 2022[8]).

Advancing trade integration across Caribbean economies requires addressing NTBs and fostering regional value chains. Current challenges related to NTBs include the co-ordination of investment codes, harmonisation of sanitary and phytosanitary measures, and the free movement of skilled people.

Building production capacity through regional value chains in strategic sectors can help Caribbean countries diversify their production, reduce over-dependency on extra-regional imports, and lower vulnerability to disruptions in GVCs while potentially creating more jobs. Some strategic areas of opportunity are linked to the green, blue, and circular economy (see Chapter 3), as well as the food sector, as Caribbean economies look for potential trade solutions to their food security challenges (Santamaría, 2024[9]). Indeed, the Caribbean relies on imports for 80% to 90% of its food needs to satisfy both local consumption and the demands of tourists (IICA, 2018[10]). Hence, intra-regional trade for food security can increase production efficiency and give consumers access to a greater variety of food at lower prices (Campos, 2024[11]) (see Box 6.1).

Box 6.1. Food production as a promising sector to boost intra-regional trade in the Caribbean

Food production represents an interesting area to boost intra-regional trade. This is a sector where the Caribbean is losing share in a global growing market. At the same time, it presents inter-related challenges, including excessive dependency on imports, high relative costs and food insecurity (Allub and Schliesser, 2023[1]). While many Caribbean economies export agricultural products, 80-90% of all food consumed in the region comes from abroad. Meanwhile, intra-regional food trade accounts for only 16.6% of total food imports (IICA, 2018[10]; Turnbull, 23 April 2021[12]). The average cost of a healthy diet in Caribbean countries in 2021 was estimated at USD 4.4 per person per day in purchasing power parity terms, which is 42% higher than in the OECD average (Arias, Brown and Hassiner, 2024[13]).

By tapping into its comparative advantages and introducing technology, the region could upgrade its agricultural and food processing value chains, the latter creating eight times more output per worker than jobs in farming (Dessina, Minsat and Delana, 2022[14]; ECLAC, 2022[8]). Agri-tech is an opportunity to increase productivity and resilience towards climate vulnerability and extreme weather events. The Inter-American Development Bank (IDB) is promoting adoption of technology use in agriculture and agro-food sectors in the Caribbean. It supports entrepreneurs and start-ups in the sectors of fruits and vegetables, coffee and cocoa, and sauces and spices (Competitiveness, 2021[15]).

The Caribbean Export Development Agency (CEDA) is advancing a positive integration agenda by working to promote value chains across Caribbean economies. For example, CEDA is helping strengthen the cocoa or chocolate value chain between the Dominican Republic and Haiti by promoting dialogue and co-operation and providing technical support to the private sector. In this context, two firms from the value chain – Makaya (Haiti) and Definite Chocolate (Dominican Republic) – collaborated to produce the first bi-national chocolate. Together, they created a chocolate collection that combines the history of cocoa and common traditions from both countries, while using recipes that highlight organic indigenous ingredients, such as coffee, cashews, and peanuts.

Source: (Caribbean Export, 2022[16]).

Caribbean countries have room to improve their position in global value chains through targeted policies in production transformation, trade facilitation and trade partnerships

The Caribbean has decreased its participation in GVCs over the past few decades. Caribbean economies have a high degree of trade openness, with an average trade-to-GDP ratio above 90% (ECLAC, 2022[8]). Nevertheless, the Caribbean's participation in world exports of goods and services fell from a peak of 0.35% in 1984 to a record low of 0.15% in 2020 before slightly recovering to 0.23% in 2022 (Figure 6.3). While Latin America also shows a declining trend, the ASEAN region has more than doubled its share in global exports, from 3.35% in 1981 to 7.45% in 2022.

Figure 6.3. Participation in world exports (percentage) of the Caribbean, Latin America, and ASEAN, 1981-2022

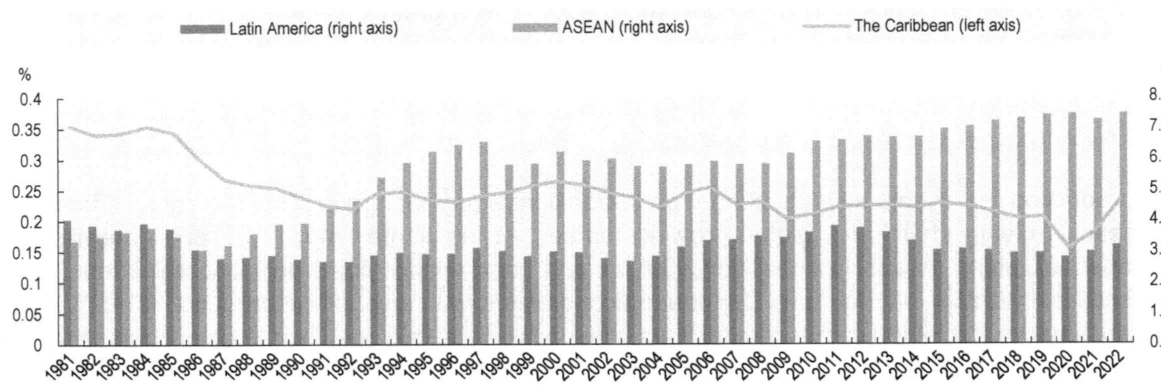

Source: Authors' elaboration based on (World Bank, 2023[17]).

StatLink https://stat.link/ptj4c8

The Caribbean faces a variety of challenges to integrate into the global market. These include: inadequate export readiness among producers; limited creation, transplant, and diffusion of technology; weak production systems; low levels of trade competitiveness; and high energy, shipping, and connectivity costs (ECLAC, 2022[8]).

Product diversification is a critical area to improve integration of the Caribbean into GVCs. The region has high levels of concentration in the number of exported products in the Export Concentration Index (UNCTADStat, 2024[18]). Ranging from 0 to 1, higher values in this index reveal that a small number of countries in the Caribbean dominate commodity exports and thus have market concentration. In 2022, the Caribbean scored 0.432, which compares to scores of 0.128 in Central America, 0.137 in South America, 0.215 in Small Island Developing States (SIDS) and 0.067 in the OECD. Nevertheless, there are significant country differences within the Caribbean average – from a low 0.177 score in Barbados and the Dominican Republic to a high 0.742 in Suriname. With the exception of oil-exporting economies, such as Trinidad and Tobago, Suriname, and more recently Guyana, goods exports in the region are often centred on tropical agricultural products and related agro-industries, including sugar, rum and tropical fruits (Allub and Schliesser, 2023[1]). With respect to services, which represent 58% of total exports in the region (see Chapter 1), the travel sector – closely linked with tourism – is the main exported service in most countries of the region. In 2023, it represented more than 50% of the total trade in services in 12 Caribbean countries and, in particular, more than 90% in The Bahamas, Barbados, Grenada, Saint Lucia and Saint Vincent and the Grenadines (UNCTADStat, 2024[18]).

Efforts to enhance production integration and global competitiveness in the Caribbean should be geared towards globally expanding sectors where the region has demonstrated potential, like the cultural and creative sector (CCS). Currently, creative industries contribute around 5% to the region's GDP and employ, on average, 3% of the region's workforce (Bauer, 2023[19]). With well-targeted regional policies, the Caribbean can seize the opportunities of this rising sector. From 2002 to 2020, global exports of cultural and creative goods more than doubled in value, reaching USD 524 billion in 2020, while global exports of creative services were estimated at USD 1.1 trillion in 2020, with a prominent role in the digital creative economy (UNCTAD, 2022[20]). Additionally, global foreign direct investment (FDI) in CCS has more than doubled over the past 20 years, growing by 118% from 2003 to 2021 (OECD, 2023[21]). The Caribbean can leverage its comparative advantages in tourism to support growth in CCS, which, in turn, can have positive externalities in its tourism sector.

An analysis of the EU Outermost Regions (ORs) shows the potential to enhance global competitiveness in the Caribbean through leveraging strategic sectors. The EU ORs include Guadeloupe, Martinique, Saint Martin, and French Guiana. They are natural partners with their Caribbean neighbours, with which they share comparable challenges – such as limited size, geographical isolation, and climate change vulnerability – and opportunities – including the rich biodiversity, cultural traditions, and natural assets. Strategic sectors in the EU ORs, like ocean economies, the agro-food sector, and the CCS, coincide with sectors where the broader Caribbean region has demonstrated potential (Box 6.2). By leveraging their local strengths, the EU ORs could collaborate with other Caribbean countries to boost these sectors and improve participation in the global economy.

Box 6.2. Spotlight on the EU Outermost Regions: Strategic sectors and the potential for internationalisation

Leveraging competitiveness through the ocean economy, agro-food, and the cultural and creative sector

Oceans are a key factor of competitiveness and internationalisation for EU ORs. Ocean-related economic activities are projected to double in 20 years, from USD 1.5 trillion in 2010 to USD 3 trillion by 2030 (OECD, 2023[22]). These estimates include both traditional industries, like the extraction and exploitation of marine living and non-living resources, maritime transport, and coastal tourism, as well as fast and innovative growth activities related to oceanic renewable energy, biotechnology and bio economy (Jolliffe, Jolly and Stevens, 2021[23]). Representing 75% of their territories, EU ORs can harness oceans and position themselves in emerging high-value activities within the ocean economy (OECD, 2023[22]). French Guiana has established a Blue Economy Strategy, while other EU ORs are in the process of developing theirs. With support from France, Guadeloupe and Martinique have initiated innovative projects and enterprises focused on repurposing sargassum for agricultural use and transforming algae into environmentally sustainable building materials.

Given their vast maritime areas, favourable climate, and biodiversity, the EU ORs are well-positioned to improve their participation in international agro-food value chains (OECD, 2023[24]). Agro-food is already among the main economic activities in EU ORs and food processing is their main industrial activity. With the global market for natural and organic food growing, Caribbean EU ORs can expand their global market share by producing high quality, traceable, and sustainable agro-food products. Guadeloupe is already promoting activities that combine sustainable farming with local high-value food products via the Agropark Caraïbes Excellence Programme, which includes an agro-processing platform, a business incubator, and a commercial hub (OECD, 2023[24]). To unlock their potential, these regions should strengthen quality infrastructure, focus on quality branding, invest in sustainable practices and new farming techniques, and connect with innovation ecosystems.

The CCS can contribute to the comparative advantage and local development of EU ORs, generate wealth through international exports, and create cultural employment (OECD, 2023[21]). Between 2002 and 2020, global exports of cultural and creative goods more than doubled in value, reaching USD 524 billion in 2020, while world exports of creative services were estimated at USD 1.1 trillion that year, a sizeable increase from the USD 487 billion value in 2010 (UNCTAD, 2022[20]). The CCS is not yet consolidated in EU ORs. Nonetheless, given that tourism is already the leading export service for most of these territories and is often deeply intertwined with the CSS, inter-sectoral synergies could be established to seize the potential that both sectors offer for internationalisation (OECD, 2023[21]).

Caribbean countries could apply co-ordinated and targeted strategies to improve trade facilitation. With the exception of the Dominican Republic, trade facilitation performance scores in the Caribbean are lower than those of LAC, the European Union and ASEAN (Figure 6.4) (OECD, 2024[25]). Trade facilitation covers the full spectrum of border procedures. It ranges from the electronic exchange of data about a shipment to the simplification and harmonisation of trade documents, to the possibility of appealing administrative decisions by border agencies (OECD, 2024[25]). Areas that need more attention in the Caribbean are automation, procedures, internal and external border agency co-operation and governance, and impartiality.

Figure 6.4. Trade facilitation performance, 2022

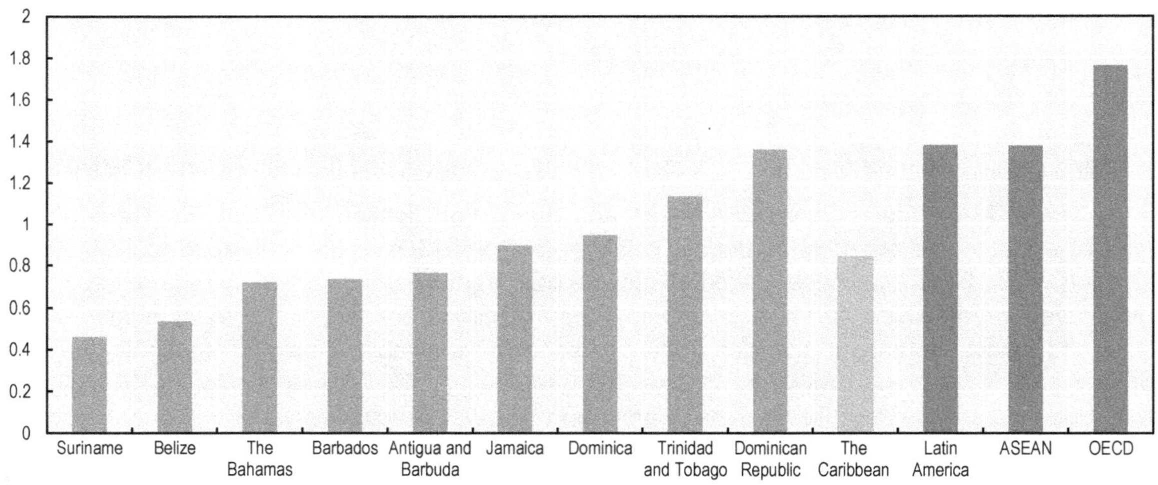

Note: The Trade Facilitation Performance is the average of the Trade Facilitation Indicators (TFI). These take values from 0 to 2, where 2 designates the best performance that can be achieved. TFIs include the following: a) Information availability; b) Involvement of the trade community; c) Advance rulings; d) Appeal procedures; e) Fees and charges; f) Documents; g) Automation; h) Procedures; i) Domestic border agencies co-operation; j) Cross-border agency co-operation; k) Governance and impartiality.
Source: Authors' elaboration based on (OECD, 2024[25]).

StatLink https://stat.link/yism0x

Although the region has several trade arrangements; there is room to improve their impact, establish agreements with new trade partners and improve market penetration. Three non-reciprocal agreements have translated into higher market penetration for the region: agreements between CARICOM countries and Canada; between OECS and the United States; and the Central America Free Trade Agreement with the United States (CAFTA-DR) (ECLAC, 2022[8]). Several countries in the region have a high concentration of exports to the United States, notably The Bahamas, Dominican Republic, Guyana, Jamaica and Saint Kitts and Nevis (Figure 6.5). In contrast, the Cariforum-European Union Economic Partnership Agreement signed on 15 October 2008[1] has not delivered the expected benefits for the Caribbean. The value of Cariforum-EU merchandise trade decreased from EUR 9.5 billion in 2008 to EUR 8.828 billion in 2020.

Figure 6.5. Main destinations of Caribbean exports, 2022 or most recent year available

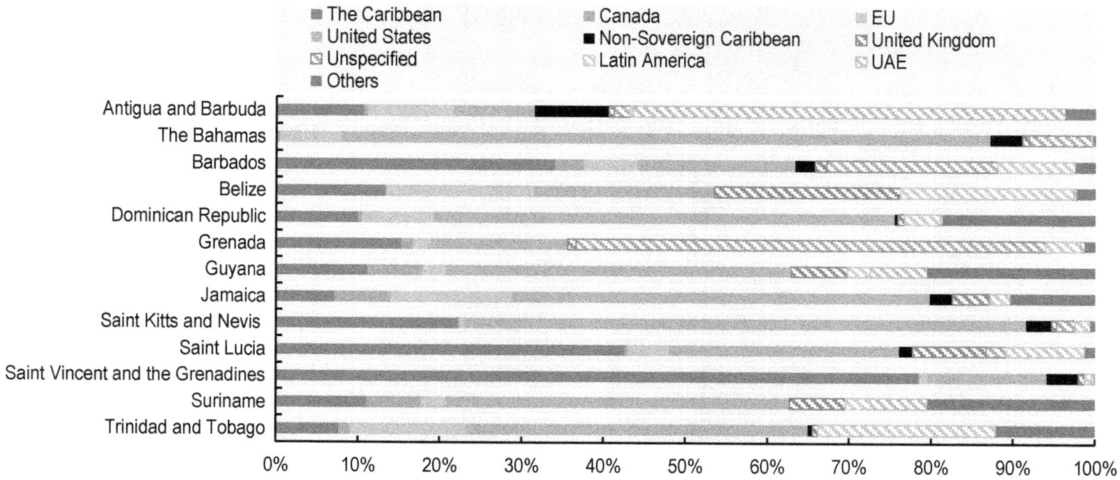

Note: Overseas territories not included in EU total. Most recent year available.
Source: Authors' elaboration based on (World Bank, 2024[26]).

StatLink https://stat.link/03iwqz

The trade relationship between the Caribbean and Latin America remains an under-exploited opportunity (Figure 6.5). The two regions are close geographically and have potential complementarities. Furthermore, the Caribbean needs food imports, industrial goods and fuels. All these factors make them potentially suitable trade partners (UN Comtrade Database, 2024[27]). However, most Latin American countries do not have trade agreements with CARICOM and thus pay high tariffs (Allub and Schliesser, 2023[1]). As a result, Latin America is not a main destination for Caribbean exports. Updating the regional integration agenda through new trade agreements with Latin America could be an interesting avenue to pursue. Estimates of a potential Latin American and Caribbean-wide free trade agreement suggest that the Caribbean would experience an 8.8% increase in such a scenario, driven by agriculture and by better access to most of the region, particularly to the Southern Common Market and Mexico (Mesquita Moreira, 2018[28]).

The potential for enhancing agro-food trade between CARICOM and SICA is significant and currently underutilised. Despite their geographic proximity and economic complementarities, trade between these regions account for just over 0.1% of LAC's agricultural trade (Santamaría, 2024[9]). SICA countries export nearly 50% of their agro-food products, while CARICOM export only 8.1% (Santamaría, 2024[9]) High tariffs on agricultural products, deficient infrastructure, and inadequate institutional response capacity hinder the development of this trade. To realise its full potential, establishing a regional trade agreement between SICA and CARICOM could help reduce tariffs, improve market access, and improve logistics and infrastructure, ultimately reducing food insecurity and supporting economic growth (Santamaría, 2024[9]).

A renewed regional agenda should prioritise the outstanding challenge of transport

Transport connectivity remains a critical challenge for the development of Caribbean nations. The transport cost intensity – or cost per ton of exporting goods – is relatively high for the Caribbean compared to other regions and country groupings, a trend that has increased in recent years (Figure 6.6). Regional logistics costs account for about 16-26% of GDP in the Caribbean compared to the OECD average of around 9%.

This renders Caribbean products relatively more expensive and therefore less competitive (Nicholson, n.d.[29]). The relatively high transport costs are primarily due to regulatory challenges, limited competition within the transport industry, and outdated transport infrastructure (Bhattacharya, 2024[30]). This, in turn, has a direct negative impact on foreign investment, trade levels and trade diversification. Indeed, estimates suggest that a 1% decline in ad valorem transport costs could increase exports from 1.5% to 8% across various sectors in LAC, demonstrating the significant impact that lower transport costs can have on boosting trade in the region (Bhattacharya, 2024[30]).

Figure 6.6. Transport cost intensity, selected regions and country groups (2016-21)

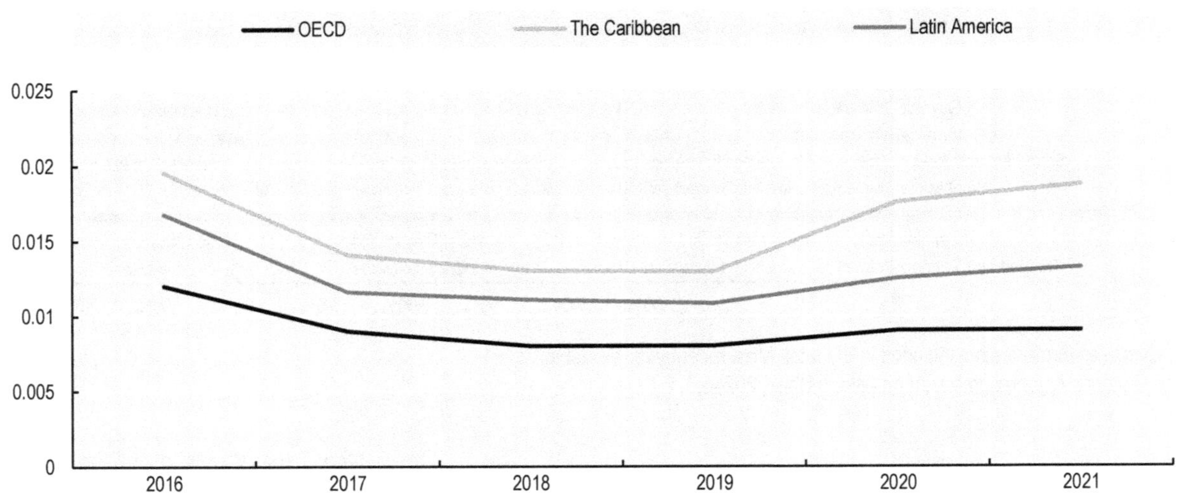

Note: Average transport expenditure in USD per 1 000 km as a ratio to their Free on Board (FOB) value of the traded goods. Formula ([transport expenditure] / [transport work in terms of value]) * 1 000. This dataset is experimental.
Source: Authors' elaboration based on (UNCTADStat, 2024[18]).

StatLink https://stat.link/a4bpyz

Some challenges that lead to high transport costs are structural, while others relate to policy interventions at the national and, above, regional levels. The geographic isolation and dis-economies of scale of Caribbean SIDS are key factors driving high transport costs. According to the UN Liner Shipping Connectivity Index, which measures connectedness to global shipping networks, remoteness is, on average, a bigger challenge for Pacific than Caribbean SIDS, though some Caribbean SIDS are still very affected (OECD, 2018[31]). While the Dominican Republic and Jamaica score comparatively well on the Index, Caribbean SIDS like Dominica, Grenada, Antigua and Barbuda, Saint Vincent and the Grenadines, Saint Lucia, and even non-island Caribbean states like Guyana and Suriname score well below. Long distances are required to transport exported goods, while ports and public administrations have high fixed costs. The low efficiency of infrastructure is another key factor, accentuated by the high costs of recovering transport infrastructure after climate disasters. The limited development of a regional vision results in inadequate transportation infrastructure, competition between Caribbean countries and poor inter-island connectivity.

Maritime inter-island connectivity is a challenge among OECS economies, where direct formal freight transport is generally unavailable. Formal maritime transport in these countries comprises large international shipping lines operating between the United States or Europe and their regional hubs in Barbados, and Trinidad and Tobago. These hubs only serve other Caribbean islands through designated feeder lines, which leads to higher freight costs between islands compared to the costs from these islands to the United States (OECD, 2022[32]). Exports of goods that rely on formal maritime transport need to be shipped through the United States, highlighting the ongoing problem of the directionality of shipping services in the Caribbean (IDB, 2018[33]). Additionally, the tax structure in the region hinders regional integration and short-sea shipping, further complicating efforts to improve connectivity and consequently trade (IDB, 2018[33]). Hence, informal maritime transport plays an important role, yet it remains fragmented and lacks organisation (IDB, 2018[33]). An analysis of different potential scenarios indicates that two viable proposals could be considered for improving inter-island trade connectivity, given their relative simplicity and low implementation costs. One proposal involves modifying an existing shipping service to run south to north through the Eastern Caribbean islands, with a liner service from Kingston to Trinidad and Tobago. The other proposal is to reduce port handling charges for Less-than-Container-Load containers (IDB, 2018[33]).

Air transport – both freight and passengers – also faces challenges. The Caribbean has several airports and routes to large origin hubs for tourism (mainly in North America and Europe). However, the overall small volume of operations and lack of large airport hubs lead to higher fixed operational costs to the region's airports, requiring higher taxes to support air transport infrastructure (Fioravanti, Granada and Veverka, 2015[34]). This can make Caribbean islands less cost-competitive with respect to larger tourism destinations. In addition, except for a recent partnership between Caribbean Airlines and Air Jamaica, airlines that serve the intra-regional market have remained as separate entities with little co-operation. This, in turn, leads to a poor level of service between islands (ACS, 2024[35]).

The Caribbean is advancing initiatives to address bottlenecks to boost transport efficiency. The ACS is steering projects for the "Mapping of Maritime Routes in the Greater Caribbean", aiming to provide information on players in the shipping industry and facilitate trade linkages between countries. It also manages the Caribbean Maritime and Port Strategy, which is building a comprehensive strategy to develop ports across the region (ACS, 2024[35]). Within the context of ACS, the Air Transport Agreement provides the legal framework for member countries to negotiate with each other for more air service options at reduced costs and prices, as well as more routes (ACS, 2008[36]). This agreement is expected to complement other tools, such as the CARICOM Multilateral Air Services Agreement.

Further initiatives are needed to optimise both intra- and extra-regional trade through integrated, resilient, and sustainable transportation systems. This calls for scaling up planning, investments and management of quality, reliable and resilient infrastructure (UN, 2024[37]). These developments should aim both to improve the connectivity of the Caribbean with the rest of the world and to improve inter-island connectivity for regional economic and value chain integration. To that end, developing a fast-ferry service between OECS islands would be an interesting policy option, although it could require public support (OECD, 2022[32]). In the case of air transport, public-private partnerships could promote regional market integration through profitable and financially sustainable regional airlines. These could provide connection routes within the Caribbean and with the rest of Latin America, which is a faster-growing market (Fioravanti, Granada and Veverka, 2015[34]). Indeed, public-private collaboration could also be useful in designing new regulatory frameworks that turn unproductive competition between Caribbean countries into better competition between private transport providers. Capacity building, or even the creation of new regional institutions, can improve co-ordination among agents, investments in technology, better data collection and analysis, and the harmonised adoption of international standards.

Harnessing the potential of regional co-operation to address common challenges and opportunities

Enhanced regional co-operation is essential to address shared challenges more inclusively, effectively and efficiently. In addition, regional co-operation can help seize development opportunities and provide quick wins, creating greater momentum to achieve full integration in the region (IMF, 2020[3]). CARICOM has 19 community institutions that promote horizontal co-operation between member states, while the ACS provides technical assistance, capacity building and promotes policy dialogue.

Some topics in this section are common to all Caribbean countries, like climate and environmental challenges or the digital transition. Others are experienced differently across countries, such as the renewable energy transition for oil-producing and oil-importing countries or intra-regional migration for origin and destination countries. In these latter cases, regional co-operation could progress through coalitions of countries having common interests.

The Caribbean can leverage its extensive co-operation in disaster risk reduction and prevention to expand towards other areas for a resilient green and just transition

Despite their relatively low carbon footprints, Caribbean countries are highly vulnerable to extreme weather events and other impacts of climate change, such as rising sea levels and changing precipitation patterns (OECD, 2024[38]) (Chapter 3). The present-day expected annual damage (EAD) for all SIDS is USD 1.64 billion (2020 values). This figure corresponds to 0.13% of total GDP in SIDS, with 49% of this EAD occurring in the Caribbean Sea. Meanwhile, half of the expected annual flooded area is in the Caribbean, where 61% of people exposed to coastal flooding for all SIDS live (Vousdoukas, Athanasiou and Giardino, 2023[39]). On top of the high human risks, high climate vulnerability affects growth rates and tourism in the Caribbean. The 6.8% contraction in GDP in Dominica immediately after "Maria", the category 5 hurricane in 2017, illustrates this impact on growth (OECD, 2022[32]).

Regional co-operation in the Caribbean is highly developed around early warning systems, and recovery and reconstruction after disasters. The Caribbean Disaster Emergency Management Agency co-ordinates emergency response for CARICOM members, generates economies of scale and facilitates logistics more systematically than would be possible by individual countries. The agency has a comprehensive strategy that supports all phases of the disaster management cycle. In addition, it is developing a regional information system for greater risk awareness and preparedness and evidence-based decision making (IMF, 2020[3]). For its part, the Caribbean Tourism Organization of CARICOM has implemented a regional monitoring and evaluation system for disaster risk management and climate change adaptation in the tourism sector with the support of the IDB. The Caribbean Catastrophe Risk Insurance Facility also provides an innovative and necessary financial mechanism to mitigate the financial costs of disasters.

Further regional efforts are needed to address other pressing environmental issues and seize the opportunities presented by the green transition. The Caribbean lacks a regional strategy to address the increasing problem of sargassum, a seaweed that has inundated shorelines in the region each spring and summer since 2011. The seaweed affects people, biodiversity (including reefs), and sea-based economic sectors, especially tourism and fishery (Rogers et al., 2023[40]). However, sargassum also presents opportunities, including its transformation into different by-products such as fertilisers, raw material for biodegradable plastics, cosmetics, electricity and biomass, and could become a resource to boost local economies' resilience (see Chapter 3).

Regional co-operation is also needed to implement Caribbean-wide policies and environmental standards to address the marine pollution of the ship industry, including from cruise ships. Individual OECS member states have levied an environmental tax for cruises as well as accommodation taxes to finance programmes that build climate resilience, but a regional strategy is still missing (Morris, 2020[41]; Virgin Islands News, 2022[42]; CNG, 2020[43]) Leveraging regional co-operation in these areas is needed to seize the high potential of the region in strategic sectors for the green transition (like the blue economy), and to enable initiatives like the Caribbean Sustainable Tourism Zone of the ACS.

New regional environmental endeavours in the Caribbean should adopt a green and just transition approach to maximise their development impact and leave no one behind. Green and just transitions are the ongoing and upcoming transitions towards achieving carbon neutrality and net zero greenhouse gas emissions by or around the mid-century, coupled with a focus on ensuring climate adaptation, resilience, and inclusiveness for all (OECD et al., 2024[44]). This concept entails maximising the positive economic and social gains of adopting more sustainable models of development while mitigating the potential negative impacts through new socio-economic opportunities, including quality jobs, enhanced public services, social protection systems, sustainable infrastructure development, new sources of affordable finance, and safe, orderly, and regular migration pathways (OECD, 2021[45]).

The digital transformation is an opportunity for the Caribbean to overcome various development challenges

Digital technologies represent an interesting opportunity for improving connectivity in a region where physical connectivity is complex and costly. In 2021, the percentage of internet users in the Caribbean region was 78% of the total population. This includes internet access from any device and connection, encompassing both fixed and mobile options (ECLAC, 2022[46]). This compares to 72% in Latin America and 89.3% in OECD countries in 2021 (Figure 6.7). While the Caribbean has made significant progress in internet adoption, the region still lags behind the more developed OECD countries.

Figure 6.7. Internet users as a percentage of the total population, regional comparison

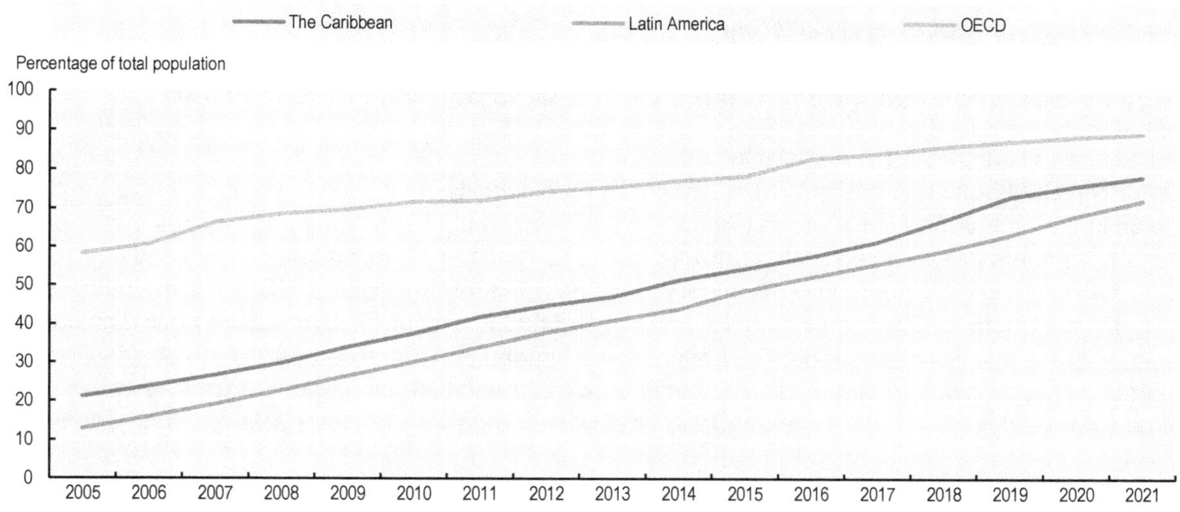

Note: This indicator includes internet use from any fixed or mobile device and connection.
Source: Authors' elaboration based on (ECLAC, 2022[46]).

StatLink https://stat.link/qvca2w

Advancing a region-wide digital transition can bring enormous development opportunities for the Caribbean. Digitalisation enhances productivity and growth in existent services and industries and supports diversification into new, higher-technology sectors. This is the case, for instance, of digital services, including financial and insurance services, IT services, digital marketing, and consultancy (OECD, 2022[32]). Digital transformation also plays a pivotal role in economic integration by reducing transaction costs, enhancing information flows and boosting competition. It can empower micro, small and medium-sized enterprises to compete better and integrate into GVCs. New, digitally-enabled technologies can also contribute to raising climate resilience by providing tools for natural disaster preparedness and emergency response, while digital connectivity can help create carbon markets (OECD et al., 2022[47]; Blanco, 2024[48]). To close the digital gap with the OECD, an estimated USD 68 billion investment is needed, with private investment playing a key role, while the public sector's involvement will be crucial in establishing public-private partnerships to reach remote areas (García Zaballos, 2020[49]).

Caribbean countries are already engaging in several digital initiatives with a regional perspective. The "Single ICT Space Project" of CARICOM is viewed as the digital layer of the CSME. It aims to create an enabling environment for regional infrastructure projects and systems through regionally harmonised ICT policy, legal and regulatory regimes (CARICOM, 2017[50]). The ACS is focusing on the digital transformation of the transport sector to increase levels of operational efficiency, build resilient supply chains and develop more integrated regional logistics. It will do this through supply chain traceability and improved connectivity among border control agencies. The United Nations Development Programme (UNDP) is leading the "Digital Support Facility for the Caribbean", which supports the development of Digital Action Plans so Caribbean SIDS can become Small Island Digital States (SIDS 2.0). The IDB confirmed its commitment to digital transformation across the region, having already mobilised some USD 480 million in the last decade for the region in this area (UNDP, 2024[51]). OECS countries are improving digitalisation policies through the Caribbean Digital Transformation Project (CARDTP). It aims to increase access to digital services, technologies, and skills by governments, businesses and individuals (OECD, 2022[32]).

However, further regional co-operation is needed for the Caribbean to fully reap the benefits of the digital transition. Some key areas where regional efforts should focus include regulatory dialogue, infrastructure investments, connectivity and free and safe data flows, cybersecurity, integrated innovation ecosystems, and space services (OECD et al., 2022[47]).

Energy co-operation can help untap the Caribbean's potential in renewables

Most Caribbean countries have relevant incentives to develop a more integrated and resilient green energy network. The Caribbean has one of the highest prices for electricity in the world, which is almost double the cost paid in the Latin American average (Figure 6.8), and it is double and sometimes triple the cost paid by average consumers in the United States (Mowla, 2024[52]). This affects export competitiveness and the cost of living for households. Energy imports account for nearly 7% of the region's GDP, limiting public sector investment in climate adaptation and social sectors. Relatedly, except for hydrocarbon-rich Trinidad and Tobago, Guyana and Suriname, most Caribbean states depend importantly on fossil fuel imports. They are therefore more exposed to external global energy shocks. In addition, the region's exposure to worsening extreme weather events can cause widespread blackouts and power outages (Goldwyn, Tiah and Mowla, 2023[53]).

Figure 6.8. Average price of electricity (1 kWh) in the Caribbean, Latin America and the OECD, 2021

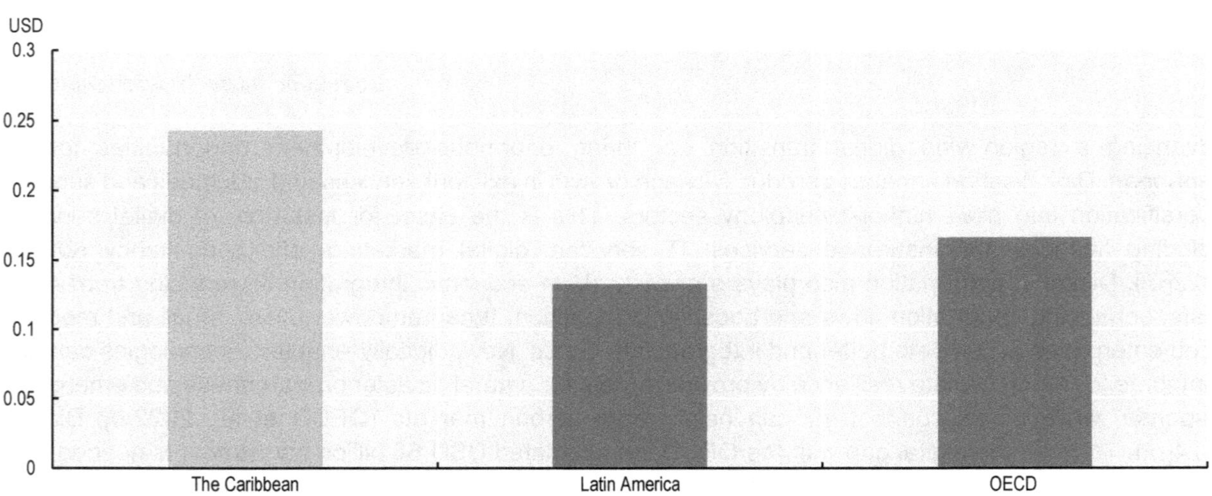

Source: Authors' elaboration based on (Cable.co.uk, 2024[54]).

StatLink https://stat.link/myax6u

Embarking on a green energy transition is a sustainable development opportunity for which the Caribbean has great potential. While installed capacity per capita in the region doubled to 100 W per capita between 2015 and 2021, this is far below its potential capacity. Moreover, it is far behind Central America and Mexico at 240 W per capita and South America at over 500 W per capita (ECLAC, 2023[55]). There is great untapped potential for growth in renewables in the Caribbean. With over 300 days of sun each year, the Caribbean could generate a potential 1 900 kWh/m^2 annually, double the capacity of Germany (CDB, 2022[56]; Goldwyn, Tiah and Mowla, 2023[53]). The Caribbean basin is estimated to have up to 751 GW of wind power (World Bank, 2020[57]). As a volcanic region, the Eastern Caribbean could also generate up to 6.29 GW of geothermal energy (Goldwyn, Tiah and Mowla, 2023[53]). With significant agricultural production, the Caribbean has an untapped potential for biomass energy. In addition, an energy transition would enable Caribbean countries to achieve their Paris Agreement commitments and generate USD 16 billion in net economic benefits in CARICOM countries by 2040 (ECLAC, 2021[58]). Nevertheless, the insufficient economies of scale, due to the small individual size of national energy markets and the lack of integrated regional energy grids, hampers the economic feasibility of many renewable energy projects (OECD, 2023[59]).

The Caribbean is taking concrete steps towards a regional energy transition. In 2013, CARICOM approved an energy policy with renewable energy and energy efficiency targets. Through the Caribbean Centre for Renewable Energy and Energy Efficiency Centre, the organisation helps member states implement the regional Energy Policy and the Caribbean Sustainable Energy Roadmap and Strategy. This aims to achieve a renewable energy electricity of 47% by 2027 (CARICOM, 2013[60]). The Caribbean Energy Working Group, established in 2023 as part of the Caribbean Initiative at the Atlantic Council, brings together stakeholders across the region to address the primary energy security challenges and enable the energy transition. Planned initiatives within the region include an undersea cable between Dominica and the EU ORs Guadeloupe and Martinique, which aims to pool the electricity grids to create a large enough demand base for the cost-effective development of geothermal power (OECD, 2023[59]).

Through regional co-operation, Caribbean countries can further advance strategies to promote regional energy integration and shared regulatory frameworks that scale up investment in renewable and resilient energy systems. The Caribbean needs USD 11 billion in investments over the next decade for the energy transition. At the same time, the necessary policy, regulatory and financial measures are similar across the region. With these observations in mind, a collective approach to creating standard tools will reduce learning and transaction costs for private suppliers and investors (Masson, Ehrhardt and Lizzio, 2020[61]). Connectedly, further focus should be given to strengthening the complementarity, integration and interconnection between the energy systems of the region. This is relevant to increasing the size of the market and making renewables more profitable, as the current small size of individual economies prevents many renewable projects from achieving the economies of scale necessary to achieve economic feasibility (OECD, 2023[62]). Further collaborative efforts could be directed towards pooling expertise, establishing concrete knowledge transfer mechanisms, and promoting scientific exchanges within the Caribbean basin and throughout the broader Latin American continent (OECD, 2023[59]).

Specifically, Eastern Caribbean SIDS, including the EU ORs, can benefit from strengthening co-operation in the development of renewable energies. Some important steps that the OECS countries, along with the EU ORs in the region, should consider to foster this regional integration are: increasing access to finance for long-term renewable projects; adopting regulatory frameworks to channel private investment; reducing red-tape to fast-track operations; improving incentive schemes for renewable energy; and harmonising standards and norms (OECD, 2023[59]). The experience of SICA's Central American Regional Electricity Market (of which Dominican Republic and Belize do not take part) could serve as a guiding example.

Leveraging co-operation for the intra-regional mobility of persons can benefit social inclusion, productivity and climate resilience

Although most Caribbean migration moves outward to North American and European countries, intra-regional migration is growing for economic and environmental reasons. The intra-regional share of immigrants in the total immigration flow to the Caribbean grew from 46% in 2000 to 56% in 2020 (Figure 6.9) (Lacarte et al., 2023[63]).

Much intra-region migration occurs for economic reasons. Countries and territories with thriving tourism industries and higher incomes attract nationals from poorer economies in the region. Haitians, for example, are by far the largest immigrant population (Lacarte et al., 2023[63]).

The growing impact of climate disasters is another cause of such migration. Three additional climate disasters annually over a five-year period are associated with an estimated 1% increase in people leaving their home countries in the Caribbean (Beltran and Hadzi-Vaskov, 2023[64]). Comparatively, the impact in South America is relatively smaller. Considering that 70% of the Caribbean population lives in coastal cities, and approximately 4.2 million people reside in low-elevation coastal areas, this cause of migration is expected to persist or worsen (UNDRR-ROAMC, 2021[65]).

Figure 6.9. Number and share of intra- and extra-regional immigrants in the Caribbean, 2000-20

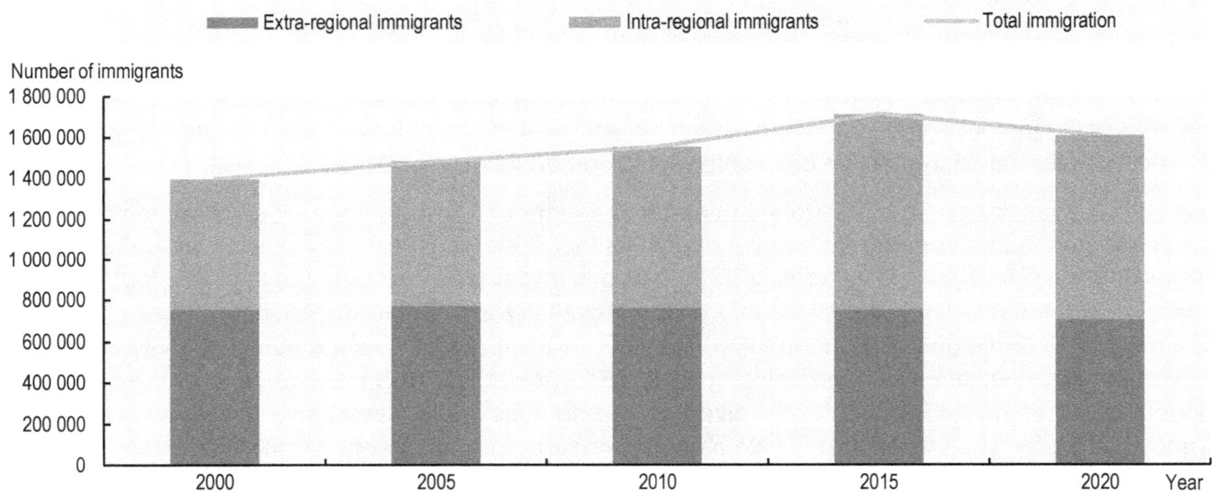

Source: Authors' elaboration based on (Lacarte et al., 2023[63]).

StatLink https://stat.link/slvc1m

Migration plays a significant role in the development of both origin and destination countries (OECD, 2017[66]). Strengthening regional co-operation in relation to the mobility of persons in the Caribbean can support the social inclusion of migrants, while bringing labour productivity gains and building climate resilience. Well-managed migration can be a powerful force for social inclusion, contributing to a more culturally diverse, resilient and cohesive society. Productivity is gained through increased access to specialised workers, knowledge and innovation spillovers, and lower costs for cross-border services. For instance, in the Dominican Republic, immigrants contribute between 3.8% and 5.3% to the country's added value, while they represent 4.2% of the population (OECD/ILO, 2018[67]). Additionally, immigrants in the Dominican Republic have a positive net fiscal impact, paying more indirect taxes and using fewer public services compared to native-born citizens (OECD/ILO, 2018[67]).

The mobility of persons also supports a smoother response to disasters and emergencies. This is true as much for people fleeing emergencies as for the temporary labour migration associated with rebuilding in the aftermath of such events (IOM, 2021[68]). This is important for two reasons. First, the Caribbean lacks regional institutions and regulatory frameworks for asylum and refugee protection. Second, some of the top-receiving countries are also highly vulnerable to climate disasters (Lacarte et al., 2023[63]). This is the case of The Bahamas, where 80% of the population lives in vulnerable coastal areas (UNDRR-ROAMC, 2021[65]).

Caribbean organisations have taken concrete strides towards more co-operation. The OECS Revised Treaty of Basseterre (2010) established complete free movement for nationals of Protocol member states. This includes authorising work without the need for a permit (Lacarte et al., 2023[63]). In a comparison between OECS and non-OECS Caribbean countries, labour productivity grew 6-7% in the OECS since the establishment of its economic union (IMF, 2020[3]). For its part, CARICOM has completed 70.6% of the required actions for the free movement of persons included in the CSME (IMF, 2020[3]).

Three key gaps must be addressed to enhance the free movement of people. First, only two countries certify service providers. Second, five of the ten categories for skilled labour still require a permit to work in all member states. Third, the Protocol Amending Agreement on Social Security still requires action before it can enter into force (IMF, 2020[3]). Challenges include non-compliance, lack of harmonised processes, inconsistent operationalisation and duplication of processes, leading to persistently high levels of irregular migration.

Regional co-operation between origin and receiving countries should focus on implementing tools throughout the migration cycle to ensure shared gains. For labour migrants, the cycle includes the stages of recruitment, the period of working abroad, and the return and reintegration phase. This final stage is crucial for enabling migrants to return to their home countries, integrate into the labour market, leverage the skills acquired abroad and achieve economic stability (IOM, 2021[68]). To capitalise on the potential productivity gains of intra-regional human mobility, new mechanisms should expand the narrow focus on high-skilled work. This would allow for more categories of high-skilled workers to seize the opportunities of intra-regional migration. Simultaneously, new mechanisms for all worker categories, including seasonal workers, should include an intersectional perspective. For instance, these should consider gender issues in human mobility, like the prevention of and protection against gender-based violence.

International partnerships to support financing for development and climate action in the Caribbean

As a small developing region, mainly composed of SIDS, and in a context of global uncertainty and compounding crisis, the Caribbean relies importantly on effective international partnerships to advance its sustainable development goals. Innovative partnerships can help the region make more efficient use of finance and leverage more public and private international development funding. Some key needed solutions include new institutional arrangements, financing frameworks adapted to the needs of Caribbean SIDS, and standards to ensure a positive impact on the region's development, particularly in relation to climate change adaptation. In addition, the Caribbean, as part of the SIDS group, has proven to have great capacity for international advocacy in the multilateral sphere. This could be catalysed in upcoming negotiations related to financing the development agenda.

Furthermore, following the Development in Transition (DiT) framework, which is mindful of the multi-dimensionality of development and the need for more inclusive international co-operation schemes, new international partnerships can play a key facilitator role in the Caribbean's development. This not only aids in catalysing additional financial resources for development but also ensures their alignment with the

SDGs and the adaptation of international efforts to each country's development challenges and specific context.

The role of international partnerships to mobilise financing for development in the Caribbean

Most Caribbean countries depend on external flows to finance development. This reliance is due to several factors, including their limited size, limited domestic financial resources, vulnerability to external shocks and major development needs. Indeed, external financial flows have played a critical role in the Caribbean in recent decades, with differentiated impacts across different sources of finance.

Official development assistance (ODA) remains an important source of external finance

ODA has been an important source of external financing for Caribbean countries, averaging 2.53% of the region's gross national income (GNI) from 2000 to 2022, and with some increases associated with the impact of specific natural disasters or the COVID-19 pandemic (Figure 6.10). This percentage is higher than the Latin American average of 1.54% (OECD, 2024[69]; World Bank, 2024[70]).

Figure 6.10. Main external financial flows to the Caribbean, 2000-23

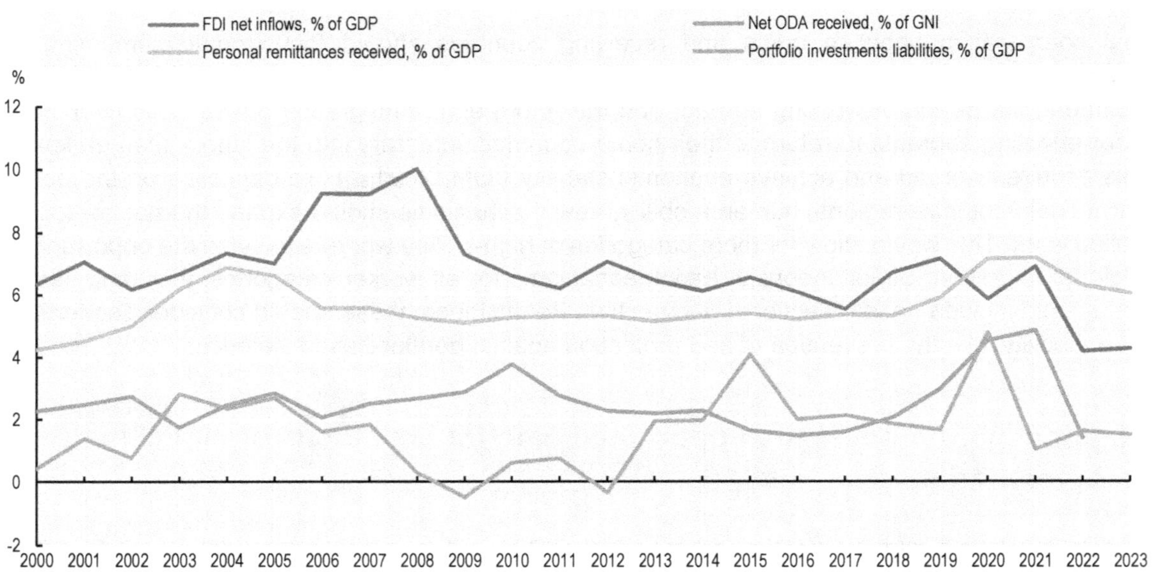

Note: GDP refers to gross domestic product, and GNI refers to gross national income. FDI refers to foreign direct investment. In 2023, Guyana was excluded from the average calculation due to its significantly higher FDI inflows as a share of GDP compared to other Caribbean countries, making it an outlier. Including Guyana in the calculations, the regional average FDI net inflows in 2023 amount to 6.8% of GDP. Countries are excluded from ODA figures when they graduate from their recipient status, specifically: Barbados and Trinidad and Tobago after 2010; Saint Kitts and Nevis after 2013; and Antigua and Barbuda after 2022. Portfolio investment liabilities are based on the authors' calculations.
Source: Authors' elaboration based on (IMF, 2024[71]; World Bank, 2024[72]; World Bank, 2024[73]; World Bank, 2023[74]).

StatLink https://stat.link/jck8h4

In 2022, 54% of ODA to the Caribbean went to Haiti. By that date, Antigua and Barbuda, The Bahamas, Barbados, Saint Kitts and Nevis, and Trinidad and Tobago were no longer eligible for ODA (OECD, 2024[69]). This underscores the importance of the ongoing discussions on the criteria for graduation from ODA. Some Caribbean countries continue to graduate as their GNIs per capita rise. As they do, they lose access to ODA even if they continue to face important development challenges and high levels of vulnerability (ECLAC/OECD, 2018[75]; Cattaneo and Piemonté, 2021[76]). In fact, the official development finance inadequately aligns with the region's evolving needs (Piemonté, Kim and Cattaneo, 2024[77]). If alternative financial resources do not adequately compensate for countries' heavy reliance on ODA, Caribbean SIDS could experience socio-economic regression and widespread negative impacts, considering the Caribbean's geostrategic significance and their key role in safeguarding oceans and biodiversity (OECD, 2024[78]).

Countries and international organisations should continue advancing discussions for the adoption of more comprehensive criteria for the allocation of ODA. In current debates and considerations of development metrics, new options, like the United Nations Multidimensional Vulnerability Index (UN MVI), are increasingly being considered pertinent for SIDS, including those of the Caribbean. The UN MVI can help reveal the heightened vulnerability of SIDS and perform better resource allocations, aligning more effectively with the priorities and financing needs of Caribbean countries (Piemonte, 2024[79]). In fact, there is no significant correlation between the UN MVI scores and GNI per capita data, showing that these two indicators are complementary (Piemonte, 2024[79]). Thus, these indexes can provide clearer insights and a deeper understanding of the risks that Caribbean countries face. In addition, international partners can also support countries in transition through the provision of tools, like the transition finance toolkit, to help them better understand, anticipate and respond to the financing challenges faced at each stage of their development, enabling them to reap the full potential of the emerging opportunities (OECD, 2024[80]).

Total Official Support for Sustainable Development (TOSSD) serves as an international standard for capturing the full range of financial flows aimed at promoting the sustainable development of developing countries. Aside from ODA, TOSSD includes financing from providers beyond DAC members and other ODA providers, activities of traditional donors that fall outside the scope of ODA, such as non-concessional loans, or outflows from multilateral organisations, both concessional and non-concessional. Moreover, TOSSD comprises expenditures for international public goods and mobilised private finance (OECD, 2024[81]). In this context, TOSSD includes South-South and Triangular Cooperation from a growing number of new and emerging providers.

To enhance the impact of limited development funds, TOSSD has focused on refining how these flows are measured, specifically in terms of their contribution to sustainable development and the 2030 Agenda more broadly (OECD, 2024[81]). Between 2019 and 2022, the Caribbean received its largest share of TOSSD flows for SDG 13 on taking urgent action to combat climate change and its impacts, which accounted for 17.2% of total resources allocated to the region. This was followed by SDG 17 on revitalising the global partnership for sustainable development, which received 15%, and SDG 10 on reducing inequalities within and among countries, which received 14.8% (Figure 6.11). These percentages for each SDG are based solely on the resources allocated, considering only TOSSD activities that align with one or more SDGs and excluding resources that may not be linked to any particular goal.

Figure 6.11. Percentages of TOSSD resources allocated by Sustainable Development Goals, 2019-22

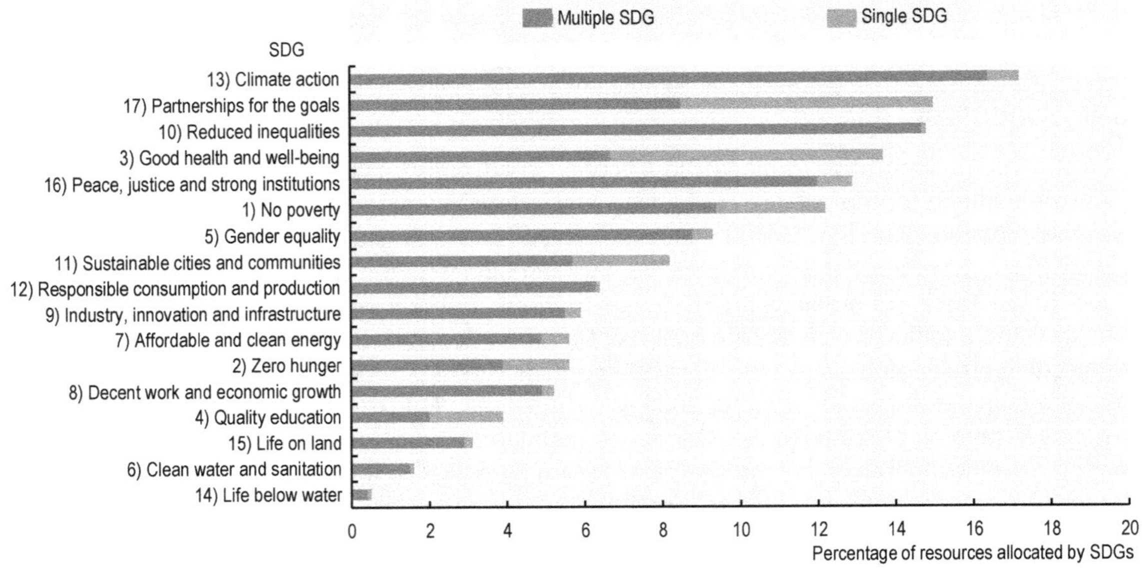

Note: The graph displays the percentage of TOSSD resources allocated to the sustainable development goals. The grey colour refers to TOSSD activities exclusively allocated to one sustainable development goal, while the blue indicates TOSSD activities allocated to multiple sustainable development goals. Hence, percentages do not sum up to 100%, as resources can be allocated to more than one SDG at the same time, resulting in overlapping allocations. The Caribbean countries in the analysis are Antigua and Barbuda, Belize, Dominica, Dominican Republic, Grenada, Guyana, Haiti, Jamaica, Suriname, Saint Lucia, and Saint Vincent and the Grenadines. The Bahamas, Barbados, Saint Kitts and Nevis, and Trinidad and Tobago are not TOSSD recipients according to the applicable method.
Source: (OECD, 2022[82]; OECD, 2024[83]).

StatLink https://stat.link/37x4tz

TOSSD data shows that South-South Cooperation (SSC) remains a relevant framework of collaboration for the Caribbean, especially with Latin American partners and, in particular, some partners from the Greater Caribbean,[2] such as Mexico and Brazil. Of the eight providers that submitted data on SSC to the Caribbean in 2022, six were Latin American countries, and another was the Central American Bank for Economic Integration (CABEI). In 2022, Brazil implemented the largest number of TOSSD activities with the Caribbean in the context of SSC (213 activities), followed by Mexico (26 activities) and Chile (14 activities). An example of the impact of these SSC efforts is the project facilitated by Brazil in 2022 for developing a method for irrigated rice planting in the Dominican Republic, which contributed to the SDGs 2 (Zero hunger), 6 (Clean water and sanitation), and 12 (Responsible consumption and production). The project aimed to establish production systems that optimise irrigation water uses by incorporating high-yielding rice varieties and environmentally sustainable technologies.

Foreign direct investment represents an important source of finance

FDI to the Caribbean has remained one of the most relevant external financial flows in recent decades. After a 10% peak in 2008, FDI as a share of GDP in 2023 stood at an average of 4.3% for the Caribbean (Figure 6.10) (excluding Guyana, which saw an extraordinary increase of FDI in 2023, reaching 42.8% of GDP), above the 2.7% average for Latin America, the OECD average of 0.1% and the world average of 0.7% for that year (World Bank, 2024[84]). The United States, the EU, the United Kingdom and Canada remain the main sources of FDI in the region, but China's FDI has been gaining ground in recent years. China has invested over USD 10 billion in the Caribbean between 2005 and 2022, both through public and private institutions (Foreign Affairs Committee, 2022[85]).

FDI shows heterogeneous trends across Caribbean countries. Guyana recorded the highest FDI inflows in the region due to foreign interest in the country's hydrocarbon sector, which concentrated 99% of FDI to the country in 2022 (ECLAC, 2023[86]). The Dominican Republic recorded FDI growth of 25% in 2022, primarily due to investments in services, which represented 76% of total FDI inflows into the country. Meanwhile, FDI to The Bahamas was up 19%, driven by intercompany loans. In contrast, FDI declined by 20% to the OECS, while Trinidad and Tobago recorded negative FDI flows as it repaid significant intercompany loans (ECLAC, 2023[86]). Citizen-by-investment programmes play an important role in attracting investments in some countries, particularly in OECS members (see Chapter 5).

Remittances are a major source of income

Remittances are significant in the Caribbean, and they have been the largest international financial flow in the region since 2020. In 2022, emigration accounted for more than half of the population in six Caribbean countries, with only The Bahamas having a net positive migration rate (Jaupart, 2023[87]). Income from these emigrants is a major flow for the region, helping to stabilise family consumption and enable investments in housing, education, food, and healthcare. Communities also invest remittances in long-term sustainability projects, including supporting small businesses, water projects, or building hospitals, counteracting some negative effects of emigration. In 2023, remittances accounted for 6.02% of the region's GDP, which was higher than ODA and FDI flows combined (Figure 6.10). These private flows have primarily originated from the United States (50.4%), though intra-regional remittance transfers are increasing, mostly from the Dominican Republic (IDB, 2023[88]; IDB, 2023[89]). Caribbean emigrants are therefore key contributors to the region's sustainable development.

New international partnerships can unleash the power of international financing for development

Following the DiT framework, the Caribbean can promote and engage in new international partnerships to catalyse international financing, ensuring its alignment with national development priorities and contributing to the SDGs and global public goods. Securing access to concessional financing for countries graduating towards higher income levels will be vital to help them address persistent vulnerabilities or specific natural disasters. International partnerships are essential to favour the positive impact of investments in key development dimensions like formal job creation, productivity growth or environmental sustainability, as well as to support aid as a catalyser for additional and varied funding sources (OECD et al., 2019[90]).

New international partnerships can provide co-ordination mechanisms to work with more tools and actors, supporting the Caribbean's efforts to raise public and private external financing and improving their development impact. For instance, the role of private finance in the Caribbean can be strengthened by mobilising it through official development interventions. This type of "blended finance" has remained relatively low in the Caribbean[3] until the significant mobilisation in 2021 of USD 1.22 billion by EU institutions towards economic infrastructure, notably for renewable energy (OECD, 2024[91]). International partnerships can have a strategic role in incentivising the flow of private finance through "de-risking instruments" that aim to share risks among multilateral, public and private actors, steering it towards key development sectors that yield profits in the longer term. New mechanisms will be needed to enhance co-ordination between different development actors and Caribbean countries, to more effectively leverage private investments and ensure their alignment with national and regional development plans.

Innovative mechanisms could be explored to engage the Caribbean diaspora to maximise the impact of remittances in development. For instance, a regional-level mechanism could promote migrants' investment in their countries of origin. The International Fund for Agricultural Development has put such a mechanism in place through its multi-donor Financing Facility for Remittances (IFAD, 2024[92]).

International partnerships can complement national development efforts by facilitating locally driven processes, promoting equal peer exchange, leveraging existing capacities and fostering the creation of new ones (OECD et al., 2019[90]). An example of this new generation of international partnerships is the IDB's One Caribbean strategy, which aims to address interconnected challenges in climate adaptation, citizen security, private-sector engagement, and food security, with a regional focus and through the inclusion of public and private stakeholders (Box 6.3).

Box 6.3. One Caribbean, the IDB's regional strategy to promote sustainable development

One Caribbean is an IDB programme for advancing sustainable and inclusive growth across the Caribbean and SIDS, notably Barbados, Belize, Guyana, Jamaica, Suriname, The Bahamas, and Trinidad and Tobago. It addresses regional challenges including frequent natural disasters, import dependency, and security issues through a unified approach that maximises resources and co-operation. This regional framework prioritises regional solutions mainly for four common challenges: climate adaptation, citizen security, private-sector engagement and food security.

The Caribbean faces a high risk of tropical storms and hurricanes, which are expected to become more frequent and severe due to climate change. This will also bring higher temperatures, longer droughts, intense rainfall and greater flooding. To tackle these issues, countries need to invest in resilient infrastructure and shift towards renewable energy to lessen their dependence on imported fossil fuels.

Secondly, citizens have consistently identified public security as the most pressing social issue in their countries, impacting public safety and domestic violence. Security concerns also burden businesses, which must allocate resources for prevention and cover costs associated with incidents.

Thirdly, limited investment and low productivity drive low growth rates in the Caribbean. The region's structure, featuring a few large enterprises alongside many small and medium-sized businesses, faces issues to increase productivity. Improved regional integration could offer economies of scale and capitalise on varied regional strengths, fostering greater private sector engagement.

Lastly, the region relies heavily on food imports, which are costly and subject to fluctuating international prices. Enhancing local agricultural production and improving trade infrastructure could lower expenses, while strategies to manage price volatility could mitigate risks to increase access to nutritious food.

In addition to these four priorities, strengthening institutions and digital transformation emerge as cross-cutting issues, as good institutions and technology are necessary conditions for project success.

Source: (IDB, 2024[93]).

Finally, new international partnerships can support the Caribbean in engaging on equal footing as peers, building and participating in multilateral and multi-stakeholder partnerships to tackle shared multi-dimensional development challenges with multi-dimensional responses (OECD et al., 2019[90]). As explained next, developing these types of partnerships will be crucial for the Caribbean's efforts towards ensuring international support for climate action, particularly for their climate adaptation needs.

The role of international partnerships to support climate action in the Caribbean

Climate action is highly relevant in Caribbean economies, as they are rich in biodiversity and largely exposed to climate threats (see Chapter 3). With USD 22 billion estimated in losses annually by 2050 caused by more frequent and intense impacts of climate change, the cost of inaction is high (UNDP, 2023[94]). However, Caribbean countries cannot address their significant mitigation and adaptation challenges alone. Moreover, they should not bear the vast financial costs of these efforts as their contribution to global greenhouse gas emissions is limited. International partnerships must seek ways to recognise the specific needs of Caribbean economies and support them in advancing their climate agenda, both through financing and technical co-operation.

Financing needs for climate action in the Caribbean are large, particularly for adaptation. For instance, the region needs approximately USD 175 billion by 2030 to fortify marine biodiversity, enhance sustainable fishing practices and bolster coastal defences against climate change (GCF, 2023[95]). ODA flows towards climate change objectives are insufficient for the region's climate financing needs. These flows have been highly variable, both in total volumes and in their distribution between mitigation and adaptation objectives. In 2022, ODA towards the Caribbean for climate change mitigation was USD 333 million (constant 2022 prices). Meanwhile, ODA for climate change adaptation reached almost USD 168 million (constant 2022 prices) (OECD, 2024[96]). In addition, adaptation projects like drought-resistant seeds, resilient buildings, environmental restoration and sea walls have struggled to attract private-sector financing.

Renewed international partnerships can help Caribbean countries harness opportunities to access vast financial resources for climate action. Three key strategies, described below, are: developing new finance instruments; providing greater access of SIDS to global climate-related funds; and mobilising the private sector.

More innovative financial instruments can support climate adaptation and build resilience

Renewed international partnerships can have a fundamental role in supporting Caribbean countries in seizing the opportunity to access vast financial resources for climate action. Emerging instruments offer innovative opportunities to raise financial resources aimed at climate goals. International co-operation and innovative financing approaches can be crucial for their development. For example, financing instruments, such as blue and green bonds, blended financing, and debt swaps, can help fund climate adaptation and resilience building (see Chapter 5).

Innovation in international partnerships is crucial. For instance, more collaboration between multilateral development banks can better support countries in developing debt operations by providing official guarantees (e.g. example of the IDB/EIB joint guarantee to a debt-for-climate operation in Barbados – see Chapter 5). Meanwhile, other partnerships can support the development of homogeneous and inter-operable green taxonomies and standards.

SIDS need more support from global climate funds

Caribbean countries should be provided with appropriate metrics and tools to access climate-related funds. Several funds have been established to support climate action, including the Green Climate Fund (GCF), the Adaptation Fund, the Climate Investment Fund and the Global Environment Facility. Indeed, green financing for SIDS has risen in recent years compared to other developing nations (Piemonte and Cattaneo, 2022[97]). However, these mechanisms often use proposed CO_2 emission reductions as criteria for investment (Piemonte and Cattaneo, 2022[97]). Consequently, as SIDS tend to have low absolute levels of CO_2 emissions, they can be disqualified from accessing these funds, even when their mitigation objectives are ambitious (OECD, 2024[38]). This suggests the need for these funds to consider new metrics that address the specific nature of SIDS.

Similarly, SIDS have significant needs for climate adaptation, biodiversity protection and land preservation. However, it is more difficult to measure the financial returns of adaptation projects and technically difficult to quantify adaptation needs. Hence, more support for SIDS is needed to make the case for adaptation and to attract more funds to these objectives (Piemonte and Cattaneo, 2022[97]). In addition, tapping into existent funds remains a challenge, given the limited administrative and technical capacities at the national level, compounded by the array of complex accreditation and project proposal procedures, which makes SIDS dependent on intermediary accredited agencies (OECD/World Bank, 2016[98]).

Renewed international partnerships to mobilise private financing

New international partnerships for climate action feature the mobilisation of private sector funds as a core element. The renewed EU-LAC partnership, for example, presents specific opportunities for the Caribbean. The European Union has led on a range of financing tools that can help address specific financing needs of the region. These include the Global Green Bond Initiative and the Caribbean Investment Facilities (now blended into the Latin America and Caribbean Investment Facility, or LACIF). These initiatives aim to provide the Caribbean and the broader LAC region with technical assistance and significant financial resources to de-risk capital market instruments towards the SDGs (Présidence de la République, 2023[99]).

The EU-LAC Global Gateway Investment Agenda (GGIA) is an ambitious initiative to promote investments in the LAC region. This initiative aims to support a fair green transition, an inclusive digital transformation, human development and health resilience. It can leverage significant additional financing for the Caribbean and favour a better alignment of private investments with the region's development priorities.

The GGIA seeks to de-risk private investment by crowding in financial actors and promoting co-operation between development institutions and private actors. To that end, it provides instruments such as guarantees, grants and loans (European Commission, 2024[100]). In this way, the GGIA aims to overcome perceptions of risk that deter private investment and help improve the investment environment for Caribbean states, both for those with and without credit ratings.

The GGIA has 39 initiatives in the Caribbean with clear areas of targeted partnership. These initiatives align with the Caribbean Maritime Intra-Regional Transport programme and the Digital for Development Hub. They also complement priorities such as promoting renewable energy systems, developing health systems and tackling sargassum issues.

The LACIF will use the European Fund for Sustainable Development Plus (EFSD+) to mobilise the GGIA. Notably, the European Union helps the Caribbean Export Development Agency to establish investment-focused initiatives. The Regional Private Sector Development Programme III, for example, supports firm competitiveness, diversification and export potential. It places a strong focus on green transition and digital transformation. For its part, the Caribbean Investment Forum has attracted the active involvement of the CARICOM Secretariat and the CDB. It explores development opportunities in agricultural technology, transitioning towards a green economy, embracing ICT, and enhancing transportation, logistics and shipping in the region.

The US-Caribbean Partnership to Address the Climate Crisis 2030 (PACC 2030), established in 2022, seeks to support climate adaptation, resilience building and the development of clean energy in the Caribbean (US Department of State, 2024[101]). The Green Shipping Challenge, launched at COP28 by Norway and the United States, seeks to align the shipping industry with the Paris Agreement. With the IDB, the United States is supporting collaboration between The Bahamas, Jamaica, the Dominican Republic, and Trinidad and Tobago to address key maritime sector emissions. These include improved port efficiencies, the development of low-emission vessels and broader associated decarbonisation (US Department of State, 2024[101]).

Other multilateral actors have also pushed forward with new mobilisation efforts. The 40th Board meeting of the Green Climate Fund (GCF), the world's largest multilateral climate fund, held in October 2024, approved more than USD 1 billion of GCF investment for 16 projects across developing countries (GCF, 2024[102]). One of these projects is the Barbados Climate Resilient South Coast Water Reclamation Project, which aims to increase Barbados' water resilience to climate change, given it is among the world's most water-scarce countries. This is a ground-breaking "debt for climate conversion" project in partnership with the IDB and the European Investment Bank, which provided guarantees. It will create fiscal space and generate savings over time, allowing the country to invest in climate-resilient infrastructure.

Equal-footing platforms can heighten the development needs of Caribbean SIDS

The Caribbean, as part of the SIDS group, has channelled common vulnerabilities into collective action in the context of international climate change negotiations. In 1990, Caribbean countries created the Alliance of Small Island States (AOSIS) that successfully lobbied for recognition of the special needs of SIDS in the text of the 1992 UN Framework Convention on Climate Change (AOSIS, 2024[103]). Since then, AOSIS has worked to place adaptation on an equal footing with mitigation and to ensure funding to help countries adapt to climate change through the Adaptation Fund and the GCF. Through AOSIS, Caribbean countries forged a unified front demanding what would then become one of the most important outcomes of COP28: the establishment of the Loss and Damage Fund, with new and additional support of at least USD 100 billion annually (UNCC, 2023[104]).

Caribbean countries have recently been active in ongoing discussions on multilateral financial architecture reforms. The Bridgetown Initiative, led by Barbados and launched in 2022, seeks to mobilise support for climate-resilient development in the Caribbean. It seeks to make more funding available for climate-vulnerable countries and emphasises the importance of financing mechanisms tailored to the specific needs and vulnerabilities of Caribbean nations, particularly in light of the increasing frequency and intensity of climate-related disasters. The Bridgetown Initiative aims to change some terms around how funding is loaned and repaid, including through Climate Resilient Debt Clauses (CRDS), through which debt repayments are automatically deferred in case of a hurricane or an extreme weather event. In this way, it seeks to stop developing nations from spiralling into a debt crisis when successive disasters like floods, droughts and storms force up their borrowing (Masterson, 2023[105]).

An array of views on critical issues related to the reform of the international financial architecture could complement the Bridgetown Initiative, as the current debt issue in the Caribbean extends beyond temporary liquidity issues and is more deeply rooted (Piemonte, 2021[106]). Jamaica, for instance, has strengthened domestic resource mobilisation and worked closely with the OECD towards improved tax mobilisation (see Chapter 5). Thanks to its progress on indebtedness, the country has achieved macroeconomic stability (Permanent Mission of Jamaica to the United Nations, 2023[107]). Antigua and Barbuda has been calling for a reconsideration of debt instruments and the need for structural reforms to upgrade policy coherence for sustainable development in the international financing architecture. This includes a Multidimensional Vulnerability Index that would allow SIDS to access concessional financing, the creation of a debt mechanism for SIDS to achieve debt sustainability and state-contingent debt instruments with disaster clauses (Government of Antigua and Barbuda, 2023[108]). The Caribbean could combine these efforts and leverage its voice in global discussions towards the transformation of the international financing architecture for sustainable development.

Building consensus among Caribbean countries would enable them to seize the opportunities presented by the main reforms to the international financing architecture. This is the case of the Paris Pact for People and Planet (4P), which was agreed upon in the context of the "Summit for a New Global Financing Pact" hosted by France in Paris in 2023 (France Diplomacy, 2023[109]). The 4P provides an inclusive forum where the 66 participating countries can discuss and build a strategic agenda, helping to guarantee that negotiations and discussions held in other multilateral forums coherently approach development, climate, and nature. It has already succeeded in improving considerations for environmental and climate issues in international financing, for example, through the World Bank's decision to devote 45% of all its financing to climate-related projects. The 4P is currently working with the United Kingdom, France, Canada and other countries to map the application of CRDS to support scale-up based on good practices. Currently, Barbados, Haiti and Jamaica are the only Caribbean members of the 4P. Enhancing alignment between Caribbean countries in the multilateral sphere is much needed in view of increasing financing needs and upcoming international negotiations, particularly the Financing for Development Conference to be hosted by Spain in 2025.

Key policy messages

Regional integration and international partnerships are crucial for driving resilient and sustainable development in the Caribbean. The region has untapped potential to boost its international position, enhance intra- and extra-regional trade, and provide innovative responses to pressing challenges like climate change. Box 6.4. presents key policy messages to help Caribbean countries focus their regional integration and international co-operation efforts towards improving development outcomes, addressing common challenges, and supporting financing for development and climate action.

Box 6.4. Key policy messages

Target trade strategies to improve development outcomes

- Strengthen co-ordination efforts across regional organisations to accelerate the implementation of regional agreements.
- Enhance trade facilitation prioritising challenging areas like automation, procedures, border agency co-operation or impartiality, and reducing non-tariff barriers, for example, through regionally co-ordinated investment codes or harmonised sanitary and phytosanitary measures.
- Promote regional value chains in strategic sectors, like the green and blue economy, or agrifood, to diversify production, reduce dependency on imports, and lower GVC vulnerability.
- Foster insertion into GVCs by targeting sectors with global growth potential, such as the cultural and creative industries.
- Strengthen market penetration within existing trade agreements and seek new agreements, particularly with Latin American countries.

Harness the potential of regional co-operation to address common challenges

- Improve intra- and extra-regional transport connectivity adopting regional strategies to scale up investments in resilient infrastructure, revise tax and regulatory frameworks to improve competition and promote agreements between national transport companies.
- Reinforce regional co-operation on disaster risk reduction and prevention incorporating digital technologies, and develop Caribbean-wide policies to address environmental challenges, such as sargassum and marine pollution.
- Advance a regional digital transition with a focus on regulatory dialogue, infrastructure investment, connectivity, data flows, cybersecurity, innovation ecosystems, and space services.
- Harmonise policy, regulations, and financial mechanisms to create an enabling environment for renewable energy investments to leverage the region's potential in this field.

Engage in international partnerships to support financing for development and climate action

- Leverage FDI and other sources of private finance, through blended finance and other risk-sharing instruments, with the support of official development interventions.
- Establish co-ordination mechanisms among development actors and Caribbean countries to mobilise private investments ensuring alignment with national and regional development plans.
- Engage in international partnerships that promote nationally driven development processes, foster knowledge exchange in equal footing, and build on existing capacities to foster new ones.
- Foster regional dialogue for a cohesive Caribbean voice in multilateral discussions, for instance on the reform of the international financial architecture for sustainable development.

Notes

[1] Except Guyana (20 October 2008) and Haiti (10 December 2009).

[2] The Greater Caribbean is a political concept created by the ACS member countries, being the most inclusive of those that define the zone bordering the Caribbean Sea. The concept therefore coincides with the ACS membership, comprising: Antigua and Barbuda, The Bahamas, Barbados, Belize, Colombia, Costa Rica, Cuba, Dominica, Dominican Republic, El Salvador, Grenada, Guatemala, Guyana, Haiti, Honduras, Jamaica, Mexico, Nicaragua, Panama, Saint Kitts and Nevis, Saint Lucia, Saint Vincent and the Grenadines, Suriname, Trinidad and Tobago, and Venezuela.

[3] Overall mobilisation for the Caribbean (USD 1 158 million) is still lower compared to larger economic regions such as Central America (USD 3 201 million) or South America (USD 13 670 million) between 2020-22.

References

ACS (2024), "Connectivity in the Greater Caribbean", webpage, http://www.acs-aec.org/index.php?q=transport/connectivity-in-the-greater-caribbean. [35]

ACS (2008), "Air transport agreement among the member states and associate members of the Association of Caribbean States", Association of Caribbean States, Port-of-Spain, http://www.acs-aec.org/sites/default/files/Final_ATA_En.pdf. [36]

Allende López, M. et al. (2020), *A Caribbean Settlement Network: Can Blockchain Ease Intra-regional Trade in the Caribbean?*, https://doi.org/10.18235/0002643. [4]

Allub, L. and R. Schliesser (2023), *Integration in the Caribbean*, CAF - Development Bank of Latin America and the Caribbean, https://scioteca.caf.com/handle/123456789/2068?locale-attribute=en. [1]

AOSIS (2024), "Member States", webpage, https://www.aosis.org/about/member-states/ (accessed on 19 April 2024). [103]

Arias, D., M. Brown and E. Hassiner (2024), "The worrying phenomenon of food insecurity in the Caribbean", World Bank blogs, https://blogs.worldbank.org/en/latinamerica/food-insecurity-caribbean#:~:text=Today%2C%20food%20insecurity%20stands%20at,meals%20or%20reduced%20food%20intake. [13]

Bauer, B. (2023), *Conectando los recursos culturales y creativos del Caribe para crear oportunidades de desarrollo turístico*, https://articles.unesco.org/sites/default/files/medias/fichiers/2023/11/ES_Caribbean%20Cultural%20Resources.pdf. [19]

Beltran, P. and M. Hadzi-Vaskov (2023), *How Climate Shocks Are Linked to Cross-Border Migration in Latin America and the Caribbean*, https://www.imf.org/en/News/Articles/2023/12/08/cf-how-climate-shocks-are-linked-to-cross-border-migration-in-latin-america-and-the-caribbean. [64]

Bhattacharya, R. (2024), *Constraints on Trade in the LAC Region*, International Monetary Fund, https://www.imf.org/en/Publications/WP/Issues/2024/02/16/Constraints-on-Trade-in-the-LAC-Region-544936. [30]

Blanco, U. (2024), "A digital leap for Caribbean islands", UNDP blog, 30 April, https://www.undp.org/blog/digital-leap-caribbean-islands. [48]

Cable.co.uk (2024), *The Price of Electricity per KWh in 230 Countries*, (database), https://www.cable.co.uk/energy/worldwide-pricing/. [54]

Campos, R. (2024), *Oportunidades para promover el comercio agroalimentario intrarregional en América Latina y el Caribe*, https://doi.org/10.4060/cc9415es. [11]

Caribbean Export (2022), *Transforming to a Greener, Smarter, Resilient Caribbean: Annual Results Report*, Caribbean Export Development Agency, St. Michael, Barbados, https://carib-export.com/es/publications/2022-annual-results-report/. [16]

CARICOM (2017), *Vision and Roadmap for a CARICOM Single ICT Space*, CARICOM, Georgetown, https://caricom.org/documents/vision-and-roadmap-for-a-caricom-single-ict-space/. [50]

CARICOM (2013), *Energy Policy*, CARICOM, Georgetown, https://caricom.org/documents/10862-caricom_energy_policy.pdf. [60]

Cattaneo, O. and C. Piemonté (2021), "Transition Finance Compendium: Challenges and recommendations for the Development Assistance Committee", *OECD Development Co-operation Working Papers*, No. 94, OECD Publishing, Paris, https://doi.org/10.1787/90f219b1-en. [76]

CDB (2022), *Keynote – Energy Transition in the Caribbean – Challenges and Opportunities*, Caribbean Development Bank, St. Michael, Barbados, https://www.caribank.org/newsroom/news-and-events/speeches/keynote-energy-transition-caribbean-challenges-and-opportunities. [56]

CNG (2020), *Caribbean News Global (CNG)*, https://caribbeannewsglobal.com/understanding-variable-tourism-levy/ (accessed on 4 September 2024). [43]

Competitiveness (2021), "Agritiech Challenge in the Caribbean", webpage, https://www.competitiveness.com/en/projects/agritech-challenge-caribbean/. [15]

Dessina, Y., A. Minsat and R. Delana (2022), "Why stronger regional value chains can help Africa rebound from economic shocks", OECD Development Matters blog, https://oecd-development-matters.org/2022/06/09/why-stronger-regional-value-chains-can-help-africa-rebound-from-economic-shocks/. [14]

ECLAC (2023), *Foreign Direct Investment in Latin America and the Caribbean*, United Nations Economic Commission for Latin America and the Caribbean, Santiago, https://repositorio.cepal.org/server/api/core/bitstreams/fd2ce029-2846-4900-a0e6-14818f6191b3/content. [86]

ECLAC (2023), *Sustainable Development Goal (SDG) 7: Regional Profile*, United Nations Economic Commission for Latin America and the Caribbean, Santiago, https://www.cepal.org/sites/default/files/23-00204b-sdg.7_web.pdf. [55]

ECLAC (2022), *CEPALSTAT Statistical Databases and Publications*, https://statistics.cepal.org/portal/cepalstat/dashboard.html?theme=4&lang=en. [46]

ECLAC (2022), *The Caribbean Outlook Summary. Recovery and Resilience - Repositioning the Caribbean post COVID-19*, United Nations Economic Commission for Latin America and the Caribbean, Santiago, https://www.cepal.org/en/publications/48379-caribbean-outlook-summary-recovery-and-resilience-repositioning-caribbean-post. [8]

ECLAC (2021), "Strategies for post COVID-19 recovery in the Caribbean", *Focus: Magazine of the Caribbean Development and Cooperation Committee*, https://repositorio.cepal.org/server/api/core/bitstreams/61858ae6-0605-4b23-a8c1-a795764c057b/content. [58]

ECLAC/OECD (2018), *Emerging Challenges and Shifting Paradigms: New Perspectives on International Cooperation for Development*, United Nations, Santiago, https://repositorio.cepal.org/server/api/core/bitstreams/414911fd-ec99-4ae8-8e0a-dd3c5a2478e0/content. [75]

European Commission (2024), *EU-LAC Global Gateway Investment Agenda*, European Commission, Brussels, https://international-partnerships.ec.europa.eu/policies/global-gateway/eu-lac-global-gateway-investment-agenda_en. [100]

Fioravanti, R., I. Granada and J. Veverka (2015), *Air Transport Sector in the Caribbean*, Inter-American Development Bank, Washington, DC, https://doi.org/10.18235/0000056. [34]

Foreign Affairs Committee (2022), *China Regional Snapshot: The Caribbean*, https://foreignaffairs.house.gov/china-snapshot-project-the-caribbean/. [85]

France Diplomacy (2023), *The Paris Pact for People and the Planet (4P)*, https://pactedeparis.org/pdf/the-paris-pact-for-people-and-the-planet.pdf (accessed on 27 March 2024). [109]

García Zaballos, A. (2020), *Digital gap in Latin America and the Caribbean*, Inter-American Development Bank, https://publications.iadb.org/en/publications/english/viewer/Annual-Report-of-the-Broadband-Development-Index-IDBA-2020-Digital-Gap-in-Latin-America-and-the-Caribbean.pdf. [49]

GCF (2024), *GCF Board's USD 1 billion for climate projects signals increased climate finance ahead of COP29*, https://www.greenclimate.fund/news/gcf-board-s-usd-1-billion-climate-projects-signals-increased-climate-finance-ahead-cop29. [102]

GCF (2023), "Plugging the finance gap in the Caribbean", 2 December, Green Climate Fund, Songdo, https://www.greenclimate.fund/news/plugging-finance-gap-caribbean. [95]

Giordano, P. (2012), "Regional Integration", in *The Oxford Handbook of Latin American Economics*, Oxford University Press, https://doi.org/10.1093/oxfordhb/9780199571048.013.0014. [5]

Goldwyn, D., E. Tiah and W. Mowla (2023), "A roadmap for the Caribbean's energy transition", *Issue Brief*, 26 September, Atlantic Council, Washington, DC, https://www.atlanticcouncil.org/in-depth-research-reports/issue-brief/a-roadmap-for-the-caribbeans-energy-transition/?_thumbnail_id=684876#:~:text=the%20roadmap%E2%80%99s%20steps.-,Drivers%20of%20the%20Energy%20Transition%20and%20System%20Transformation,-. [53]

Government of Antigua and Barbuda (2023), *Statement by the Honourable Gaston Browne, Prime Minister, at the High-level Dialogue on Financing for Development*, United Nations, New York, https://estatements.unmeetings.org/estatements/10.0010/20230920090000000/tV32tvvz19xc/wGTmWcREt0dj_en.pdf. [108]

IDB (2024), "One Caribbean", *IDB website*, https://www.iadb.org/es/inicio/bidimpact/one-caribbean (accessed on 4 September 2024). [93]

IDB (2023), *Migration, Integration, and Diaspora Engagement in the Caribbean*, Inter-American Developmet Bank, New York, https://www.migrationpolicy.org/sites/default/files/publications/mpi-idb-caribbean-report-2023-final.pdf. [89]

IDB (2023), *Remittances to Latin America and the Caribbean in 2023*, Inter-American Development Bank, Washington, DC, https://publications.iadb.org/en/publications/english/viewer/Remittances-to-Latin-America-and-the-Caribbean-in-2023.pdf. [88]

IDB (2020), *Progress and challenges of the integration agenda*, Inter-American Development Bank, https://publications.iadb.org/en/publications/english/viewer/CARICOM-Report-Progress-and-Challenges-of-The-Integration-Agenda.pdf. [2]

IDB (2018), *Short sea shipping network and finance model for the Caribbean*, CPCS Transcom Limited; Trevor Hamilton and Associates, https://doi.org/10.18235/0001253. [33]

IFAD (2024), *The Financing Facility for Remittances*, International Fund for Agricultural Development, Rome, https://www.ifad.org/en/ffr. [92]

IICA (2018), "The Caribbean market seeks to strengthen trade links by eliminating non-tariff barriers", 23 October, Inter-American Institute for Cooperation on Agriculture, Turrialba, Costa Rica, https://iica.int/en/press/news/caribbean-market-seeks-strengthen-trade-links-eliminating-non-tariff-barriers. [10]

IMF (2024), *Balance of Payments Analytic Presentation by Indicator: Supplementary Items, Portfolio Investment, Net Incurrence of Liabilities (Excluding Exceptional Financing), US Dollars*, (database), https://data.imf.org/?sk=7a51304b-6426-40c0-83dd-ca473ca1fd52&sid=1393552803658. [71]

IMF (2020), "Is the whole greater than the sum of its parts? Strengthening Caribbean regional integration", *Working Paper*, International Monetary Fund, Washington, DC, https://www.imf.org/en/Publications/WP/Issues/2020/01/17/Is-the-Whole-Greater-than-the-Sum-of-its-Parts-Strengthening-Caribbean-Regional-Integration-48930. [3]

IOM (2021), *Mechanisms for Labour Migration in the Caribbean*, International Organization for Migration Regional Office for North America, Central America and the Caribbean, San José, https://publications.iom.int/system/files/pdf/Labour-Mechanisms-Caribbean.pdf. [68]

Jaupart, P. (2023), "International migration to the Caribbean", *Background paper for the World Development Report 2023: Migrants, Refugees, and Societies*, World Bank, Washington, DC, https://thedocs.worldbank.org/en/doc/3c5cf49b10dd0607472f4a2fb8a063ce-0050062023/original/WDR2023-Caribbean-Background-Paper-FORMATTED.pdf. [87]

Jolliffe, J., C. Jolly and B. Stevens (2021), "Blueprint for improved measurement of the international ocean economy: An exploration of satellite accounting for ocean economic activity", *OECD Science, Technology and Industry Working Papers*, No. 2021/04, OECD Publishing, https://doi.org/10.1787/aff5375b-en. [23]

Lacarte, V. et al. (2023), *Migration, Integration, and Diaspora Engagement in the Caribbean: A Policy Review*, Migration Policy Institute and Inter-American Development Bank, Washington, DC, https://www.migrationpolicy.org/sites/default/files/publications/mpi-idb-caribbean-report-2023-final.pdf. [63]

Lund, S. et al. (2019), *Globalization in Transition: The Future of Trade and Value Chains*, McKinsey Global Institute, https://www.mckinsey.com/featured-insights/innovation-and-growth/globalization-in-transition-the-future-of-trade-and-value-chains. [6]

Masson, M., D. Ehrhardt and V. Lizzio (2020), *Sustainable Energy Paths for the Caribbean*, Inter-American Development Bank, Washington, DC, https://doi.org/10.18235/0002236. [61]

Masterson, V. (2023), "The Bridgetown Initiative: Here's everything you need to know", 13 January, World Economic Forum, Cologny, Switzerland, https://www.weforum.org/agenda/2023/01/barbados-bridgetown-initiative-climate-change/. [105]

Mesquita Moreira, M. (2018), *Connecting the dots: A road map for better integration in Latin America and the Caribbean*, Inter-American Development Bank, https://doi.org/10.18235/0001132. [28]

Morris, C. (2020), *St Lucia Star*, https://stluciastar.com/st-lucias-new-tourism-tax-how-does-it-stack-up-to-other-destinations/ (accessed on 4 August 2024). [41]

Mowla, W. (2024), "Accelerating the energy transition in the Eastern Caribbean", *Issue Brief*, Atlantic Council, Washington, DC, https://www.atlanticcouncil.org/in-depth-research-reports/issue-brief/accelerating-the-energy-transition-in-the-eastern-caribbean/. [52]

Nicholson, G. (n.d.), "Transport, logistics and competitiveness in Latin America and the Caribbean", Association of Caribbean States, Port-of-Spain, http://www.acs-aec.org/index.php?q=transport/transport-logistics-and-competitiveness-in-latin-america-and-the-caribbean. [29]

OECD (2024), *Aid (ODA) disbursements to countries and regions [DAC2A]*, (database), https://data-explorer.oecd.org/vis?fs[0]=Topic%2C1%7CDevelopment%23DEV%23%7COfficial%20Development%20Assistance%20%28ODA%29%23DEV_ODA%23&pg=0&fc=Topic&bp=true&snb=11&df[ds]=dsDisseminateFinalDMZ&df[id]=DSD_DAC2%40DF_DAC2A&df[ag]=OECD.DCD.FSD&df[vs]=1.0&pd (accessed on 9 October 2024). [69]

OECD (2024), "Helping Small Island Developing States graduate to success", *OECD Policy Briefs*, OECD Publishing, Paris, https://www.oecd.org/en/publications/helping-small-island-developing-states-graduate-to-success_8f2910aa-en.html. [78]

OECD (2024), "Mobilised private finance for development", *OECD Data Explorer*, (database), https://data-explorer.oecd.org/vis?fs[0]=Topic%2C1%7CDevelopment%23DEV%23%7COfficial%20Development%20Assistance%20%28ODA%29%23DEV_ODA%23&pg=0&fc=Topic&bp=true&snb=11&vw=tb&df[ds]=dsDisseminateFinalDMZ&df[id]=DSD_MOB%40DF_MOBILISATION&df[ag]=OECD.DCD.FSD&d. [91]

OECD (2024), *RioMarkers: Aid activities targeting global environmental objectives*, (database), https://data-explorer.oecd.org/vis?fs[0]=Topic%2C0%7CDevelopment%23DEV%23&fs[1]=Topic%2C2%7CDevelopment%23DEV%23%7COfficial%20Development%20Assistance%20%28ODA%29%23DEV_ODA%23%7CFlows%20on%20individual%20projects%20%28CRS%29%23DEV_ODA_FIP%23&fs[2]=Marker%. [96]

OECD (2024), *Small Island Developing States*, https://www.oecd.org/en/topics/sub-issues/small-islands-developing-states.html (accessed on 5 September 2024). [38]

OECD (2024), *Total Offical Support for Sustainable Development (TOSSD) - Methodology*, https://tossd.org/methodology/. [83]

OECD (2024), *Total Official Support for Sustainable Development (TOSSD) website*, OECD Publishing, Paris, https://www.tossd.org/. [81]

OECD (2024), "Trade Facilitation", OECD website, https://www.oecd.org/en/topics/sub-issues/trade-facilitation.html. [25]

OECD (2024), "Transition finance", OECD website, https://www.oecd.org/en/topics/sub-issues/investment-for-trade-and-economic-development/transition-finance-toolkit.html. [80]

OECD (2023), "Innovative agro-food industries in the EU Outermost Regions", *OECD Development Policy Papers*, No. 49, OECD Publishing, Paris, https://doi.org/10.1787/0d615c8d-en. [24]

OECD (2023), "Innovative oceans: Drivers of internationalisation for the EU Outermost regions", *OECD Development Policy Papers*, No. 51, OECD Publishing, Paris, https://doi.org/10.1787/e28cc1f5-en. [22]

OECD (2023), "Leveraging cultural and creative sectors for development in the European Union outermost regions", *OECD Local Economic and Employment Development (LEED) Papers*, No. 2023/21, OECD Publishing, Paris, https://doi.org/10.1787/950f214a-en. [21]

OECD (2023), *Making renewable energies drivers of competitiveness in the EU Outermost Regions*, OECD Publishing, https://doi.org/10.1787/6169e85d-en. [62]

OECD (2023), *Production Transformation Policy Review. Spotlight on Guadeloupe's Internationalisation*, OECD Development Pathways, OECD Publishing, Paris, https://doi.org/10.1787/ac8c5b0d-en. [59]

OECD (2022), *Development Strategy Assessment of the Eastern Caribbean*, OECD Development Pathways, OECD Publishing, Paris, https://doi.org/10.1787/f1566c7a-en. [32]

OECD (2022), *Total Official Support for Sustainable Develoment (TOSSD) - Data Visualisation tool*, https://tossd.online/. [82]

OECD (2021), "The inequalities-environment nexus: Towards a people-centred green transition", *OECD Green Growth Papers*, https://doi.org/10.1787/ca9d8479-en. [45]

OECD (2018), *Making Development Co-operation Work for Small Island Developing States*, OECD Publishing, Paris, https://doi.org/10.1787/9789264287648-en. [31]

OECD (2017), *Interrelations between Public Policies, Migration and Development*, OECD Publishing, Paris, https://doi.org/10.1787/9789264265615-en. [66]

OECD et al. (2024), *The role of the G20 in promoting green and just transitions*, https://doi.org/10.1787/548e71cd-en. [44]

OECD et al. (2022), *Latin American Economic Outlook 2022: Towards a Green and Just Transition*, OECD Publishing, Paris, https://doi.org/10.1787/3d5554fc-en. [47]

OECD et al. (2019), *Latin American Economic Outlook 2019: Development in Transition*, OECD Publishing, Paris, https://doi.org/10.1787/g2g9ff18-en. [90]

OECD/ILO (2018), *How Immigrants Contribute to the Dominican Republic's Economy*, International Labour Organization, Geneva/OECD Publishing, Paris, https://doi.org/10.1787/9789264301146-en. [67]

OECD/UNCTAD/ECLAC (2020), *Production Transformation Policy Review of the Dominican Republic: Preserving Growth, Achieving Resilience*, OECD Development Pathways, OECD Publishing, Paris, https://doi.org/10.1787/1201cfea-en. [7]

OECD/World Bank (2016), *Climate and Disaster Resilience Financing in Small Island Developing States*, https://doi.org/10.1787/9789264266919-en. [98]

Permanent Mission of Jamaica to the United Nations (2023), *Statement by Senator the Honourable Kamina Johnson Smith, Minister of Foreign Affairs of Jamaica, at the High-level Dialogue on Financing for Development*, Permanent Mission of Jamaica to the United Nations, New York, https://estatements.unmeetings.org/estatements/10.0010/20230920090000000/tV32tvvz19xc/HoRJ1MQsF3rf_en.pdf. [107]

Piemonte, C. (2024), "Using the new UN MVI to identify and fill in vulnerability financing gaps in SIDS", OECD, Paris, https://one.oecd.org/document/DCD(2024)16/en/pdf. [79]

Piemonte, C. (2021), "External Debt in Small Island Developing States (SIDS): One-year into the COVID-19 crisis, where do we stand?", OECD, Paris, https://one.oecd.org/official-document/DCD/DAC(2021)23/en. [106]

Piemonte, C. and O. Cattaneo (2022), "SIDS' Access to Green Funds", OECD, Paris, https://one.oecd.org/official-document/DCD(2022)34/en. [97]

Piemonté, C., J. Kim and O. Cattaneo (2024), *Financing sustainable development in the Organisation of Eastern Caribbean States: A Transition Finance Diagnostic*, OECD Publishing, https://doi.org/10.1787/62a4deae-en. [77]

Présidence de la République (2023), *Chair's Summary of Discussions at the Summit for a new Global Financing Pact*, Présidence de la République, Paris, https://www.elysee.fr/admin/upload/default/0001/15/4748a23641c5b2d55a47d63d7ed2e16963c11195.pdf. [99]

Rogers, F. et al. (2023), "Toxic gas, livelihoods under threat and power outages: How a seaweed causes chaos in Caribbean", 11 April, The Guardian, https://www.theguardian.com/environment/2024/apr/11/toxic-gas-livelihoods-under-threat-and-power-outages-how-sargassum-seaweed-causes-chaos-in-caribbean. [40]

Santamaría, V. (2024), *Opportunities and challenges for agrifood trade between Central American Integration System and Caribbean Community countries*, Inter-American Development Bank, https://doi.org/10.4060/cc9421es. [9]

Turnbull, D. (23 April 2021), "Food security in the Caribbean", IICA blog, https://blog.iica.int/index.php/en/blog/food-security-caribbean. [12]

UN (2024), *The Antigua and Barbuda Agenda for SIDS (ABAS) – a Renewed Declaration for Resilient Prosperity*, Fourth International Conference on Small Island Developing States, https://sdgs.un.org/sites/default/files/2024-04/SIDS4%20-%20Co-Chairs%20FINAL.pdf. [37]

UN Comtrade Database (2024), *Imports Trade Data*, (database), https://comtradeplus.un.org/#state=eyJpZCI6ImVhOWIzMzdjLTUwZDMtNGMxNi04ZWM0LWY4Yjc4MWM5MGIxZiIsIm1ldGEiOnsiaW50ZXJhY3Rpb25UeXBlIjoicmVkaXJlY3QifX0%3d&client_info=eyJ1aWQiOiI2ZjI5MjA2Zi1hNTU5LTRkNmEtODJkMi1iNDI3NjFiZTg0M2MtYjJjXzFhX3NpZ251cF9zaWduaW5fY29td. [27]

UNCC (2023), "Caribbean island states forge unified front ahead of COP28", 13 October, UN Climate Change News, https://unfccc.int/news/caribbean-island-states-forge-unified-front-ahead-of-cop28. [104]

UNCTAD (2022), *Creative Economy Outlook 2022*, United Nations Publications, https://unctad.org/system/files/official-document/ditctsce2022d1_en.pdf. [20]

UNCTADStat (2024), *Data Centre*, (database), https://unctadstat.unctad.org/datacentre/. [18]

UNDP (2024), "Leaders from Caribbean small islands set priorities to ensure a digital transformation that leaves no one behind", 1 May, Press Release, United Nations Development Programme, Port-of-Spain, https://www.undp.org/trinidad-and-tobago/press-releases/leaders-caribbean-small-islands-set-priorities-ensure-digital-transformation-leaves-no-one-behind. [51]

UNDP (2023), "How countries in Latin America and the Caribbean are financing their climate goals", 19 October, United Nations Development Programme, New York, https://climatepromise.undp.org/news-and-stories/how-countries-latin-america-and-caribbean-are-financing-their-climate-goals. [94]

UNDRR-ROAMC (2021), *Regional Assessment Report on Disaster Risk in Latin America and the Caribbean (RAR 2021)*, United Nations Office for Disaster Risk Reduction, Geneva, https://www.undrr.org/es/publication/undrr-roamc-informe-de-evaluacion-regional-sobre-el-riesgo-de-desastres-en-america. [65]

US Department of State (2024), “U.S.-Caribbean Partnership to Address the Climate Crisis 2030”, webpage, https://www.state.gov/pacc2030/ (accessed on 11 July 2024). [101]

Virgin Islands News (2022), *Virgin Islands News*, https://www.virginislandsnewsonline.com/en/news/cruise-passengers-need-to-pay-their-fair-share-of-environmental-levy-hon-flax-charles (accessed on 4 September 2024). [42]

Vousdoukas, M., P. Athanasiou and A. Giardino (2023), “Small island developing states under threat by rising seas even in a 1.5 °C warming world”, *Nature*, Vol. 6, pp. 1552-1564, https://doi.org/10.1038/s41893-023-01230-5. [39]

World Bank (2024), “Foreign direct investment, net inflows (% of GDP)”, *World Bank Group Data*, (database), https://data.worldbank.org/indicator/BX.KLT.DINV.WD.GD.ZS. [72]

World Bank (2024), *WITS Database: Trade Flow Export*, World Bank, Washington, DC, https://wits.worldbank.org/CountryProfile/en/Country/WLD/Year/2021/TradeFlow/Export. [26]

World Bank (2024), *World Bank Group Data*, https://data.worldbank.org/indicator/NY.GNP.MKTP.CD?locations=ZJ. [70]

World Bank (2024), *World Bank: World Development Indicators (Foreign direct investment, net inflows (% of GDP))*, World Bank, Washington, DC, https://data.worldbank.org/indicator/BX.KLT.DINV.WD.GD.ZS. [84]

World Bank (2024), *World Development Indicators: GDP Current US$*, World Bank, Washington, DC, https://databank.worldbank.org/reports.aspx?source=2&series=NY.GDP.MKTP.CD&country=#. [73]

World Bank (2023), “Exports of goods and services (BoP, current US$)”, *World Bank Group Data*, (database), https://data.worldbank.org/indicator/BX.GSR.GNFS.CD. [17]

World Bank (2023), “Net ODA received (% of GNI)”, *World Bank Group Data*, (database), https://data.worldbank.org/indicator/DT.ODA.ODAT.GN.ZS. [74]

World Bank (2020), “Offshore wind technical potential in the Caribbean Islands”, (infographic), World Bank, Washington, DC, https://documents1.worldbank.org/curated/en/261081586847581050/pdf/Technical-Potential-for-Offshore-Wind-in-Caribbean-Islands-Map.pdf. [57]

www.ingramcontent.com/pod-product-compliance
Lightning Source LLC
Chambersburg PA
CBHW061208240926
51846CB00006B/1155
9789264530386